IN THE FOOTSTEPS OF JUDAS
AND OTHER DEFECTORS

In the Footsteps of Judas and Other Defectors

The Gospels, Acts, and Johannine Letters

B. J. OROPEZA

Apostasy in the New Testament Communities
VOLUME 1

CASCADE *Books* • Eugene, Oregon

IN THE FOOTSTEPS OF JUDAS AND OTHER DEFECTORS
The Gospels, Acts, and Johannine Letters

Apostasy in the New Testament Communities, vol. 1

Copyright © 2011 B. J. Oropeza. All rights reserved. Except for brief quotations in critical publications or reviews, no part of this book may be reproduced in any manner without prior written permission from the publisher. Write: Permissions, Wipf and Stock Publishers, 199 W. 8th Ave., Suite 3, Eugene, OR 97401.

Cascade Books
An Imprint of Wipf and Stock Publishers
199 W. 8th Ave., Suite 3
Eugene, OR 97401

www.wipfandstock.com

ISBN 13: 978-1-61097-289-5

Cataloging-in-Publication data for series:

Oropeza, B. J., 1961–

    Apostasy in the New Testament communities / B. J. Oropeza.

    xviii + 304 p. ; 25.4 cm. Includes bibliographical references and indexes.

    Contents:
        v. 1, In the Footsteps of Judas and Other Defectors: The Gospels, Acts, and Johannine Letters.
        v. 2, Jews, Gentiles, and the Opponents of Paul: The Pauline Letters.
        v. 3, Churches under Siege of Persecution and Assimilation: The General Epistles and Revelation.

    ISBN 13: 978-1-61097-289-5 (v. 1); 978-1-61097-290-1 (v. 2); 978-1-61097-291-8 (v. 3); 978-1-61097-206-2 (vols. 1–3)

        1. Apostasy—Biblical teaching. 2. Apostasy—Christianity. 3. Bible N.T.—Theology. I. Title. II. Series.

BS2395 O55 V.1 2011

Manufactured in the U.S.A.

To Jared and Justin

μειζοτέραν οὐκ ἔχω χαρά

Contents

Preface ix

Abbreviations xii

Introduction 1

1 The Gospel of Mark: The Message of Persecution and Obduracy for the Markan Community 11

2 The Gospel of Matthew: Law Breakers, False Prophets, and Final Judgment 48

3 Luke-Acts: Perseverance and Temptation among Jews and Gentiles in the Plan of God 98

4 The Gospel of John and the Epistles of John: Defectors from the Johannine Community 160

Conclusion 229

Bibliography 235

Ancient Sources Index 259

Author Index 292

Subject Index 297

Preface

This three-volume work is my attempt to do a complete study on the subject of apostasy in the New Testament, which is the main reason for its sizeable length. The study adds and expands on my previous papers and publications on the subject. In these volumes I examine the entire New Testament attempting to address defection from the emerging Christian faith according to the respective authors or community's point of view. Volume one focuses on the Christ-communities of the Gospels, Acts, and Johannine letters. Volume two examines the Pauline communities including the undisputed, disputed, and Pastoral Letters. In volume three I cover the general epistles of Hebrews, James, 1 and 2 Peter, and Jude, and then end with the book of Revelation. In order to appreciate my sustained argument, the reader is encouraged to look at all three volumes.

The entire work is motivated by the possibility of diverse opinions within the New Testament communities about falling away, a prospect that I mentioned but was not able to develop in *Paul and Apostasy: Eschatology, Perseverance and Falling Away in the Corinthian Congregation* (2000). Similar to my previous monograph, this current work does *not* intend to serve or defend theological positions such as Calvinism or Arminianism. And for the record, in case someone wishes to peg down my own theological presuppositions, my religious background includes a nominal Roman Catholic upbringing, and then I fell away to secularism while growing up, but then I returned to faith and attended a Pentecostal church during my college years, was schooled primarily in the Reformed tradition, worked at a parachurch institute, lived and worshipped among Anglicans at St. John's College in Durham, England, attended and served at a Presbyterian church while belonging to the Free Methodist denomination, have taught at Quaker and Wesleyan universities, and am currently finishing my research at a German university in which the theological department is mostly Lutheran and Catholic. If my perspective in this book turns out to be eclectic, at least you know why!

Preface

Over the course of the several years that it has taken me to write this book, new studies continue to be published that interact with my own, and I regret to say that I have not been able to keep up with all of them, especially the ones that are coming out just now. Be that as it may, I hope my scholarly peers will find this study engaging and that students, seminarians, ministers, and informed audiences in religious studies will likewise benefit from it. May this book provide you with insight, wisdom, learning, and thoughtful reflection and application.

In the process of producing this work many have assisted along the way. A very special thanks goes out to my colleagues, friends, and academic readers who have taken time to provide me with feedback and criticisms on various pre-published versions of chapters and selections in this three-volume study. These individuals include Paul Anderson, Richard Ascough, Bart Buhler, Scott Caulley, David deSilva, Don Garlington, Robert Hall, David Horrell, Roy Jeal, Judith Lieu, Fred Long, Lynn Losie, James McGrath, Mark Nanos, C. K. Robertson, Kenneth Schenck, Kay Smith, Jerry Sumney, Kenneth Waters, Robert Webb, Adam Winn, and Karen Winslow.

As well, at Azusa Pacific University I was able to participate at the Center for Research on Ethics and Values (CREV) headed by Carol Lambert, where I presented drafts of some of my chapters to fellow colleagues for their feedback. The CREV participants in fall 2006 included Ruth Anna Abigail, Mark Eaton, Carole Lambert, Daniel Park, Carrie Peirce, Karla Richmond, and Kay Smith; and in fall 2008 the participants were Mark Eaton, Randy Fall, Emily Griesinger, Craig Keen, Carole Lambert, Annie Tsai, and Steven Wentland. A special thanks goes out to them all. I hope I have not left out anyone! I was also fortunate enough to be awarded the Beverly Stanford Hardcastle Fellowship Award for 2009–2010, which will provide me with an upcoming semester for research, time off teaching, and a research assistant. I would like to thank Mark Eaton for chairing the award committee and making this possible, and a very special thanks to my assistant, Maranatha Wall.

I would also like to thank the APU School of Theology, headed by David Wright, Russell Duke, and now Scott Daniels (deans), Bill Yarchin and Kenneth Waters (assistant deans), and Kay Smith (chair of biblical studies), for their support and providing me with various types of assistance, time for research, and great colleagues. Colleagues that I have not mentioned already that deserve special mention for helping me with ideas and resources to this book are Ralph Martin, Roger Oakland, and Don Thorsen. I also give a warm thanks to administrative assistants Sheryl Lindsay, Pat Losie, Marilyn Moore, and Laura Smith Webb.

Finally, at APU I also wish to thank Kimberly Battle-Waters and again Carol Lambert for providing me with opportunities to get away to the beautiful Franciscan

Preface

monastery in Malibu, California, for the annual Faculty Writer's Retreat. Friends, students, and assistants that have helped directly or indirectly with this book and deserve honorable mention include Sybil Schlegel, Eric Ciampa, Breonna Wharton, Garret Granitz, Claire Moellenberndt, and Jessica Chessum.

For my sabbatical at the University of Tübingen, I wish to thank Professor Dr. Michael Theobald of the Katholisch-Theologischen Fakultät for graciously inviting me to do research and use the facilities of the Bibliothek des Theologicums, Dr. Thomas Schmeller of the Universität Frankfurt for helping arrange this connection; and Dr. Thomas Scott Caulley, director of the Institut zur Erforschung des Urchristentums, and Dr. Hermann Lichtenberger of the Evangelisch-Theologischen Fakultät, who were kind enough to invite me to present a paper on my research at their seminar. In Tübingen, Timothy Sailors and Petra Keller also deserve special mention for their friendship and assisting me with daily living protocols and use of the university housing and facilities. Finally, to my sons Jared and Justin, I love you and will see you again long before this book goes to print!

B. J. Oropeza
University of Tübingen, Germany
Azusa Pacific University, California
Fall 2009

Abbreviations

MODERN SOURCES

AB	Anchor Bible
ABD	*Anchor Bible Dictionary*, edited by D. N. Freedman, 6 vols. (New York: Doubleday, 1992)
ABRL	Anchor Bible Reference Library
AGJU	Arbeiten zur Geschichte des antiken Judentums und des Urchristentums
AM	Athenäums Monografien
AnBib	Analecta biblica
ANRW II	*Aufstieg und Niedergang der römischen Welt*, part II: *Principat*
ANTC	Abingdon New Testament Commentaries
AsJ	*Asbury Journal*
ATD	Das Alte Testament Deutsch
AUSS	*Andrews University Seminary Studies*
BBB	Bonner biblische Beiträge
BDAG	Danker, F. W., W. Bauer, W. F. Arndt, and F. W. Gingrich, *A Greek-English Lexicon of the New Testament and Other Early Christian Literature*, 3rd. ed. (Chicago: University of Chicago Press, 2000)
BDB	Brow, F. S. R. Driver, and C. A. Briggs, *A Hebrew and English Lexicon of the Old Testament* (Oxford: Clarendon, 1907)
BDF	Blass, F. A. Debrunner, and R. W. Funk, *A Greek Grammar of the New Testament and Other Early Christian Literature* (Chicago: University of Chicago Press, 1961)
BECNT	Baker Exegetical Commentary on the New Testament
BETL	Bibliotheca ephemeridum theologicarum lovaniensium
BIBALDS	BIBAL Dissertation Series
BIS	Biblical Interpretation Series
BIW	The Bible in Its World
BKAT	Biblischer Kommentar, Altes Testament
BNTC	Black's New Testament Commentaries
BRS	Biblical Resource Series
BSac	*Bibliotheca sacra*

Abbreviations

BSR	Biblioteca di scienze religiose
BT	*The Bible Translator*
BU	Biblische Untersuchungen
BWANT	Beiträge zur Wissenschaft vom Alten und Neuen Testament
BZ	*Biblische Zeitschrift*
BZNW	Beihefte zur Zeitschrift für die neutestamentliche Wissenschaft
CBET	Contributions to Biblical Exegesis and Theology
CBQ	*Catholic Biblical Quarterly*
CBQMS	Catholic Biblical Quarterly Monograph Series
CBR	*Currents in Biblical Research*
CCom	Concordia Commentary
CCR	Cambridge Companions to Religion
CEPBT	Contemporary Evangelical Perspectives, Biblical Theology
CH	*Church History*
CNT	Commentaire du Nouveau Testament
CNTOT	*Commentary on the New Testament use of the Old Testament*, edited by G. K. Beale and D. A. Carson (Grand Rapids: Baker Academic, 2007)
CompNT	Companions to the New Testament
ConBNT	Coniectanea biblica: New Testament Series
CRBR	*Critical Review of Books in Religion*
CSJH	Chicago Studies in the History of Judaism
DLNT	*Dictionary of the Later New Testament and Its Developments*, edited by R. P. Martin and P. H. Davids (Downers Grove, IL: InterVarsity, 1997)
DPL	*Dictionary of Paul and His Letters*, edited by G. F. Hawthorne and R. P. Martin (Downers Grove, IL: InterVarsity, 1993)
EBib	Etudes bibliques
EdF	Erträge der Forschung
EDNT	*Exegetical Dictionary of the New Testament*, edited by H. Balz, G. Schneider, 3 vols. (Grand Rapids: Eerdmans, 1990-93)
EKK	Evangelisch-katholischer Kommentar zum Neuen Testament
EpC	Epworth Commentaries
ESEC	Emory Studies in Early Christianity
ETL	*Ephemerides theologicae lovanienses*
ETR	*Evangelical Theological Review*
EvQ	*Evangelical Quarterly*
ExpTim	*Expository Times*
FF	Foundations and Facets
FN	*Filología Neotestamentaria*
FRLANT	Forschungen zur Religion und Literatur des Alten und Neuen Testaments
GTA	Göttinger theologischer Arbeiten
HBT	*Horizons in Biblical Theology*
HCS	Hellenistic Culture and Society
HKNT	Handkommentar zum Neuen Testament

Abbreviations

HNTC	Harper's New Testament Commentaries
HTKNT	Herders theologischer Kommentar zum Neuen Testament
HTR	*Harvard Theological Review*
HTS	Harvard Theological Studies
HUT	Hermeneutische Untersuchungen zur Theologie
HvTSt	*Hervormde teologiese studies*
IB	*The Interpreter's Bible*, edited by G. A. Buttrick et al., 12 vols. (New York: Abingdon-Cokesbury, 1951–57)
IBS	*Irish Biblical Studies*
ICC	International Critical Commentary
IVPNTC	IVP New Testament Commentary Series
IRT	Issues in Religion and Theology
ISBL	Indiana Studies in Biblical Literature
ITS	*Indian Theological Studies*
JAAR	*Journal of the American Academy of Religion*
JBL	*Journal of Biblical Literature*
JETS	*Journal of the Evangelical Theological Society*
JPSSS	Journal of Pentecostal Studies Supplement Series
JSNT	*Journal for the Study of the New Testament*
JSNTSup	Journal for the Study of the New Testament Supplement Series
JSOTSup	Journal for the Study of the Old Testament Supplement Series
JSSM	Journal of Semitic Studies Monograph
JTS	*Journal of Theological Studies*
KEK	Kritisch-exegetischer Kommentar über das Neue Testament
LCL	Loeb Classic Library
LD	Lectio divina
LEH	Lust, Johan, Erik Eynikel, and Katrin Hauspie, *A Greek-English Lexicon of the Septuagint*, rev. ed. (Stuttgart: Deutsche Bibelgesellschaft, 2003)
LES	Library of Ecumenical Studies
LIntI	Luke the Interpreter of Israel
LNTS	Library of New Testament Studies
LSJ	Liddel, H. G., R. Scott, and H. S. Jones, *A Greek-English Lexicon*, 9th ed. (Oxford: Clarendon, 1996)
LUÅ	Lunds universitets årsskrif
NAC	New American Commentary
NEchtB	Neue Echter Bibel
NGS	New Gospel Studies
NIB	*New Interpreter's Bible*
NIBCOT	New International Biblical Commentary on the Old Testament
NICNT	New International Commentary on the New Testament
NIDNTT	*New International Dictionary of New Testament Theology*, edited by C. Brown, 4 vols. (Grand Rapids: Regency Reference Library, 1975–85)
NIGTC	New International Greek Testament Commentary
Neot	*Neotestamentica*

Abbreviations

NovT	*Novum Testamentum*
NovTSup	Supplements to Novum Testamentum
NTDH	Neukirchener theologische Dissertationen und Habilitationen
NTL	New Testament Library
NTM	New Testament Monographs
NTR	New Testament Readings
NTS	*New Testament Studies*
NTTh	New Testament Theology
NTTS	New Testament Tools and Studies
NTSI	The New Testament and the Scriptures of Israel
OBO	Orbis biblicus et orientalis
OBT	Overtures to Biblical Theology
OrChrAn	Orientalia christiana alalecta
ÖTKNT	Ökumenischer Taschenbuch-Kommentar zum Neuen Testament
OTL	Old Testament Library
PBTM	Paternoster Biblical and Theological Monographs
PC	Proclamation Commentaries
PFES	Publication of the Finnish Exegetical Society
PRSt	*Perspectives in Religious Studies*
RB	*Revue biblique*
RechBib	*Recherche Biblique*
RelAT	Religion in the Age of Transformation
RelSRev	*Religious Studies Review*
RevExp	*Review and Expositor*
RHR	*Revue de l'histoire des religions*
RNT	Regensburger Neues Testament
RNTS	Reading the New Testament Series
RRelRes	*Review of Religious Research*
SANT	Studien zum Alten und Neuen Testaments
SB	Sources bibliques
SBB	Stuttgarter biblische Beiträge
SBEC	Studies in the Bible and Early Christianity
SBLDS	Society of Biblical Literature Dissertation Series
SBLMS	Society of Biblical Literature Monograph Series
SBLSP	*Society of Biblical Literature Seminar Papers*
SBLSymS	Society of Biblical Literature Symposium Series
SBS	Stuttgarter Bibelstudien
SBT	Studies in Biblical Theology
SC	*Second Century*
SE	*Studia Evangelica*
SF	*Social Forces*
SFE	Sage Focus Editions
SNTSMS	Society of New Testament Studies Monograph Series
SNTW	Studies of the New Testament and Its World
SocR	*Sociology of Religion*

Abbreviations

SP	Sacra pagina
SPNT	Studies on Personalities of the New Testament
SRC	Studies in Religion and Culture
SSSRMS	Society for the Scientific Study of Religion Monograph Series
STDJ	Studies on the Text of the Desert of Judah
Str.B.	Strack, Hermann Leberecht, and Paul Billerbeck, *Kommentar zum Neuen Testament aus Talmud und Midrasch*, 6 vols. (Munich: C. H. Beck, 1922–61)
TANZ	Texte und Arbeiten zum neutestamentlichen Zeitalter
TDNT	*Theological Dictionary of the New Testament*, edited by G. Kittel and G. Friedrich, translated by G. W. Bromiley, 10 vols. (Grand Rapids: Eerdmans, 1964–76)
ThH	Théologie historique
THKNT	Theologischer Handkommentar zum Neuen Testament
TNTC	Tyndale New Testament Commentaries
TTE	*The Theological Educator*
TU	*Texte und Untersuchungen*
TZ	*Theologische Zeitschrift*
TynBul	*Tyndale Bulletin*
UM	*Urban Mission*
USQR	*Union Seminary Quarterly Review*
VT	*Vetus Testamentum*
VoxT	*Vox Theologica*
WBC	Word Biblical Commentary
WTJ	*Westminster Theological Journal*
WUNT	Wissenschaftliche Untersuchungen zum Neuen Testament
ZNW	*Zeitschrift für die neutestamentliche Wissenschaft und die Kunde der älteren Kirche*
ZTK	*Zeitschrift für Theologie und Kirche*

SCRIPTURES AND ANCIENT SOURCES

'Abot R. Nat.	*'Abot de Rabbi Nathan*
1 Clem.	*1 Clement*
1/2 En.	*1/2 Enoch*
2 Bar.	*2 Baruch*
Acts Thom.	*Acts of Thomas*
Add Esth	Additions to Esther
Ambrose, *Virg.*	*Concerning Virgins*
Apoc. Ab.	*Apocalypse of Abraham*
Apoc. Dan.	*Apocalypse of Daniel*
Apoc. El.	*Apocalypse of Elijah*
Apoc. Pet.	*Apocalypse of Peter*
Apuleius, *Metam.*	*Metamorphoses* (*The Golden Ass*)
Augustine, *Doctr. chr.*	*Christian Instruction*

Abbreviations

Augustine, *Fel.*	*Against Felix*
Augustine, *Nat. orig.*	*The Nature and Origin of the Soul*
CD	*Damascus Document*
Clement of Alexandria, *Quis div.*	*Salvation of the Rich*
Cyprian, *Laps.*	*On the Lapsed*
Cyprian, *Tr. Nov.*	*Treatise against Novatian*
Cyprian, *Unit. Eccl.*	*The Unity of the Catholic Church*
Did.	*Didache*
Eusebius, *Hist. eccl.*	*Ecclesiastical History*
Gos. Jud.	*Gospel of Judas*
Gos. Thom.	*Gospel of Thomas*
Herm. Mand.	*Shepherd of Hermas, Mandates*
Herm. Sim.	*Shepherd of Hermas, Similitudes*
Herm. Vis.	*Shepherd of Hermas, Visions*
Hippolytus, *Haer.*	*Refutation of All Heresies*
Ign. *Eph.*	*Ignatius, To the Ephesians*
Ign. *Eph.*	*To the Ephesians*
Ign. *Magn.*	*To the Magnesians*
Ign. *Phld.*	*To the Philadelphians*
Ign. *Rom.*	*To the Romans*
Ign. *Smyrn.*	*To the Smyrnaeans*
Iranaeus, *Haer.*	*Against Heresies*
Jerome, *Comm. Matt.*	*Commentary on Matthew*
John Chrysostom, *Hom. 1 Cor.*	*Homily on the First Epistle to the Corinthians*
Jos. Asen.	*Joseph and Aseneth*
Josephus, *Ag. Ap.*	*Against Apion*
Josephus, *Ant.*	*Jewish Antiquities*
Josephus, *J.W.*	*Jewish War*
Jub.	*Jubilees*
Justin, *Dial.*	*Dialogue with Trypho*
Lactantius, *Inst.*	*The Divine Institutes*
Lucian, *Alex.*	*Alexander the False Prophet*
LXX	Septuagint
Mart. Ascen. Isa.	*Martyrdom and Ascension of Isaiah*
Mart. Habib	*Martyrdom of Habib the Deacon*
Mart. Pol.	*Martyrdom of Polycarp*
MT	Masoretic Text
Origen, *Cels.*	*Against Celsus*
Origen, *Comm. Jo.*	*Commentary on the Gospel of John*
Origen, *Comm. Matt.*	*Commentary on the Gospel of Matthew*
Origen, *Princ.*	*First Principles*
Philo, *Alleg.*	*Allegorical Interpretation*
Philo, *Conf.*	*On the Confusion of Tongues*
Philo, *Flight*	*On Flight and Finding*

Abbreviations

Philo, *Names*	*On the Change of Names*
Philo, *Spec.*	*On the Special Laws*
Pliny, *Nat.*	*Natural History*
Ps.-Clem.	*Pseudo-Clementines*
Ps.-Longinus, *Sub.*	*On the Sublime*
Pss. Sol.	*Psalms of Solomon*
Quintilian, *Inst.*	*Institutio oratoria*
Sib. Or.	*Sibylline Oracles*
Sus	Susanna
T. Ab.	*Testament of Abraham*
T. Dan.	*Testament of Daniel*
Tg. Eccl.	*Targum Ecclesiastes*
T. Gad	*Testament of Gad*
T. Isaac	*Testament of Isaac*
T. Job	*Testament of Job*
T. Jos.	*Testament of Joseph*
T. Jud.	*Testament of Judah*
T. Levi	*Testament of Levi*
T. Naph.	*Testament of Naphtali*
T. Zeb.	*Testament of Zebulun*
Tertullian, *Marc.*	*Against Marcion*
Tertullian, *Nat.*	*To the Heathen*
Tertullian, *Praescr.*	*Prescription against Heretics*
Tertullian, *Scorp.*	*Antidote for the Scorpion's Sting*

Introduction

A perplexing question for our times involves the problem of human difference, which seems to be at the heart of human evil, whether it be racism, hatred, prejudice, genocide, religious wars, oppression, or injustice. If cultural conflicts lie at the heart of human societies, then perhaps, as Miroslav Volf maintains, we ought to have as the center of our theological reflection the notions of identity and otherness.[1] The idea of social identity has become vitally important for our age, and perhaps the more we learn about "the other," the more chances will arise for promoting peace among people of different cultures, nations, and religions. My study accepts this challenge from an angle that is often neglected—religious apostasy. Defectors from religious communities have often been polarized as "the other" in contrast to those of "us" who participate in major religious communities.

Although it is my personal wish that contemporary communities understand themselves and others with more insight, sympathy, and open dialogue, this study does not necessarily have as its main goal the incentive to place all apostates in sympathetic light. Rather, it intends to provide a thorough examination aiming at more clarity on how apostasy is viewed in the various New Testament communities and hopefully open up further discussions on the issue.

By "apostasy" I mean foremost the phenomenon that occurs when a religious follower or group of followers turn away from or otherwise repudiate the central beliefs and practices they once embraced in a respective religious community.[2] Quite often the words "apostate" and "defector" are the terms used by these communities to label persons that have abandoned the group's core values and teachings. For

---

1. Volf, *Exclusion and Embrace*, 17.

2. For discussions on the history of interpretation of apostasy (primarily Christian) see Oropeza, *Paul and Apostasy*, 1–34; Peterson, "Perseverance and Apostasy," 119–25; Davis, "Perseverance of the Saints," 213–28. For general overviews (primarily Jewish and Christian), see e.g., Dov, "Apostasy," 3.201–15; Kippenberg, "Apostasy," 1.353–56; Preston, "Expulsion," 5:233; Schereschewsky, "Apostate," 377–79; Ermoni, "Abjuration," 1.98–104; Foakes-Jackson, "Apostasy," 1.623–25; Van Hove, "Apostasy," 1.624–26; Starbuck, "Backsliding," 2:319–21.

simplicity's sake this study will use "apostasy" and "defection" interchangeably even though some scholars argue that the former emphasizes religious and theological falling away and the latter stresses a sociologically oriented and less negative departure. Likewise the apostate is sometimes considered more actively against the religious group he or she once espoused than is the defector.[3]

A distinction between apostates and dissidents or so-called "heretics" must be made even though the terms may frequently overlap in meaning.[4] The heretic deviates from beliefs and practices of a host religion but often remains within the religious community; the apostate normally abandons the religion altogether.[5] Perhaps in the New Testament it is not expedient to use this meaning for the term "heretic" because, as a number of scholars argue, this word often presupposes in Christian circles an established embodiment of teachings identifying "orthodoxy" from which the heretic has deviated.[6] A standard of this sort developed within Christian communities over the process of several centuries and was eventually codified by the ecumenical creeds. In the first-century world of the New Testament, however, no elaborate creed existed for the emerging Christians. Hence "false teachers," "dissidents," and similar terms are more appropriate for my purposes and will be used in this work.

A number of studies demonstrate that contemporary and ancient religious groups frequently lose followers who repudiate their former beliefs.[7] While it is

---

3. On possible distinctions see further, Bromley, "Social Construction of Contested Exit Roles," 19–47; Wilson, *Leaving the Fold*, 3–4, 9–11, 22, 120. On New Testament terms related to apostasy see, e.g., Oropeza, *Paul and Apostasy*, 218–19n113; Brown, "Concept of Apostasy"; Bauder, "Fall, Fall Away," 1.606–11; Mateos, "Analisis semantico," 57–92; Humbert, "Essai d'une Théologie du Scandale," 1–28; Stählin, *Skandalon*; idem, "σκάνδαλον, σκανδαλίζω," 7.338–58; Schlier, "ἀρνέομαι," 1.469–73; idem, "ἀφίστημι, ἀποστασία, διχοστασία," 1.512–14; Wilckens, "ὑποκρίνομαι," 8.563–71; idem, "ὕστερος," 8.592–601; Michaelis, "πίπτω," 1.161–73; Braun, "πλανάω," 6.228–53; Wolter, "παράπτωμα," 3.33–34; Giesen, "σκανδαλίζω," 3.248–50.

4. On the development of the Greek word for heresy (αἵρεσις), see Von Staden, "Hairesis and Heresy," 76–100; Simon, "Greek Haresis to Christian Heresy," 101–16. For early Jewish heresy see Stern, *Jewish Identity*, 109–12; Goodman, "Function of the Minim," 1.501–10; Horbury, "Benediction of the minim," 19–61; Cohen, "Virgin Defiled," 1–11.

5. In agreement with Wilson, *Leaving the Fold*, 12–13, 22. Clear-cut distinctions between heretics as repudiating beliefs and doctrines and apostates repudiating ethics and practices cannot be demonstrated consistently in earliest Christian writings, as will become evident in this study, especially when we examine Jude and 2 Peter.

6. On the development of heresy in Christian traditions, see, e.g., Desjardins, "Bauer and Beyond," 65–82; Wilson, *Leaving the Fold*, 11–16, 135; Segal, *Two Powers in Heaven*, esp. 5; and the classic treatment by Bauer, *Orthodoxy and Heresy*.

7. For contemporary examples, see, e.g., Partridge and Reid, *Finding and Losing Faith*; McKnight and Ondrey, *Finding Faith, Losing Faith*; Jindra, *Konversion und Stufentransformation*, 229–305; Francis and Katz, *Joining and Leaving Religion*; Bromley, *Falling from the Faith*; idem, *Politics of Religious*

virtually impossible to count with certainty the number of apostates in religious communities past and present,⁸ Stephen Wilson nonetheless canvasses numerous examples from early Jewish and Christian sources to conclude that such phenomena is by no means rare: "Their numbers are significant enough . . . for us to grant them a more prominent role in the religious life of the ancient world than they have heretofore been given."⁹

If evidence for ancient religious apostasy seems infrequent, this may be due in part to the reluctance of religious communities to publicize accounts of defectors from their ranks. Few groups wished to capitalize on their failures, and apostates did not normally write about their own apostasies or label their departures as such. Wilson, for example, brings up Eusebius' admittance of open reluctance in writing about Christians who fell away during the persecution of Diocletian in the early fourth century; Eusebius thinks it would be improper and unprofitable to describe such "melancholy misfortunes" and determines not to mention those who "have made utter shipwreck of their salvation" (Eusebius, *Hist. eccl.* 8.2.2–3).¹⁰

Moreover, clearly defined and universal boundaries did not always exist between ancient Jews, Christians, and "pagans" so as to make lucid exactly when individuals had stepped over the line from Christian to Jewish beliefs or vice versa. To complicate things even more for us, all the earliest Christ-followers were Jewish.¹¹ The early disciples of Jesus were often thought to be another Jewish sect belonging to emerging Judaism (e.g., Acts 18:12–16).¹² Hence, boundaries between the Christ-followers

---

Apostasy; Barbour, *Versions of Deconversion*; Sherkat and Wilson, "Preferences, Constraints, and Choices," 993–1026; Hadaway, "Five Types of Apostates," 26–34; Brinkerhoff and Mackie, "Casting Off the Bond," 235–53; Hunsberger, "Apostasy," 21–38.

8. For examples of apostasy in early Christianity, see Sato, "Martyrdom and Apostasy," 619–34; Bardy, *Conversion au Christianisme*, 294–351; Guignebert, "Demi-Chrétiens et l'Eligise Antique," 65–102; Wilson, *Leaving the Fold*, 66–99. For examples in early Judaism, see Feldman, *Jew and Gentile in the Ancient World*, 79–83 who holds to a minimalist view. For a non-minimalist perspective see Wilson, *Leaving the Fold*, 23–65.

9. Wilson, *Leaving the Fold*, 133.

10. Ibid., 8–9. Translation in quotes of Eusebius by Lake, *Eusebius*.

11. On the history of research related to Jewish Christians, see, e.g., Paget, "Definition of the Terms Jewish Christian," 22–52; Skarsaune, "Jewish Believers in Jesus in Antiquity," 3–21; Jackson-McCabe, "What's in a Name?," 7–38.

12. Here I am using the term "sect" to refer to a splinter group of religious adherents that have deviated or broken away from a more dominant religious group. For further nuances, definitions, and discussions related to the term, see, e.g., Wilson, *Religious Sects*; idem, *Magic and the Millennium*; Stark and Bainbridge, "Of Churches, Sects, and Cults," 117–33; idem, *The Future of Religion*; Chalcraft, *Sectarianism in Early Judaism*.

and other Jews were not explicitly clear; the dividing line between "Christianity" and "Judaism" developed over the process of many decades and perhaps even centuries.[13]

The level of Greco-Roman influence within early Christian and Jewish communities was likewise interpreted differently depending on the issue. John Barclay provides three master descriptors for how we are to understand the Hellenization of ancient Jews from the Diaspora: (1) Assimilation: social integration into the majority society. Jewish integration with Hellenistic culture could range anywhere from their being socially aloof to Gentiles, to formal contacts, to attending sporting events, to intimate contact and education in Hellenism, to the complete abandonment of Jewish distinctives. (2) Acculturation: exposure to non-material facets of Hellenistic culture such as cardinal virtues, linguistic, literary, and educational aspects. Jewish familiarity in this regard could range from their having no facility in Greek, to acquaintance with Greek values, to familiarity with literature (e.g., rhetoric and philosophy), to scholarly expertise. (3) Accommodation: the degree one permits the knowledge of acculturation to shape one's heritage, which for ancient Jews could span from antagonism towards Hellenistic culture, to reinterpreting but maintaining some uniqueness in Judaism, to the complete submersion of that uniqueness.[14] These categories help us discern boundaries in which ancient Jews became Hellenized and abandoned ancient Judaism.

One of Barclay's important conclusions is that we cannot determine who was an apostate but only who was *considered* an apostate by someone else labeling that person as such.[15] The religious communities may claim that someone has become an apostate for abandoning the group even though, from the perspective of the so-called apostate, he or she was still faithfully serving God. Paul's radical change from Pharisee to follower of Christ exemplifies this point. He was perceived in certain Jewish sectors as an apostate due to his alleged abandonment of Mosaic Law (Acts 21:21, 28), and yet from his own perspective, he believed his change was something positive and ordained by God (Gal 1:13–16; Phil 3:4–8; cf. Acts 9:1–20). Even so, the concept of apostasy within a religious group need not be entirely relative. Barclay

---

13. For a second century view of this departure, see Dunn, *Parting of the Ways*; for a later view suggesting the break during the Theodosian era (fifth century) see Boyarin, "Justin Martyr Invents Judaism," 427–61. A pre-70 view is argued by Jossa, *Jews or Christians?* For a continuing relationship between early Jews and Christians, see Becker and Reed, *Ways That Never Parted*.

14. Barclay, "Paul among Diaspora Jews," 89–120. See other examples of boundaries and elusiveness in McKnight, *Light among the Gentiles*, 18–19. Differently Cohen, "Crossing the Boundary," 13–33, brings out seven ways Gentiles showed affection to Judaism, which range from "admiring some aspect of Judaism" to "converting to Judaism and 'becoming a Jew.'" Essentials of early Jewish identity are discussed in, e.g., Schiffman, *Who Was a Jew?*; Stern, *Jewish Identity*.

15. E.g., Barclay, "Who Was Considered an Apostate," 80–98, esp. 80–81.

selects a sampling of Jewish writings from the Second Temple Era, and in the midst of examining diverse perspectives on which particular acts constitute apostasy, he finds out that a rising consensus exists in relation to idolatry and the infringement of Jewish food laws. These violations more or less are consistently associated with apostasy.[16]

Although further probings into Second Temple literature are needed to confirm Barclay's study, his model nevertheless is helpful for discerning boundaries related to the Hellenization of ancient Jews from the Diaspora. The scheme is less successful for determining apostasy in early Christian literature because many of these writings are addressed to Gentile audiences who belong to the Hellenistic society.[17] Their struggle is in the opposite direction: a striving to divest themselves from pagan influences in an effort to conform to the values of the minority group of Christ followers who used Jewish scriptures and teachings for guidance. For them apostasy involves a reverse assimilation back to the cultural mores they once embraced; they are unlike ancient Jews whose struggle was to maintain their distinctiveness and not be swallowed up by the majority culture.

In any case, if a tentative consensus on apostasy can be reached by Barclay regarding Jews from the Diaspora, and every religious movement has its boundaries, then my study will attempt to identify where the lines are drawn against apostasy within the emerging Christian communities in the New Testament. It may be the case that, similar to Diaspora Jews, the early Christian communities mark their boundaries differently while at the same time maintaining a unified position on other core issues. It is my aim to explore these writings and bring into sharper relief how these communities perceived apostasy.[18]

My task for this study, then, is fourfold.

First, I am challenged to *identify the communities* from which the warnings against defection arise, and identify the persons thought to be apostates from these respective communities. The chapters in this book and the following volumes will recognize whenever possible the author, audience, and apostates within the various communities being addressed in the New Testament. Quite often this pursuit involves surmising the community situation and potential opponents. This is often

16. Ibid., 91. Stern, *Jewish Identity*, 106-9, marks Jewish boundaries in relation to "limited apostates" (those who reject few commandments such as dietary rules, Sabbath, and circumcision) and "comprehensive apostates" (those who worship *avoda zara* and reject the entire Torah) based on the Talmud and other Jewish literature.

17. Helpful here in evaluating Barclay's work is Wilson, *Leaving the Fold*, 114-18.

18. Although this will not be done by using Barclay's model for Diaspora Jews, the concept of assimilation will in a number of cases assist our interpretation of the New Testament communities and their respective situations.

stated in the beginning sections of each chapter, which often engage or rely on other scholarly works. It may turn out that not every community discloses their defectors but that certain churches or individuals are thought to be heading towards apostasy.

Second, I will examine the *perceived nature of apostasy within the respective communities.* Important inquiries in this regard are related to finding out what type of apostasy is being warned against and how do the defectors, if there are any, fall away. Issues such as divisions among community members and leaders, their rejection of community teachings, denying Christ during persecutions, or committing immoral acts that place them "out" of the religious community may be some important topics to consider. From this vantage point we might be able to observe whether the apostasy is subjective and relative to claims of the New Testament authors, or whether there are some objective and universal aspects to the claims. Moreover, sometimes apostasy may be implied in light of preventative measures or exhortations the community is supposed to follow. In this case a person might be deemed apostate who resists or rejects these measures. Relevant passages in the respective New Testament writings will be examined with these types of questions in mind. The majority of each chapter will be focused on interpreting such passages.

Third, the chapters address *the perceived consequences of apostasy*. In a word, what will happen to those who turn away from the community and its message? If the biblical writers normally understand apostates as "out" of the community, relevant concepts related to this phenomenon such as expulsion from the community and divine judgment must be probed. Related to the consequences of defection is the potential for restoration. Once the person or group has fallen away, does the author or community make it possible for them to be restored to the community and a right standing with God? Often passages related to the second coming of Christ (*parousia*) and final judgment will be read in light of such consequences. Intricacies about final judgment, however, will not normally be pursued (e.g., I am not interested in questions that probe the nature of hell, how long the wicked might stay there, and whether annihilationism is more humane than eternal conscious punishment).

Finally, with the results of this investigation from all three volumes I will *compare the various New Testament communities' views of apostasy* to highlight similarities and differences. This final point will be made possible by a comprehensive study of the entire New Testament corpus on apostasy; a task that has been rarely attempted.[19] The results of the complexity, unity, and diversity related to apostasy

---

19. As far as I know, in the past fifty years the most influential historical-critical study on apostasy that covers the entire New Testament corpus is Marshall, *Kept by the Power of God*. His outcome tends to be univocal, highlighting similarities between New Testament authors as he attempts to steer a middle position between Berkouwer, *Faith and Perseverance*, who for Marshall minimizes the real danger

among New Testament communities in the gospels will be noticed at the conclusion of this volume, but a canonical comparison cannot be appreciated until we reach the conclusion of volume three, after all the relevant communities of the New Testament have been covered.

It is extremely difficult to attempt a one-size-fits-all method of interpretation as I attempt to cover a range of literature that includes everything from third-person narratives (e.g., Acts) to apocalyptic visions (e.g., Revelation). My method throughout the volumes will be somewhat eclectic. In my view the interpretation of apostasy in the New Testament should include at least the following influences and interactions: 1) historical settings and situations, hence my prompting of historical-critical and social inquiries; 2) exhortations and authoritative statements attempting to persuade audiences, hence my prompting of literary/intra- and intertextual inquiries; and 3) language about human relationships with God, that is, theological inquiries.[20] These three venues will be frequented in this study. Of course this does not mean that other methods of interpreting biblical apostasy are not important, but, lest my study become almost twice its present length, I have chosen for the most part not to use other methods.[21]

This study frequently interprets passages intertextually, that is, by virtue of insights derived from the source materials used by the respective authors, whether by

---

behind warning passages, and Bultmann, *Theology of the New Testament*, who minimizes assurance and maximizes human effort (cf. Marshall, 200–207). Due to the age and modest length of Marshall's work, it is quite evident that a more extensive and up-to-date study is in order. Other books that aim towards covering the whole New Testament on the subject include Schreiner and Caneday, *Race Set before Us*; and Claybrook, *Once Saved, Always Saved?* Schreiner and Caneday's work is less comprehensive than Claybrook's, but their study is more academically oriented than the latter even though it is written for a somewhat popular audience. Unfortunately, Claybrook's work avoids footnotes and interacting with scholarship. Both works are motivated by conservative biblical-theological assumptions, concerns, and agendas that conform all the scriptures to a univocal position on apostasy and perseverance. They come to virtually opposite conclusions on the issue, perhaps indirectly demonstrating a limitation with such approaches that do not seem to progress much further than classic systematic-theological debates between Calvinists and Arminians. Studies such as Dunn, *Unity and Diversity in the New Testament* demonstrate diversity of viewpoints among the New Testament writers. They did not all think alike on every issue (e.g., Gal 2:1–14); hence their perspectives may not be alike on every aspect of apostasy.

20. On this level it will become evident that questions related to soteriology (e.g., justification/righteousness, perseverance or "staying in" salvation), ecclesiology (e.g., community fellowship, election), and eschatology (e.g., second coming/Parousia, divine judgment) will dominate some of our discussions.

21. For studies on apostasy using social-scientific, cultural-anthropological, and ideological approaches, see, e.g., deSilva, "Hebrews 6:4–8," 33–57, 225–35; idem, "Exchanging Favor for Wrath," 91–116; Oropeza, "Apostasy in the Wilderness," 69–86; idem, *Paul and Apostasy*, esp. 34–53; Barclay, "Deviance and Apostasy," 114–27; Salevao, *Legitimation in the Letter to the Hebrews*; Neyrey, *Ideology of Revolt*.

citation formula (e.g., "it is written"), by referencing without formula, or by echo.[22] Fruitful studies may come out of my examining catchwords or phrases that point to passages in Israel's scriptures or other traditions. It is assumed that the original contexts of these words and phrases have informed the New Testament authors and influenced their choice of words and the manner in which they convey their arguments.[23] Without trying to make an ironclad set of rules for determining the existence of allusions/echoes, I do believe that context, clarity, persuasiveness of the case being made, and assumptions about the original author's purposes and arguments become important factors for evaluating their plausibility in a selected pericope. These echoes, whether consciously or unconsciously created by the author, should be examined on a case-by-case basis, and the reality and strength of them determined as such.[24] Some common themes that occasionally surface in this study and speak to apostasy are the spiritual obduracy of God's people, God's people experiencing a new exodus and wilderness journey, and the idea of two ways, one righteous and the other unrighteous, set before God's people.[25] I attempt to connect some of the dots behind the texts to unearth subtexts that seem to show a connection between Israel's ancient stories, prophecies, and teachings and the later New Testament stories, teachings, and exhortations.[26]

A final word about terminology is in order. The timelines related to identifying Christianity as distinct from Judaism are notoriously difficult to determine. The name "Christian" (Χριστιανός) developed in the first century (Acts 11:19; 26:28; 1 Pet 4:16), but it is not entirely clear when this designation became the universally normative one for identifying those communities who believed in Jesus as the

---

22. By interextuality I mean the method of interpretation by which a text (here biblical) may recite, echo, reconfigure, recontextualize, or amplify other texts outside itself. For a helpful resource explicating intertextuality, see Robbins, *Exploring the Texture of Texts*, 40–70. Though I recognize that some scholars make distinctions between "allusion" and "echoes," I think it more prudent to use the words interchangeably.

23. See, e.g., Stegner, "Romans 9:6–29," 37–52.

24. My expectations, then, are more flexible than the seven tests of Hays, *Echoes of Scripture*, 29–32.

25. The writings of Isaiah will stand out prominently in this study in regard to the first and second motifs. An Isaianic preponderance is not arbitrary since its importance to New Testament studies is well recognized. Sawyer, *Fifth Gospel*, for example, shows that about 100 verses from Isaiah are quoted or clearly alluded to in the gospels, Paul, and Revelation. See also Moyise and Menken, *Isaiah in the New Testament*.

26. Although my own focus in this regard will mostly center on Israel's scriptures, much more could be said about potential echoes and influence from Greco-Roman literature, Targums, Rabbinic thought, Qumran texts, Philo, Josephus, and other sources, which provide clues as to how New Testament authors interpret words and handle parallel language and thoughts. But such inclusions would have required me to write more than three volumes related to this project!

Christ.²⁷ Other early names for the faithful include "the way" (Acts 9:2), "Nazarenes" (Acts 24:5), and the "church" (1 Cor 15:9), just to name a few.²⁸ I will sometimes use the term "Christians" to describe New Testament communities, but what I technically mean is that they are "emerging" Christians whose identity was not necessarily separated in a complete sense from Jewish religious roots and identity. I will also use the term "believers" quite frequently to designate Christ-followers.

By "author" I mean the person or persons who wrote the New Testament writing under examination. By "readers," "audience," or "auditors," I normally mean the community or communities that were the original recipients of a given New Testament text.²⁹ By my use of "we" and first-person plurals I am often referring to myself rhetorically, though admittedly I am sometimes extending my words to the readers of this study in hope of a shared opinion.

This first of three volumes examines the four gospels. Mark is given priority in the Synoptic Gospels, and so is covered before Matthew. I have combined Luke and Acts because these writings are attributed to the same author and communicate very similar themes. I have included the Johannine epistles with my study of John's gospel with the conviction that these writings come from the same community and perhaps convey the same or similar phenomena regarding apostasy.

---

27. Leaning towards a later date than the Antioch reference in Acts 11:26 is Horrell, "Label Χριστιανός," 361–81. Other early references to the Christians appear in Tacitus, *Annals* 15.44; Suetonius, *Nero* 16.2; Pliny, *Epistulae* 10.96.1–3; *Did.* 12.5; Ign. *Eph.* 11.2; Ign. *Rom.* 3.2; *Mart. Pol* .3.2; 10.1; 12.1–2.

28. See other designations for the first community of Christ (Jerusalem) in Bauckham, "James and the Jerusalem Community," 56–60.

29. The word "community," however, may not always refer to the recipients. Context will determine its meaning.

1

The Gospel of Mark

The Message of Persecution and Obduracy for the Markan Community

The traditional view of the community behind Mark's gospel suggests that it was written in Rome somewhere between the middle to late 60s CE.[1] According to the church father Papias and later sources, John Mark authored the gospel using the "memoirs" of Saint Peter.[2] A close relationship between Peter and Mark is assumed in 1 Pet 5:13, and internal evidence from Mark's gospel is said to support a Gentile or Roman audience. Among other arguments the text contains Latinisms[3] and assumes the reader lacks familiarity with certain Jewish customs and Aramaic words.[4] Mark, who is probably Jewish Christian,[5] may be writing this gospel primarily for an audience who already follows Christ, but it is also possible that non-Christians heard and read it.[6]

---

1. Contemporary scholarship often dates this gospel either during or right after the Jewish war with Rome (c. 66–70 CE): see list of supporters in Guelich, *Mark 1–8:26*, xxxi.

2. Irenaeus, *Haer.* 3.1.1; Eusebius, *Hist. eccl.* 2.15.1–2; 3.39.14–16; 6.14.5–7; Collins, *Mark*, 7–10, 96–102.

3. Mark 5:9; 6:37; 12:42; 15:15–16, 39.

4. E.g., 3:17; 5:41; 7:3–11, 34; 15:22, 34, 42. On the other hand, the gospel probably assumes that the audience is familiar with Israel's scriptures: cf. Mark 1:2–3; 4:12; 7:6f, 10; 8:18; and so on.

5. In the New Testament he apparently grows up in Jerusalem and his mother's house is an early center for the Christ-followers (Acts 12:12). His relative is Barnabas, who is said to be a Levite (Col 4:10; cf. Acts 4:36), and he assists Barnabas and Paul on their mission, which includes preaching in the synagogues (Acts 13:5, 13; cf. 12:25; 15:37, 39). On Mark see further Philemon 24; 2 Tim 4:11; Jefford, "Mark," 4.557–58.

6. Beavis, *Mark's Audience*, 171–72, raises this possibility regarding Mark's audience. Gundry, *Mark*,

In the Footsteps of Judas and Other Defectors

A number of scholars, however, question the biblical Mark as author of this gospel and posit that the community behind the text originates from Galilee.[7] If from Galilee, the community may be more Jewish than traditionally assumed. The followers could be awaiting the second coming or redefining the kingdom of God in relation to Galilee.[8] A polemical reading of the gospel suggests for some that this community was highly interested in reaching Gentiles with the good news, and they opposed believers in Jerusalem, considering the original disciples to be embracing false teachings.[9] The gospel shows the demise of the disciples from insiders to outsiders.[10] Werner Kelber presents the Twelve as originally insiders (Mark 1:1–4:34), but they grow spiritually blind, with their hearts hardened (4:35—8:21) to the extent that they become Jesus' opponents and do not understand his upcoming suffering in Jerusalem (8:22—10:52). Then they misunderstand his role as Messiah and associate God's kingdom with the temple in Jerusalem (11:1–13:37). In the final section of the narrative, the disciples fall away from Jesus and remain in Jerusalem instead of going to Galilee; the latter location is where the resurrected Jesus is to meet them, but the women fail to relay to this message to the disciples (14:1—16:8). Such a reading suggests the Markan community as Galilean Christians who opposed some false teachings arising from the Twelve and an apostate church in Jerusalem.

This scenario for the Markan community is highly questionable. First, the ending of Mark 16 leaves the impression that Jesus sought to restore the disciples after they abandoned him during his arrest (16:7–8; cf. 14:27–31, 50).[11] Even though the text finishes abruptly in 16:8, the shorter ending of Mark does not leave us with the impression that Jesus has abandoned his disciples for abandoning him.[12] Jesus promises his disciples that he would meet them in Galilee after he had risen from the dead (14:28; cf. 16:7), and Mark's audience would have no doubt regarded Jesus' words as

---

1026, goes further to argue that Mark was primarily written to non-believers as religious propaganda.

7. For the Galilean view, see, e.g., Roskam, *Purpose of the Gospel*. Other popular provenances include Syria or Alexandria. See further discussions on the Markan provenance and communities in Peterson, *Origins of Mark*; Black, *Mark*, chs. 3–5; Collins, *Mark*, 96–102; Matera, *Saying about Mark*.

8. On the first view, see, e.g., Marxsen, *Mark the Evangelist*; and the second, see, e.g., Kelber, *Kingdom in Mark*.

9. For a convenient synopsis of major supporters, see Matera, *Saying about Mark*, 42–46.

10. On various opinions related to insiders and outsiders in Mark 4, see Beavis, *Mark's Audience*, 70–75.

11. The longer ending of Mark 16 that extends to verse 20 is found in the Majority Text (e.g., KJV, NKJV) and other witnesses but is not found in important Greek manuscripts such as ℵ and B. I do not consider the longer ending to be authentic. See discussion in Metzger, *Textual Commentary*, 102–7.

12. Contrast the view that sees Peter's denials as a last hope for the disciples that failed: Kelber, *Oral*, 128–29.

reliable.¹³ If so, then reconciliation between the risen Christ and his disciples may be assumed. Moreover, Mark's gospel was not written in a vacuum: both its author and audience would know from oral tradition and possibly even surviving witnesses that these same disciples became the first leaders in the early church. Second, while Galilee plays a major role in Mark (and Matthew), this may be due to the original disciples' sentiment for the area: it is the place where Jesus and his earliest followers originate.¹⁴ The region is also associated with a prophetic mission to the Gentiles. Galilee becomes the headquarters for the apostolic commission to go out and preach the gospel, reflecting the Isaianic call for Israel to be a light to the nations.¹⁵ The importance of Galilee, then, has more to do with its prophetic significance than the identification of Mark's community. Third, the Markan emphasis on the disciples' failures probably suggests the author's pastoral intentions on discipleship rather than a desire to refute rival church leaders. Stephen Barton writes cogently regarding Mark's gospel: "it is *a priori* far more likely that he [Mark] is concerned to pass on the tradition in a way that will summon his readers to faith and instruct them in the way of true discipleship rather than to engage in acts of subtle literary character assassination designed to undermine the leaders of neighboring churches."¹⁶

A relevant question related to a specific community addressed in Mark's gospel is whether one can be really known at all. Unlike the Pauline epistles, no community is explicitly named as the recipients in this writing. In fact, a stationary and ongoing communal aspect of Christian living found in the other gospels seems to be lacking in Mark.¹⁷ Richard Burridge demonstrates how the gospels resemble Greco-Roman biographies, and as such they may have been intended for wide circulation.¹⁸ Moreover, Richard Bauckham challenges the community perspectives of the four

---

13. See Collins, *Mark*, 801. This reunion is not referring to the *parousia* because the main text on the *parousia* assumes that in the future Christ's disciples are faithfully proclaiming the gospel; i.e., the restoration of the disciples has already taken place (13:9–13). See further Stein, "Short Note," 445–52; Tannehill, "Disciples in Mark," 156–57n39; cf. 151–52.

14. If we assume for a change that Papias was right and the Markan account reflects the thoughts of Peter, a fisherman from Galilee, this would seem to be one reason for the gospel's sentiment of the region.

15. Matt 4:15/Isa 9:1–2; 26:32; 28:7, 10, 16–20; Mark 13:10; 14:28; 16:6–7/1:24; cf. Isa 42:6; 49:6; 60:1–3.

16. Barton, "Can We Identify," 184. Barton, however, is reluctant to identify a specific community to Mark.

17. E.g., Matt 18:15–20; John 13:12–17, 35; Luke 22:19; Acts 2:42–47. Cf. Rhoads, *Reading Mark*, 104–8. Rhoads opines that Mark establishes a "network" of Jesus followers.

18. Burridge, *What Are the Gospels?*; idem, "About People," 113–45.

gospels by stressing, among other things, that their circulation was not limited to specific communities.[19]

Nevertheless, we consider the task of identifying a community behind Mark (and other gospels) to have some positive interpretative value. There seems to be a reason behind our author highlighting topics and issues such as suffering, spiritual obduracy, discipleship, explanation of Aramaic terms, and reinterpreting the Torah in relation to foods, and the reason does not appear to be explained entirely by our suggesting that this gospel was widely circulated and has evangelistic or theological agendas. The author lived within a specific community of Christ-followers that no doubt had concerns begging to be addressed, and a text about Jesus and his early followers would seem to be a proper vehicle for which to address them, regardless of whether the writing was intended to stay within the community or not. These and other issues point us in the direction that Mark is addressing a particular community and not just generic Christians. Even if this gospel were written with a number of communities in mind, this would not rule out that the author could have orchestrated his work in a way that stresses or at least addresses some of the needs of his own community. If the author of Mark's gospel radiates with instructions about discipleship, it seems less plausible to me that he would have in mind an audience he does not know than a community that he does know.

A COMMUNITY IN THE MATRIX OF ROMAN PERSECUTION

Mark's audience was expected to learn from the disciples' mistakes and lack of faith as well as their successes.[20] In this sense the stories function implicitly as exhortations. In a negative sense they warn against apostasy: Christ-followers should always be careful not to abandon Christ as did the disciples when facing external pressures (e.g., 14:50, 66–72). In a positive sense the narratives encourage authentic discipleship: being a true follower of Jesus involves a willingness to confess him as the Christ even in the midst of suffering. If the traditional provenance and date of this gospel are accepted, perhaps the Markan stress on suffering is related to Nero's persecution of Christians that reportedly involved ghastly tortures.[21] There seems to be no

---

19. Bauckham, "For Whom Were Gospels Written?," 9–48. For a discussion of the debate, see Klink, "Gospel Community Debate," 60–85.

20. Their failures will be addressed below; some of the commendable things they did include their decision to leave all and follow Jesus (1:17–20; 2:14; 10:28–30); their desire to learn from Jesus (4:10; 13:3–4); their endowment and obedience to preach the gospel, heal the sick, and cast out demons (6:7–13); Peter's confession of Jesus as the Christ (8:29); and so on.

21. Cf. Eusebius, *Hist. eccl.* 2.25.1–8; 3.1.2; 4.26.9; *1 Clement* 5.2–5; Tertullian, *Apology* 5, 21; *Nat.* 1.7; Lactantius, *Inst.* 21.

definitive arguments against Rome as the matrix for the community, and internal evidence supports a situation of persecution (e.g., 4:17; 8:34–38). Tacitus in his *Annals* mentions that during Nero's persecution certain members of the Christian sect were arrested, and on disclosure, many others were apprehended (*Annals* 15.44). This record seems to coincide with Markan warnings about persecution and the betrayal of family members during the end times (e.g., Mark 13:12). It appears that Roman Christians would not be able to trust one another if some from among their own group could betray them to Roman authorities. Such a situation may have prompted our author to emphasize the negative role Jesus' own family members play in the narrative (3:21, 31–35; cf. 6:1–6; 10:28–30). Likewise it brings into sharper relief the roles of Peter and Judas, who as Jesus' close followers, deny (Peter) and betray (Judas) their teacher (14:21, 43–46).

It seems that Nero needed a scapegoat to blame for the fire in Rome, and the way a Christian might avoid punishment was to deny that he/she was a Christian.[22] Peter does something similar in Jerusalem by denying that he knows Jesus (14:66–71). In addition, Jesus' sayings about losing one's life to save it, taking up one's cross, not being ashamed of Jesus, and mutilating one's body parts rather than being thrown into *Gehenna* may have been quite relevant to the community, which perhaps faced threats and tortures when under interrogation to reveal the whereabouts of others. If the early Christian and non-Christian records mentioned above are not too distorted, the martyrdoms of Christians under Nero included crucifixions, burnings, and being ravaged by wild dogs.

We suggest, then, that the Markan community lives in Rome in the mid to late 60s CE. In this situation, or not long after it, the Christians in Rome (c. 64–67 CE) needed a narrative and characters that would help them through their own crisis. They needed to see disciples who failed Christ much the way some of them had failed by betraying fellow believers and denying Christ out of fear of imprisonment, torture, and death. Under these extreme circumstances perhaps a number of them still believed but were too fearful to confess their allegiance to Christ before authorities. Some probably returned to Christian meetings but struggled with guilt and questions about their personal faith. Others perhaps wanted to return but feared rejection. No doubt some of the loyal members perhaps questioned the faith and motives of those who had failed in one way or another. Some loyalists possibly considered

22. See Griffin, "Nero," 4.1076–81, esp. 1080. Compare Pliny's record of Christians renouncing Christ in his *Epistulae* 10.96–97. A public renunciation of Christ, though, is not necessarily the same thing as denying Christ. The former may assume that the Christian admitted to being Christian, and then after being arrested or tortured by the Roman authorities, he or she renounces Christ. The latter assumes the Christian denies being Christian when asked by Romans if he or she is Christian; hence, no arrest or torture is necessary.

apostasy to be final, and so they believed that those who had shown themselves to be disloyal to the group should not be allowed to participate in community gatherings. In sum, Mark's audience in Rome is probably quite familiar with persecution and failures.[23] Hence, *Mark's gospel may be written not only to the faithful but also the unfaithful, the past defectors and traitors from Nero's persecution who still wanted to remain in the Christian community. For them, Mark's gospel would highlight failure as an incentive for their restoration.* The brief ending of Mark leaves open an implicit question about the possibility of their renewal—as the risen Jesus still remembers a remorseful Peter after his three denials, they might come to realize that Christ remembers them and wants them to participate fully in his community. *Their failure does not need to be fatal.*

SPIRITUAL BLINDNESS "SO THAT" THE OUTSIDERS MAY NOT REPENT (MARK 4:10-12/ISA 6:10-11)

A number of interpreters have noticed that the Synoptic Gospels present a new exodus exemplified in the Isaianic tradition, with Jesus appearing as a suffering servant (Mark), a Davidic servant (Matthew), or a servant and prophet like Moses (Luke) who delivers and leads his people who are called "the way" (cf. Isa 11; 40–55; 61; 63). The Isaianic new exodus may have developed as a prominent motif for the early followers of Jesus because, during his final supper with his disciples, Jesus himself said that his blood would be "poured out for many," intimating his fulfilling the role of the Isaianic servant of the new exodus (Mark 14:24; cf. Isa 52–53; esp. 52:13, 15; 53:5–6, 11–12). Mark's gospel opens by citing Isa 40 (and Mal 3:1), a passage related to the restoration of God's people and making ready a way in the wilderness (Mark 1:1–4). As Ricki Watts demonstrates, this opening functions as a pivotal hermeneutic framework for the rest of the gospel. Both Mark and the Isaianic new exodus are structured in terms of proclaiming good news (e.g., Mark 1:1), a journey in the "way" with "blind" followers (e.g., Mark 6:52), and an eventual arrival in Jerusalem (e.g., Mark 11:1).[24] The Markan narrative reconfigures from Isaiah "the way" (ὁδός) as a route Jesus takes to his own Passion in Jerusalem and that his disciples are to follow; it is the way of suffering and death (e.g., 8:27—10:52).[25]

23. In general agreement with Iersel, "Failed Followers," 244–63.

24. Cf. Watts, *Isaiah's New Exodus*, 119–21, 370–74. For a summary of various Isaiah references and allusion in the early chapters of Mark, see Schneck, *Isaiah in the Gospel*, 252–53. For a study of passages relevant to the Isaianic new exodus, see Barstad, *Way in the Wilderness*; Oropeza, "Echoes of Isaiah," 87–112; Anderson, "Exodus Typology," 177–95.

25. Cf. Swartley, *Israel's Scripture Traditions*, 111–12; Best, *Following Jesus*, 16. Marcus, *Mark*, 2.589–92, traces the dual theme of suffering and power in Deutero-Isaiah and Mark.

More specifically in relation to the motif of spiritual obduracy, the Isaianic tradition is influential for our understanding of those who are blind and deaf to the parables in Mark 4:10–12. The passage refers to Isa 6:9–10, and here Jesus affirms the disciples as insiders who are given the "mystery" of the kingdom of God; the outsiders who hear the message receive everything in parables: "So that while seeing they may see and not perceive, and while hearing they may hear and not understand, lest they turn again and it should be forgiven them" (Mark 4:12). The Isaianic passage is related to Israel's apostasy from God and may provide insight on interpreting apostasy in Mark. Variations of Isa 6:9–10 are also cited in Matt 13:13–17; Luke 8:9–10; Acts 28:25–27; and John 12:38–41.[26] Other Isaianic passages related to spiritual blindness are echoed in 2 Cor 3:14—4:4 and Rom 11:7–8. This motif, it seems, became prominent among early Christians as way to explain why a number of Jews rejected Jesus as the Christ: they were spiritually blinded and thus were hindered from following in the way of the prophetic new exodus.

Mark's version of Isa 6:9–10 poses some interesting paradoxes. First, the crowd who is unable to perceive Jesus' words in this text gladly hear him later on (Mark 12:37). Second, Jesus' opponents in Mark are able to understand his parables without any apparent explanation of their meaning (12:12). Third, the disciples who are supposedly enlightened to such mysteries often do not understand his sayings and parables (4:10–11; cf. 4:34; 6:52; 8:14–21; 9:32). If the parables are intended to provide vividness in storytelling fashion, as commonly assumed, it seems rather odd that here Jesus claims they obfuscate meaning to the outside listeners. This has led some interpreters (perhaps correctly so) to understand "parables" (παραβολή) in Mark 4:10 as inclusive of the concept of "riddles."[27] The reference to Isa 6:9–10 follows neither the Masoretic text nor the Septuagint. The MT reads:

> Go and say to this people, hearing you hear but do not understand, and seeing you see but not perceive. Make fat the heart of this people, and its ears make heavy, and shut its eyes; lest it see with its eyes, hear with its ears, and its heart understand, and turn, and one heals it.

The LXX reads a little differently:

> Go and say to this people, hearing you shall hear and not understand, and seeing you shall see and not perceive. For the heart of this people has

---

26. Kellenberger, "Heil und Verstockung," 274–75, adds also John 9:39 to the gospels list. For the saying's authenticity as a Jesus *logion* see Hultgren, *Parables of Jesus*, 460. Parallel charts of this passage in the Synoptics and *Gos. Thom.* 9 are conveniently presented by Hultgren, 184, 186.

27. The word may have been developed from the Hebrew מָשָׁל, which can be understood as a parable, proverb, or riddle (e.g., Ezek 17:2; Hab 2:6): cf. Jeremias, *Parables of Jesus*, 17–18; Guelich, *Mark 1–8:26*, 208.

grown fat, and their ears have heard heavy and their eyes they have shut. Lest they perceive with their eyes, and hear with their ears, and understand with their heart, and turn, and I shall heal them.

An important distinction between the MT and LXX is that the latter places more responsibility on the people than the former. The MT indicates that spiritual blindness happens as a judgment from God. The LXX softens this language by using future tenses ("shall see," "shall hear") to emphasize this message as a prediction in response to the people's hardened state prior to the prediction ("For"/γὰρ). Whereas the MT places an emphasis on divine hardening of the heart via the message of the prophet (i.e., "make fat"/ הַשְׁמֵן), the LXX uses the more passive "has grown fat" (ἐπαχύνθη). The LXX uses "lest" (μήποτε) in a different sense than the MT (פֶּן): the hardening does not rest on God's active purpose for the people but as a result caused by the people themselves who, because of their dulled hearts, no longer understand and thus cannot be healed.[28] The LXX also makes clear that God is the healer, but the MT is ambiguous.

In certain ways Mark's citation of Isa 6:9-10 resembles the Targum of Isaiah by using the third person in Isa 6:9b (the LXX and MT use the second person) and the idea of passive forgiveness instead of healing.[29] Moreover, the word μήποτε ("lest") may have been derived from אמלד, which can mean "in order that not," "lest perhaps," or "unless." Jeremias opts for the last definition, supporting his case by maintaining that later Jewish sources use Isa 6:10 in terms of a promise of forgiveness.[30] Mark 4:12 begins with "that" (ἵνα), which has been understood in multiple ways, but perhaps the most common are: 1) telic/purpose—"in order that"; 2) consecutive/result—"with the result/to the effect that"; or 3) fulfillment—"so that (the prophecy might be fulfilled)."[31] This gospel uses the same word to address a fulfillment of

---

28. Evans, *See and Not Perceive*, 63, interprets the concept lucidly: "The people hear with difficulty and have shut their eyes *so that they* do not have to perceive with their eyes, hear with their ears, discern in their heart, and repent."

29. Manson, *Teachings*, 76–79, has been influential in stressing the importance of the Isaianic Targum for this saying of Jesus.

30. Jeremias, *Parables of Jesus*, 15. Jeremias (17) refers to rabbinic examples given in Str.B. 1.662–63; cf. *b. Megillah* 17b; *y. Berakot* 2.4:5. Kaufmann, *Targum Lexicon*, only uses "lest" and "perhaps" as meanings behind אמלד.

31. For a list of scholarly supporters of each position, see Schneck, *Isaiah in the Gospel*, 105–13. See further Lampe, "ἵνα," 2.188–89. Some interpreters argue that ἵνα is wrongly derived from the Aramaic ד, and so "who" may have been the original meaning. See Hultgren, *Parables of Jesus*, 7; and for major supporters of this view, see Watts, *Isaiah's New Exodus in Mark*, 187. Another option is that the Mark/Isaiah passage is to be read ironically. If so, the people are hardened "because the last thing they want is to turn and have their sins forgiven!" Translation from Hollenbach, "Lest They Should Turn," 312–21. This interpretation, while possible, would not seem to be sufficient to explain entirely the obduracy theme derived from Isaiah (see below).

Scripture in 9:12, which can lend support to the third option. For Jeremias, Mark 4:11–12 refers to outsiders seeing everything obscure, "in order that they (as it is written) may 'see and yet not see, may hear and yet not understand, unless they turn and God will forgive them.'"[32] This position is attractive to some interpreters because it softens the harsh language of 4:11–12, which might otherwise resemble a negative form of predestination: i.e., Jesus speaks in parables to the outsiders for the purpose of blinding them from understanding.

Craig Evans, however, questions why Matthew and Luke, which both tend to tone down the harsh language of Isa 6:9–10, omit Mark's μήποτε from their respective versions if "unless" were the proper interpretation of this word: "apparently Matthew and Luke were not aware of any such meaning in Mark and so found the clause, if not unacceptable, at least undesirable and so omitted it."[33] The combined use of "that" (ἵνα) and "lest" (μήποτε) tends to support a final or telic meaning to Mark 4:12, a point Matthew Black has argued cogently—the ἵνα clause is "continued and reinforced" by the μήποτε clause.[34] If the former normally means "in order that" and the latter normally means "lest," then the normal and harsher meaning is to be preferred over more unusual ones.[35] In other words, *the outsiders have their spiritual senses dulled "in order that" they would not perceive Jesus' parables "lest" they come to repentance*. This interpretation appears to be correct, but it raises new questions. Why would God deliberately harden the outsiders to prevent them from repentance, and are they held responsible for their unbelief and apostasy? We will turn to the Isaianic text to help us pursue some possible answers.

APOSTASY AND THE OBDURACY MOTIF IN ISAIAH AND MARK 4:10-12

The prophet in Isaiah claims to have seen the Lord in glorious splendor and hear him ask for a volunteer to speak before Israel (Isa 6:1–13).[36] He agrees to be God's spokesperson, but his message will be one of judgment. Israel will become "blind" and

---

32. Jeremias, *Parables of Jesus*, 17.

33. Evans, "Function of Isaiah 6:9–10," 130.

34. Black, *Aramaic Approach*, 212–14; see also Tuckett, "Mark's Concerns," 19.

35. Marcus, *Mark*, 1.300 correctly suggests, "it strains credulity that two rare meanings should be assigned to *hina* and *mēpote* when their usual meanings yield good sense and correspond to their regular Markan significance (for *hina* cf. 1:38; 2:10; 3:2, 9–10, 12, 14 etc., for *mēpote*, cf. 14:12, the only other Markan example)."

36. This throne room scene, along with Ezekiel 1 and 1 Kings 22:19–22, became influential in later apocalyptic writings and Merkavah mystics. On the influence of Isaiah 6:1–13 in Second Temple literature, see Hannah, "Isaiah within Judaism," 22–27.

"deaf" through the prophet's words. To a certain extent God has disowned apostate Israel, calling them "this people" (Isa 6:8) instead of "my people" (1:3; 3:12; 5:13).[37] His judgment of divine obduracy would last until the land becomes desolate, but there will be a hope of restoration afterward (6:13). If we backup to Isa 1–5, God calls heaven and earth as a witness in affirming that Israel has become apostate: they rebelled against him, forsaking the Holy One of Israel (1:2–4, 20, 23). They have committed injustices and murder, neglected the socially oppressed, and have become companions of thieves by taking bribes (1:15–17, 21–23; 5:7). Their worship has become hypocritical because they practice idolatry and immorality; they follow fertility rituals related to Baal and bow down to objects made by their own hands (1:29–31; 2:6–9, 18). An ox knows its master and a donkey its feeding troughs, but the Israelites are said not to know their Master and the source of their spiritual nourishment, which is wisdom derived from God's law. Instead the people have become wise in their own eyes, senseless drunkards, exploiting the weak, and have rejected God's law (1:2–4; 5:11–24).[38] They are also filled with pride and hold their Lord in contempt and derision (2:11–17; 3:8–9, 16; 5:14–24).[39] The relevant passages in Isaiah echo Deuteronomic blessings and curses in relation to covenant keeping (Deut 28–30).[40] If the Israelites choose to be obedient, they will eat from the best of the land; if they rebel, they will be devoured by the sword (Isa 1:18–20). They have chosen to be disobedient, and so God declares their punishment—their enemies will devastate their land (1:5–9, 20; 3:1–9, 25–26; 5:5–6, 13–30; 6:11–13).

Prior to the indictment we find in Isa 6, it is clear from chapters 1–5 that the ancient Israelites have already neglected God and divine wisdom, and God holds them responsible for this negligence.[41] He will now confirm them in their willful ignorance—they will become even more obdurate and foolish than they were before. After King Uzziah's death (Isa 6), the wise counselors of God's people turn their backs on divine guidance and seek human wisdom instead. When facing the threat of foreign oppression, the counselors submit to the advice of Egyptians (19:1,

---

37. Cf. Vriezen, "Essentials of the Theology of Isaiah," 128.

38. On the wisdom motif in Isaiah, see further Whedbee, *Isaiah and Wisdom*; Martin-Achard, "Sagesse de Dieu," 137–44.

39. For various facets of Israel's rebellion and vice doings in Isaiah, see Vriezen, "Essentials of the Theology of Isaiah," 134–35.

40. See further, Oropeza, "Echoes of Isaiah," 100–101, 105, 111.

41. While some think that Isaiah's calling in ch. 6 precedes the prophecies in chs. 1–5, either the author or a later editor thought it better to place it in the order of the received text. Isaiah 1–5 precedes Isaiah 6, it seems, to show the reason and justification of God's judgment in ch. 6. On this issue see also Evans, *See and Not Perceive*, 42.

11–12; 29:14; 30:1–7, 9–11; 31:1–3; cf. 5:24; 7:9–13).[42] Israel's teachers are portrayed as drunkards whose ability to educate the people has been reduced to teaching children very elementary principles (28:5–13). We can adduce from these passages that Israel's leaders were responsible for leading Israel's people astray, and so they face divine judgment, which includes spiritual obduracy (cf. 28:7, 12; 29:9–14; 30:1, 9–11; 48:4–8). The people have become like the idols in which they trust that neither see nor hear (42:16–20; 44:9–20; 46:5–7; 48:1–8; cf. Pss 115:4–8; 135[134]:15–18).[43] Watts astutely writes regarding this theme in Isaiah, "Having rejected Yahweh their maker, he will now confirm them in their decision by recreating them, as it were, in the image of the gods they have chosen."[44] This perspective might be considered as almost a type of "magic" reciprocation for wrongdoing that appears in Israel's traditions in which the measure of folly a person commits is measured back to them (e.g., Exod 1:15–16; 11:4–5; Esth 7:9–10).[45] Perhaps this notion is captured better by the idea of *lex talionis*,[46] though here it would not be "an eye for an eye, tooth for a tooth" but, as it were, *a blind eye for a blind eye.*

Israel's blindness will eventually be removed as God restores a remnant of his people who go through a new exodus journey in the wilderness (Isa 35:1–10; 42:16–19; 43:8; 61:1–11; 63:17; cf. 29:18–19; 30:20–22; 32:1–5; 33:17–22). Through the Isaianic servant, God reverses Israel's blindness imposed earlier in Isa 6: "I Yahweh, have called you in righteousness . . . to open the eyes of the blind, to bring out prisoners from the dungeon, from the prison those who dwell in darkness" (42:6–7).[47] Although Israel's election is affirmed via God restoring a remnant of the people he has chosen (1:9; 10:20–22; 11:11; 46:3; cf. 6:13), equally valid is the observation that many Israelites deliberately remained disobedient to God before God hardened them.

These observations draw us to a certain perspective regarding Israel's obduracy and apostates in Isaiah. Although the prophet's preaching instigates spiritual blindness in Isa 6:10–11, this happens as a result of the people's refusal to turn to God and keep his covenant. Israel's callousness, then, is not an arbitrary act of God, but a judgment resulting from their own apostasy. Even though God takes initiative to harden

---

42. See Wildberger, *Jesaja*, 3.1078.

43. For this insight I am indebted to Beale, "Isaiah VI 9–13," 257–78, esp. 258.

44. Watts, *Isaiah's New Exodus and Mark*, 191.

45. In these references the firstborn of Egypt are slain by God after Pharaoh attempts to slay the firstborn of Israel, and Haman is hanged on the very gallows he intends for Mordecai.

46. On *lex talionis* in the relevant passages of Isaiah, see further Goldingay, *Isaiah*, 60–61; Watts, "Mark," *CNTOT*, 150, 152.

47. Quote is from McLaughlin, "Their Hearts Were Hardened," 20.

In the Footsteps of Judas and Other Defectors

Israelite hearts, this judgment happens because of Israel's prior disobedience.[48] Not only is this phenomenon portrayed in Isa 1–6, but if there is any credence to the correlation between king Uzziah's death and Isaiah's vision in 6:1, then other accounts of that era confirm that immediately prior to and during this period in Israel's tradition-history, the people of Judah practiced idolatry, while northern Israel experienced corruption and political upheaval (cf. 2 Kgs 15:4, 27–30, 35; 2 Chr 27:2b; Amos 1:1; 2:4—4:11; Hos 1).[49] Even so, Israel's spiritual dullness seems only partial; God can still appeal to his people to repent (Isa 1:16–20; 8:16–20; 9:8–13; 28:16; 30:15; 31:6).[50] In fact it is possible that the original intention of the judgment in Isa 6 was open-ended in hope of getting Israel to repent after hearing the message, much like the people of Nineveh repented at God's judgment pronounced by Jonah. This may function as a type of reverse psychology.[51]

Jesus' reference to Isa 6 probably prompted his original followers to recollect something about the tradition-history of Israel and the Isaianic situation, namely, that Israel's previous disobedience and apostasy led to divine hardening. In Mark this obduracy continues with those who are outside the community of Jesus' followers (Mark 4:10–12). Deliverance from the spiritual inability to perceive the words of Jesus will require the crowds to become insiders. Like the community of early Jesus followers, they must repent of their wrongdoings in the face of God's in-breaking kingdom and follow Jesus in the way of the new exodus (cf. 1:2–4, 14–15, 17–18, 20). *Mark's gospel probably assumes Israel is still in some sense apostate, and as a result of this, obduracy as a form of divine judgment remains in effect from Isa 6 for all those who do not embrace the gospel message of Jesus.* To break free of this vicious cycle, the people from Judea, Jerusalem, Galilee and the surrounding areas must repent at the

---

48. After writing a draft of this chapter, I was pleased to learn that Meadors, *Idolatry and the Hardening of the Heart*, has confirmed similar thoughts to my own by studying the concept of divine hardening in Israel's scriptures and the New Testament: he concludes, among other things, that God's hardening of "sensory depletion" is not arbitrary but a consequence of divine judgment and is symptomatic of idolatrous sin. It brings about chastisement that aims to incite repentance; salvation is still possible for those whom God hardens (173–77).

49. Isaiah 6 is situated in the year of King Uzziah's death (also known as Azariah). If understood in relation to the kings of Judah, Uzziah's death was followed by his sons Jotham and Ahaz. Meanwhile in Northern Israel, King Pekah had formed an alliance with Rezin of Aram and waged war against Judah, who under Ahaz, requested assistance from Tiglath-pileser III of Assyria (2 Kings 15:32—16:9; Isa 7–9). This era marked Assyrian dominance in which Northern Israel was eventually destroyed (c. 745–21 BCE). Judah persisted under Ahaz's son, Hezekiah. On the dating of these events, see Horn and McCarter, "Divided Monarchy," 165–75.

50. Hence, we must question whether it is entirely accurate to say that because Israel *will not* repent, this stubbornness progresses to the point in which Israel *cannot* repent: e.g., Eakin, "Spiritual Obduracy," 94 cf. 89, 92; von Rad, *Old Testament Theology*, 2.152.

51. Cf. Lehnert, *Die Provokation Israels*.

The Gospel of Mark

message of John of the Baptist (1:4) and Jesus (1:15; cf. 6:12). Whereas Luke stresses that the "crowds," sinners, and tax collectors need repentance (Luke 3:3, 7–14; 5:32), and Matthew emphasizes that Pharisees and Sadducees must bear "fruit" worthy of genuine repentance (Matt 3:2, 8–11), Mark centers more generally on Israel needing repentance. To be sure, idolatry was no longer a major problem in Palestine as it was in the time of Isaiah, but as we noticed earlier, Israel's rebellion also included pride, exploitation, indifference toward God and his word, and various immoral deeds that would still be relevant for the people of Jesus' time. The gospel message required repentance from such things—the command to love God with all fervency and love one's neighbor as oneself stood at the heart of kingdom living (cf. Mark 12:28–32).[52] The crowds' inability to see and hear, then, comes as a result of divine judgment, but this judgment is not placed squarely on the shoulders of their forefather's apostasy back in the days of the Hebrew prophets. They, too, are responsible for their own sins and stubbornness. But they are not alone—as we will observe below, even Jesus' family and closest followers are spiritually calloused.

PROPORTIONAL HEARING IN THE PARABLES OF JESUS (4:9, 23–25)

Jesus' repetitive phrase "He who has an ear, let him hear" seems rather hollow if all outsiders *cannot* hear with spiritual understanding (Mark 4:9, 23; cf. 4:3, 33; Luke 4:8b; 14:35b; Matt 11:15; 13:9, 43b; *Gos. Thom.* 8, 21, 63, 65, 96). After the crowd's blind and deaf obduracy is affirmed in Mark 4:10–12, the narrative awkwardly claims that Jesus spoke parables to the crowd, "just as they were able to hear" (καθὼς ἠδύναντο ἀκούειν, 4:33). This seems to suggest that some of them were able to understand and respond, and they had been listening in on his parables since 3:21.[53] Later on, Jesus does the very thing he does not do in 4:10–12 and 4:34—he explains his teaching to the crowd (7:14–15).[54] Moreover, there is no indication that the

---

52. On the importance of such ethics in Mark see esp. Breytenbach, "Identity and Rules of Conduct," 49–75.

53. Jesus speaks "to them" (4:21, 23), addressing both outsiders (cf. 4:33–34) and insiders (cf. 4:11). Guelich, *Mark 1–8:26*, 256–57, on the other hand, suggests a superficial hearing in 4:33 based on 4:34. Marcus, *Mark*, writes that in "the pre-Markan parable collection the audience here was limited to the disciples," and they were able to hear "'according to their God-given ability to hear.'" But the Markan redactor "has drawn the crowd of 'outsiders' mentioned in 4:11–12 into the audience, and for *them* the meaning of the phrase must be 'according to their *inability* to hear with true understanding'" (1.325). In my view the parable of the Sower suggests a variety of responses to Jesus' parables and teachings (see below), but even so, the tension between 4:10–12 and 4:33 might suggest that two or more sources were used by the Markan redactor.

54. Baird, "Pragmatic Approach," 205, observes that in the Synoptics Jesus explains twenty-eight of his parables to the Twelve or the larger body of disciples, but he also explains thirteen to the either

scribes do *not* understand the parable Jesus gives them in 3:23–27. The parables in 7:14–15 and 12:1–12 in fact suggest that his opponents *do* understand them, whereas his own disciples do not always understand the parables (7:14–18; cf. 8:14–18).[55] Despite the capstone explanation in 4:10–12, then, no consistent pattern seems to exist between outsiders who do not understand the interpretation of the parables in Mark and disciples or insiders who supposedly do understand them. Even the very parable that is used in conjunction with 4:10–12, the parable of the Sower (4:1–9), was probably not understood clearly by any of Jesus' followers, and that is why they need to ask about its interpretation (4:10). The wisest listeners hearing this parable for the first time would have inevitably run into difficulties trying to understand it. The word "seed" has various metaphorical meanings in Jewish tradition, including the Law (2 Esd 9:31–37), humankind (Jer 31:27–38), and evil (2 Esd 4:28–32), and in other parables of Jesus the seed can be understood as God's kingdom (Mark 4:26–32). Since the term had multiple meanings, how could any of Jesus' disciples have known with confidence that the seed represented the word in this particular parable? The parable would indeed be mysterious in relation to the kingdom of God for the listener who did not obtain its interpretation from Jesus (4:11a).[56]

Along with these thoughts we should take into consideration that not all parables would have been equally difficult to comprehend. Some parables are not understood (e.g., 4:10, 34), some are understood by listeners but do not change the listeners (e.g., 12:1–12), and others are apparently understood with positive results. The more difficult parables would naturally pique curiosity among hearers who were genuinely seeking truth, and so this would prompt them to further inquiry, whereas those who were indifferent or opposed to Jesus would not care to discover the meaning. Perhaps the crux of the issue is not the initial ability of the listeners to understand Jesus' parables, but their willingness to seek out a parable's true meaning and believe and obey its content after finding out. What is meant by Jesus' saying to "hear" in 4:9 and 4:23 is that his parables and teachings require a deeper level of understanding than what is stated on the surface. Although the *Shema* is not directly echoed in the frames of the parable of the Sower, Jesus' call for his audience to "hear" is similar to the Jewish pattern of linking the concepts of hearing with obeying (Mark 4:3, 9, 23; cf. Deut 6:4–8; Ezek 3:7, 11, 27; 12:2; Rev 2:7, 11, 17, 29;

---

crowd of onlookers or his opponents or both.

55. The text may be showing irony here. Even though Jesus speaks privately with his disciples about his teachings (unlike the outsiders), they still have difficulties understanding him. Robbins, *Jesus the Teacher*, 137–38, notes a parallel irony in Plato's *Theaetetus* 152C, where Protagoras speaks things in dark sayings to commoners but speaks the truth secretively to his disciples.

56. Cf. Boucher, *Mysterious Parable*, 48.

3:6, 13, 22; 13:9; Jas 1:22–25). The listeners are to seek the meaning of the parable and then produce good fruit as a result (cf. Mark 4:20). They must obey and put to practice what they learn.[57]

Likewise this call involves a challenge to the audience; they could either accept or refuse the teaching of God's messenger. *Those whose hearts were fully hardened would not receive Jesus words, but others might be able to receive them in varying degrees.*[58] William Lane puts it well when he writes, "There was *veiling* (or partial disclosure) before the multitude and *disclosure* (but only partial understanding) to the disciples."[59] Not every case of obduracy is the same. Some have hardened their heart to the point of blaspheming the Spirit (cf. 3:22–30), whereas others, such as Jesus' followers (cf. 6:52; 8:17–18), have partially hardened hearts. Perhaps the crowd's own obduracy extends this entire spectrum. For Mark the crowd probably represents Israel who as a whole did not fully accept the good news of the kingdom of God as preached by John the Baptist and Jesus. Because of this the people as a group is viewed as obdurate sharing an affinity with apostate Israel in Isaianic times. Nevertheless, individuals from among the people are only partially callous; it seems that they are still able to believe and repent. The crowd's hearing of the parables, then, does not assume categorical incomprehension in every case. On the contrary, the parable of the Sower (4:3–8, 13–20) illustrates that even though many do not "hear" properly or continue in the word (i.e., the first three types of sowing and seeds), a minority does (the fourth type) and yields much fruit (4:8, 20). Ultimately as the parable of the Sower itself affirms, there is mixed reaction to the word. If all the hearers among the crowd were excluded from arriving at the truth of Jesus' parables, the leading parable he mentions would not make good sense. The Markan Jesus expects at least some of his hearers from among the crowd to produce good results (4:9).

An important corollary to this is that the charge of Jesus at the beginning and end of the parable for the outsiders to "hear" (4:3, 9) and his warning for all listeners to "take heed" (βλέπετε) in relation to hearing (4:24) presuppose that regardless the extent of God's involvement in making the people obdurate, the listeners' choices are still the responsibility of the listeners.[60] In relation to this he declares to his audience

---

57. See Pesch, *Markusevangelium*, 1.248.

58. Instructive here is Boucher, *Mysterious Parable*, 53, who writes that Mark 4:9, 23 points to "the connection between the obliqueness of revelation and the need for personal decision in the matter of faith; the revelation of the kingdom is indirect *in order* to make faith possible, in order to give room for that personal decision."

59. Lane, *Mark*, 173.

60. The same word (βλέπετε) is given to his disciples when warning them not to commit apostasy during the upcoming time of testing (e.g., 13:33, 37) and to the crowd in Jerusalem when warning them

that to the one who has will more be given, and to the one who has not, what that person has will be taken away (Mark 4:25). The saying suggests that the measure of receiving is proportional to the measure in which one hears.[61] All listeners must pay attention to what they hear, for the measure they receive will be in proportion to what they do with what is given them.[62] In this saying we may have an implication that helps our understanding of who become insiders and who remain outsiders. *God accepts those who seek to implement the words of Jesus, and God hardens those who harden themselves against the message.* Divine hardening is a response to self-hardening.[63] Madeleine Boucher perceptively says, "One might say that God confirms the believer in his belief, and the unbeliever in his disbelief—thus the interplay between the will of God and the will of man. Faith is at once a human decision and a divine gift."[64]

If the paradox of human freedom and God's sovereign purposes is a problem for us, this does not mean it was an issue for Mark, who seems oblivious to tensions between divine hardening and human responsibility.[65] The crowd's lack of faith seems to be based on a combination of God's sovereign plan via Isaiah as well as the crowd's own volitional shortcomings. Despite their obduracy that was given as divine punishment, they must hear and repent. Mark 14:21 is a prime example of this—Jesus claims he must die in fulfillment of scripture and this will happen so that he may become an atonement for his people (cf. Mark 10:45; 14:24; Zech 13:7; Dan

---

against the scribes (12:37b–38).

61. Variations of the *logion* in Mark 4:25 were used in multiple settings (Matt 7:2; 13:11–12; 25:29; Luke 6:38; cf. *Gos. Thom.* 41). Both Mark and Luke connect the *logion* to sayings of exposing light and the revelation of everything that was previously hidden (Mark 4:21–22, 24–25; Luke 8:16–18). Here the meaning is that the mysteries of God's dominion, including the interpretation of Jesus' parables, will inevitably be revealed. In Matthew the saying contrasts the disciples who "have" and others who "have not" (Matt 13:11–12). In the Matthean parable of the Talents, the saying reappears in the mouth of a master who justifies taking away the talent from the wicked and slothful servant and giving it to the good and faithful servant who has ten talents (Matt 25:29). All three gospels place the saying in close proximity to the parable of the Sower. Matthew's version in fact follows immediately after the parable (Matt 13:11–13).

62. Compare the thought with the wisdom sayings in Prov 1:5; 9:9 and for more examples, see Gundry, *Mark*, 217; Str.B., 1.660–62.

63. See, e.g., Hanges, Review of *Prädestination und Verstockung*, 262.

64. Boucher, *Mysterious Parable*, 54.

65. Röhser, *Prädestination und Verstockung*, esp. 68–69, in relation to Pauline and Johannine theology may present some insight to this paradox by using metaphors such as "Raum" and "Spielraum" to affirm that humans are permitted freedom within divine limits and determination. The term "In-Wirken" relates to a type of enclosed area determined by God's will, and within which humans can do free actions. For Röhser, there is no real contradiction between the two ideas. On the paradox see further various perspectives in Barclay and Gathercole, *Divine and Human Agency*; Carson, *Divine Sovereignty*.

7:21–25; 9:26f; Isa 53), while at the same time Judas is held responsible for his act of betraying Jesus even though this act irretrievably sets Jesus on his course to fulfill God's purposes.

APOSTASY IN THE PARABLE OF THE SOWER (4:1–9, 13–20)

The parable of the Sower is found in the Synoptic Gospels and a variation appears in the *Gospel of Thomas* (Mark 4:1–20; Matt 13:1–23; Luke 8:4–15; *Gos. Thom.* 9).[66] Similar to this parable, Isa 55:10–11 associates the word of God with a seed and Isa 6:13 mentions a holy "seed," which implies a remnant of God's people. Humans are also associated with seeds and plants in *4 Ezra* [2 Esd] 8.41–44; 9.31.[67] Even so, there is not enough evidence to solidify passages from Isaiah or *4 Ezra* as the definitive background to this parable.[68] Its origin is perhaps best explained as originally spoken by Jesus.[69] In the parable there are four different outcomes related to the sowing of God's word. The explanation of the parable relates these outcomes to those who hear the word. Some hear it and then Satan steals the word sown in them (i.e., those beside the road); some hear and receive the word but do not persevere (those sown on rocky ground); some hear the word but do not produce fruit (those sown among the thorns); and some hear it, accept it, and do produce fruit (those sown on good soil).[70]

Mary Ann Tolbert compares the scribes, Pharisees, and religious leaders in Jerusalem with those related to the first seed that is eaten by birds representing Satan.[71] The disciples, especially Peter, James, and John, represent those sown on

---

66. Hultgren, *Parables of Jesus*, 184–85, determines that the *Gospel of Thomas* version of this parable is "gnosticized" and probably derives from a different tradition than the Synoptics.

67. On possible Isaianic connections with the parable of the Sower, see Bowker, "Mystery and Parable," 300–317. In *4 Ezra* the sower illustration is related to some seeds that do not come up from the ground or take root. It is declared to "Ezra" that all the "seeds" sown in the world will not be saved, and so he intercedes that this would not be the case.

68. Gundry, *Mark*, 210, for example, observes that in Isaiah 55:10–11 the word is compared with the rain and snow, not the seed.

69. Black, *Aramaic Approach*, 63; Gundry, *Mark*, 209, address Semitic aspects of the parable lending support to its authenticity. It is possible that the interpretative section of the parable, however, was developed by the early Christians. See Hultgren, *Parables of Jesus*, 189–90, 459–60 for discussion.

70. The soil and seed are confusing in this parable; sometimes the soil is the hearer, other times the seed seems to be the hearer: see Allison and Davies, *Matthew*, 2.400–401. It seems that "seed" can refer to both the word and hearer.

71. Though interestingly Satan is the one who takes away the word (4:14). Given 4:10–12 one could argue that he, too, plays an active role in hardening hearts (cf. 2 Cor. 4:4). Perhaps this is evidence that the parable of the Sower and the reference to Isa 6 were not always used together when Jesus originally uttered the *logia*.

rocky soil. They accept the word for a season but then fall away in a time of "oppression and persecution" (Mark 4:17)—they abandon and deny Jesus at his arrest. Herod and the rich man of 10:17–22 are compared with the third seed in which wealth and the cares of life choke it. The fourth seed that bears fruit represents the ideal disciple.[72] Such parallels may provide some insight on how the parable is used in Mark, but as an authentic parable of Jesus the original referents may have been more general, depicting four types of responses to the good news about the kingdom. This parable, if anything else, demonstrates that God's word impacts its listeners differently: some reject it, and others accomplish great things for God's kingdom because of it, and many others fall in between these two poles. It is not clear that Mark intended the meaning of the parable's four seeds and soils to be applied merely as a tit-for-tat correlation with religious authorities, failed disciples, the affluent, and ideal followers, respectively. The seed that is consumed by Satan, for example, can refer to all outsiders who reject the gospel, not just religious leaders.

The second seed/soil pertains to apostasy in particular. Mark uses the word σκανδαλίζω to describe the falling away of those sown on the rocky soil (4:17). The same word describes the disciples abandoning Jesus at his arrest and relate to his earlier warnings (14:27, 29; cf. 9:42–47).[73] The disciples' apostasy, however, is only temporary. As we have argued already, they are restored at the end of Mark's gospel. The idea of restoration is not found in the parable. The ones sown on rocky ground paradoxically grow where there is not "much soil," and they have "no depth" (4:5).[74] Did the seeds penetrate the soil at all? One thing is clear; the imagery portrays them as not having deep and firm roots,[75] and so when the sun scorches them they wither for lack of moisture. What may be represented here is the shallowness of the listeners' reception of the word. It is perhaps reading too much into this passage to discern that these listeners are clearly inauthentic believers; they are in the process of growth, receiving but not continuing in the gospel message. Other sayings in Mark

---

72. Tolbert, *Sowing the Gospel*, 153–62. Donahue and Harrington, *Mark*, 142, suggest a wordplay on the rocky ground and the name of Peter, who is later called "Satan" (Mark 8:33). The parable may reflect his failure when tested. Malina and Rohrbaugh, *Synoptic Gospels*, suggest the normal yield for sowing was two-fold to five-fold rather than 30- to 100-fold and that the sower would be very careless if he let some of the seed fall on unproductive soil (160). On the former point, the exaggerated increase might stress the notion of productivity. On the second point, the parable does not center so much on the nature of sowing but on the responses of the people who hear the word.

73. On σκανδαλίζω see below on Mark 9.

74. Differently than Mark and Matthew's versions, Luke 8:13 avoids the problem by claiming this seed as sown on a "rock" (πέτρα) rather than on "rocky ground" (πετρώδης).

75. They fall away, not having any root "in themselves" (Mark 4:17a): Allison and Davies, *Matthew*, 2.384, seem correct by writing that these seeds "have not sent down firm roots." Luz, *Matthew* 2.248f, finds parallels in Isa 40:24; Sir. 23:25; 40:15; Wis 4:3–4; *Herm. Sim.* 9.1.6; 9.21.3.

suggest, in any case, that Jesus' bona fide disciples could fall away (14:21, 27, 50)—he warns his closest followers against apostasy on several occasions (8:15, 17, 34–38; 9:42–49; 10:15; 13:5–6, 13, 37; 14:38).[76]

Stephen Wilson derives some insights from a sociological study by Stuart Wright who examined religious defection by surveying ninety people from new religious movements (half of them defected).[77] From the latter's study, Wilson distils three types of apostates that he connects with early Jewish and Christian apostasy: (1) Gradual defectors: people who drift apart from their community slowly and leave the group cumulatively "in response to the routine business of defining their position in the world."[78] They lose their ties with the group through various circumstances such as intermarriage, ambition, and social advancement. In this category he includes the apostate Christians in the writings of Hermas and Cyprian, among others. (2) Precipitate defectors: those who make a sudden decision to leave the community. Quite often the abruptness of their departure involves deception or disillusionment. In this category he includes Paul's change from a Pharisee and the Christians who defected according to Pliny the Younger. (3) Antagonistic apostates: those who become fervent opponents against the community from which they departed. Julian the apostate and betrayers in Christian traditions would seem to fall into this category.[79]

Wilson's three categories might inform our understanding of apostasy in Mark. The second seed/soil connects fairly well with Wilson's second category of precipitate defectors. Perhaps significantly, Wilson connects this category with deception and Christians who were persecuted by Roman officials in the late first and early second centuries. The defectors in Jesus' parable receive the word and start off with much enthusiasm but do not have a mature depth in the gospel message. They convert quickly but then fall away quickly when persecution takes place. Later on Jesus will warn his disciples about being deceived by false teachers during an impending time of affliction and persecution in which personal endurance and God's intervention will be needed to preserve the faithful (13:5–6, 21–23; cf. 13:12–13, 20). Christian believers will betray one another (Mark 13:12, 22; cf. *1 Clem.* 5:2), and Jesus' disciples must be watchful so that they do not to fall away during the upcoming time of

---

76. On Jesus' warnings against the authorities, see Mark 3:29; 12:9, 40; 14:62, and see further the warning motif in Rhoads, *Reading Mark*, 122–24.

77. Wilson, *Leaving the Fold*, 121–23; cf. Wright, *Leaving Cults*. Wright's three categories that are developed by Wilson are the covert (those with strong ties with outsiders and ambiguous discontents), overt (those who make a strong reaction toward certain beliefs or policies), and declarative (those whose departure from the group becomes confrontational).

78. Wilson, *Leaving the Fold*, 124.

79. Ibid., 124–25.

testing (cf. βλέπετε: Mark 13:5, 9, 23, 33, 37; cf. 14:38).[80] A combination of deception and persecution are thus perceived as factors that cause believers to abandon their faith in Mark 13. If the disciples continue to grow and put to practice Jesus' parables and teachings, they will be better equipped to shun deception when it comes their way. In essence their "roots" will grow deeper. Spiritual immaturity, then, may play a factor in both the second seed and Wilson's precipitate defectors. The more inexperienced in the word the believer is, the more prone that believer is to apostasy. In any case, and independent of Wilson's observations, in Mark the aspects at work against those who believe the word but then fall away are affliction/oppression (θλῖψις) and persecution (διωγμός).[81] The theme of persecution and suffering is prominent in Mark (e.g., 8:34; 10:30), and in this parable apostasy through persecution is probably being stressed because in the community's situation of Mark's day, Nero's attack on the Christians was their reality. *The meaning behind the second seed and soil no doubt serves as a warning to all Christ-followers, especially those within the Markan community—they must not fall away in times of hardship and persecution.*

Wilson's third category of antagonistic apostates perhaps reflects the nature of Judas' acts in 14:10–11, 18–21, 43–45. Judas does not simply betray Christ but opposes the leader he once served by handing him over to the authorities. Then again, is Judas' act a better fit with Wilson's first category? If the third seed/soil that is choked by riches, desires, and concerns related to the world implies that this seed/soil at one time received the word before being choked, then Wilson's description of gradual defectors might relate here. Perhaps teachings related to the rich young ruler (10:17–31) and Judas' selling out his rabbi for a sum of money (14:1–11) spoke to the problem of affluence among early Christians. Problematic with this association is that, unless the concept of chocking implies death, this seed has not perished like the first two seeds; it just does not yield fruit.[82] Still, further inferences may be drawn from this. For example, the fig tree in Mark 11:14 that does not yield proper fruit is cursed by Jesus, and the tenants in 12:2 are to perish for not giving the appropriate share of their produce to the land owner. Such passages may suggest that

---

80. See the chapter on Matthew below for more on apostasy in the Olivet discourse of Matthew 24/Mark 13.

81. Matthew 13:21 follows Mark in this reading, but Luke uses "temptation" instead (πειρασμός). On διωγμός see further Acts 13:50; Rom 8:35; 2 Thess 1:4; 2 Tim 3:11; *Mart. Pol.* 1.1.

82. France, *Mark*, 191, notices, perhaps correctly, a progression from the first seed that died, the second that lived but later died, and the third that lived but does not bear fruit. Differently, Collins, *Mark*, 352, thinks that the cares of life, etc. suggest that some in the community of Christ practiced an ascetic lifestyle. Perhaps more correctly, these and other seeds may be seen in light of various experiences related to the community of faith and their mission activities: cf. Pesch, *Markusevangelium*, 1.244.

The Gospel of Mark

those in Israel who do not yield proper obedience to God will be visited with divine punishment.

The parable of the Sower would seem to function for Mark's community in at least a threefold way. First, it may have provided them with a reason why many do not accept the gospel: Satan steals the word from their heart (4:15). Second, it warned the believers against falling away through suffering and persecution (4:17). Third, it encouraged believers to be productive followers of Christ (4:18–20). The parable demonstrates to the auditors that the proper response to the message of Jesus is to receive and obey it rather than allow Satan, suffering, persecution, or the concerns of this world to consume or obfuscate that message. At this early stage in the gospel, the readers can already see that even though many "outsiders" reject Jesus' message and possess hardened hearts akin with apostate Israel in the Isaianic tradition, the same thing could happen to "insiders," the very followers of Christ. They, too, are susceptible to apostasy.

CROWDS, OPPONENTS, AND BLASPHEMY OF THE HOLY SPIRIT (3:22–30; 4:10–12, 21–36)

In Mark's gospel Jesus faces conflicts with Satan, unclean spirits, disease (e.g., 1:13–14, 23–27, 34; 3:11; 5:8 13; 17 25), nature (e.g., 4:37–41; 6:48–51; 11:13–14), and even with his disciples (e.g., 6:52; 14:21, 27).[83] Moreover, Jesus' own family and hometown do not recognize his identity and fail to comprehend his message (3:21, 31–35; 6:1–6). At his trial the crowd in Jerusalem ultimately rejects him, and he is mocked during his suffering and crucifixion (15:8–15).

It is rather difficult to determine a consistent function for the multitudes in Mark's gospel. We do not know, for instance, to what extent the people comprising the crowd in 2:29–34 and 3:7–10 make up the crowd of outsiders in 4:1–12, 21–36. In the various Galilean episodes in which crowds appear, their role alternates from those who experience Jesus' miracles[84] to those who hear Jesus' teachings (2:13; 3:32–35; 6:34; 7:14–15; 8:1–9). This pattern is repeated on Jesus' way to Jerusalem (10:1, 46–52), and the multitudes hear him gladly once he is there. They become a "retarding factor" in keeping the religious leaders from harming him (11:18, 32; 12:12).[85] Nonetheless the chief priests are able to manipulate a crowd to demand his crucifixion (15:8–15; cf. 14:43). Hence, the crowds seem to play various roles throughout the gospel, and their precise identity is not always clear. Mary Thompson is perceptive in

---

83. See Rhoads et al., *Mark as Story*, 76–78.
84. 1:32–34; 2:1–12; 3:7–11; 5:21–34; 6:34–44, 54–56; contrast 7:33; 8:23.
85. For the quote see Thompson, *Role of Disbelief*, 157.

In the Footsteps of Judas and Other Defectors

asserting that "the crowd is used in whatever way the author chooses."[86] The identity of the insiders likewise is not always clear: 4:10 mentions both the twelve and "those around" Jesus. Are these other disciples of Jesus, or people from among the crowd who decide to inquire about his parables, or both? The distinction between insiders and outsiders, then, may be an emerging distinction.[87] The multitudes do appear to be outsiders for the most part, or as Best puts it, "the unevangelised mass."[88] The outsiders in chapter 4 probably include both religious opponents and the people they influence.

In Mark's gospel, and in Matthew's parallel, those who are in danger of committing the blasphemy of the Holy Spirit are not followers of Jesus but Jesus' opponents (Mark 3:28–29; cf. Matt 12:31–32).[89] They are not identified as Christ's followers.[90] James Williams suggests that the term "holy spirit" was associated with the "spirit of prophecy" and "presence" of God from the Tannaitic perspective, and the blasphemous act of Jesus' opponents had to do with their "perverted evaluations" of what the Spirit was accomplishing through Jesus. In other words the opponents reject the definitive sign of God's impending kingdom that brings forth prophetic words and deeds. Moreover, since the Spirit is related to divine healing and preaching associated with the forgiveness of sins, and the opponents' problem is one of unforgiveness—both of others and their own need to be forgiven—they could not comprehend "the true nature of God's disposition toward and work in the world."[91] This perspective works contextually with Mark's version of the incident, and it attributes the unpardonable sin to Jesus' unbelieving opponents, the religious leaders. The accusation of Jesus being demonized is given twice in the narrative, perhaps suggesting a repetitive charge (Mark 3:22; 3:30).[92] Similarly, the Matthean parallel

86. Ibid., 158.

87. Cf. Watts, *New Exodus in Mark*, 202, who uses the phrase "emerging division" and says that this is nevertheless consistent with divisions found in Deutero-Isaiah (e.g., Isa 65:8–16; 66:5) and Malachi. For more examples of the various insider identities in Mark, see Strecker, "Messiasgeheimnistheorie," 92; Tuckett, "Mark's Concerns," 14.

88. Best, *Following Jesus*, 29.

89. Luke 12:10, however, paints a different portrait of the unpardonable sin (see below in Luke-Acts).

90. Thompson, *Role of Disbelief*, 52–53, observes that the hostile trend of authorities against Jesus does not vary in Mark's gospel: "With the Jewish officials, there is no progressive alienation. . . . There is no progression, no reconciliation and no recognition of who he is or what his message may mean. These officials have freely and deliberately hardened their hearts. Therefore they have refused to understand."

91. Williams, "Note on the 'Unforgivable Sin,'" 75–77, who pays homage to Moore, *Judaism*, 1.237, 437. Contrast *Jub.* 15.33–34, which claims the only unpardonable sin is to be uncircumcised.

92. Also, it is possible that the imperfect ἔλεγον in 3:22 and 3:30 implies that the scribes "kept on saying" Jesus performed exorcisms through the help of demonic powers. Cf. Lane, *Gospel of Mark*, 136. But Mark uses the word and tense quite frequently (cf. 2:16, 24; 3:21; 4:41; 5:31; 6:14–15; 6:35; etc.). Even so, Matthew uses the same tense at least in 9:34. Luke does not use the imperfect for his parallel

includes two separate incidents where the opponents' claim that Jesus performs exorcisms by demonic powers (Matt 9:32–34; 12:24).

The result of persistent stubbornness exemplified by the escalating resistance towards Jesus' message portrayed in Mark 2–3 functions as the ground for why divine hardening takes place in 4:10–12. Both Mark and the Isaianic background echoed here emphasize Israel's leaders as the culprits in rejecting divine guidance, which results in the divine hardening and blinding of God's people (Mark 3:1–4:12/Isa 1–6; Mark 7:1–13/Isa 29:13; Mark 12:1–12/Isa 5:1–7). The prior resistance of these leaders towards Jesus and his miracles in Mark 2–3 fits well with the following pericope in which Isa 6:9–10 is quoted in relation to those "outside" who do not comprehend his parables. Mark's gospel probably assumes that its audience will connect the dots between the outsiders' spiritual blindness in 4:10–12 and Jesus opponents who harden their heart in Mark 2–3 (e.g., 3:5–6).[93] It becomes quite evident that the unpardonable sin of blaspheming the Holy Spirit is the end result of persistent obduracy, and the crowds who are influenced by these leaders are likewise obdurate, though not to the point of being unpardonable. For the Markan community, the upshot of all this is that, if one's blaspheming of the Spirit is not apostasy but persistent hardness of heart that ultimately leads one to attribute to the devil the miraculous signs of God's Spirit through Jesus, and *if Jesus' warning against the unpardonable sin is not addressed to his followers but opponents, then the failed members of Mark's community could take comfort in knowing that their apostasy is not fatal. Denying Christ and betraying other Christians for fear of persecution are forgivable sins.*

OBDURACY AND APOSTASY AMONG JESUS' FAMILY AND FOLLOWERS (3:21, 31–35; 6:52; 8:17–18; 14:21, 27, 50, 66–72)

Opponents and crowd aside, Jesus' own family members are viewed as obdurate (Mark 3:21, 31–35).[94] Unlike the other Synoptic texts (e.g., Matt 1–2; Luke 1–2), Mark's portrayal of Jesus' relatives is quite negative. First, his mother and brothers attempt to take him away from his ministry, thinking he is out of his mind (Mark

in 11:15.

93. When they accuse Jesus of demon possession, Jesus responds by speaking to them "with parables" (ἐν παραβολαῖς), a phrase that is used in Mark to address either Jesus' opponents or those "outside" (Mark 3:23; cf. 4:2, 11; 12:1).

94. In 3:21 οἱ παρ' αὐτοῦ most likely refers to family ties (Prov 31:21; Sus 33; Josephus *Ant.* 1.193; BDAG, 756–57). Contrast Wansbrough, "Mark 3, 21," 233–36, who thinks it refers to the followers of Jesus who attempt to calm down the crowd that is out of control with enthusiasm. This interpretation, among other difficulties, leaves no explanation for the arrival of Jesus' family in 3:31 and expunges the parallel negative perceptions of Jesus in 3:21 and 22. See further Lambrecht, "Relatives of Jesus," 244–45n6; France, *Mark*, 165–67.

In the Footsteps of Judas and Other Defectors

3:21).⁹⁵ They possibly agreed with his opponents that he is demon possessed.⁹⁶ We cannot ignore that a Markan sandwich related to his unbelieving family members is placed at the front and back end of a narrative where Jesus' work is attributed to demonic powers (3:22–30). This would appear to insinuate that they, too, had blasphemed the Holy Spirit.⁹⁷ On the other hand, the fact that they do not attribute his behavior to Beelzebul but to insanity may suggest that their unbelief had not reached the level of being unpardonable. Second, rather than affirming his family as insiders, Mark has them remain on the "outside" (3:32), and Jesus declares that his true family are those insiders who do the will of God (3:31–35). It probably follows from this that the outsiders, including his family, represent people who do not obey the will of God.⁹⁸

Cilliers Breytenbach aptly determines that doing God's will in Mark refers to following Jesus as the messianic Son of God and following what has been written in the scriptures, especially the Deuteronomic code (Mark 7:9–10/Deut 5:16; Mark 10:6/Deut 24:1; Mark 10:19/Deut 5:16–20; Mark 12:19/Deut 25:5–6). The *Shema* and command to love God and neighbors stand out in the text (Mark 12:28–34/ Deut 6:5–6; cf. Lev 19:18).⁹⁹ The relatives of Jesus may have tried to follow God's commands, but like the rich young ruler they failed to follow Jesus. Third, his close ties in Nazareth reject him in unbelief (cf. σκανδαλίζω, Mark 6:3)¹⁰⁰ prompting him to claim that his own hometown dishonors him (6:1–6). Significantly the redactor in 6:4 adds that this dishonor comes from his own "relatives" (συγγενής). Fourth, the disciples are commended for forsaking everything for the sake of the gospel, including family ties (10:29–30).

This negative portrait of Jesus' kin in Mark has suggested to some scholars that Mark's community was set at odds with Jesus' family and James.¹⁰¹ More likely Jesus' prophetic claim that family members will betray one another in the upcoming crisis is probably in view here (13:12). Mark's gospel attaches "persecutions" as a

---

95. Here ἐξίστημι (3:21) probably means that "he has lost his senses": cf. BDAG, 350 (for examples see Oepke, "ἐξίστημι," 2:459–60). Another possibility is that they thought he had committed apostasy: ἐξίστημι can refer to abandoning something or changing one's opinion: see LSJ, 595, for examples in Greco-Roman literature (special thanks to my colleague Kay Smith for this tip). In this case they would seem to agree with Jesus' opponents that he was a blasphemer and violator of the Law (e.g., 2:7, 23–28).

96. See Lohmeyer, *Evangelium des Markus*, 77.

97. On this thought, see Crossan, "Mark and the Relatives," 89.

98. Cf. Tolbert, *Sowing the Gospel*, 160.

99. Breytenbach, "Identity and Rules of Conduct," 63.

100. In reference to this verse, among others, Stählin, "σκάνδαλον, σκανδαλίζω," 7.349, writes that "σκανδαλίζεσθαι ἐν αὐτῷ can be the opposite of πιστεῦσαι εἰς αὐτόν."

101. E.g., Crossan, "Mark and the Relatives of Jesus," 112–13; Pesch, *Markusevangelium*, 1.224; see further supporters and discussion in Myllykoski, "James the Just," 80–81.

phenomenon associated with the abandonment of family members (10:30), unlike its Synoptic parallels (Matt 19:29; Luke 18:29–30). One's own family members could become a stumbling block that discourages perseverance in following Christ (Mark 13:13). *Family ties must therefore be shunned if such relationships lead astray the faithful from following Jesus.* Wright's sociological study on modern defectors reveals the necessity that tight-knit religious groups have affective relationships that resemble surrogate families. Ties within the group must be strong because external social and family ties can become significant factors that draw away practitioners from their religious commitment. This phenomenon is likewise seen in certain sources of antiquity as grounds for apostasy, as Wilson evinces (e.g., Philo, *Spec.* 1.316; Cyprian, *Laps.* 9.1–5).[102] In view of the likelihood that some of the Markan community members may not have remained faithful to Christ during Nero's recent persecutions but betrayed other members by disclosing information to their captures (Tacitus, *Annals* 15.44), and these disclosures probably included relatives and close relationships, the importance of loyalty to Christ even above one's own kin needed to be stressed. Even so, Mark does not view all familial ties negatively (e.g., 7:10–13; 10:19). Family members are to be honored, but not at the price of falling away for their sake.

Spiritual obduracy also plagues Jesus' disciples in Mark 6:52 and 8:17–18. Their shortcomings may be juxtaposed with minor characters in the narrative: the friends of the paralytic (2:5), the woman with a hemorrhage (5.25–34), the Syrophoenician woman (7:24–30), blind Bartimaeus (10:46–52), the woman who anoints Jesus (14:7–8), and the Roman centurion who proclaims Jesus as the son of God when Jesus dies (15:39) all act more faithfully than the disciples. Notably also, Simon of Cyrene's taking up of Jesus' cross (15:21; cf. 8:34) is something the disciples will not do, and Joseph of Arimathea's care for the burial (15:42–46) is something we might expect family and close friends to do (cf. 6:29).[103] Tannehill rightly says, "If certain minor characters in the narrative do what the disciples should but do not do the contrast increases our sense of the disciples' failure."[104] In the narrative the disciples' hardness of heart is highlighted on boat rides: they are fearful of a storm in 4:35–41, fearful of wind and ghosts in 6:45–52, and hardened in 8:14–21. Perhaps an indirect message to the audience is that they should not follow the disciples' fearfulness but exercise faith when facing turbulent circumstances, characterized in those passages as a journey across the sea. The second and third stories both take place after Jesus feeds a multitude of people in the wilderness (6:30–44; 8:1–13). With this setting, Mark seems bent on intimating the exodus narrative by echoing either the harden-

---

102. Wright, *Leaving Cults*; Wilson, *Leaving the Fold*, 122; cf. 125.

103. Cf. Tannehill, "Disciples in Mark," 152.

104. Ibid., 137.

ing of Pharaoh (e.g., Exod 7:13; 9:7) or of the wilderness generation (Deut 29:3) and associating such obduracy with Jesus' followers. Mark 8:17–18 is also framed between stories in which Jesus heals the deaf and blind (7:31–7; 8:22–26), which may be set in contrast with the disciples' spiritual inability to hear and see (8:18).[105] The disciples suffer from callousness similar to the outsiders in 4:10–12, and as the narrative continues, they all fall away. Judas betrays Jesus (14:10–11, 18–21, 43–46), Peter denies that he knows Jesus (14:66–72), and the other disciples abandon Jesus at his arrest (14:27–31, 37–38, 50–52).[106] *The disciples' obduracy leads to their apostasy.*

When Jesus predicts their apostasy (σκανδαλίζω) in Mark 14:27, he cites Zech 13:7: "Strike the shepherd and the sheep will be scattered." The verse is associated with a time of restoration related to the Davidic house (Zech 12:10—13:1) and 13:7 continues that the LORD will turn his hand against the "little ones" (MT).[107] In Mark, Jesus probably identifies himself in the role of a good shepherd who is struck down as part of God's divine plan, a thought that pertains to his arrest and crucifixion. At that time his disciples will abandon him (cf. 14:50). Their apostasy takes place despite their privileged status and empowerment to preach repentance, cast out unclean spirits, and heal the sick (Mark 3:14–19; 6:7–13).

Peter's three denials happen not only because he is afraid of being arrested (14:54, 66–72) but also because of his lack of prayer (14:31–42). At Gethsemane Jesus warns him along with James and John that they must watch and pray not to fall into temptation (14:38), essentially a plea for them not to defect (cf. 13:5, 9, 23, 33, 37).[108] Prayer and watching are seen as keys to how temptation could be overcome, but in a reverse manner, Peter and his companions fall asleep.[109] Immediately after the Gethsemane scene, the disciples forsake Jesus, and Peter denies him to the extent of cursing and swearing by oath (14:71), an aspect our author may have added to allude to early Christian persecutions in which defectors would use curse formulas to renounce Christ (cf. Acts 26:11).[110] Peter saves his physical life at the expense of

---

105. Cf. ibid., 147.

106. On the disciples' apostasy in Mark, see further Kingsbury, *Conflict in Mark*, 89–117.

107. The Qumran text's elaboration of the passage interprets it in an eschatological framework with the shepherd possibly as the Teacher of Righteousness, but then again this shepherd could be a wicked leader (CD-B 19.5–21). See Watts, "Mark," 232–33.

108. So Feldmeier, *Petrus*, 55. On the general theme of watching in Mark, see Best, *Following Jesus*, 147–61.

109. A noticeable pattern of reversal of expectations in the gospels may be viewed in the narratives about Peter. One classic case of this is when he denies that he will deny Jesus (14:29–30). As Wiarda, *Peter*, 34–41, properly maintains: "Peter is portrayed as saying or doing something in relation to Christ based on an certain understanding of what is appropriate . . . only to receive correction or be proven wrong" (34).

110. Lampe, "St. Peter's Denial," 352, relates Peter's denials to three early interrogations Christians

being ashamed of Jesus and failing to take up his cross and follow him (cf. Mark 8:34–38).

Peter's defection is not the same as Judas' betrayal. The former claims he does not know Jesus. This denial is of the sort that the community in Mark were probably tempted to succumb to when interrogated by their persecutors. Judas does not deny Jesus this way; he affirms that he knows Jesus and is willing to point him out to the authorities. Hence, Mark's community is able to distinguish between two kinds of failures: denial and betrayal. Peter's failure results in remorse implied by his crying, but Judas shows no regrets for his betrayal. He is brazen up to his final scene where he kisses his rabbi and makes sure his captors lead him away securely (14:43–45). Judas wants to make sure that Jesus does not escape; otherwise he would lose his betrayal money.[111] In keeping with this gospel's view of apostasy, it would seem that Judas has gained temporal wealth in this life at the price of losing eternal life (cf. 8:35–38). We are left with a strong impression that Peter is restored (implied in 16:7), but Judas is condemned (cf. Mark 14:21; see Luke-Acts below). This distinction in judgment is not based on the way they forsake Jesus but apparently on the basis that one repents and the other does not.[112] The impact of Judas' betrayal may have resonated deeply with the original audience who heard this gospel. Judas belonged to the inner core of Jesus' disciples and yet turned away from Jesus. When Judas responds, "Surely not I?" after Jesus claims one of his disciples would betray him (Mark 14:19), the audience probably reflected on their own potential as defectors.[113]

The disciples' falling away would seem to function in a threefold manner for Mark's community. First, it gives warning to the audience that even Christ's closest followers can turn away from him, but even if that should happen, it would not nullify Jesus as Messiah and Son of God—at the end of Mark's gospel, God vindicates Jesus and raises him from the dead. Second, as we have argued earlier, the disciples'

---

faced when being persecuted (cf. *Mart. Pol.* 9–10; Pliny, *Epistulae* 10.96.3). The thesis is stimulating but Gundry, *Mark*, 921, vigorously contests it. More relevant is the Lukan Paul's claim in Acts 26:11 that as a former persecutor of the church, he would force Christ-followers to "blaspheme," that is, curse or renounce Christ.

111. See Evans, *Mark*, 423. A remorseful Judas is found only in Matthew's gospel.

112. To be sure, it is quite possible our narrator implies that Judas' betrayal was predicted in the scriptures (cf. Ps 40[41]:9–10 LXX/Mark 14:18, 20–21), but this is not much different than the certainty of the prediction that all of Jesus' disciples would fall away according to Zech 13:7 (cf. Mark 14:27). Peter and the other disciples in fact challenge that inevitability and are later proven wrong (14:29–31). Whatever else this might suggest about divine foreknowledge, none of the disciples, Judas included (cf. 14:21b), are excused of personal responsibility for their failures, and it is always possible that Jesus' words in 14:21 are intended to get Judas to repent. This is perhaps how Matthew's version is understood (see below).

113. In agreement with Vogler, *Judas Iskarioth*, 55–56.

restoration is also implied at the end of the narrative (14:28; 16:7). *Mark's community was probably able to relate to the disciples' failures, and if such failures were not the end of the story, then the narrative may have provided them with hope for their own recovery from apostasy.* Finally, if Mark's community pondered on the defections of Peter and Judas, they may have applied the stories to their own backslidden state and be left with a decision—they could choose to be remorseful like Peter and be restored, or they could be recalcitrant like Judas.

In sum, the Markan community learns from the examples of unfaithful followers of Jesus. The disciples abandon Jesus, an unknown young man (Mark?) deserts him, and the women followers look from afar when he was crucified and at the empty tomb they flee in fear rather than proclaim that he has risen (15:40; 16:1–8). On a positive note, the audience learns from Jesus' example the importance of self-denial, faith, watchfulness, and prayer. By following Jesus they learn how to avoid spiritually obduracy and its eventual consequence, apostasy. As Tannehill affirms, "The more clearly the reader sees that the disciples represent himself [sic], the more clearly the necessary rejection of the disciples' behaviour becomes a negation of one's past self. The recognition of the disciples' failure and the search for an alternative way becomes a search for the new self who can follow Jesus faithfully as a disciple."[114] Mark's gospel ends with incompletion, perhaps formulating a rhetoric of suspense that prompts the ancient audience to pick up where the women left off. The good news of Jesus' resurrection still needs to be proclaimed, and his followers in Rome should not be fearful but ready to confess him before others.

PERSECUTION AND LOSING ONE'S LIFE TO SAVE IT (8:34–38)

A significant pericope of Jesus that warns against apostasy is related to persecution (8:34–38). On the way to Jerusalem, Jesus speaks about his upcoming death and resurrection three times (8:31–9:1; 9:30–50; 10:32–45), and after each prediction he teaches his followers lessons related to discipleship, servanthoood, and suffering (8:35; 9:35; 10:43–45).[115] In the first of these lessons he challenges his followers to take up their crosses in self-denial and follow him (8:34).[116] As a subtext the thematic purpose of the exodus way is finally exposed in 8:31–38: the faithful must follow

---

114. Tannehill, "Disciples in Mark," 142. Best, *Following Jesus*, 246 is also noteworthy: "While Mark pictures the historical disciples as challenged to journey after Jesus it is not his primary purpose to record how they reacted but to summon his own community to enter more seriously on the same journey."

115. See Rhoads, *Reading Mark*, 45.

116. Notice that γάρ connects 8:35 with 8:34. The three subsequent times γάρ appears in verses 36, 37, 38 make 8:34–38 a tightly knitted pericope related to suffering and warning against apostasy.

Jesus on his journey to Jerusalem, and that path will involve suffering and death, but it will eventually produce new life when Jesus is raised from the dead. Jesus elaborates on what cross-bearing entails: "for whoever wishes to save his life will lose it, but whoever loses his life for my sake and the gospel's will save it" (Mark 8:35; cf. Matt 10:39; 16:25; Luke 9:24; 17:33; John 12:25).[117] Here "life" (ψυχή) refers to the essential person that survives death. The saying is found in all four gospels, which vouches for its authenticity as a saying that originates from the Jesus of history.[118] The saying is often repeated by the church fathers also, often in relation to martyrdom and persecution.[119] It is considered an example of antithetic parallelism, a common mode of speaking related to Jesus sayings.[120] Jesus' preference for this type of speech may stem from the way it communicates urgency and the mnemonic ease with which it could be remembered.[121] *The saying in 8:35 encourages the disciples, especially when facing persecution and martyrdom, to look beyond the temporal life and receive eternal life, and conversely, it warns them against keeping their temporal life at the expense of losing eternal life.*

If a person should gain the entire world this would not be worth the value of his or her life in the age to come (8:36–37). The idea finds a parallel thought in Ps 48[49]:7–8, where there are intimations about life after death. Redeeming a life (נפש/ψυχή) is costly, and no price is great enough for it (Ps 48[49]:13, 15).[122] The

---

117. For a comparative list and other possible allusions to the saying in the NT, see Rebell, "'Sein Leben Verlieren,'" 202–18, esp. 206. For parallels from primarily Greco-Roman traditions, see Beardslee, "Saving One's Life," 61–64.

118. Schmidt, "Zum Paradox vom Verlieren," agrees but argues the ground saying of Jesus from Luke's version (Luke 9:23; 17:33), and he removes it from a martyrdom matrix to one that favors life and encourages right behavior in the kingdom of God (esp. 332, 351). But oral tradition and the repetitiveness of the saying might suggest that Jesus said these words in various settings and contexts, some no doubt related to persecution and martyrdom. An either/or approach would seem to be insufficient for New Testament examples of the saying. Certainly, many of the church fathers interpreted the saying as persecution/martyrdom (see next footnote). On the saying's authenticity, see further Rebell, "Sein Leben Verlieren," 202–18; Dinkler, "Jesu Wort," 77–98; and for possible Aramaic renditions, see Meier, *Marginal Jew*, 3.61, 63.

119 E.g., Tertullian, *Scorp.* 9; Cyprian, *Epistulae* 55[48].7; *Treatises* 9; *On the Glory of Martyrdom* 17; Hilary of Poiters, *On the Trinity*, 10; Ambrose, *Auxentius* 8; John Chrysostom, *Hom. 1 Cor.* 32[11]; Jerome, *Epistulae* 108.19; Augustine, *Nat. orig.* 2.17; *Mart. Habib*. See also other allusions to the saying in, e.g., *Herm. Vis.* 2.2; *Herm. Sim.* 9.26.3; Clement, *Strom.* 4.6; Tertullian, *Marc.* 4.21; Ambrose, *Virg.*, 2.4[25]; Augustine, *Doctr. chr.* 3.16.

120. For examples, see Jeremias, *New Testament Theology*, 14–15; cf. 8.

121. So ibid., 20.

122. For possible parallels in Jewish traditions, see Josephus, *J.W.* 1.18.3[357]; *2 Bar.* 51.15; *b. Tamid* 32a; *'Abot R. Nat.* B §35; Str.B. 1.587–88; and for Greco-Roman similarities, see Marcus, *Mark*, 2.626; Gundry, *Mark*, 455.

consequence of losing eternal life in Mark 8:35 is further explicated in the following verses and chapter 9.

Jesus goes on to warn that *in the age to come the Son of Man will be ashamed of those who denied him in the present age* (Mark 8:38; cf. Luke 12:8–9; Matt 10:32–33; 1 John 2:28; 2 Tim 2:12; *Herm. Sim* 8.6.4; 9.21.3).[123] This saying has apocalyptic leanings and refers to life gained or lost on judgment day once the *parousia* takes place.[124] At this judgment Jesus will be ashamed of his former followers who were ashamed of him, and he will disassociate himself from them.[125] *In essence, the disciples are warned that to deny Christ before others will result in their being denied by Christ at his second coming. He will disown them. This refers to a negative verdict and loss of eternal life.*

More than this, Jesus' followers must not be ashamed of his "words" (Mark 8:38; cf. Luke 9:26).[126] This probably refers to their putting to open practice the message of the gospel that Jesus proclaims (cf. Mark 8:35; 10:29), which would include ethical precepts such as loving God and others (12:28–34), keeping God's commands (10:17–19), and forgiving others (11:25).[127] It is not enough for them to confess Christ: their lifestyle needs to match that confession.

During the final week of Jesus in Jerusalem, Peter and the other disciples turn into prime examples of people who save their temporal life and are afraid of being identified as followers of Jesus (14:27, 50, 66–72). They are restored, however (14:28 cf. 14:72; 16:7), and so they do not face the eventual punishment of losing eternal life. Differently, Judas becomes a prime example of gaining the wealth of the world at the expense of eternal life (8:36–37; cf. 14:10–11). Jesus warns Judas that he will suffer a fate so terrible that it would have been better for him not to be born (14:21). This does not seem to be referring to his physical death. Mark's gospel gives

---

123. This particular saying goes back to an Aramaic original in which the Markan words for "ashamed" and Matthean/Lukan "deny" were almost indistinguishable: so Jeremias, *New Testament Theology*, 7. Nevertheless, the concepts of honor and shame in this passage are comparable to Greco-Roman contours, affirming Mark's gospel as "a Jewish document in a Greco-Roman world," according to Robbins, *New Boundaries*, 241. On the authentic presence of the "Son of Man" phrase in this saying, see Lambrecht, "Note on Mark 8.38," 117–25. Beasley-Murray, "*Parousia* in Mark," 565–81, relates Mark 8:38 to the Parousia and the Son of Man/judgment scene of Dan 7. See also *1 En.* 46.6; 48.8–10, and further Barrett, "I Am Not Ashamed," 19–50.

124. Compare with Meier, *Marginal Jew*, 3.58: "those who cling at all costs to this present life will lose it at the final judgment, while those willing to sacrifice their present lives to follow Jesus wholeheartedly will receive a fuller, lasting form of life at the final judgment."

125. On the aspect of disassociation, see Malina and Rohrbaugh, *Synoptic Gospels*, 182.

126. Some manuscripts omit λόγους (e.g., p[45vid], W), but the longer reading is generally sound and preferable: see Metzger, *Textual Commentary*, 84, 124.

127. See further the fuller listing of ethical criteria in Breytenbach, "Identity and Rules of Conduct," 62–71.

no information on the death of Judas—he remains alive and recalcitrant in his final appearance in this text. The audience can surmise that eternal punishment will await him in the age to come.[128]

The saying of Jesus in 8:34–38 would challenge all followers of Jesus who experienced persecution to be unafraid of their tormentors and unashamed of Jesus. Taking up one's cross includes self-denial and willingness to die; in essence, the audience must follow the example of Jesus. These words would be especially relevant for Mark's community, which possibly witnessed firsthand some of its members put to death by crucifixion in Rome.[129] Such an audience would be emboldened to reaffirm their commitment to Christ and his teachings, realizing that this present life is not all there is. Jesus' conquest of physical death through the resurrection demonstrates that there is more life to come.

CAUSING OTHERS AND ONESELF TO APOSTATIZE (9:42–50)

Another warning against apostasy is found in 9:42–50 when Jesus speaks of the potential for "little ones" to "fall away" (σκανδαλίζω). The verb σκανδαλίζω has ancient meanings conveying entrapment, ensnaring, causing a downfall, and, together with its noun form (σκάνδαλον) in the LXX, it frequently results in the destruction of God's people or human life (Josh 23:13; Judg 2:3; 8:27, Ps 105:36; 139:5–6; 140:9; Hos 4:17; Wis 14:11).[130] In the gospels it often connotes the notion of falling away (e.g., Mark 4:17; 14:27, 29; Matt 18:1–4; Luke 17:1–2). For those who cause little ones to fall away, it would be better for them if a millstone were tied around their necks and they be cast into the sea (Mark 9:42; cf. Rev 18:21). This probably suggests a colorful nuance for σκανδαλίζω, metaphorically depicting the casting of a stumbling block before one's path so as to cause that person to fall (cf. Sir 27.23; *Pss. Sol* .16.7; 1 Pet 2:8; Rom 9:33; Rev 2:14).[131] In this case those who cast the block will themselves suffer a fate worse than being tied to a heavy block and thrown into the Sea of Galilee to drown. *A fate worse than drowning turns out to be suffering damnation in the fires of Gehenna* (cf. Mark 9:43–50).[132] We are dealing here with an act so

---

128. For a Synoptic approach to Judas' end, see the section in Luke-Acts below.

129. On this thought see Incigneri, *Gospel to the Romans*, 242–43.

130. Cf. Humbert, "Essai d'une théologie," 1–2: "σκάνδαλον, au sens concret primitif, signifierait donc <<la détente d'un piège >>." For the softer meaning as an "offense"/"to offend," see Matt 17:27. For further studies on the term, see Mateos, "Analisis semántico," 57–92; Iersel, "Het begrip σκάνδαλον κτλ," 33–41; Stählin, *Skandalon*; Giesen, "σκανδαλίζω," 3.248–50.

131. See *LEH*, "σκανδαλίζω," "σκάνδαλον," and further, Stählin, "σκάνδαλον, σκανδαλίζω," 7.341.

132. For the concept of *Gehenna* and its association with eschatological damnation, see Milikowsky, "Which Gehenna?," 238–49.

vile as to send the culprits to hell. They do not merely cause others to stumble by sinning but by committing apostasy.

Various identities have been given to the "little ones"[133] who believe in Jesus, including "children,"[134] those who are "weak in faith,"[135] "defenseless disciples,"[136] the "lowborn,"[137] and "people with the least social status and power."[138] We may add to this list another option: Zech 13:7, which Jesus cites in Mark 14:27, mentions the sheep or shepherd boys as the "little ones."[139] With this meaning in mind, Jesus may be referring to his followers in the imagery of sheep who follow his lead as the shepherd.[140] Contextually, the term points back to the earlier pericope in which Jesus sets a child before the disciples and says, "Whoever receives such a child in my name receives me" (9:33–37). The "little ones" in 9:42 would seem to include little children but not exclusively so given that he addresses disciples in verses 41 and 43–48. Matthew's version of the warning also has a child present (Matt 18:1–7), but Luke places the saying in a setting dealing with adult Christian relationships and forgiveness (Luke 17:1–4). Mark 9:42 indicates that those who are vulnerable to falling away are individuals who "believe," that is, those trust in Christ, bear his name, and belong to him. The situation in Mark's Rome possibly involved family heads of households who apostatized and in their fear of being persecuted, they discouraged and destroyed the faith of their children by refusing to let them gather with the Christians.

The warning spills over into 9:43–50, in which the subject involves disciples whose body parts cause them to fall away. If their hand, foot, or eye causes them to stumble (σκανδαλίζω), they should sever the member from their body rather than be thrown into *Gehenna*. What type of apostasy is the pericope indicating? A parallel passage in Matt 5:28–29 suggests sexual immorality (cf. *Pss Sol* 16.7), and Robert Gundry compares the sin in Mark 9 with later Jewish writings in which the "hand"

---

133. The phrase also can be rendered as "one of the least of these who believe" (ἕνα τῶν μικρῶν τούτων τῶν πιστευόντων).

134. Evans, *Mark*, 70.

135. Grant and Luccock, *Mark*, 7.751.

136. Schweizer, *Mark*, 198.

137. Malina and Rohrbaugh, *Synoptic Gospels*, 186.

138. Rhoads, *Reading Mark*, 119.

139. The LXX refers to sheep only, but the MT uses "little ones" (צֹעֲרִים). See BDB, 858; Smith, *Micah–Malachi*, 282.

140. The Qumran sect may interpret the little ones of Zech 13:7 as those who enter into God's covenant. In this text it is not clear if they are associated with the "poor" among God's metaphoric flock who in the age of visitation will escape the messiah's punishment against apostate covenant breakers (CD-B 19.5–21). So Watts, "Mark," 232; cf. CD-B 19.16. Apparently, the "poor" of the flock are compared to Ezekiel's faithful remnant with the mark of "tau" on their foreheads (CD-B 19.11–14; cf. Ezek 9:1–11).

is associated with masturbation, the "foot" with common adultery (foot may be a euphemism for the penis), and playing with children may be related to pederasty (*b. Niddah* 13a–b; cf. *m. Niddah* 2.1): "Jesus may therefore build on a Jewish tradition that condemned pederasty and prescribed cutting off the hand of a masturbater and the penis of an adulterer."[141] But there are problems with this interpretation. Although sayings about masturbation, adultery, and pederasty may have been known orally for many years before recorded, these sayings from the Talmud and similar sources were written down at a later time than the words of Jesus. Mark's Gentile audience, in fact, probably would not have been able to decipher such a meaning from Mark 9. Moreover, there is no condemnation anywhere in Israel's scriptures or the New Testament concerning masturbation.[142] If this practice could send a person to everlasting "fire," we might expect it to be clearly condemned somewhere in these texts. Moreover, the effectiveness of the saying breaks down when we realize that cutting off one hand will not necessarily stop a person from masturbating.[143] Also, the sayings call people to be maimed, not eunuchs.[144]

Other options for the sin committed in this passage include pederasty or sexual vice *in general* (e.g., Mark 9:36–37, 42), unbelief (9:42), or sins related to pride, selfishness, division, and haughty ambition (9:33–34, 50b).

More clearly, the imagery of salt with fire at the end of the passage may be referring to a purification related to suffering and persecution (9:49).[145] If so, then perhaps the entire pericope centers on this notion, and the primary agent of stumbling relates to denying or abandoning Christ through cowardice in the face of such affliction. This understanding would also seem to bridge 9:42 with 9:43–50:[146] Those who cause the little ones to stumble are not only external persecutors, but

---

141. Gundry, *Mark*, 524f, but also see his qualifications. On this reading, gouging out the offensive eye would seem to be related to sexual lust (cf. Matt 5:28–29). Collins, *Sexual Ethics*, 67–68, 189, referring to the same passage, considers masturbation a vice that excludes individuals from the kingdom of God. On this position, see also Deming, "Mark 9.42–10.12," 130–44; Collins, *Mark*, 450–52.

142. For a refutation of alleged passages, see Oropeza, "What Is Sex?," 41–43.

143. And although severing one's penis may stop adultery, the foot/penis euphemism is not a good one, for the body parts in this text assume pairs, whether hands, feet, or eyes. Losing one testicle would seem to be a better comparison.

144. So Marcus, *Mark*, 2.696–97.

145. Cf. Hooker, *Saint Mark*, 233. Evans, *Mark*, 73, is on target when he comments that the fire in 9:49 is different from that which is mentioned in 9:48: "Jesus does not salt anyone with the fire of Gehenna. But the evangelist is not remiss in placing these two sayings one after the other, for both carry with them eschatological implications. The one who becomes ensnared in the temptations of the world will be cast into Gehenna, whose fires are never quenched [9:47–48], but the one who submits to the purifying fire of Jesus [9:49] will escape Gehenna."

146. Differently, Marcus, *Mark*, 2.695, thinks 9:43 begins the offenses caused by Christians.

In the Footsteps of Judas and Other Defectors

Christ-followers who betray fellow believers to the persecutors. Both the betrayer and persecutor are in danger of a fate worse than drowning. That fate is disclosed in 9:43–47—presumably at the eschaton they will be thrown into *Gehenna*. We notice also the similar of wording related to judgment in 9:42 (καλόν ἐστιν αὐτῷ) and 14:21 (καλὸν αὐτῷ), the latter describing Judas' upcoming punishment on account of his betrayal. An example of persecution that relates to torture and maiming is found in 2 Macc 7, in which the eldest of seven sons who are martyred under Antiochus Epiphanes has his hands and feet cut off.[147] Later on in that story there is hope of life after death in view of resurrection. The echo is considerable and fits well with a community that has probably experienced persecution, torture, betrayal, and apostasy.

Moreover, for the disciples to be at peace with one another (9:50) might suggest that a reconciliation ought to take place in which repentant traitors are welcomed back into the community and forgiveness is established (cf. 11:25). The mandate for forgiveness is so important that believers cannot expect to be forgiven by God if they do not forgive others (cf. 11:25).[148] Then again, and perhaps more relevant to the narrative, 9:50 may simply function as Jesus' closing comment to the disciples' earlier argument amongst themselves (9:33–34). At any rate, the main weakness with our interpreting 9:43–47 as persecution and torture is that the person cuts off his or her *own* hand and foot, as the second person imperatives suggest (ἀπόκοψον, ἔκβαλε); it is not done by a torturer or executioner. *The meaning of 9:43–47, then, is perhaps wider than disciples committing apostasy because of persecution; it is probably meant to refer to any kind of sin or temptation that may cause a Christ-follower to fall away.*

Derrett ascribes the warnings of being thrown into *Gehenna* fire (i.e., "other worldly punishment") as a method of helping the disciples root out any disloyalty: "Fear of punishment was universally understood in the ancient world to be the most general means whereby people, whose loyalty was unstable and good behaviour undependable, could be attached with reasonable certainty to their leader for the time being."[149] The imagery of amputating one's body parts recalls fire and salt (cf. 9:43, 48–50): cauterization to prevent bleeding to death, and salt to treat the wound and prevent gangrene, sepsis, and "worms." As fire and salt preserved the amputated person from dying, so those who "amputate" what might cause them to apostatize will be preserved for eternal life; this will prevent them from the "worms" and eternal fire

---

147. See, e.g., Iersel, "Failed Followers," 252; Evans, *Mark*, 71.

148. See Breytenbach, "Identity and Rules of Conduct," 71. Mark 11:26 emphasizes the point of reciprocal unforgiveness, but this verse is not found in the earliest witnesses.

149. Derrett, "Law in the New Testament," 25, who argues from the ancient world that amputation was seen as a substitute for the death penalty. See also Hooker, *Saint Mark*, 231–33.

of hell.¹⁵⁰ The concept of being salted with fire (9:49) probably has in mind prophetic imagery of a fiery judgment that will punish the wicked and yet at the same time refine the righteous.¹⁵¹ Other New Testament writings addressed to Rome (Romans) or originating from that city (1 Peter) speak of Christ-followers as living sacrifices (Rom 12:1–2) and undergoing suffering in the form of a fiery ordeal (1 Pet 4:12). Along these lines also, if the concept of "little children" in Mark 9:42 originates from Zech 13:7, then it is significant that in Zech 13:8–9 God declares that two-thirds of the people in the land will be cut off and perish but one-third will be tried in fire as silver and gold. They will call on the LORD's name and be called "his people." Here again a judgment comes upon God's people in which many perish, but fire is seen as a cleansing agent for a faithful remnant who survive.

The words attributed to Jesus in this pericope would be entirely relevant for the Markan community whose members may have been tortured and lit on fire during Nero's persecutions. Even so, if the persons are supposed to cut off their own body parts, this language may be understood as hyperbole related to danger of committing sins that lead to apostasy and eternal judgment. Such sins must be severed from a believer's life if they prevent the person from obtaining eternal life.¹⁵² Clearly, eternal destinies are at stake; according to the Markan Jesus, the consequence of apostasy is eternal punishment (Mark 9:43, 45 cf. 10:17, 30; Matt 18:7–9; Isa 66:24).

CONCLUSION

We have suggested that the community of Mark's gospel is in Rome and has suffered under the persecutions of Emperor Nero.¹⁵³ As a result of this, a number of believers may have denied their identity as Christians when facing persecution, and other members betrayed the identity and whereabouts of other Christians. The community was probably quite familiar with apostasy. Mark's gospel is a call for both the faithful and unfaithful Christians to learn from the life and teachings of Jesus. Through this narrative they learn that spiritual obduracy plays a major role in apostasy. The multitudes and religious leaders of Jesus' day reject Jesus' teachings, and as punishment for their refusal to "see," God dulls their spiritual senses in a *lex talionis* manner akin with the way he judges apostate Israel in Isaianic tradition (Mark 4:10–12; cf. Isa 6:9–10). This obduracy reaches its crescendo when the religious authorities and

---

150. Cf. Derrett, "Law in the New Testament," 28–29.

151. Cf. Isa 43:2; *Pss Sol* 15.4–5; *Sib Or* 2.252–54; 1QH 14.17–18; Marcus, *Mark*, 2.698.

152. Contra Schweizer, *Mark*, 199, who denies punishment in hell in this passage and uses other texts that are hardly relevant here (Rom 11:32; 1 Tim.2:4) in an attempt to refute the more obvious reading.

153. See also Irenaeus, *Haer.* 3.1.1; Eusebius, *Hist. eccl.* 2.15.1–2; cf. 1 Pet. 5:13.

the crowd they influence bring about Jesus' death in Jerusalem. Spiritual obduracy eventually leads to the religious leaders' blasphemy of the Spirit of God by their rejection of the miraculous signs Jesus performs. They attribute his miracles not to the Spirit of God but to the power of the demonic (Mark 3:22–30).

Jesus' own family members are also hardened, but they have not blasphemed the Spirit. Instead they think Jesus has gone mad (3:21, 31–35). Their negative portrait in Mark probably arises from the community's situation in which family members betrayed and led astray their Christian relatives (cf. 13:12). Individuals from the crowd of outsiders can become insiders, however, by seeking further into the teachings and parables of Jesus, obeying them, repenting, and following Jesus. Insiders, on the other hand, can also suffer from spiritual obduracy as did the disciples (6:52; 8:17–18). Their lack of such things as insight, watchfulness, and prayer eventually leads to their apostasy when Judas betrays Jesus. They abandon Jesus at his arrest and Peter denies that he knows him (14:27, 49–50, 66–72; cf. 14:37–38). A glimmer of hope in the form of restoration is held out for these followers at the end of Mark's gospel (16:7; cf. 14:28). But not for Judas. Unlike Peter, Judas remains hardened until the end (14:21; cf. 14:44f). The Markan community would be instructed by these stories that their apostasy is not unpardonable. Apostasy is not the same thing as blaspheming the Spirit. Failures in the community of Mark may have resembled the followers of Jesus, whose obduracy was only partial. Spiritual myopia may have led to their abandoning him, but they could still be restored if they are remorseful and refuse to be recalcitrant.

The nature of apostasy in Mark centers on persecution and suffering. The disciples fall away for fear of persecution. Moreover, in Jesus' parable of the Sower, the second seed/soil depicts those who believe the gospel message with enthusiasm, but due to persecution they fall away (4:5–6, 16–17). The Markan narrative uses new exodus imagery to describe the journey of the believers: they are to follow the way with Jesus, and Jesus' way is suffering and the cross, which Jesus reveals to the disciples in 8:34–38: in the context of impending persecution they must take up their crosses and not seek to save their physical life. The believers who attempt to save their mortal life will lose eternal life, and if they are ashamed of confessing Jesus in this age, Jesus will be ashamed of them in the age to come by disowning them. The final consequence for committing apostasy will be exclusion of that life in the age to come. More specifically, their punishment is portrayed by the fires of *Gehenna*. Both believers and non-believers alike must not cause other Christians, whether children or adults, to fall away, or they will suffer a fate worse than drowning (9:42). And if the believers' body parts are leading them to commit apostasy, they are to amputate the offending part rather than be cast into *Gehenna* (9:43–47). Such imagery would make sense to Christians in Rome who perhaps experienced firsthand Christian betrayals, children falling away because of defecting parents, and tortures and burnings inflicted on them by their tormentors. Be that as it may, persecution is not viewed as the only source of apostasy—Mark 9:42–50 suggests beyond persecution that any sin that leads to defection must be severed. As well, the third seed/soil of Jesus' parable views wealth and worldly concerns as other factors that can lead to spiritual failure (4:7, 18–19). The ultimate example of this is Judas, who did not betray Jesus for fear of persecution but because of greed (14:10–11).

2

The Gospel of Matthew

Law Breakers, False Prophets, and Final Judgment

Matthew's gospel exhorts its audience repeatedly through the teachings of Jesus.[1] The traditional interpretation of this gospel claims that Matthew, a former tax collector who became one of the twelve apostles, wrote this gospel or at least compiled various *logia* of Jesus in Aramaic. In this view it was written about 65–67 CE.[2] The majority of scholars today reject this date, often noting Matthew's dependence on Mark and its theological concerns that relate to second-generation Christians. They place it sometime around 85 CE, most likely after Matthew had already died.[3] Scholarship, however, has moved away from the Eighteen Benedictions, more precisely the so-called *birkat ha-minim* Benediction 12 that pronounces a curse on Nazarenes, a marker separating Jews from Jewish Christians and allegedly affecting Matthew's community.[4] The date of this separation supposedly took place in the

---

1. Perhaps correctly, Stanton, *Gospel for a New People*, 3, 380, affirms that Matthew does not have one overriding concern but writes broadly with pastoral and catechetical concerns.

2. Eusebius *Hist. eccl.* 3.39.16; cf. 3.24.6; 5.8.2; Irenaeus *Haer.* 3.1.1.

3. For scholars in this camp, which are the majority, see in Gale, *Redefining Ancient Borders*, 4–5; Schnelle, *Einleitung*, 222. On the traditional side, see Gundry, *Matthew*, 599–609. DeSilva, *Introduction*, opines that the original collection of Aramaic sayings of Jesus may have been compiled by Matthew, but a disciple of Matthew fashioned these with "other Jesus sayings familiar to the community" (including Mark's gospel), and presented the life and teachings of Jesus in a way that was "more complete than any of the sources on their own" (235).

4. E.g., Davies, *Setting of the Sermon*. A post-70 CE date is still maintained by those who read Matthew's situation in light of Johanan ben Zakkai and the Yavneh (Jamnia) community. After Jerusalem's destruction he may have been pivotal in consolidating Jews and helping form rabbinic Judaism. Yavneh may have struggled against Jewish Christians regarding the Law: cf. Gale, *Redefining*

80s CE. The author of Matthew's gospel, at any rate, cannot be specifically identified through internal evidence. This ancient biographer of Jesus appears to be educated, familiar with Jewish thinking, and is very likely a Jew.[5] Matthew's gospel is certainly the most Jewish of the four gospels,[6] and even though it speaks negatively about Gentiles,[7] it nonetheless supports a Gentile mission (28:18–20; cf. 8:11–12; 10:18; 12:18–21; 21:43; 24:14; 25:32; 26:13).[8] Negative portrayals of the Pharisees, more numerous and intense than the other gospels, may suggest this sect as representative of the major opponents against Matthew's group.[9] They are considered foolish guides, blind leaders of the blind (15:13–14; 23:16–17, 19, 24, 26) and are sometimes teamed up with the scribes (5:20; 12:38; 15:1; 23:2).[10] The issue with these religious leaders may have centered on the question of Jesus' authority (7:29; cf. 5:20).[11]

The Matthean community probably lived in an urban setting, and the high values related to money in this gospel may suggest a somewhat wealthy congregation (10:9; 25:14–30; cf. 5:3; 14:21; 22:9; 27:57).[12] Whereas certain scholars maintain that this community originates from Antioch or somewhere in Syria,[13] others posit Galilee or some other provenance.[14] Perhaps Alan Segal is correct by extending the

---

Ancient Borders, 21, and see *y. Shabbat* 15d. For criticisms of this perspective, see Hagner, "Matthew: Christian Judaism," 276–78.

5. On Matthew as Jewish see the relevant articles in Balch, *Social History of the Matthean Community*; and further, Carter, *Matthew: Storyteller*, 28; Evans, "Jewish Christian Gospel," 242.

6. e.g., Matt 5:17–20; 10:5–6; 15:21–28; 23:3, 23; see further Evans, "Jewish Christian Gospel," 240–77, esp. 242–45; Gale, *Redefining Ancient Borders*, 15–40.

7. 5:47; 6:7, 32; 10:18; 18:17; 20:19, 25; 24:9.

8. Some aspects related to Gentiles may include an avoidance of Aramaic (e.g., Mark 1:13/Matt 4:2; Mark 5:41/Matt 9:25; Mark 7:34/Matt 15:30; Mark 7:11/Matt 15:5) and the problem with the author apparently not understanding the Hebrew poetry behind Matt 21:5–7 (but for rebuttal, see Ehrman, *New Testament*, 109). Some Semitic words are translated (Matt 1:23; 27:33, 46), while others are not (5:22; 6:24; 10:25; 27:6). Overman, *Matthew's Gospel*, 109–13, presents Matthew's negative view of outsiders (e.g., Matt 10:16–17; contrast Matt 12:30 with Mark 9:40; Luke 9:50).

9. Matt 3:7; 9:34; 12:14, 22–32, 38–42; 15:1, 7, 12–14; 16:1–12; 21:43–45; 22:15; 23:1–36; cf. 5:20; 6:1–16.

10. The scribes, along with chief priests and elders, are seen as being involved with the execution of Jesus (Matt 16:21; 26:57; 27:41). For more on the opponents of Jesus in Matthew, see Carter, *Matthew: Storyteller*, 229–41; Meier, *Marginal Jew*, 3.289–613.

11. Cf. Kingsbury, *Matthew as Story*, 125–26.

12. Ibid., 152–53, notices the number of times Matthew uses the word "city" (26) as opposed to village (4). Contrast Mark: city (8), village (7). On the community's wealth, Gale, *Redefining Ancient Borders*, 64–86, notices such things as a preponderance of teachings related to landowners and business people (e.g., 5:25f; 6:19; 13:45f; 20:1–6) and how Matt 25:14–30 uses "talents" rather than lesser monetary units found in the parallel of Luke 19:11–27.

13. E.g., Mark 3:8/Matt 4:24 "Syria"; cf. Ign. *Smyrn.* 1:1; Ign. *Phld.* 3:1; *Did.* 7:1, 8:10:5, 16.

14. Cf. Kingsbury, "Conclusion," 264, who compiles the conclusions of the contributors in Balch's book and observes a trend towards Galilee (Kingsbury himself, however, opts for Antioch: *Matthew as*

boundaries of this community anywhere from Antioch to Galilee.[15] To this region we add the possibility that the Matthean community is not merely one group in one location but a cluster of communities in different locations.[16] Hence, Matthew's audience appears to be in some sense Jewish, and there seems to be no good reason why his community could not be understood as being in more than one city.[17] The kind of "Jew" Matthew addresses may be surmised better by looking further into this gospel's view of the Law.

KEEPING THE LAW AND THE PROPHETS IN THE MATTHEAN COMMUNITY (5:17–20)

A more specific identity for the opponents behind the Matthean community has been the subject of much debate, often centering on the Law as presented in Matt 5:17–20:

> Do not think that I have come to abolish the Law or the Prophets; I came not to abolish but to fulfill. For amen I say to you, until heaven and earth pass away, one iota or one stroke will not pass from the Law until all takes place. Therefore whoever breaks one of the least of these commands and teaches so to others, that person will be called least in the kingdom of heaven. But whoever does and teaches them will be called great in the kingdom of heaven. For I say to you, that unless your righteousness exceeds that of the scribes and Pharisees, you will never enter into the kingdom of heaven.

Gerhard Barth's classic treatment of the Matthean situation argues that Matthew's group faced opponents on two fronts: antinomians on the one hand and the "Rabbinate" on the other. The Matthean group upholds the Law, contrary to the antinomians who claim "the Law" and "the Prophets" are abolished (cf. 5:17–20), and the group also holds the love commandment at the center of Jesus' interpretation of the Law, unlike the rabbis (7:12; 22:34–40; cf. 12:1–14; 15:16–20; 23:23). For Barth the former opponent is a group related to Hellenistic Christianity (but not the

---

Story, 148). On Galilee as the provenance, see also Overman, *Matthew's Gospel*, 159–60, who suggests Tiberias or Sepphoris as the location. Gale, *Redefining Ancient Borders*, 41–63, argues for Sepphoris. Stanton, *Gospel for a New People*, 378, views the community in Syria. Favoring Antioch is Gundry, *Matthew*, 609. For an overview of various provenances, see Allison and Davies, *Matthew* 1.138–47.

15. Segal, "Matthew's Jewish Voice," 19, 26–27.

16. For a similar view, see Stanton, *Gospel for a New People*, 50–51. In response to Bauckham, *Gospel for all Christians*, who attempts to undermine the view of distinct gospel communities, see the preceding chapter on Mark; and Mitchell, "Patristic Counter-Evidence," 36–79.

17. To avoid complexity, however, we will use the singular "community."

Pauline community or Gnosticism), which is both libertine and charismatic—they are workers of lawlessness (7:15–23; cf. 24:11–12, 24).[18] The Pharisees, however, are even characterized as lawless in 23:28.[19] Incidentally for Matthew, to commit lawlessness is to deviate from God's will and not bear the fruit of righteous living (7:17; 12:33; 13:41; 21:43; 24:12).

More recently it has been argued that Paul's Law-free gospel was defeated at Antioch against Peter and James with the latter apostles influencing the Matthean community. Matthew is said to contend against Paul's gospel.[20] To be sure, Matthew and Paul may have different perspectives about the Law, but both epitomize it through the command of loving one's neighbor as oneself (Matt 22:34–40; Rom 13:8–10), and both condemn a form of lawlessness that can lead to apostasy (Matt 7:21–23; 2 Cor 6:14; 2 Thess 2:3, 7–9; cf. 1 Tim 1:9). Nowhere in Matthew's gospel is it affirmed that Christ's followers must be circumcised, the main point of contention Paul has with his opponents in Galatia (e.g., Gal. 5:1–6; 6:12). Also, the idea that Paul's view was defeated by the other apostles in Antioch remains questionable. It runs counter to the Book of Acts, which does not portray Paul against James in the years following the decision at the Jerusalem meeting (Acts 15:1–30, 35; cf. 18:22; 21:17–26). Of course, in these passages Luke seems to paint with a broad brush over problems between Paul and other apostles. He does not always shy away, however, from mentioning Paul's disputes with other Christian workers (e.g., Acts 15:1–2; 15:36–41). One assumption behind the Matthew-versus-Paul view seems to be that Paul rather than Luke is correct about his relationships with the other apostles.[21] Is this really the case given that Paul's letters are loaded with rhetorical language intended to persuade his audiences to his way of thinking? The perspective that Matthew is against Paul requires us to interact with many assumptions and inferences about Galatians 2 and Acts and the Law.

Perhaps a better option is that the antinomian opponents in Matthew have taken Paul's teachings to an extreme. This seems to have been a problem in some churches after Paul had died (cf. 2 Pet 3:15–16). We suggest that Matthew's group faces a conflict with what they perceive to be false prophets who claim to be Christ's followers and have antinomian and charismatic tendencies. While an opponent in

---

18. Barth, "Matthew's Understanding," 94–95, 73–105, 160–64.

19. Differently, Sand, *Gesetz*, argues that Matthew comes against libertine tendencies within his own community.

20. See Sim, *Gospel of Matthew*; idem, "Matthew's Anti-Paulinism," 766–83; idem, "Matthew 7.21–23," 325–43.

21. On the general integrity between Acts and Paul see Hemer, *Book of Acts*; Talbert, *Reading Acts*, 233–50.

the post-Pauline tradition remains possible, we simply do not have enough evidence to support this identity with any confidence.

Even so, Matthew's group does seem to face opponents on two fronts.[22] The false prophets are one of the rivals. What group is the other?

Contemporary scholarship now views Matthew's community as one of various competing religious groups during the first century, and it primarily contends against formative Judaism, an emerging group of that time.[23] Matthew's community is identified as an *ekklesia* while the opponents congregate in "their synagogue" (4:23; 9:35; 10:17; 12:9; 13:54); the former believes that Jesus fulfilled the Law and Prophets, thus becoming a true teacher of the Law with his community as the true Israel.[24] A growing number of scholars suggest that when Matthew wrote his gospel his community still operated within formative Judaism.[25] The community is said to be post-70 CE Christian Jews who live according to Mosaic Law and Jesus' teachings, are not strongly involved in Gentile missions, and have not broken away from emerging Judaism even though they may be experiencing some conflicts with the mainstream.

Passages such as 23:2–3 may suggest this reading. Here Jesus says to his disciples that they are to do and keep everything the scribes and Pharisees tell them because they sit on the chair of Moses, but they must not do their works.[26] Donald Hagner, however, argues that even though the community would consider itself to be the true Judaism of its day, it reflects more a Christian group from *our* perspective.[27] The community had already broken away from formative Judaism, and the latter considered the Matthean group to be apostate. For Hagner the community is best defined as "Jewish Christian" rather than "Christian Jewish." The former refers "to Jews who have come to faith in Jesus as the divine κύριος, who affirm their faith as the fulfillment of the scriptures, whose experience involves a degree of newness that transcends the synagogues and temple, and who believe that by following the teaching of Jesus, their Messiah-Teacher, they fulfill the righteousness of the Torah."[28]

22. On this facet we generally agree with Barth (see above).

23. Cf. Overman, *Matthew's Gospel*, esp. 105, 156–57, who in addition suggests that Matthew's Gospel represents a minority community, which responds to the dominant group represented by the Pharisees who perhaps wielded political authority in Galilee.

24. Cf. ibid., 16–19, 153–58, 98–99.

25. Proponents of this view include, e.g., Saldarini, *Matthew's Christian-Jewish Community*; Sim, *Gospel of Matthew*; Overman, *Matthew's Gospel*; Dobbeler, "Auf der Grenze," 55–79. Contending with this view is, e.g., Deines, "Not the Law," 53–84.

26. We see through other passages like 15:1–9; 16:6, 11–12; 23:8–10, 16–22 that Jesus denounces their teachings. A discussion of recent developments is given by Deines, "Not the Law," 53–57.

27. Hagner, "Matthew: Apostate," 193–209.

28. Ibid., 196.

Apart from passages that seem to portray continuity ("old") and discontinuity ("new") with emergent Judaism based on the eschatological age having begun (9:16–17; 13:52; cf. 12:28; 13:17; 21:41, 43), certain teachings in Matthew would be considered offensive, or at least problematic, for Judaism of that time. Jesus' authority, for example, appears to rank supreme over the Torah so that the Torah is to be interpreted through him (e.g., 5:22, 28, 32, 34, etc.).[29] Obedience is also centered on Jesus, and he turns out to be even greater than the temple (12:6), lord of the Sabbath (12:8), and contrasts his yoke with the yoke of Torah (11:28–30). Moreover, Matthew presents the Messiah as a unique manifestation of God who will judge the nations at the end of time (1:23; 10:32–33; 11:27; 16:27; 25:31–32; cf. 18:20; 28:18–20), and yet this Messiah dies as a criminal, the act of which provides a way of forgiveness from sin.[30]

Warren Carter responds that Hagner's case of "newness" through Christ is overstated, especially in Christology: among other things, God has been "with" his people before, not just through his Christ (cf. Deut 2:7; Isa 43:5; Ezek 34:30/Matt 1:23), Isa 7:14 refers to a royal human figure, the term "son of God" does not break boundaries with ancient Judaism, and Jesus is seen more as giving a hermeneutical key to interpreting the law's intent via love and mercy.[31] But Carter's response does not squarely face the impact of Matthew's implications about Jesus. To be sure, Isa 7:14 refers to a royal birth in Ahaz's lineage, but Matthew uses the text as support for Jesus' virgin birth (Matt 1:23–25). This insinuates uniqueness about Jesus as God's son, highlighted again by passages such as 11:27 and 28:19, which virtually equate Jesus with his heavenly Father. Such an understanding about Jesus would no doubt be considered offensive to synagogue teachers of the time and blurring boundaries between God and human. In terms of who would have called the Matthean community "apostate" (presumably here meaning their abandonment of prior commitment to the way of life of formative Judaism), possibly the synagogue officials would label early Christ-followers this way, but Matthew's gospel gives us no direct examples of this.[32] The religious officials nonetheless consider Jesus to be blaspheming (Matt 9:3;

---

29. For continuity with the Law see, e.g., 5:17–20; 8:4; 9:20; 14:36; 23:2–3, 23; 24:20. For discontinuity see e.g., 5:21–48; 7:12; 8:3, 22; 9:10–11; 11:11–15, 28–30; 12:1–14; 15:1–11; 16:19; 17:24–25; 18:18. See further Deines, "Not the Law," 58–70.

30. Cf. Hagner, "Christian Judaism," 267–79; idem, "Matthew: Apostate," 200–205.

31. Carter, "Matthew's Gospel," 155–79.

32. Carter points out this aspect in his response to Hagner (ibid., 176–77). Among other things, he employs the view of Barclay, "Who Was Considered Apostate," 91, in which apostasy among Diaspora Jews can be generalized under the breeches of idolatry and food laws to claim that Matthew does not violate either of these (e.g., Matt 15:2–20 omits the words of Mark 7:19, its parallel). But his view assumes that Matthew's perspective of Jesus does not infringe on typical Jewish notions of deity. If they did, would not this be interpreted by Matthew's opponents as serving another deity, and hence associated with idolatry?

26:65). Although he did not curse or speak contemptuously about the divine name, which would be understood as blasphemy (cf. Lev 24:10–16; *m. Sanhedrin* 7.5), his words were probably interpreted by the authorities as assuming divine prerogatives and thus held in contempt of God's singularity (Matt 26:63–65; cf. Mark 14:61–64).[33] Quite possibly the Matthean group's confession of Jesus as Son of God, Lord, and Son of Man who sits at God's right hand and will judge the world would be viewed by local synagogue leaders in a similar way (cf. e.g., Acts 7:54–58; cf. 6:11).

The verdict is still out on whether or not this community had entirely broken away from the synagogue by the time Matthew's gospel was completed.[34] If the community is more specifically a cluster of communities, as we have surmised, then it is quite possible that the Matthean Christ-followers from different localities experienced variegated degrees of conflicts with local synagogue leaders. It might be safer to say they were in the process of breaking away. In any case, *the Matthean community most likely would have considered itself to be Jewish and fulfilling the true intention of the Law through Jesus its founder. For the disciples of Jesus, doing righteousness and following God's will require not only obedience to the Father but also hearing and obeying Jesus' teachings, which center on the Law* (7:21–27; 12:50; 21:28–31; 26:42; cf. 5:20; 6:1–18; 7:12).[35] Jesus is the key to interpreting "the Law" and "the Prophets" (5:17–20)—the predictions from "the Prophets" in the holy scriptures find fulfillment in Jesus,[36] and "the Law" finds ultimate meaning in Jesus who actualizes that which the Law requires by virtue of his life and teachings (7:12; 22:36–40).

What can be agreed on by the majority of scholars is that Matthew's community was both Jewish and Christian. Its contention was against a more dominant Jewish group representative of Pharisaic teachings.[37] This group, along with the other group identified as false prophets who claim to follow Christ, are the two major opponents of Matthew's community.

---

33. See Luz, *Matthew*, 3.430–32. On blasphemy see further Bock, *Blasphemy and Exaltation*, 51–66; Brown, *Death of the Messiah*, 1.520–23.

34. The majority view seems to be that the group had not entirely broken away from Judaism: cf. the summary on Matthean scholars in Kingsbury, "Conclusion," 265, 268–69.

35. Cf. Luz, "Jünger," 151–52.

36. On the importance of Matthean Christology in relation to Israel's scriptures, see e.g., Luz, *Matthew*, 1.163.

37. See community summaries in McKnight, "Matthean Community," 724–25; Kingsbury, "Conclusion," 264–65.

The Gospel of Matthew

WARNINGS TO CHRIST-FOLLOWERS IN THE SERMON ON THE MOUNT (MATT 5–7)

The message of the Sermon on the Mount not only teaches its audience how to live righteously, but it also warns against negative repercussions that could happen as a result of unrighteous living. The people being addressed are both disciples and the crowd (5:1–2; 7:28–29).[38] The dual audience makes our interpretation of the sermon rather complex: on one level it refers to Christ-followers, on another to the people of Israel, who are the people of the Law. A number of warnings are noteworthy.

First, the audience is described as the "salt of the earth" (5:13). The imagery of salt can refer to a number of things, including sacrifices and covenant (Lev 2:13), preservation and purification (Mark 9:49–50), seasoning (Luke 14:34), fertilization (Luke 14:35), and wisdom of speech (Col 4:6). Salt is used because it is an essential ingredient for everyday life (cf. Sir 39:26; Pliny, *Nat.* 31.102).[39] "Salt" for the disciples relates to their righteous deeds as a witness before outsiders (cf. Matt 5:16), and for the Jewish crowd it also refers to their responsibility to be God's people to the nations (cf. Matt 5:14–16; 10:16; Isa 42:6; 51:4–5; Phil 2:15).[40] If the salt becomes tasteless or "foolish" (μωραίνω) it is to be cast out and trampled underfoot. The uselessness of salt may refer metaphorically to the followers of Jesus losing their identity and becoming failures.[41] The notion of being cast out probably reflects a punishment related to their failing to bear "good fruit" (Matt 3:10; 7:19; cf. 8:12; 22:13; 25:30). This metaphor has the audience's good works in mind with the assumption that their righteous deeds become a strong incentive for the Gentiles to turn to God and Christ (cf. 1 Pet 2:12; 3:1, 16; John 13:35; 2 *Clem.* 13.1–5). The punishment of being trampled underfoot seems directed to the crowds as Israelites and possibly alludes to Jerusalem's destruction for failing to be a city set on a hill to give light to the Gentiles. On another level the punishment may warn Jesus' followers of eschatological pun-

---

38. Cf. Luz, *Matthew*, 1.182

39. See Hagner, *Matthew*, 1.99–100.

40. The aspect of being a light probably echoes foremost the prophetic notion of Israel becoming a light for the Gentiles (Isa 42:6; 49:6; 51:4; cf. 60:1–3).

41. Bertram, "μωρός κτλ," 4.837–39, associates μωραίνω here with apostasy, but salt is connected with "the indestructibility of salvation" (439). That salt can lose its saltiness may be impossible (cf. *b. Bekhorot* 8b) unless it is mistaken for another mineral such as gypsum. Luz, *Matthew*, 1.206, however, suggests that moisture can take away from the taste of salt. On failed disciples see further, Betz, *Sermon on the Mount*, 158, and on loss of identity, cf. Hagner, *Matthew*, 1.100. If apostasy is suggested here, then ἐν τίνι ἁλισθήσεται ("how will it be made salty again?" BDAG, 44) might hint at the possibility of no restoration for the apostate. But other translations of the phrase are possible, such as "with what shall one salt?" or "with what will God salt?" (cf. Betz, 159). The phrase in any case is rhetorical and meant to give a reason for the salt being cast out. It is evident that Matthew's Gospel accepts that defectors can be restored (cf. Matt 26:75; 28:7–10, 16–20).

ishment that might happen to them if they do not produce righteousness (cf. Matt 7:21–23; 25:1–13).⁴² The disciples likewise are to be involved in missions rather than pleasing themselves.

Second, anger towards one's brother or sister not only results in earthly punishments (5:21–26) but also eschatological judgment in "hell," i.e., the fiery *Gehenna* (5:22; cf. 5:29f; 10:28; 18:6–9; 23:5, 33). Third, if a body part causes one to lust and commit adultery, then it is better to amputate the offending part than to be cast into *Gehenna* (5:28–30). In 5:29–30 σκανδαλίζω may refer to apostasy (cf. Mark 9:42–47) or more generically as sin if we consider that this message relates to both the crowd and disciples. Fourth, God will not forgive the person who will not forgive others (Matt 6:14–15; cf. 18:21–35; Mark 11:25, and see below). Fifth, the manner in which a person judges others will be reciprocated to that individual by God (or Christ) on the day of judgment (Matt 7:1–2).⁴³ Here the aspect of judging (κρίνω) is interpreted with the nuance of "condemn"; otherwise, "so that you are not judged" would not make proper sense.⁴⁴ The parallel in Luke 6:37 stresses this aspect by adding καταδικάζω: "condemn not and you will not be condemned."⁴⁵ It follows that a negative judgment will be rendered to those who judge negatively.

Sixth, two ways are set before the audience of the sermon: the wide path that leads to eschatological destruction and the narrow path that leads to eternal life (Matt 7:13–14; cf. Luke 13:23–30). A number of Jewish traditions use similar language related to two ways as does Ancient Near Eastern, Egyptian, and Greek traditions.⁴⁶ The *Didache* 1–6 (e.g., 1.1, 5) also portrays the motif and possibly comes from the same community;⁴⁷ likewise, Jas 5:19–20 communicates the motif to Jewish Christ-followers. The passage in Matthew probably recalls the covenant of Moses in Deut 30:15–19, in which the people of Israel must choose to keep God's covenant, which brings life and blessings, or disobey it, which brings death and curses. The main distinction is that Jesus has reinterpreted Moses' Law to the extent that righteousness and obedience to God's will now center on keeping Jesus' teachings, and

---

42. The notion of treading a winepress under one's foot is sometimes associated with eschatological judgment (e.g., Isa 63:2–6).

43. Betz, *Sermon on the Mount*, 491, is right to show that the future tenses in 7:2 refer to the eschatological future and are similar to the reciprocation found in the Beatitudes (cf. 5:5–9).

44. Cf. Allison and Davies, *Matthew* 1.669.

45. In the Lukan context, the verse applies to being merciful and forgiving one's enemies (Luke 6:35–37).

46. Ps 1:6; Wis 5:6–7; *1 En.* 91. 18–19; *2 En.* 30.15; *T. Jos.* 1.3; *2 Bar.* 85.13; Philo, *Agriculture* 102–4. See further Betz, *Sermon on the Mount*, 521, and respective footnotes for a myriad of sources. The motif of two gates, however, is rare according to Luz, *Matthew*, 1.370 (cf. *T. Ab.* 8).

47. See e.g., Draper, *Didache*; Sandt, *Matthew and the Didache*.

he will soon interpret his upcoming death and the forgiveness it provides in terms of covenant language (Matt 26:26–28). The way, then, to the narrow path that leads to eternal life is by following Jesus. The gate is possibly at the end of the journey rather than its beginning. It opens up to the fully realized eschatological kingdom, and the wider gate opens up to *Gehenna*. But it is equally possible that the gates and paths are simply two metaphors speaking about the same reality so that our decision over sequence is unnecessary.[48] Perhaps the most disturbing aspect about the saying is that "many" go on the wrong path and into the wrong gate, and "few" find the right way. The Matthean community might see itself as the minority group, but more correctly the two ways do not divide neatly along the lines of those who are Christ-followers and those who are not. Ulrich Luz brings this out in a sobering manner by comparing 7:13–14 with the "many" in 7:22 who call Jesus Lord but do not enter God's kingdom:

> The many who go on the broad way are for him [Matthew] obviously not only the Jewish scribes, not only Israel's majority that does not follow Jesus, not only the "others" from whom one has separated, or, as in the *Didache*, the unbaptized whose way one has abandoned by being baptized; the "many" are Christians, members of the community. . . . The community is on the move; it is on the way that leads to life. It is constantly faced with the choice of the two ways. Being a Christian and being baptized does not mean that one has the comforting assurance of salvation; it means that one has the chance of being confronted daily with the choice between the broad way and the difficult ways of the Sermon on the Mount.[49]

Seventh, the listeners must watch out for false prophets that could lead them astray (7:15–20; cf. 24:4–5, 11, 23–26; see below); such deceivers will be thrown into the fires of *Gehenna* (cf. 7:19). Eighth, the audience is instructed that it is not enough to do miraculous deeds in Jesus' name but one must do God's will, that is, produce righteous deeds and follow Jesus' teachings; otherwise, one could expect to be rejected much the way false prophets are excluded from the kingdom (7:21–23).[50] Finally, the sermon ends with a comparison between a wise and foolish builder. Whoever puts to practice Jesus' words is like a wise builder establishing a house on a firm foundation ("rock") that withstands the storms. Whoever does not put to practice the words of Jesus is compared to a foolish builder whose house is

---

48. On the former view see, e.g., Gibbs, *Matthew*, 383. On the latter, Michaelis, "ὁδός," 5.70–75.

49. Luz, *Matthew*, 1.372.

50. Here obviously the sermon discourse is more specifically relevant for the Christ-followers than the crowds.

built on sand and is destroyed by the storms (7:24–27).⁵¹ The metaphoric "winds" of the storms may refer to coming afflictions and persecution the disciples would face; those whose foundation is flimsy will become fearful and commit apostasy during times of testing (13:21; cf. 8:24–26; 14:29–31). The metaphor of "floods" may have special relevance to eschatological judgment in Matt 24:38–39 (cf. Luke 17:27; Isa 29:6; Ezek 38:22; 1QH 3.14; *2 Bar.* 7–12; *Sib. Or.* 3.689–92).⁵² The warning appeals to "everyone" who hears Jesus words, whether crowds or followers (7:24). They all must obey Jesus' teachings if they are to endure trials and stand on the day of final judgment.

Even though these sayings were directed at a general Jewish audience in the text, *the Matthean community no doubt considered all these sayings to be relevant for their own ethical conduct. Namely, if they did not believe and practice these sayings, they would be violating the Law and could expect to be punished on judgment day.* For them, to disregard these teachings would be to commit apostasy or reveal one's true character as an insincere follower of Christ in solidarity with the false prophets the sermon condemns (7:15–23). They believed that Christ-followers who are disobedient to these instructions will be considered "least" in the kingdom of heaven, i.e., they will be excluded from the heavenly kingdom. *Thus the Christ-followers must endeavor to stay on the right path because it is always possible that they might be led astray by false prophets or fall away through behavior that contradicts Jesus' teachings. If they failed to remain on the narrow path, they would be among the "many" who will face eschatological ruin* (7:13–14).

One possible example of apostates in the Sermon on the Mount is given in 7:6 (cf. *Gos. Thom.* 93): "do not give what is holy to the dogs or cast your pearls among swine." In its immediate context this saying would seem to suggest that one must not only be ready to give non-hypocritical correction to others (cf. Matt 7:5) but also be discerning regarding the readiness of others to receive the correction.⁵³ Both dogs and pigs were considered unclean animals by Jews, and it is possible that this passage

---

51. The house may be understood as one's "house of life": so Betz, *Sermon on the Mount*, 567. The parallel in Luke 6:47–49 is spoken to Jesus' disciples (cf. Luke 6:20). Betz, interestingly connects the foolish person in Matt 7:26 (μωρός) with similar wording in the sermon, including μωραίνω in 5:13 (567). This provides us with a kind of *inclusio* related to people who are saltless salt.

52. Gregg, *Final Judgment Sayings*, 81–82, among other arguments, draws our attention to these and other passages in relation to metaphoric floods to determine in Matt 7:24–27 that the storm represents final judgment. He may be correct regarding flood metaphors, but I would add that the upcoming trials the disciples would face are preludes to the final eschaton and should not be excluded from the metaphoric "winds" and "floods," especially when we notice that these terms and their accompanying verbs are all plurals rather than singulars (". . . καὶ ἦλθον οἱ ποταμοὶ καὶ ἔπνευσαν οἱ ἄνεμοι καὶ προσέκοψαν τῇ οἰκίᾳ": 7: 25a, 27a).

53. Cf. Wilson, "Third Form of Righteousness," 315.

refers to sinners among the Gentiles (cf. Matt 15:21–27).[54] Mark Nanos, however, adduces from early Jewish sources that the connection between "dog" and "Gentile" is actually quite rare.[55] The Petrine author associates beasts, including dogs and pigs, with the false teachers and apostates (2 Pet 2:22 cf. vv. 12, 16; Jude 10; *Gospel of Truth* 33.15–16), and other early Christian sources associate dogs with outsiders, apostates, and false teachers (Phil. 3:2; Rev. 22:15; *Did.* 9.5; Ign. *Eph.* 7.1; cf. *Smyrn.* 4.1; *Ps.-Clem. Recognitions* 2.3; 3.1.2). The "pigs" in Matt 7:6 probably identify in a vituperative way persons who reject teachings related to the gospel of the kingdom (the "pearls" and what is "holy") and trample them underfoot, connoting disdain for such instruction and hostility towards those who perpetrate it. Together with "dogs" this verse may have been understood in early Christian circles as inclusive of false teachers and apostates (cf. Heb 10:29). For the Matthean author it would be especially ironic and insulting for the Pharisees to be labeled as unclean animals. Perhaps his community associated the animals in 7:6 to be inclusive of antagonistic rivals from emergent Judaism, false prophets, apostates, and hostile outsiders.

"FORGIVE US AS WE HAVE FORGIVEN OTHERS . . . AND LEAD US NOT INTO TEMPTATION": THE LORD'S PRAYER (MATT 6:9–13; CF. LUKE 11:2–4)

The importance of the disciples' perseverance is implied in the Lord's Prayer (Matt 6:9–13; cf. Luke 11:2–4; *Did.* 8:1–3). The prayer is eschatologically focused with the petitioner requesting that the Father's "kingdom come" and "will be done" on earth as in heaven.[56] The request may be understood as a petition for God's kingdom and purposes to be fulfilled on earth (Matt 6:10), implying this world's present condition as incomplete and looking forward to future renovation. This perspective is similar to the Jewish Kaddish, an Aramaic prayer that looks forward to God's kingdom:[57]

> Exalted and hallowed be his great name in the world which he created according to his will. May he let his kingdom rule in your lifetime and in

---

54. See Allison and Davies, *Matthew*, 1.675–77.

55. Nanos, "Paul's *Reversal* of Jews," 1–33. Contra Str.B. 1.724–25.

56. See further Meier, *Marginal Jew*, 2.302. Contrast Gundry, *Matthew*, 106, who views the "Thou" aspects of this prayer as referring to the present and not the eschaton. Notice the helpful qualification in Manson, *Sayings of Jesus*, 169: "The petition certainly has an eschatological sense. . . . But it need not be an exclusively eschatological petition. There is a sense in which the Kingdom comes whenever and wherever God's will is acknowledged and obeyed on earth."

57. Translation from Jeremias, *New Testament Theology*, 198. The question remains open whether this prayer was known in the first century given that it first appears in liturgy several centuries later: cf. Duling, "Kingdom of God," 4.52.

your days and in the lifetime of the whole house of Israel, speedily and soon. Praised be his great name from eternity to eternity. And to this, say: Amen.

That the Father's "will be done," as James Dunn points out, assumes that sometimes "God's will is not done on earth, and that there will always be a tension between the divine will and the actuality of human structures and relationships until the kingdom comes."[58] Gerhard Lohfink relates the will of God in the Lord's Prayer to the divine "Heilsplan."[59] This might be a correct notion for 6:10, but the divine "will" (θέλημα) is not limited to God's salvific plan or sovereign purpose in human history; in Matthew's gospel there is also an ethical dimension to it. Humans appear to be free to follow or reject God's will, and obedience is required to accomplish the former option (7:21; 12:50; 18:14; 21:31). Jesus becomes the prime example of submission to God's purposes at Gethsemane when he prays, "not my will but your will be done" (26:42). Conversely, Christians who do not submit to Gods' will are excluded from God's kingdom (7:21).

With this perspective in mind, a longing for the eschatological messianic banquet in terms of inclusion and exclusion becomes more evident in the "we" petitions of the Lord's Prayer. It is possible, perhaps even likely, that the first "we" petition in 6:11 is for the Father to provide the petitioner with bread "for tomorrow" or "for the coming day [ἐπιούσιος] . . . today [σήμερον]."[60] Accordingly, this aspect of the Lord's Prayer encourages the disciples to pray for the bread of the future today—the food that exemplifies the believers' participation in the coming messianic banquet is to be requested in the here and now.[61] This view emphasizes the request for spiritual blessings associated with God's eschatological kingdom, and such an interpretation is to be preferred over any request for tomorrow's physical food, which is something Jesus specifically tells his disciples *not* to be concerned about (Matt 6:25–34).

If elements of 6:10–11 relate to kingdom yearnings, then 6:12–13 are implicit appeals for the petitioners not to be excluded from kingdom blessings. The "we" petition in 6:12 is a request that God forgive us our wrongdoings in proportion to

58. Dunn, "Prayer," 621–22.

59. Lohfink, "Präexistente Heilsplan," 110–33, compares Matt 6:10 with Acts 22:14, Eph 1:3–14, and passages in the *Apoc. Ab.* to write: "So wie der Heilsplan vor den Augen Gottes im Himmel in urbildlicher Dimension 'geschieht', soll er auch auf Erden geschehen" (130).

60. If this is the case, then "daily" may not be the original meaning of this word. Contrast Luke 11:3. Jeremias, *New Testament Theology*, 199, refers to the *Gospel of the Nazoreans* (mentioned in Jerome, *Comm. Matt.* 6.11) as an example of the Aramaic מחר ("tomorrow"), standing behind ἐπιούσιον in Matthew 6:11.

61. Jewish sources associate bread with the eschatological return of manna (Exod 16; Ps 77 [78]:24–25; 2 Esd 1:19; cf. Rev 2:17; *Sib. Or.* 7.149; 2 *Bar.* 29.8).

our forgiving others who have wronged us.⁶² The Lord's Prayer is followed by Jesus' exhortation that if his followers forgive others, they too will be forgiven (6:14–15). While the other gospels and Paul affirm such forgiveness, Matthew adds that if they do not forgive others, they will not be forgiven by God in the eschaton (Matt 6:14–15; 18:21–35; cf. Sir 28:2–5).⁶³ Failure to forgive others would seem to jeopardize one's own forgiveness from God, and in this sense it may be related to apostasy or it shows one's own experience of forgiveness to not be genuine. Jesus' parable on forgiveness in 18:21–35 fleshes out 6:14–15 and is intended to get the audience to forgive others. Arland Hultgren rightly affirms that the goal of the parable is, "Since you have been forgiven so much, how can you not forgive the other person?"⁶⁴ Manson suggests it is not that humans can purchase God's forgiveness by forgiving others, but that "a forgiving spirit in man [sic] is an essential condition of his receiving God's forgiveness."⁶⁵

Perhaps the rationale for 6:15 can be found elsewhere in the Sermon on the Mount. We notice that the one who is angry at a brother or sister is in danger of hell fire, and it is crucial to be reconciled with the person (5:21–26). The goal of being "perfect" includes loving one's enemy (5:43–48), and the one who judges others will be judged by the same standard (7:1–2). These sayings probably assume that forgiving others will be necessary in order to carry out the teachings, and those who are not willing to forgive are not keeping Jesus' teachings faithfully. An inference that can be drawn from 7:12 is that *an unwillingness to forgiven stands the Golden Rule on its head*: those who expect to receive forgiveness from others and God are themselves not willing to forgive others who have wronged them. Hence, by violating the command to treat others as they would want to be treated, such individuals break the most fundamental teaching of Jesus and all that is commanded in the Law and the Prophets (7:12; cf. 5:18–19; 22:36–40). The practice of forgiving others would be one more way of keeping Jesus' command to love one's neighbor, and indeed, to love one's enemy.⁶⁶

---

62. I accept the aorist ἀφήκαμεν rather than the present tense ἀφίομεν/ἀφίεμεν. On witnesses for each, see Metzger, *Textual Commentary*, 13. While ὡς in 6:12 is perhaps a Matthean redaction in this verse, the concept of reciprocal forgiveness is confirmed in the following the verses (6:14–15). On 6:14 as an authentic Jesus saying, see Pesch, *Markusevangelium*, 2.207 (Mark 11:25).

63. On being forgiven in relation to forgiving others see Luke 17:3–4; Col 3:13; Talbert, *Reading the Sermon on the Mount*, 117.

64. Hultgren, *Parables of Jesus*, 29.

65. Manson, *Teaching of Jesus*, 308–11.

66. Meier, *Marginal Jew*, 2.301, adds an astute comment: "Making God's final forgiveness of individual believers depend on their forgiveness of others in the present moment may create problems for Christian theology. But, since Jesus was not a Christian theologian, he seems sublimely unconcerned about the problem."

In the third "we" petition the audience is to pray, "Lead us not into temptation, but deliver us from the evil one" (Matt 6:13; cf. Luke 11:4; *Did.* 8.2; Polycarp, *Phil.* 7.2).[67] Problematic with this petition is the idea of God leading human petitioners into temptation, which seems to be a point that James counters or tries to correct: "Let no one say when . . . tempted, I am being tempted by God" (Jas 1:12–14). Some have suggested that the original wording in the Lord's Prayer may have included an Aramaic causative (*hafel*) that suggested permission rather than direct cause.[68] If so, the original meaning would be, "Allow us not to enter into [a time of] temptation" (cf. *b. Bekorot* 60b; John 17:15). Nevertheless, Jesus' temptation in the wilderness involves being led by the Spirit of God to be tempted by Satan (Matt 4:1; Mark 1:12; Luke 4:13),[69] and this perspective suggests that both the divine and demonic are involved in times of testing (cf. Job 1–2; 1 Kgs 22:22; *Jub.* 48:15–18).[70] Whether directly or indirectly, then, God is still in some sense involved with periods of testing.[71] Hence, it is not incorrect to assume the simple rendering, "lead us not into temptation."

The prayer against temptation finds its closest parallel with Jesus' words at Gethsemane (cf. Matt 26:39–42; Mark 14:35–36; Luke 22:42). The only other Matthean instance of the word πειρασμός ("temptation") appears when Jesus warns his disciples to watch and pray lest they enter into temptation (Matt 26:41).[72] The disciples fail to do so and end up forsaking Jesus during his arrest. Temptation in Matthew seems to indicate a period or time of testing similar to the coming eschatological tribulation when Christ-followers will succumb to apostasy (see Matt 24 below).[73]

---

67. For parallels in the early church fathers see Fitzmyer, "Lead Us Not," 265–67.

68. E.g., Meier, *Marginal Jew*, 2.301; Jeremias, *Prayers of Jesus*, 105. Similarly the causative hifil in Hebrew is argued by Carmignac, "Fais que nous n'entrions pas," 218–26.

69. Luke 4:13 is the only text that uses the same word for temptation as in Matt 6:13: πειρασμός.

70. Could Jesus' temptation in the wilderness have led to his apostasy? The Synoptic tradition probably assumes the affirmative, but how so in Matthew's version, where he is intimated as virtually God's equal? Later theological speculations argue for Christ's impeccability as Deity, but Matthew's text does not seem to ponder Jesus' capability or incapability of sinning in this light.

71. Referencing Israel's scriptures and early Jewish sources, Fitzmyer, "Lead Us Not," 263–65, argues that such texts, along with biblical texts of Jesus' own temptations, have a "protological" way of describing God's activity. God is not the origin or source of the temptation but causality of the temptation is attributed to him.

72. On "temptation" as the proper translation of πειρασμός for Matt 6:13 and Luke 11:4, see Porter, "Mt 6:13 and Lk 11:4," 359. On apostasy and πειρασμός see Luke 8:13.

73. An objection to this interpretation is that πειρασμόν does not contain the definite article τόν, which would make it read *the* temptation and be related to the great tribulation period or messianic woes. Allison and Davies, *Matthew*, 1.613, correctly respond that the anarthrous πειρασμόν does not necessarily indicate a general temptation as opposed to a particular period of testing; moreover, the

In Jesus' own prayer at Gethsemane he requests that the Father spare him from impending suffering on the cross. Oscar Cullmann's comment on this passage is perceptive: "In expressing the purely human wish that the cup may pass from him, Jesus . . . by his example indirectly authorizes us in the Our Father to pray that temptation may also pass us by."[74] If Cullmann is correct, then certain temptations could be avoided by making the request known before God or praying the Lord's Prayer.[75] To this effect, early Jewish and Christian writers seem to agree that God provides a way for his followers to escape temptation (cf. Ps 17:30 LXX; Sir 33:1; 1 Cor 10:13; 2 Pet 2:9). *One reason for the Christ-followers to pray against temptation is because it can potentially cause them to fall away from their faith and thus be excluded from God's coming kingdom.*

BECOMING SEVEN TIMES WORSE THAN BEFORE: THE RETURN OF THE UNCLEAN SPIRIT (MATT 12:43-45; CF. LUKE 11:24-26)

Situated in between Matthew's version of blaspheming the Holy Spirit and the parable of the Sower is the story in Q about the return of the unclean spirit (Matt 12:43–45; cf. Luke 11:24–26). The saying apparently comes from an Aramaic source and perhaps originated from Jesus, who was famous for his exorcisms. The term "unclean spirit" is a Jewish way of referring to demons.[76] While this pericope about demons flows naturally from the prior Beelzebul accusation in Matthew and Luke, only Matthew's version places it almost directly before the parable of the Sower. Whereas Luke's context makes the passage relevant to individuals and decision-making (Luke 11:23), Matthew's version addresses an "evil generation" associated with Jesus' opponents (Matt 12:38–42).[77] Luke's version of the saying suggests that others performed exorcisms apart from Jesus, but they "scattered" rather than "gathered" with him (Luke 11:19, 23). In this version the saying functions primarily as a warning against exorcists who did not align themselves with Jesus. Luke, it seems, needed a ground for justifying Jesus' exorcisms as a unique sign of God's kingdom:[78]

---

early church writers considered themselves as already living in eschatologically turbulent times making the distinction between general and particular temptation moot. For other instances of πειρασμός in the Gospels, see Mark 14:38; Luke 4:13; 8:13; 11:4; 22:28, 40, 46.

74. Cullmann, *Prayer in the New Testament*, 65.

75. The alternative understanding is that temptations are inevitable, and so prayer is a request for believers not to succumb to temptation when in the midst of one.

76. On the Aramaic origin of the passage, see Luz, *Matthew*, 2.216.

77. Cf. Carter, *Matthew and the Margins*, 278; Keener, *Matthew*, 369.

78. Jesus does not condemn anyone who casts out demons in his name (Luke 9:49f), but he does seem to come against those who apparently do not use his name (Luke 11:23).

even though other exorcists cast out unclean spirits, their inability to provide those they cure with correct teachings on God's kingdom allow for the nomadic demons to once again inhabit the individuals from whom they had been expelled.

Once the unclean spirit is cast out, it goes into dry regions (i.e., the desert) and finds no rest. Returning to its former host, it finds the home swept and put in order. Matthew's version adds that the house is empty. The implication may be that the unclean spirit could return to the house now that it is unoccupied. The spirit brings along seven other demons more wicked than itself, and together they possess the individual so that the person's latter state is worse than the former.

The saying has more than one layer of meaning. Matthew and his community probably would make the story applicable to the false prophets who cast out demons in Jesus' name (cf. Matt 7:22), and later Christians may have understood it as a warning for those who convert to Christianity but then commit apostasy. If they are not spiritually alert, they could find themselves backslidden in which their "last state" is "worse than the first."[79] Jesus may have originally spoken these words as a way of cautioning those who were formerly demon possessed. It is not enough that they are healed; they must also accept Jesus' message and follow him. If their body or "house" is not occupied with his teachings, they might find themselves in a worse state than before (cf. John 5:41; *Acts Thom.* 46; Irenaeus, *Haer.* 1.16.3).[80] A change needs to take place for those who are set free from demonic powers, or else they could find themselves possessed again by more powerful spirits. As such, *the original purpose of Jesus' logia may have served as a warning for those whom he personally healed. They must not neglect his teachings.*[81]

The predicament of seven more spirits entering into the same host does not necessarily mean that the host would now do seven times the amount of unrighteous activities that he or she used to do. It is a way of describing how an individual or people could become more callous to God than they had been previously. If the

---

79. See 2 Pet 2:20; *Herm. Sim.* 9.17.5–18.2; *Herm. Vis.* 4.2; *Apoc. Pet.* 3; *1 Clem.* 46.8; Irenaeus. *Haer.* 4.27; cf. Matt 26:24; Mark 14:21; *1 En.* 38.3.

80. Jeremias, *Parables of Jesus*, 198, says it well: "The relapse is not something predetermined and inevitable, but something for which the man himself [*sic*] is responsible. The house must not remain empty. . . . A new master must reign there, the word of Jesus must be its rule of life, and the joy of the Kingdom of God must pervade it." See also Jeremias, *New Testament Theology*, 154: Logically speaking, Matthew 12:44 is intended to be conditional—"*if* the demon returns and finds the house empty, *in that case* he will return with sevenfold reinforcements . . ." Jeremias associates this with "half-hearted repentance."

81. In Matthew the saying takes on another meaning at a corporate level with "this evil generation" (Matt 12:45c), an addendum that was probably added by the author and influenced by Jesus' previous answer to the scribes and Pharisees as belonging to the wicked generation that seeks a sign (Matt 12:38–42).

number seven is understood figuratively here, it refers to complete apostasy, pointing back to the unpardonable sin (Matt 12:30-32), forward to spiritual obduracy (13:11-15), and anticipating the coming judgment on those who refuse to believe the message and ministry of Jesus (12:36-42). In essence the idea of becoming "worse" (12:45) and having one's spiritual insight "taken away" (13:11-12) are conceptually close. They both convey obduracy toward God's kingdom and messenger.

Given Matthew's perspective, if the Law and the Prophets find their ultimate meaning in the life and teachings Jesus, then it becomes important for us to investigate Matthew's quotes and allusions to the Law and the Prophets as they relate to apostasy. For a Jewish audience, Matthew's repetitive use of Israel's scriptures as being fulfilled through the life and teachings of Jesus buttresses the authority of his gospel message and lends credibility to the plight of his community as opposed to that of his Pharisaic opponents from the local synagogue. In this case we find examples of apostate behavior committed not only by those who work lawlessness, and thus contrary to the Law, but also and primarily by those who refuse to hear God's messenger, and thus contrary to the Prophets. Matthew 12:43-45 alludes to the prophet Isa 34-35 (cf. Isa 34:14 LXX; cf. Isa 34:9-10; 35:1; 13:21).[82] The passage shares parallels with Matt 12:43-45 related to demons, a desert, and looking for rest.

Through the lens of Isaiah we thus see in the exorcism stories of Matt 12 an overturning of the social order with Jesus casting out demons and giving sight to the blind. It is the simple folk, those whom Jesus normally heals, who are receiving spiritual insight. On the other hand, *the leaders of God's people, typified by the scribes and Pharisees, become progressively obdurate, seven times worse than before.* J. D. Kingsbury notes that Matthew's gospel uses the words "see" and "hear" about 230 times. These concepts suggest a "rhetoric of comprehension" in which Matthew's interest is to draw the readers into a seeing and hearing relationship with Jesus so as to receive him as Messiah and do God's will.[83] With this approach in mind, the parable of the Sower in Matt 13:1-23 functions as an exhortation to the disciples and Matthean audience to be like the fourth seed that was sown in good soil (13:8, 23) and understand kingdom teachings so that they might produce much fruit.[84] This seed recalls the fertile vegetation in Isa 35 and Jesus' ministry of restoration in Matt 12. Differently, the second seed that withers because of the sun's heat (Matt 13:5-6, 20-21) points the readers back to the dry abode of demons mentioned in Isa 34 and Matt 12:43-45.

---

82. Wildberger, *Jesaja*, 3.1347 defines the terms in Isa 34:14 (MT) as demons (צִיִּים), phantoms (אִיִּים), lilith (לִילִית), and goats/goat spirits (שָׂעִיר); cf. Lev. 17:7; 2 Chr 11:15; BDB, 973.

83. Kingsbury, "Rhetoric of Comprehension," 359-561, 376.

84. Ibid., 366-67, 377.

OBDURACY AND THE TURNING POINT (13:10-17)

Matthew 13:10–17 associates speaking in parables with the blindness motif of Isa 6:10–11, similar to Mark 4:10–12.[85] The passage helps set into sharp relief the later distinction between those who understand Jesus' parables and those who do not. And similar to Matt 11:27 spiritual knowledge is hidden,[86] but this time the crowd is in view with the mysteries of the kingdom hid from them but revealed to Jesus' disciples (Matt 13:11; cf. Mark 4:11–12).[87] We are left with questions that interact with Mark's parallel: Is the crowd obdurate because they do not do God's will, or because not doing God's will is an outcome of their obduracy? Matthew 13:10–17 differs from Mark 4:10–12 in a number of ways that help us answer this question:[88]

(1) Matthew's version has the disciples asking Jesus why he speaks to the crowd in parables (13:10), whereas in Mark the disciples ask Jesus about the interpretation of the parable in order to understand it themselves.

(2) Jesus' response in Matthew is that "it has been given" to the disciples to know the mysteries of the kingdom of heaven, but to "them," the crowd, "it has not been given" (ἐκείνοις δὲ οὐ δέδοται) to know these mysteries (13:11).[89] In Mark's version those who are near Jesus and are privileged to know the "mystery" are contrasted with those "outside" who are given parables only.

(3) Matthew 13:12 adds Jesus' saying that the one who "has" (i.e., ears to "hear" and obey spiritual knowledge [cf. 13:9]) will be given more, but the

---

85. Immediately before Jesus' teachings on parables, Matthew has Jesus affirming that his true family members are those who do the Father's will (Matt 12:46–50), which is also true of Mark 3:31–35, but Luke includes the passage shortly after the parable's explanation (Luke 8:19–21), and he transforms the idea of doing the will of God into hearing and doing God's word (cf. Luke 8:18).

86. The severity of divine judgment in Matt 11:25–27 must be tempered with human responsibility in 11:28–30: Jesus invites the weary to "come" to him, affirming that his benefits are open to all who seek him in humility (cf. 7:7–8). The assumption in 11:25–27 is not that God arbitrarily blinds certain individuals from spiritual revelation but that God hides such insight from the proud who deserve their punishment, as the haughtiness of Capernaum and other unrepentant cities represent (10:20–24, esp. 23). God's disdain for the proud, often typifying the religious leaders, and his favor on the humble, are both affirmed here (e.g., Prov 16:18–19; cf. Matt 23:11–12; Jas 4:6).

87. Nevertheless, since this passage stands in close proximity with the scribes and Pharisees who oppose Jesus in 12:24, 38–42, it is probable that these religious leaders are among the crowd.

88. For a more thorough study, see Evans, *See and Not Perceive*, 108–13.

89. The passive voice of δέδοται demonstrates divine involvement with the obfuscation (cf. 11:27), but this is not to be confused with predestination, contrary to Wiefel, *Evangelium nach Matthäus*, 250. God reciprocates according to a person's own hearing and obeying (cf. Matt 13:12). On Matt13:15 (cf. Isa 6:10), Luz, *Matthew* 2.247, rightly says, "μήποτε maintains Israel's guilt and not God's predestination. If Israel were to repent, then God would truly heal it!"

one who "has not," from that person will be taken away even that which the person has.[90] Mark includes this saying at the end of the parable of the light under a bushel (Mark 4:25).

(4) Matthew 13:13 uses ὅτι ("because" "that") rather than Mark's ἵνα ("in order that") to introduce the crowd's inability to see, hear, and understand the parable.

(5) Matthew 13:14 adds that this fulfills Isaiah's prophecy and then proceeds to cite the Septuagint version of Isa 6:9–10. Mark does not follow the LXX as closely.[91] The LXX reinforces human responsibility by mitigating the command form in Hebrew, "Make fat the heart of this people," to "For the heart of this people has grown fat,"[92] and "they have shut their [own] eyes."

(6) In contrast to those who are blind and deaf, Matthew includes that the disciples are blessed because they see and hear, and many prophets and righteous individuals longed to see and hear what the disciples are experiencing (13:16–17).[93]

In Matthew the contrast between the disciples and the crowd is evident in points 2, 3, and 6 above. The disciples see and hear spiritual knowledge, but the crowd does not. Mark omits such thoughts and plagues the disciples with spiritual blindness even after they receive Jesus' interpretation of the parable (e.g., Mark 6:52).[94] The disciples are definitely portrayed in a better light in Matthew. Yet Matthew's version affirms that the crowd's lack of spiritual sensitivity happened as a result of their own disobedience (points 4 and 5), unlike Mark's version, which indicates that God blinded them. Kingsbury suggests that Matt 13 marks the turning point of the narrative. The Israelites have generally rejected the Messiah's earlier missions (cf. Matt 4:17, 23; 9:35; 10:1–8; 11:1), and now he charges them with blindness and turns towards his disciples in 13:10–17.[95] Among other things, Jesus' earlier pattern of

90. Allison and Davies, *Matthew* 2.391, correctly distill from this saying that "knowledge is rewarded with knowledge, ignorance with ignorance. Like begets like." See also Dodd, *Parables of the Kingdom*, 110: "who possesses spiritual capacity will enlarge that capacity by experience."

91. Evans, *See and Not Perceive*, 107, observes that the first quote in Matt 13:13b is a paraphrase of Mark 4:12, and 13:14b–15 is derived from the LXX.

92. Van Elderen, "Purpose of Parables," 188, notices how Matthew's use of aorist tenses from the LXX reinforces the idea of precondition: they already are blind.

93. The beatitude in 13:16 may be echoing Isa 52:15.

94. For Matthew's contrast with Mark on the concept of "understanding," see further Barth, "Matthew's Understanding," 108–12; but see qualifications in Luz, "Jünger," 148–49.

95. Kingsbury, *Parables of Jesus*, 130. Similarly, Rothfuchs, *Erfüllungszitate des Matthäus-Evangeliums*, posits Matthew 13:35–36 as the turning point from all Israel to Jesus' disciples (cf. 13:11, 16, 51).

teaching and preaching to the crowd now turns to "speaking" (λαλέω), which is more apologetic in nature (cf. 23:1), and they are described as "them," suggesting they stand outside the sphere of those who receive revelation and kingdom promises from God. Matthew also introduces the word παραβολή in chapter 13, where he also discusses the crowd's obduracy.[96] Jesus proceeds to turn away from them to his disciples in 13:36.[97] For Matthew, the crowd is clearly responsible for its own obduracy. If they would not shut their "eyes," they would perceive spiritual insight and bear good fruit as a result, which, for this gospel, involves doing righteous deeds associated with keeping the law of Jesus (cf. 7:12–26; 12:33, 50; 13:41–42; 21:43; 23:28–29).

The disciples' blessing in 13:16–17 possibly implies that the crowd is now cursed, but these multitudes who listen to Jesus cannot be categorized so easily. Jesus typically teaches and heals people from among the crowds before and after 13:10–17,[98] and sometimes they are portrayed in positive way (9:8, 33; 14:5, 14; 15:31–32; 21:8–11). Their spiritual obduracy should not be taken as all-inclusive, especially when the parable of the Sower affirms that a portion of the seeds that are sown (associated with the word of the kingdom: 13:19) produce fruit. Moreover, in 15:8–9 Jesus quotes Isa 29:13, another passage related to obduracy, when addressing the scribes and Pharisees who are compared to the disobedient "people" in the Isaianic citation. The Pharisees are viewed as not being planted by God (i.e., they do not belong to God) and as blind leaders of the blind. Divine judgment awaits them: they will be "uprooted" and along with their followers will end up in the "pit" (Matt 15:13–14).[99] Their kingdom would be "taken away" from them because they did not "hear" and bear good fruit; it would be given to the Gentiles who believe (8:10–12; 21:43; cf. 28:19).

Matthew 13:10–17, then, probably provided the Matthean community with some sort of legitimation as the disciples' successors. Through the passage they could affirm themselves as blessed with divine insight and their opponents with spiritual blindness. In this manner the passage operates as an apologetic for the early Jewish Christians about their compatriots' unbelief, which for them was influenced and exemplified by local synagogue leaders of the Pharisaic tradition.

---

96. Cf. Kingsbury, *Parables of Jesus*, 131.

97. See Phillips, "History and Text," 121–28.

98. cf. Matt 5:1; 7:28; 11:7; 12:46; 15:10; 17:14; 19:2; 20:29.

99. On Israel as a planting of God, see Isa 5:1–7; 60:21; 61:13; Jer 45:4; *Pss Sol* 14:2–4; CD 1.7. On judgment or calamity related to the pit/*sheol*, see Isa 24:18; 38:18; Psa 7:15-16; 16:10; Prov 26:27; *T. Reub* 2:9; Gnilka, *Matthäusevangelium*, 2.25.

WARNINGS OF APOSTASY TO THE DISCIPLES
(10:28, 32-33, 38-39; 13:20-21; 16:24-27; 18:1-14)

A number of warnings against apostasy and judgment are likewise addressed to Jesus' followers.

First, together with the crowd they are warned in the Sermon on the Mount of eschatological consequences related to violating the law of Jesus.

Second, along with everybody else who hears the parable, the disciples have the potential of becoming like the second seed/soil of the parable of the Sower: it receives the word of the kingdom immediately and grows on rocky soil but falls away due to afflictions and persecution (13:5-6, 20-21). The word for falling away in 13:21, σκανδαλίζω, sometimes involves temporal offenses in Matthew (15:12; cf. 17:27) and the opposite of believing in Jesus (Matt 13:57; cf. Mark 6:3; Luke 7:23).[100] It also is used for the disciples' abandonment of Jesus at his arrest (Matt 26:31, 33-35; cf. 26:56, 70-75) and in an eschatological warning to them of upcoming persecutions and deceptions: in those days betrayals will take place, many will fall away, and their love will grow cold because of so much lawlessness (Matt 24:10-12, see below).[101] The latter references convey the meaning of σκανδαλίζω in 13:21.[102] The third seed/soil that bears no fruit because of the worries of this world and deception of wealth (13:7, 22) might also be relevant to apostasy given the importance of Jesus' teaching on avoiding worry (6:19-34) and various teachings against materialism and wealth (8:18-20; 10:8-10; 13:4-6; 19:16-30).[103] Since this gospel stresses the importance of bearing good fruit, the idea of bearing no fruit may be tantamount to bad fruit, which for followers of Jesus would amount to apostasy and condemnation (Matt 3:10; 7:17-20; 12:33; 21:19, 41-43; cf. Jude 12; *Herm. Sim.* 4.4). Such sayings against materialism would be entirely relevant for a community like Matthew's, thought to be fairly wealthy.

Third, Matthew records several other warnings related to persecution. Jesus teaches the Twelve that discipleship includes persecution and their willingness to suffer even to the point of martyrdom (Matt 10:16-39). They can expect to be brought

---

100. *BDAG*, 926 has the meaning in such verses as being repelled by Jesus or refusing to believe in him or "becoming apostate" from him.

101. Hartman, *Prophecy Interpreted*, 169-70, notes the use of the same word (σκανδαλίζω) in the eschatological setting of Daniel 11:41LXX.

102. Kingsbury, *Parables of Jesus*, interprets the person represented by the second seed as not fully understanding the word "in the true sense of the term" (57). This might point to a recent convert rather than a mature follower of Christ. In any case, the disciples who followed Jesus during his short earthly ministry would be considered new converts from *our* perspective.

103. Matt 16:26 is another possible reference to wealth, and this one is related to apostasy. The verse, however, is set in the context of persecution.

before the courts (συνέδρια: cf. e.g., Acts 5:27; 23:1), governors, and scourged in the synagogues as transgressors of the Law (10:17-18; cf. 23:34; 2 Cor 11:24; Acts 22:19; *m. Makkot* 3.12). Jesus exhorts them not to fear their persecutors who are able to kill only their bodies (10:26, 28a, 31) but fear instead God who is able to cast both body and soul into *Gehenna* (10:28b; cf. Luke 12:4-5; 4 Macc 13:14-15; 2 *Clem.* 5.4).[104] If they are to be saved for God's everlasting kingdom, they must persevere through persecutions until the "Son of Man comes" or they are martyred (Matt 10:22b; cf. 10:21b; 10:23b, 28, 39; 24:13). In this passage, and again right after he first reveals that he will be killed in Jerusalem, Jesus affirms the necessity of the disciples taking up their cross and being willing to lose their life to save it; the converse is for them to lose eternal life to save their mortal life (Matt 10:38-39; 16:25-26; cf. Mark 8:34-38).[105] They should realize that they will have to answer to God for negative actions; at the eschaton God will judge everyone, including disciples, according to their deeds (Matt 16:27). Jesus likewise warns them that gaining the world is not worth the price of losing eternal life (16:26). Such language reflects a temptation similar to what Jesus faced with Satan in the wilderness: the devil tempts him with the kingdoms of the world if Jesus would worship him (Matt 4:1-11; cf. Luke 4:1-13). Moreover, Jesus affirms that if his disciples confess him before others, he will reciprocate by accepting them on judgment day, but if they deny him before others this will be reciprocated with their being denied: at the *parousia* Christ will claim that he does not know them and they will be excluded from his eschatological kingdom (Matt 10:32-33; cf. 7:21-23; Luke 12:8-9; 2 *Clem.* 3.2). *To deny Christ is to commit apostasy and be eternally condemned. These particular warnings of Jesus speak to persecution and pertain to his disciples.*[106] The stakes are eternal rather than

---

104. While Gregg, *Final Judgment Sayings*, 148-49, affirms that 10:28 refers to final judgment, it is possible that the parallel in Luke 12:4-5 refers to punishment immediately after death and unrelated to the resurrection of the body (e.g., Luke 16:19-31; 23:43). Milikowsky, "Which Gehenna?," 238-49, argues that resurrected bodies are a reward for the righteous only (cf. Luke 14:14; 20:35f). For distinctions between Matt 10:28 and Luke 12:4f, see further Gregg, 150-53.

105. A distinction here is that 10:39 contrasts find (εὑρίσκω) and lose, whereas 16:25 contrasts save (σῴζω) and lose. The latter follows Mark (cf. Mark 8:35; Luke 9:24). The former still has the gaining of one's life in mind (find = obtain, BDAG, 412); Luz, *Matthew*, 2.116, claims the nuance of εὑρίσκω "is something that one cannot procure for oneself, but only receive," and so Matthew is thinking about eternal life. In 10:39 death is associated with hell (cf. 10:28). Luke 17:33 contrasts the idea of preserving life (περιποιέω, ζῳογονέω) and losing it. John uses loving and hating life (φιλέω, μισέω) in contrast to losing and keeping it, respectively.

106. Barrett, "I Am Not Ashamed," 23, observes that Q (Matt 10:32-33; Luke 12:8-9) differs from Mark 8:38 by adding a promise for the confessor of not losing a reward and by using the concept of denying rather than being ashamed. All three Synoptics agree "in that the language they use is appropriate to the situation of Christians in time of persecution."

temporal, and so the Matthean community should continue to confess Christ openly even through it struggles with hostile outsiders and local synagogues.

Fourth, Jesus mentions the possibility of "little ones" falling away (Matt 18:6–7, 10). Given the importance of straying sheep in the context (18:12–14), I suggest, as in Mark 9:42, that the "little ones" is another term for metaphoric sheep (cf. Zech. 13:7 MT), and hence, Christ-followers who are susceptible to going astray (cf. Matt 26:31). This group probably highlights the church's weaker members, such as believing children, youths, slaves, uneducated, poor, and marginalized believers. Whoever causes them to fall away will suffer a severe judgment worse than drowning (18:6). Their potential to apostatize is linked with the parable of the Stray Sheep, in which the shepherd leaves ninety-nine sheep to go after the one that went astray (Matt 18:10–14; cf. Luke 15:3–7).[107] Matthew's version affirms that it is not the will of the Father that one of these little ones be destroyed eschatologically via their going astray (Matt 18:14), and yet this does not necessitate their safe return. While the readers hope that the lost sheep will be found again, the conditional phrase in 18:13a, "if he [the shepherd] happens to find it" (ἐὰν γένηται εὑρεῖν αὐτό), leaves open the possibility that he may not. The assumption in this verse provides no guarantee that every apostate eventually returns to the fold of Christ-followers. Although the "world" is to blame for tempting them to fall away (18:7; cf. 13:41),[108] the disciples are also warned about their treatment of these little ones (18:10). The warning to them may be that *if these believers are despised (καταφρονέω) by their leaders, that is, looked down upon or treated with contempt, they could end up leaving the congregation and become lost eternally (18:11–14).*[109] This thought segues to the next pericope about Christians sinning against other Christians (18:15)[110] and the proper means for ex-

---

107. Overman, *Matthew's Gospel*, 101, following Pesch, *Matthäus als Seelsorger*, correctly notices that in Luke 15:3–7 the lost (ἀπόλλυμι) sheep has been changed to a straying (πλανάω) sheep in Matt 18:12–14. Luke relates the lost sheep to a missionary emphasis and need for repentance among tax collectors and other sinners; Matthew relates the lost sheep to church members who have strayed from the community and its norms. Earlier in Matt 10:6 there is nonetheless a missionary emphasis with "lost sheep" identified as the "house of Israel" and the crowds (cf. 9:36; 15:24).

108. A more general sense of the plural τὰ σκάνδαλα in 18:7 (and 13:41) is likewise found in the parallel Luke 17:1 but without direct mention of "the world" as the cause of stumbling. Romans 16:17 relates the plural σκάνδαλα more specifically to divisive people and false teachers within the church, whereas the LXX often relates it to idolatry or the nations/Gentiles or both (e.g., Josh 23:13; Hos 4:17; Wis 14:11). Jdt 5:1 uses it in a literal sense related to military battle.

109. On this meaning for καταφρονέω, see 1 Cor 11:22; 1 Tim 4:12; 6:2; Titus 2:5; BDAG, 529. In this context ἀπόλλυμι means eternally lost or perishing in the final judgment (Matt 18:14; cf.18:6; 5:29; 16:25).

110. I accept "against you" (εἰς σέ) as original in this verse (D, L, W, *TR*, Lat., Syr.): cf. Luke 17:1–4. Two strong witnesses (ℵ, B) omit these words, but this might be due to an attempt at making the "sin" more general in the passage, or accidental: see Metzger, *Textual Commentary*, 36. In another passage

pelling a member from church (18:15–20). The passage shares some similarities with Pauline warnings against knowledgeable Christians causing weaker Christians to sin and fall away (cf. 1 Cor 8:10–13; Rom 14:13–21), and similar to Matt 18, Paul accepts that expelling a member from the congregation is sometimes necessary (1 Cor 5). Differently than Paul, Matthew's conflict does not center on idol meats. It seems to deal with self-serving leaders who abuse their authority and neglect and mistreat weaker members (cf. Matt 18:1–3, 10). In contemporary religious groups the prominence of defections that take place on the membership level due to disillusionment with leaders is well attested.[111] We may be seeing an ancient example of this being warned against in Matt 18.

Fifth, the disciples are also cautioned against becoming the cause of their own stumbling. Matthew 18:3 possibly attests to the need for conversion if one interprets στρέφω as "convert" rather than "turn" (see NASB, KJV; John 12:40). The attractiveness of this translation is that no one would be able to enter the kingdom of heaven without being converted. This meaning in 18:3, however, would seem to be rather odd given that Jesus is addressing his disciples ("you") and the "little ones" in 18:6 identify believers that are already followers of Jesus. This verse more likely means that the disciples need to "turn" in the sense of changing their flawed thinking about who is the greatest in the kingdom of heaven (18:1). To follow Christ requires humility, not self-exaltation, and if the disciples lack childlike humility they will not enter the kingdom of heaven. They must change their attitude or they will suffer final judgment. *This passage therefore stresses a warning specifically to the disciples, unlike its Synoptic parallels that address a similar warning to "whoever"* (Mark 10:15; Luke 18:17). The redaction in Matthew possibly unveils conflicts the community experienced with teachers in the synagogue. In this case the Matthean group might have thought itself to be the "little ones" who were despised by their leaders in the synagogue. Possibly, some of the Christ-followers had abandoned faith earlier in the community's history as a result of being poorly treated.

More than this, Matt 18:8–9 warns the disciples that if their body parts are causing them to fall away (σκανδαλίζω) it would be better for them to cut off the body member than perish in hell.[112] The saying relates to individuals in terms of committing adultery in 5:27–30, but here in 18:8–9 the sin is not specified. On at

---

on apostasy (Matt 24:10–12), Christians will betray Christians, and they will hate one another (the opposite of Jesus' command to love).

111. E.g., Brinkerhoff and Mackie, "Casting Off the Bond," 235–53; Jacobs, *Divine Disenchantment*; Wilson, *Leaving the Fold*, 122–23.

112. Schnackenburg, *Gospel of Matthew*, 173, makes a distinction in meaning between the ideas of temptation related to "lapse of faith" (Matt 18:6–7) and "grave sin" (18:8–9). In either case, in this context, both lead to destruction in hell (18:8b, 9b, 14).

least a secondary level there seems to be hints that the body represents the community of Christ-followers. In 18:15–20 the expulsion of the sinner is probably for the sake of the spiritual preservation of the community. The community may be viewed as a metaphoric body, and so the cutting off of one of its body parts can refer to its expelling a member, lest the whole body be contaminated and destroyed because of the sinning person's influence. Corporate body imagery related to the church, however, is found more clearly in Paul than Matthew.[113]

Finally, in Matt 24–25 teachings about a great apostasy that will take place before Jesus' *parousia*, the watch motif and parables related to it, and the possibility of certain people being on the wrong side of the great divide at final judgment all speak to the impending dangers that could happen to the disciples (see below). The potential reality of Jesus' disciples committing apostasy is thus present throughout Matthew, and the Matthean community would be informed that Satan, false prophets, other believers, and the "world" itself would tempt Christians to fall away.

AUTHORITY AND APOSTASY AMONG THE DISCIPLES (18:15–20; 26:31, 33–35, 56, 70–75; 27:3–5)

Not only does Matthew portray the disciples as blessed perceivers of spiritual insight (13:11, 16–17), but they also have the authority to "bind" and "loose." Peter is granted the ability to give authoritative Halakah (16:16–18),[114] and the disciples have authority to shun church members who refuse to recant sin after being confronted a few times (Matt 18:15–20; cf. John 20:23; *Did.* 15:3; Tertullian, *Modesty* 21; Origen, *Comm. Matt.* 12:14).[115] Here the binary terms "binding"/"loosing" may refer to the ability to expel and restore to fellowship; the terms are held in contrast to Pharisaic authority to "banish" (bind) and "recall" (loose) with judiciary power (cf. Josephus, *J.W.* 1.5.2 [111]).[116] Some sort of ancient excommunication is meant in Matt 18:15–20 because the impenitent sinner is to be excluded from all church

---

113. On the connection between excommunication and the cutting off of body parts see also Pesch, *Matthäus als Seelsorger*, 32.

114. On binding and loosing in relation to Peter, see further Allison and Davies, *Matthew* 2.635–40, 787.

115. Büchsel, "δέω," 2.60, opines that binding and loosing in Matt 16:19 and 18:18 relate to expelling a member from one's congregation, and the terms have the meaning of imposing or removing a ban and is derived from the Aramaic אֲסַר and שְׁרָא. While this interpretation may be correct for Matt 18:18, it does not appear to be the best interpretation for 16:19, which has more to do with revelation/teaching than banning. On early Jewish excommunication, see 1QS 5.24–6.1; CD 9.2–8; Josephus *Ant.* 4.8.15 [219]; Josephus, *Life* 49.

116. Cf. Manson, *Sayings of Jesus*, 210. Prohibiting and permitting are other respective nuances. On binding and loosing in early Judaism, see Keener, *Matthew*, 455; Str.B. 1.730–38.

fellowship (ἐκκλησία). That this individual is to be treated like a "Gentile" and "tax collector" would mean that such a person is to be shunned, that is, excluded from the community.[117] The transgressor has been confronted by two or three witnesses and still refuses to repent (cf. Deut 17:6; 19:15; Lev 19:17).

At first glance this thought does not fit well with Jesus' earlier teaching on the importance of having compassion for lost "sheep" (Matt 18:12–14) and his next teaching that focuses on manifold forgiveness (18:21–35). Moreover, the notion of the shunned individual being treated like a Gentile and tax collector fits awkwardly with Jesus being a friend of sinners and tax collectors (9:9–10). Obviously, in 18:10–15 Matthew does not mean that the disciples should continue to embrace the unrepentant church member similar to the way Jesus welcomes sinners to his own ministry in other contexts. Otherwise, the passage would be encouraging church members to rebel against church leaders in order to receive special treatment in the church! Matthew 18:17 involves a church setting rather than missionary evangelism, and the offending person is supposed to be a believer, not an outsider. No doubt, "Gentile" and "tax collector" are used negatively here, as in 5:46–47 and 6:7. The negative connotation would make sense to Matthew's Jewish-Christian audience, who probably understood tax collectors as traitors and non-Christian Gentiles as outsiders. Regarding the larger context, in 18:12–14 the stray "sheep" are believers in Jesus ("little ones") who fall away or otherwise leave the church (18:12–14)—there is no evidence that they have been expelled. And those who receive forgiveness in 18:21–22 apparently *ask* for mercy and forgiveness as the related parable implies (cf. Matt 18:26, 29; Luke 17:3–4).

Hence, in relation to the excommunication that takes place in 18:15–20, Overman correctly posits that even though forgiveness is emphasized in Matt 18, "if all else fails, the institution of discipline and expulsion" is necessary (cf. 18:15–20).[118] Bornkamm goes a step further by writing that such discipline involves "final exclusion of the obdurate sinner from the congregation and thus salvation; the possibility of a later repentance is not being considered."[119] This may be correct if the Matthean community's expulsion resembles that of the Pauline community in 1 Cor 5:1–13, albeit Paul still holds out the possibility of the expelled individual's restoration (1 Cor 5:5b). *The disciples thus have authority backed up by heaven to confirm a member's apostasy by expelling such a person from their church. They also have the ability*

---

117. cf. Allison and Davies, *Matthew*, 2.785, who affirm the exclusion is from a local congregation/community, not the universal church.

118. Overman, *Matthew's Gospel*, 101. On the legitimacy of expulsion see further Forkman, *Limits of the Religious Community*, 124–32.

119. Bornkamm, "Authority to 'Bind,'" 42.

to forgive these members, and so restoration from apostasy and heinous sins is possible. The restoration of the lost sheep confirms the possibility of restoration after apostasy (Matt 18:12-14). The importance of proper procedures related to expulsion may hint at some of the experiences individuals faced in the Matthean community in reference to the synagogue, or possibly these guidelines betray their own excommunication of those whom they thought to be false prophets.

Other portrayals of the disciples in Matthew's gospel are not so flattering. In 13:36, despite their eyes that "see," the disciples still need explanation to understand Jesus' parables, just as in Mark. They understand by virtue of Jesus' good instructions. If Mark emphasizes that the disciples have hardened hearts, Matthew claims they possess "little faith" (Matt 8:26; 14:31; 16:8; 17:20), are fearful (14:30), and some doubt even after Jesus' resurrection (28:17).[120] Similar to Mark's gospel, the disciples abandon Jesus at his arrest (Matt 26:31, 33-35; cf. 26:56), and even though Peter is called first, walks on water, and is identified as the blessed "rock" who possesses the keys to the kingdom (4:18; 14:28-31; 16:17-19; 14:28-31), he becomes a stumbling block (σκάνδαλον) to Jesus (16:23b), and is also called "Satan" (16:23a). Peter becomes a σκάνδαλον in the sense of being an obstacle to Jesus' path to do God's will. In this way he acts like Satan (4:1-11) and therefore must get "behind" Jesus so that he does not block Jesus' path.[121] Jesus' rebuke may also be considered a warning to Peter: he must follow behind Jesus; failure to do so might cause Peter to stumble in his own spiritual walk. In a sense this does happen to him later on when he denies Jesus (26:69-75). Nevertheless, Peter's going out and weeping bitterly after his denial may be viewed in contrast to Judas going out and hanging himself after betraying his teacher (26:75; 27:5).[122] It is evident that Matthew's gospel accepts that defecting disciples can be restored if Peter and the others (minus Judas) are commissioned by Jesus after they had forsaken him (26:75; 28:7-10, 16-20). Their restoration in Matthew is clearer than in Mark.

Perhaps the most celebrated disciple-turned-apostate is Judas Iscariot. In Matthew, he is numbered among the Twelve, and Jesus gives him authority over unclean spirits and sicknesses (Matt 10:1-8; cf. Mark 6:7-13; cf. 3:13-19). Judas is instructed with the Twelve to preach the kingdom of heaven to the lost sheep of Israel, and he must be alert and not commit apostasy on account of impending per-

---

120. Barth, "Matthew's Understanding," 116, notes that while the disciples have little faith (ὀλιγόπιστος), the crowd (non-disciples) possess unbelief (ἀπιστία; 13:58; 17:17). Matthew 17:17, however, may include disciples. For more on the disciples in Matthew, see Zumstein, *Condition du Croyant*; Luz, "Jünger," 141-71; Meier, *Marginal Jew*, 3.40-285; Kingsbury, *Matthew as Story*, 129-45.

121. Cf. Hagner, *Matthew*, 2.480.

122. So Brown, *Death of the Messiah*, 1.644.

secutions (Matt 10:25-39; 24:9-10), false prophets (7:15-23; 24:11, 23-24), or moral failure before the Son of Man's return (24:12-13, 42-51). Likewise, he is given spiritual insight and authority to bind and loose, just like the other disciples (13:10-17; 18:16-20). In essence, Judas is as much a follower of Jesus as the other disciples, and he is graced with the same privileges as the rest of the Twelve. Judas would seem to be an example of a follower who fails morally because he covets money; he surrenders Jesus over to the authorities for thirty pieces of silver (26:14-16; cf. 26:21-25, 46-50). After Judas bargains with the chief priests to have Jesus arrested, unlike the other disciples who call Jesus "Lord" (26:22), Judas calls him "rabbi" (cf. 26:25, 49), a name the Matthean Jesus prohibits and attributes to the hypocritical scribes (cf. 23:7-8). An indirect message for those in the Matthean community is that they also, like Judas, could fail morally and become disobedient to Jesus if they are not alert.

After Jesus' arrest, Judas confesses his betrayal and Jesus' innocence before the authorities, throws away his money, and hangs himself (27:3-10; esp. vv. 3-5). Matthew's gospel is the only one that records these turn of events, which leaves open for us a possibility that Judas' repentance was genuine, and his act of suicide may be considered some sort of atonement for sin, in keeping with certain Jewish traditions (e.g., 4 Macc 17:11-24; cf. *Gen. Rabbah* 27.27).[123] It is possible in the narrative that Judas seeks divine forgiveness at the price of his own life. With this perspective in mind, Judas' suicide may not be considered a wrongful act by Matthew. James Tabor and Arthur Droge write, "Judas was his own judge *and* executioner. Matthew shows no trace of disapproving of the means of death as such. On the contrary, the implication is that Judas's act of self-destruction was a result of his remorse and not an additional crime."[124] In other traditions, however, the act of suicide seems condemned (e.g., Josephus, *J.W.* 3.8.5 [361-82]; *m. Sanhedrin* 10.2), and even if we grant the genuine repentance and suicidal "atonement" for Judas, these ideas create tensions with Jesus' "woe to that man" judgment on him in Matt 26:24 (see further in Luke-Acts below). A possible resolution may be that Jesus pronounces judgment on Judas with the intention of getting him to repent, and his warning succeeds—Judas becomes exempt from divine punishment in 26:24 because of his remorse. This possibility, however, rests on two crucial assumptions: (1) that Judas' remorse is to be equated with sincere repentance; and (2) that suicide for Matthew neither leads to, nor is a result of, divine punishment. It seems just as likely for us to suggest that Matthew foresaw the suicide of Judas as something negative and as

---

123. See Allison and Davies, *Matthew* 3.561-63; Luz, *Mattthew* 3.470. On Judas as a scapegoat, see Drewermann, "Fürbitte für einen Verzweifelten," 29-43.

124. Tabor and Droge, *Noble Death*, 113.

part of Jesus' condemnation of the betrayer in 26:24.[125] Moreover, the point of the 27:3–5 is not to affirm the innocence of Judas but the innocence of *Jesus*. Pilate and Judas are responsible for Jesus' death, and yet they both maintain his innocence of any wrongdoing, a claim the religious authorities do not contest (27:3–4, 23–24).[126] *Judas' eternal destiny remains ambiguous, then, in Matthew.* It ranges from the possibility of his genuine repentance (27:3–5) to his untimely death as a confirmation of future divine judgment against him (26:24; cf. 27:5). Perhaps this uncertainty about his end evoked the audience of this gospel to draw their own conclusions. Whereas sources such as Mark perceive the betrayer's eternal fate in negative terms, Matthew's gospel may be suggesting for its audience that Judas' final destiny is best left in God's hands. Even so, Matthew does not regard Judas' betrayal as an act of goodwill but one of treachery. If Judas is ultimately found innocent, it would be on the basis that he had repented of his betrayal.

REJECTED AFTER ACCEPTING THE WEDDING INVITATION (22:1–14)

The parable of the Wedding Banquet is a prominent passage about inclusion and exclusion related to God's kingdom (Matt 22:1–14; cf. Luke 14:15–24; *Gos. Thom.* 63–65).[127] Significant in the story is that not only do many reject the invitation to the wedding feast, but one man accepts it and is rejected at the banquet, possibly suggesting for Matthew's audience that outward acceptance of Jesus' message is not good enough to secure one's place in the eschatological kingdom, and some who claim to be Christ-followers will be rejected when Christ returns.

In the parable Jesus compares the kingdom of heaven to a king who prepares a banquet for his son's wedding. He gives out an original invitation that is rejected. Then he invites the guests again, providing them with more information about the feast, but they still refuse to come and others end up mistreating and killing his servant-messengers. The king sends an army to kill the murderers and burn their city, and he gives another invitation through his servants to invite whomever they could find, good and bad, to the wedding. A certain man who attends the feast does not wear a wedding garment; he is cast into outer darkness where there is weeping

---

125. Even so, if Matthew considered suicide to be wrongful, this would not necessarily mean that all the emerging Christians thought the same way. It is not until the time of Augustine (c. 354–430) that the equation of suicide with damnation is etched firmly in the Christian imagination.

126. Luz, *Matthew*, 3.471, notices Pilate's wife as another person declaring Jesus' innocence (Matt 27:19).

127. In Luke the message is set in the context of Jesus eating at the house of a ruler belonging to the Pharisees. There are significant differences between the Matthean and Lukan texts, and neither Luke nor Thomas includes a saying resembling Matt 22:14.

and gnashing of teeth (Matt 22:1–14). The parable is related to the parable of the Wicked Tenants (21:33–43)—both stories involve a powerful lord who has a son and sends his servants to communicate a message to recipients who reject the message. As a result, the original recipients are rejected and new ones are favored. Jesus in fact proclaims that God's kingdom will be taken away from the Pharisees and chief priests and given to another nation that will produce proper fruit (21:43).[128] The parable of the Two Sons (21:28–32) is also relevant to the Wedding Banquet and Wicked Tenants parables. These parables imply that God is rejecting the religious leaders and those who follow them because they have not done the Father's will (Two Sons), have not produced good fruit (Wicked Tenants), and have rejected God's message and messengers (Wicked Tenants; Wedding Banquet). He will accept the lowly and Gentiles to be included in his kingdom (21:31–32, 41–43; 22:9–10).

It is possible that the wedding garment the guest is supposed to wear to the feast in 22:11–13 is a robe of righteousness, as in Isa 61:10.[129] The concept of righteousness plays prominently in this gospel (3:15; 5:6, 10, 20; 6:33; 13:43; 21:32; 25:46; 27:19), and it is related to doing God's will, bearing good fruit, and obeying God's messenger. If this interpretation is correct, then the person who is improperly dressed may be committing unrighteous deeds. But this interpretation may not be necessary. There may be a more realistic and practical reason why the guest is not properly attired.

One explanation for the man's improper garments centers on the notion that he is unprepared. The invitation came later than expected, and so the man had no time to put on the appropriate clothing.[130] The wedding feast represents the messianic banquet found in apocalyptic literature,[131] and the guest's condemnation of being cast out of the feast means that he is banished from God's kingdom and eschatologically punished. Possibly, his judgment for being unprepared resembles the kind found in various crisis stories in Matthew (24:37–39, 43–51; 25:1–13). The stories function as warning-exhortations to the early listeners. They must be ready to accept the invitation of Jesus and be ready when he returns at the *parousia*; those who are not prepared and commit unrighteous deeds will be punished (Matt 24:48–51; cf. 1 Thess 5:4–8; Rev 3:3–5; 16:5; 22:12). In the Matthean community the *parousia* may have remained important for paraenetic purposes not only because of its imminence but because it would be the final separator between the righteous and unrighteous,

---

128. Precisely how the kingdom will be taken away from them seems to be related to Jerusalem's destruction in 70 CE (22:7; cf. 21:41). See Lutz, *Matthew*, 3.41, 54.

129. Righteousness is also associated with garments in other ancient Jewish and Christian traditions (Job 29:14; *Bar.* 5:2; *Sir.* 27:8; *Asc. Isa.* 1:5 [D, E]; Eph 6:14; Rev 3:4; 6:11; 7:9; 19:8; Irenaeus, *Haer.* 4.36.6; 5.35.1).

130. See Jeremias, *Parables of Jesus*, 188.

131. *1 En.* 60:7–24; 62:14; *4 Ezra* 6:49–52; *2 Bar.* 29:3–6; Isa 25:6; Rev 19:9; cf. Matt 8:11–12; 26:29.

including those within the mixed body of the church (22:10–14; cf. 13:24–30, 36–43; 47–50; 21:28–32, 40–44; 24:37–39, 45–51; 25:1–13, 19–46).[132]

Richard Bauckham, however, suggests that the issue of the man's garment is related to social contempt for the occasion (cf. Irenaeus, *Haer.* 36.6).[133] That the king makes ready the feast (Matt 22:4, 8) means that the preparations are advanced enough so that the guests can now begin their travelling to the banquet. It was perhaps expected that not all of them would arrive at the beginning of the feast; such occasions would last an entire week. The man is improperly dressed (perhaps wearing soiled or common clothes) not as a result of insufficient time but because he is not willing to honor the king or his son's wedding and rejoice at the occasion, an act that shows contempt and has political ramifications. In this sense he is not any more worthy than those who earlier refused the king's invitation (an act that would no doubt be interpreted as an insurrection). An important point in the parable is that "those who are unworthy of entering the kingdom of God are not only those who spurn the Gospel invitation but also those who ostensibly accept it while rejecting what it really represents."[134] This aspect of the parable brings to mind the Christians who say "Lord, Lord," but are rejected on judgment day because they fail to do the will of the God (7:21–23). Here we have either an apostate or false Christian depicted. In either case the Matthean community would perhaps recognize the mixed nature of congregants that confess Christ.

The saying "many are called, but few are elect" (22:14)[135] seems misplaced given that only one individual is rejected from among the "all" and "as many as" who are given a second invitation (22:9–10).[136] Ben Meyer may be correct to suggest that the

---

132. Cf. Meier, "Matthew," 4.623.

133. Bauckham, "Parable of the Royal Wedding," 471–88.

134. Bauckham, 488.

135. The adjectival "chosen" (ἐκλεκτοί) in this verse is perhaps better translated as "elect." In the Second Temple era "elect" was frequently used as a fixed term for God's corporate people (cf. 1QS 6.1–11; CD 4.3–4; 1QH 2.13; Sir 46:1; 47:22; Wis 3:9; Tob 8:15; *1 En.* 5.7–8; *Jub.* 1.29; 1 Chr 16:13LXX).

136. If 22:14 is understood in terms of some sort of divine pre-selection, it makes an extremely bad fit with its context because the parable intends to stress the king's inclusiveness rather than exclusiveness. The king is *not* very selective of those whom he invites to his son's feast, and those originally invited are *not willing* to come, even after a second invitation (22:3–4; cf. 21:29). In the end it seems to be the choice of those who refuse to attend the wedding and wear improper attire that governs why they are not "chosen." Räisänen, *Idea of Divine Hardening*, 90, writes perceptively, "The reason that only few are chosen is the attitude of the 'many.'" The contextual implication is clear enough: a large number attended the feast, whereas the saying in 22:14 seems to suggest almost the exact opposite: that many receive the invitation but few attend. We do well to suspect the saying as a Jesus *logion* that may have not been originally spoken in connection with this parable. The saying appears in a different context in certain manuscripts of Matt 20:16 (e.g., C, D, *Byz*, Latin, Syriac), confirming our suspicion that this may have originally been a floating *logion*.

word "few" (ὀλίγοι) functions as a Semitic idiom in terms of a correlative comparative with πολλοί conveying the sense of "more/fewer" or "all/not all" (cf. 2 Esd 8:3; Num 26:54; 35:8; Exod 16:17–18 with 2 Cor 8:15).[137] There are also other examples in Matthew where "many" essentially means "all" (Matt 8:11; 20:28; 26:28). The saying is intended to convey that everyone is called (κλητοί), in other words, "invited"[138] to be present at the messianic banquet and the kingdom related to it, but not everyone will participate in it. As in 24:22–31, it is significant that the term "elect" (ἐκλεκτοί) is found in an eschatological context that functions as an exhortation. The elect refers to those among the messianic community who will be accepted at the final judgment.[139] Whatever else they saying in 22:14 might mean, it serves as a warning to early Christ-communities; they must not fall away from their faith before the end takes place (cf. Matt 24:13; *Barn.* 4:14; Irenaeus, *Haer.* 4.15.2; Tertullian, *Modesty* 9.14). A person may outwardly respond to the kingdom invitation and yet still be rejected later on if they despise or abandon what it represents.

PERSECUTION, FALSE PROPHETS, AND APOSTASY IN THE OLIVET DISCOURSE (24:4–28; CF. 7:15–23)

In the Olivet Discourse or "Little Apocalypse" (Matt 24; cf. Mark 13; Luke 21:10–36), the disciples can potentially fall away due to persecutions, lawlessness, being led astray by false prophets, and not being watchful.

Jesus assures his disciples that, due to the severity of the impending tribulation, God will shorten the days for his elect community's sake (Matt 24:22; cf. Mark 13:20). He will not allow the distress and persecutions they undergo to persist indefinitely; otherwise no one would be preserved from physical harm ("no flesh" would be saved, Matt 24:22). The assurance Jesus gives is that, despite persecutions and

---

137. Meyer, "Many (=All) Are Called," 89–97. Similarly, Jeremias, *New Testament Theology*, 130–31; idem, "πολλοί," 6:536–45, notes the phrase's Aramaic origin, in which the plural πολλοί ("many") would represent "all" because Semitic languages do not have a word to describe totality in a plural sense. He argues that a parallel passage in *4 Ezra* 8:3, "many have been created but few will be saved," does not make sense unless one substitutes "all" for "many." The phrase is intended to convey an incalculable number of people created.

138. In agreement with the interpretation of κλητοί by Nolland, *Matthew*, 891.

139. The "elect" perhaps alludes to the Isaianic identification of Israel during its prophetic restoration as elect and called by God (Isa 41:9; 42:1–6; 43:10; 44:1–2; 45:4; 48:12–15; 49:1; 54:6). The Servant of God is likewise elect/chosen, whom Matthew interprets as Jesus (Matt 12:18–21/ Isa 42:1–4), and so the Matthean community would probably view their election both in terms of their Jewish heritage and their being followers of Christ. We seem to have in seminal form the notion that the elect community is elect through Christ, the chosen one predicted in the Isaianic scriptures. Luke fleshes out a similar implication by using the term to describe both Christ as the Elect One and God's people as the elect (Luke 9:35; 18:7–8; 23:35).

martyrdoms that his followers will face (Matt 24:4–9; cf. Mark 13:12; Luke 21:16), the tribulation will have its end before his followers are completely wiped out.[140] God will intervene to rescue them before too much time elapses. The promise of God preserving his elect is probably connected with prophetic promises that a remnant of God's people would survive exiles and future calamities they might face (e.g., Dan 12:1; Isa 10:20–22; 11:11–16; 37:31–32; Joel 2:32; Mic 4:6–7; Zeph 3:11–13). It seems that the survival of a remnant often characterizes the messianic age (e.g., Isa 8–11; Jer 23:3–6; Ezek 34:1–11). Likewise God demonstrates through such preservation of the elect community his promise to Abraham of future descendants (Gen 15:4–5; 17:1–8).

Despite God's promise of preserving the Christian church as a corporate entity, individual believers within this community must persevere throughout this temporal life; only the ones who endure to the end will be saved (Matt 24:13; cf. 10:22b; Mark 13:13; Luke 21:19). The preferred reading of τέλος here is the "end of the age" (cf. Matt 24:6, 14; Dan 12:12–14 [Theodotion]; *4 Ezra* 6:25; 7:27; 1 Cor 1:8) over the meaning of death or the end of one's physical life, as in Matt 24:22 (cf. Rev 2:10). Even so, both ideas seem to be present in 24:13 because the suffering Jesus' disciples would face includes potential martyrdom (cf. Matt 24:9–10; 10:22–39; Mark 13:7–13). If martyrdom is inevitable for some of the disciples, then the salvation of one's life here must mean something more than just physical preservation.[141] The discourse predicts that many will fall away (σκανδαλίζω, 24:10a). There will be betrayals and hatred among the Christ-followers, the advent of many false prophets who will lead astray many, and an increase of lawlessness in which the love of many believers will cease to be practiced (Matt 24:10b–12; cf. 10:21–22; 2 Thess 2:3; *Did.* 16.3–5). More precisely, their love "will be extinguished."[142] It is quite evident that Matt 24:10a is not describing a group of apostates independent of other groups that are not considered apostates in 24:10b–12. Betrayals, hatred, deception, and failed love all characterize the ways believers will fall away from their faith. Hence, the individual Christ-followers must not assume that they are exempt from committing apostasy simply because Jesus promises that the church as a whole will never be destroyed. The eschatological forecast is bleak: *many Christians will be deceived and become apostate. They will turn away from Jesus' command to love God and love their neighbor as themselves; they will*

---

140. On shortening the time of the end see, e.g., *2 Bar.* 20:1–2; *4 Ezra* 2:13; 4Q385; Sir 36:10.

141. Marshall, *Kept by the Power*, 74, notices that if this verse were referring to physical preservation, it would amount to a tautology in which the person's physical life would endure until the end of the person's physical life.

142. On ψύχω, see BDAG, 1100; Josephus, *J.W.* 5.472. See conceptual parallel in Rev 2:4–5.

In the Footsteps of Judas and Other Defectors

"hate one another" instead.[143] The followers of Jesus must therefore persevere in faith to the end of the age or the end of their physical life, whichever comes first. Failure to do so would constitute apostasy and loss of eternal salvation.

Other apocalyptic sources also claim that before the end time reaches its culmination there will be a great trial in which many among God's people will commit apostasy, persecution will increase, the world will become increasingly wicked or more idolatrous, and there will be treachery among close relatives.[144] Jesus' instruction in the Olivet Discourse may then suggest a larger conflict than merely first-century Christian trials and persecutions; the text characterizes a number of conflicts taking place between the Maccabean and Constantinian eras.[145] In any case, Luz is correct when he affirms that Matthew has dealt with the topics of false prophets and apostasy earlier (e.g., 7:15–23; 18:6–9), but now in this apocalyptic text these issues are highlighted in "extremely drastic colors. That indicates that we are dealing here not simply with a traditional apocalyptic topos but with a real and pressing experience of the churches."[146]

The discourse continues that Jesus' followers must beware of being led astray by false messiahs and false prophets (Matt 24:4–5, 11, 23–24, 26; cf. Mark 13:5–6, 21–22). Matthew mentions false prophets in this discourse more than Mark,[147] and since earlier he included a pericope that teaches against false prophets (Matt 7:15–23), the prevalence of this subject in Matthew's gospel has sparked the imagination of scholars to determine whether these false prophets can be identified as Pharisees, Zealots, Essenes, Paulinists, or charismatics.[148] We suggest they are antinomian and false Christians but not apostates.

Matthew 7:22–23 (cf. 7:13–14) shares some common thoughts with Luke 13:24–27, where a different audience is in view:[149] "someone" (τις) asks Jesus if few

---

143. On the importance of the love command in relation to keeping the Law, see Matt 22:36–40.

144. *4 Ezra* 5.1–2; 11.42; *1 En.* 80.7; 91.7; 93.9; 100.1–2; *2 Bar.* 70.2–7; *Jub.* 23.16–24; *T. Levi* 14–15; *T. Zeb.* 9; *Sib. Or.* 3.273–79; *Apoc. El.* 1.13–14; 3.1, 5; 4.15–25; 5.1; 4Q375, 378; *m. Sotah* 9:15; cf. Deut 13; 18:22. For more examples, see Hartman, *Prophecy Interpreted*, 28–30; Russell, *Method and Message*, 274–75.

145. For a list of parallels, see Hartman, *Prophecy Interpreted*, 145–77; Frend, *Martyrdom and Persecution*.

146. Luz, *Matthew*, 3.194.

147. See Barth, "Matthew's Understanding," 159–64. Matthew 24:24 may depend on Mark 13:22, or it derives from the same source, so this verse is probably less important for identifying Matthean opponents.

148. See the relevant discussion above under the sub-heading, "KEEPING THE LAW AND THE PROPHETS IN THE MATTHEAN COMMUNITY (5:17–20)."

149. Matthew 7:15–25 also loosely parallels a saying of Jesus in Luke 6:43–49, but the latter is not associated with false prophets.

will be saved, and Jesus responds with the necessity to enter the "narrow" door, for once the door is shut, the householder will say to those who knock, "I do not know you." Those who are rejected in Luke's version seem to be unfaithful Jews of the towns and villages where Jesus preached on his way to Jerusalem; they ate and drank with him but did not really follow him (Luke 13:22, 26). Unlike those who are rejected in Matt 7, they do not perform any miracles or great works, and they are workers of "unrighteousness" (ἀδικία, Luke 13:27) rather than "lawlessness" (ἀνομία). The "many" who are rejected in Matt 7:22 are not exclusively Jews, Gentiles, or apostates; they seem to identify false prophets who speak in Jesus' name, as the context suggests (Matt 7:15-23). The scene depicts judgment day in which Jesus is viewed as the judge of the people (cf. 16:28; 19:28; 25:31-46).[150] These prophets perform exorcisms and other powerful deeds in the name of Jesus, but they are rejected by him.[151] In the Olivet discourse there will be "many" such prophets arising before the end takes place (24:11).

The false prophets respond to Jesus with the double vocative "Lord, Lord," which functions as an emphatic appeal often directed towards God (Matt 7:22; cf. LXX Pss 129:3; 108:21; 139:8; Amos 7:2-4; Add Esth 13:9; 14:17; 2 Macc 1:24; Philo, *Conf.* 34 [173]). Jesus, as the Lord of his subjects, does not publicly give these clients any honor or recognition for their public claim, "Lord, Lord," because they do not honor him by doing his Father's will (cf. Matt 10:32-33; 15:7-9; Luke 6:46; 13:23-27). The Lord instead shames them by not allowing them into the kingdom; in essence, as Jerome Neyrey puts it, he slams the door in their face.[152] Often in visions or theophanies God calls individuals as his own for special services by using the double vocative of their name.[153] When "Lord, Lord" is addressed to Jesus, it is found on the lips of those who are disobedient to him and are excluded from his community (Matt 7:22; 25:11; cf. Luke 6:46). It may function as a rhetorical device that points to the reversal of God calling an individual. The disobedient who use the double vocative in Matthew's gospel are disowned, dishonored, and excluded from God's kingdom.[154] After the first century the saying "not all that say to me 'Lord,

---

150. Differently, Betz, *Sermon on the Mount*, 555-56, argues that Jesus is not the judge; he is an advocate for the people in Matt 7:21-23. For the phrase "on that day" (7:22) as referring to the eschaton, see Matt 24:19, 22; 25:31; 26:29.

151. Regarding exorcisms, differently in Mark 9:38-39 and Luke 9:49-50, those who apparently do not belong to Jesus and yet cast out demons in Jesus' name are *not* denounced. They do not appear to be associated with the false prophets.

152. Cf. Neyrey, *Honor and Shame*, 225-26.

153. Gen 22:11; Exod 3:4; 1 Sam 3:10; Acts 9:4; *Apoc. Ab.* 9.1; *2 Bar.* 22.2; *Jos. Asen.* 14.7.

154. This does not mean, however, that the saying, "Lord, Lord," possesses some magical property that excludes one from God's kingdom. The ones who are excluded have already shown themselves to

Lord'" was not only related to false or inauthentic teachers[155] but was also used for exhortational purposes or in reference to apostates (e.g., *2 Clem.* 4; Cyprian, *Unit. eccl.*15; *Tr. Nov.* 9).

The false prophets' punishment involves departing from the Lord's presence (Matt 7:23; cf. 25:41). The phrase "depart from me . . ." echoes Ps 6:8–9 and is originally directed against the psalmist's enemies who are workers of lawlessness. The LXX version of the Psalms frequently associates "workers of lawlessness" with enemies who persecute God's people or the psalmist; these enemies will be punished (Pss 13[14]:4; 52[53]:5; 58[59]:3, 6; 63[64]:3; 93[94]:4; 124[125]:5; 140[141]:9). Matthew's allusions to the psalm suggest that the ones who are being judged practice lawlessness and will be punished as God's enemies. They are in essence sentenced to hell (Matt 13:41–42; 23:28, 33–36; cf. 24:12; 2 Thess 2:3, 7–12). A person's position in or out of the kingdom of heaven is contingent upon their doing the Father's will, which takes on an ethical dimension in this passage. Consequently the false prophets are practicing lawlessness, not necessarily teaching a collection of false doctrines independent of moral precepts. The righteous, on the other hand, produce good fruit by doing God's will (obeying God), which means that they work righteousness and put to practice the law of Jesus (Matt 7:15–27; cf. 5:17–20).

Jesus also says to them, "I never recognized you; depart from me, you who practice lawlessness" (7:23). Variations of this declaration may have been spoken as excommunication formulae[156] in which the general meaning is probably, "I do not wish to have anything to do with you."[157] Nevertheless, their being denied access to the kingdom of heaven may be related to Jesus declaring that he will deny those who deny him (Matt 10:33; cf. Luke 12:9), and so "I do not know you" would seem to suffice (cf. Peter's denials in Matt 26:70, 72, 74). At any rate, the nuance given in Matt 7:23 is that Jesus "never" (οὐδέποτε) recognized as his own the ones he is excluding.[158] D. A. Carson argues that these individuals have "spurious" rather than genuine faith.[159] While it is possible that "I never recognized you" essentially means,

---

be disobedient to God.

155. E.g., Justin, *Apol.* 1.16 (Christians only "by name"); Clement of Alexandria, *Miscellanies* 7.12 (of Gnostics).

156. Matt 25:12; cf. 10:32; 18:15–20; Luke 12:8; *2 Clem.* 4.5; 4Q175 15–17.

157. Cf. Manson, *Sayings of Jesus*, 125, 177. Alternatively, Luz, *Matthew* 1.445–46, views the declaration as a legal testimony rather than a banishment formula; consequently, those who do not do God's will are denied fellowship.

158. Allison and Davies, *Matthew* 1.717, claim that the "never" probably refers back to the "protracted period of ministry presupposed by 7.22." Along these lines: Amos 3:2; John 10:14; 1 Cor 8:3; 2 Tim 2:12, 19.

159. Carson, "Reflections on Christian Assurance," 17.

The Gospel of Matthew

"I never endorsed your miracles and deeds that you performed," the second-person plural "you" should be taken seriously. Hence, the perspective that they never belonged to Jesus seems correct. If so, the false prophets in this passage may be characterized as inauthentic—they were never truly followers of Jesus. If we assume this reading, however, it is incorrect for us to infer from the passage that *every person who claims to be a Christ-follower and is ultimately rejected by Jesus was never a genuine believer in the first place*.[160] Several points from Matthew's relevant texts argue against such a grand inference.

First, the many Christians who will fall away in 24:10-12 are not themselves the false prophets; rather, the false prophets are the ones who have led them astray. Second, the passage states in reference to these apostates that their love for God and others will be extinguished (24:12). The most plausible inference to draw from this is that at one time they genuinely loved God and obeyed Jesus' love command. Third, we can affirm the possibility that individuals from among God's elect community could be deceived by the false prophets (cf. 24:24; see below). Fourth, the warnings in the apocalyptic discourse are given to Jesus' disciples in the narrative: *they* must constantly beware of being deceived by false prophets and committing apostasy; they will be saved only if they endure to the end (24:4, 13).[161] Finally, the expulsion formula for the false prophets, "I never recognized you" (οὐδέποτε ἔγνων ὑμᾶς) in 7:23, is not repeated again in 25:12, which uses instead, "I do not know you" (οὐκ οἶδα ὑμᾶς). The context of the latter suggests a more general rejection of Christians who are unprepared for Jesus at his second coming; the latter verse leaves open the possibility that at one time Jesus *did* know them. It follows from these observations that *even though Matthew's gospel may suggest that false prophets are inauthentic Christ-followers or have spurious faith, the same cannot be said about the many apostates. On the contrary, at least in the Olivet discourse, they are Christians who obey Christ's commands, love God, but will fall away.* Such a view matches the phenomenon of apostasy we find described or warned against in many other New Testament writings,[162] and incidentally, even the phenomenon of false teachers who once had genuine faith does not go unnoticed in 2 Pet 2:1.

---

160. The general thrust of Carson's article unfortunately travels in this direction.

161. Will the warnings themselves prevent the disciples from falling away after hearing them? This certainly does not happen in the narrative: after hearing these warnings, they still fall away (Matt 26:31, 56) and even though they are eventually restored, the same cannot be said with any confidence about Judas. This aspect of the disciples hearing the warnings of upcoming apostasy and then committing apostasy anyway is likewise found in the parallel passages in Mark (e.g., 13:5; 14:27, 50), and here Judas is condemned without any indication of his remorse (Mark 14:21).

162. E.g., Gal 5:4; 1 Cor 10:12; 2 Cor 11:29; 1 Tim 1:19-20; Heb 10:29; Jas 5:19-20; Jude 22-23; but contrast 1 John 2:19.

In the Footsteps of Judas and Other Defectors

For the Matthean community the false prophets are perceived as professing Christian belief or at least giving lip service to Christ's name, and they allegedly work miracles but practice antinomianism (cf. Matt 7:15–23; 24:24). A trend towards false teachers who practice lawlessness or immorality may be seen in other Christian communities of the late first century,[163] perhaps confirming the omen that "many" such prophets would arise (24:11). The Matthean group may have had its share of encounters with such individuals, some of which were possibly itinerate preachers, and others perhaps distorting Pauline teachings on grace and freedom from the works of the Law (cf. 2 Pet 3:15–17). Beyond this we do well not to speculate on a one-size-fits-all identity for these prophets. Matthew 24, in common with other apocalyptic traditions, forecasts false prophets and mass deception during the end times.[164] A growing number of deceivers were to be expected at the close of the age, and perhaps the Matthean community knew that such warnings should be understood as ground for avoiding *anyone* who would attempt to seduce them, not *just* the antinomians.

The Matthean Jesus also warns that great wonders will arise from the false prophets for the purpose of deceiving the very elect, if possible (Matt 24:24; cf. Mark 13:22). God will preserve a remnant by ending those days before there is no elect community left (Matt 24:22).[165] The hypothetical "if possible" in 24:24 (εἰ δυνατόν)[166] normally leaves open the chance that something may or may not happen (Matt 26:39; Acts 8:22; 20:16; 27:39; Rom 2:18; cf. Mark 9:23).[167] Morna Hooker ar-

---

163. E.g., 2 Tim 3:1–5; Jude 4; 2 Pet 2:1–22; 2 John 8–10; Rev 2:14, 20–22.

164. 2 Bar. 48.34; Apoc. Ab. 31.4–8; Apoc. El. 1.13–14; 4.15; Apoc. Dan. 9:10–16; T. Lev. 10.2; 16.3; T. Jud. 21.9; CD 5.20; 7.21; 4Q 339; 340; 2 Thess 2:9–11; Rev 13:11–14 16:13; 19:20; Herm. Mand. 11.1 [43]: cf. 1 Tim 4:1–3; 1 John 2:18–19; Did. 16.3.

165. Mark 13:20 stresses election by using τοὺς ἐκλεκτοὺς οὓς ἐξελέξατο. This may be a somewhat redundant way of emphasizing God's intervention, or it may be narrowing down a smaller group (οὓς ἐξελέξατο) among the elect (τοὺς ἐκλεκτούς). If the verse highlights physical death, the latter would make sense given that many in the community would be killed. If this is the case, then perhaps God has chosen a remnant among the elect community who will physically survive the tribulation period.

166. In Mark 13:22, Schreiner and Caneday, *Race Set before Us*, 159–60, argue that it is the false prophets who suppose the possibility of leading the elect astray: "Therefore, so far from suggesting possible apostasy of God's elect, Mark 13:22 actually affirms the opposite." But this view is unlikely given the repetitive warnings for the disciples to "beware" of apostasy and deception (cf. Mark 13:5, 9, 23, 33, 37). Likewise, the position is difficult to maintain in the parallel passage of Matt 24:24 because Jesus warns the disciples not to be mislead. He also affirms that many will fall away in the coming crisis (24:4, 10–12).

167. In the case of Matt 26:39/Mark 14:35, Jesus' prayer request is not granted by the Father; he still suffers on the cross. The negative result of εἰ δυνατόν in this case, however, is not really counter evidence. It can be adduced from the narrative that Jesus would not have earnestly made the request in the first place, spending hours doing so, if he did not believe in the possibility that things could have turned out differently for him.

gues that based on the "continual failures on the part of the twelve men whom Jesus has chosen, it is clear that he believes that such a thing *is* possible."[168] Perhaps more precisely, individuals from among the elect could be deceived and commit apostasy without the entire community itself falling away. In 24:22 the promise that the elect community will be preserved seems to relate primarily to deliverance from physical harm, and yet 24:9 affirms that some Christ-followers will be killed. It seems that the physical preservation of the community as a whole does not necessitate such protection for every individual.

Even so, 24:22 may include preservation to final salvation and access to God's heavenly kingdom. The corporate community in this case may be set in contrast against the singular "he/the one" (ὁ . . . οὗτος σωθήσεται) in 24:13. The elect community is promised an ultimate deliverance, but the Christian *individual* must endure until the end to be saved. God's care for the corporate elect, then, does not necessarily mean that every person within the community will be preserved from deception. Some in fact *will* be deceived and apostatize (24:10–12). Both the preservation of the corporate elect and the apostasy of the individual are affirmed without any apparent recognition of the tension between the two. In this manner the possibility of falling away from the community resembles the Deuternomistic tradition that stresses both Israel's election and yet repeatedly warns the people against apostasy (cf. Deut 32).[169]

It is possible that the persecution doublet in Matt 10:17–22 and 24:9–13, as well as other evidence that early Christians committed apostasy and betrayed one another (cf. Tactitus, *Annals* 15.44.4; *1 Clem.* 5; *Did.* 16.3–5), reflects the time of Nero's persecution in 64 CE.[170] Mark's gospel, which is situated in Rome, would seem to reflect this persecution especially well (see Mark above). On the other hand, because the Neronian persecutions took place in Rome, this does not account for the gospels' locating the coming conflict in or around Jerusalem. The coming tribulation in the Olivet discourse reflects some events related to the Jewish war with Rome in the late 60s CE (cf. Matt 24:1–3, 15–21; cf. Mark 13:14; Luke 21:20; Eusebius, *Hist. eccl.* 3.5.3). The Matthean community members, in any case, interpreted Matt 24 as culminating in the suppression of wickedness, the Messiah's return, and God establishing his dominion on earth. *Their community would seem to be affirmed*

---

168. Hooker, *Mark*, 317.

169. Alternatively speaking, the elect might refer to the Jewish people or Jewish Christian remnant, such as found in other apocalyptic messages (e.g. Rev 7, 12). But if so, this perspective would not seem to resolve the tension—the disciples whom Jesus warns in the discourse are themselves Jewish, and unless they are not part of the elect community, his prediction that some of his followers will be deceived, fall away, and killed in the upcoming tribulation pertains to them. At all events the responsibility of every Christ-follower to persevere and be watchful is mandated.

170. Cf. Taylor, "Love of Many," 352–57.

through the Olivet discourse—they belong to God's elect community even if they are experiencing estrangement from local synagogues. At the same time, they would be instructed through Jesus' warnings that their election provides no guarantee against personal apostasies. If Jesus predicted that many of his followers will fall away, then each of them must persevere if they are to be finally saved.

THE "WATCH" MOTIF: ESCHATOLOGICAL EXHORTATIONS TO BE PREPARED (24:4, 42–51; 25:1–10)

Jesus exhorts his disciples to be watchful and productive during the coming eschatological crisis (Matt 24:4; cf. 26:41; Mark 13:5, 9, 23, 33; Luke 21:8). The imperatival "watch"/"beware" often conveys a warning that, if not followed, results in the possibility of Christians being led astray or falling away into eschatological ruin.[171] The word βλέπετε stands out more prominently in Mark's gospel,[172] whereas Matthew's text favors using προσέχετε[173] and γρηγορεῖτε.[174] In the Olivet Discourse spiritual wakefulness will be necessary for the Christians who await Jesus' returns, and this idea exemplifies the stories related to Christ's coming as a Thief in the Night and the Ten Virgins (Matt 24:42–51; cf. Mark 13:33–37; Luke 12:34–40/ Matt 25:1–13; cf. Luke 12:35–36). Matthew's version of these stories adds that severe judgment awaits those who fail to watch.

The uncertainty in relation to the time of Jesus' return requires his followers to always be prepared for it. At that time a bifurcation will take place between faithful and unfaithful Christians (Matt 24:37–44), which is depicted again when Jesus contrasts the behavior of a servant who is left in charge of the master's home (24:45–51).[175] The servant may act in an unfaithful way, violating Jesus' love commandment by physically abusing fellow servants (cf. 22:37–41; 18:28–30) and getting drunk instead of staying alert (cf. Luke 21:34–36; 1 Thess 5:7; 1 Cor 6:10). The master's coming will take the servant by surprise and he will be punished severely with the hypocrites (Matt 24:48–51; cf. 8:12; 25:30). The Lukan parallel uses "unbelievers" rather than "hypocrites" (Luke 12:46). In the New Testament the former word is

---

171. Mark 8:15; 12:38; Luke 8:18; Acts 13:40–41; Gal 5:15; 1 Cor 10:12, 18; Phil 3:2; Heb 3:12; 12:25; 2 John 8; cf. 1 Pet 4:7; *Did.* 16; *Gos. Thom.* 21; Ign. *Eph.* 10; Irenaeus, *Haer.* 36.3.

172. Mark 4:24; 8:15; 12:38; 13:5, 9, 23, 33; cf. Matt 24:4.

173. Matt 7:15; 10:17; 16:6; cf. Luke 12:1; 20:46; 21:34; Acts 20:28.

174. Matt 24:42; 25:12; 26:38; cf. Mark 13:35; Acts 20:31; 1 Cor 16:13. Matthew's use of βλέπετε in 24:4 is perhaps borrowed from Mark or the same source as Mark (cf. Mark 13:5; Luke 21:8).

175. A stress is on the behavior of the *one* servant, who is called "that servant" (24:46, 48). He could decide to behave either faithfully or unfaithfully. There does not appear to be two different servants in the story. See further, Hultgren, *Parables of Jesus*, 162–63.

The Gospel of Matthew

used of those who suffer eschatological retribution and separation from God (Rom 11:20; Heb 3:12, 19; Rev 21:8). The latter in Matthew probably refers to Israel's religious leaders, who are repeatedly labeled as hypocrites (e.g., Matt 23:13–15, 23, 25, 27–29).[176] More specifically, punishment against the servant is described in terms of torture—he will be cut in two (Matt 24:51a; cf. 1 Sam 15:33; Sus 55–59; Heb 11:37).[177] His portion will be in the place where there is "weeping and gnashing of teeth" (Matt 24:51b), a phrase in Matthew representing hell (Matt 8:12; 13:42, 50; 22:13; 25:30; cf. Luke 13:28). The unprepared servant is the one who violates Jesus' law of love and practices vices such as drunkenness. That servant will be treated like an apostate and removed from God's kingdom. The implication behind the story is clear: *the unfaithful Christian servant will end up eschatologically condemned along with the religious leaders who oppose Jesus*. Through this message the disciples, and by extension *the Matthean community, are warned to be spiritually and morally ready for Jesus' return at that close of the age* (24:42, 44), or else suffer terrible consequences. Matthew's audience should therefore mimic the behavior of the faithful servant who works in his master's household and is loyal to what his lord commissions him to do.[178] Such a servant will be rewarded at the eschaton (Matt 24:45–47).

If the Thief in the Night story was originally given by Jesus to his disciples (24:43)[179] and perpetrated by Matthew's Jewish-Christian community, other adaptations are given primarily to Gentile-Christian audiences. Paul reaffirms to the Thessalonians a tradition they already knew—the Day of the Lord will come as a thief in the night (1 Thess 5:1–4).[180] When the world is saying "peace and safety" there will come upon them sudden destruction (5:3). Paul's congregation is encouraged to be sober instead of drunk and asleep like the outsiders (5:5–7). The notion of a society at peace prior its swift destruction recalls Jesus' words about people feasting and marrying, unaware of the coming flood in Noah's day (Matt 24:37–39). Unlike Paul, however, Matthew's text addresses the thief in the night not in relation to judgment that will fall upon an unbelieving society; rather it will fall on believers who

---

176. Matthew's term may have derived from the same word as unbeliever in Aramaic: cf. Marshall, *Luke*, 544.

177. See further, Str.B. 4.737–39; 4.739.

178. Relevant here is Strobel, *Untersuchungen*, who argues for the importance of the waiting motif from Hab 2:3–4, which influenced the early church in relation to their need to remain faithful and righteous during eschatological delay. Matthew may be operating under the assumption that "my lord delays his coming" shows the servant to be unfaithful, unlike the righteous person of Habakkuk who lives by faithfulness.

179. On the saying's authenticity see Hultgren, *Parables of Jesus*, 159–60.

180. On comparisons between the Little Apocalypse of the gospels and 1 Thess 4–5, see Hartman, *Prophecy Interpreted*, 178–205.

are not prepared for the second coming. Similar to Matthew, Rev 3:3 warns church members in Sardis against spiritual lethargy. If the Christians are not alert, the Lord will come upon them as a thief and they will not know what time he will arrive. Those in this church who have not "soiled" their garments will be clothed in white and not be blotted out of the book of life (Rev 3:4–5). In 2 Peter, knowledge about the Lord's return as a thief involves the destruction of earth's elements in preparation of a new heaven and earth. Such judgment ought to stir up the believers to live in holiness and godliness (2 Pet 3:10–14), and similar to Matt 24, they are warned to be on guard (φυλάσσω) so that they do not get led astray by lawless (ἄθεσμος) people (2 Pet 3:17; cf. Matt 24:4–5, 11–12).

The parable of the Ten Virgins also centers on the aspect of Christ-followers being ready for the *parousia*. On that day a division between wise and foolish maidens will take place. Five of the ten virgins fail to take oil for their lamps during the night, and when the bridegroom finally appears they need to purchase oil but do not make it back before the door is closed to the wedding feast (here again representing the messianic banquet: Matt 8:11–12; 26:29; Luke 14:15; 22:28–30). The burning lamps and oil may not have any deeper meaning apart from providing light for the virgins at night. Then again, they might be associated with the concepts of Jewish-Christian standards of the Law, or with good works (cf. Matt 5:14–16), or with righteousness, faithfulness, and life (cf. Prov 13:9; cf. 20:20; 24:20; Job 18:5–6).[181] The foolish virgins' lack of oil, in any case, makes the main point of the story: they were not prepared for the bridegroom when he finally arrived. The parable still seems to be governed by Jesus' Olivet Discourse and exhortation for his disciples to be prepared for his second coming (Matt 24:3, 42, 44). Hence, the foolish virgins point to unprepared Christian disciples. This is spelled out more clearly in the parallel passage in Luke even though no virgins are mentioned in this particular rendition (Luke 12:35–48).

These stories provide its Christian audience with warnings that reinforce ideas already learned from the "Little Apocalypse." *The disciples must be vigilant at all times and persevere until the end, not succumbing to the abundance of sin, loss of love, betraying attitudes, and false prophets characteristic of the age in which the tribulation occurs.* In short, they must not behave like an apostate or else they will suffer the fate of one. No doubt Christians in the Matthean community would have applied

---

181. See Manson, *Sayings of Jesus*, 244, for the first interpretation; Luz, *Matthew* 2.235, for the second; and Lövestam, *Spiritual Wakefulness*, 115–17, for the third. Incidentally, both the thief in the night saying and the ten virgins are set at night. Does this signify a period of much "darkness" or apostasy before Jesus' return? Another interpretation is that the night represents the present fallen age as distinguished from the age to come (Isa 21:11f; *Sifre Num.* 6:24; *Mekilta Exod.* 14:31; Rom 13:11–14; Gal 1:4; cf. Lövestam, 9f, 85–88). If the night has multiple meanings, perhaps an allegorical interpretation for the ten virgins is in order, and Luz's interpretation that relates the lamps to light may be accepted.

these teachings to themselves: they must be prepared for Jesus at his second coming, for a separation between wise and foolish Christ-followers is going to take place at that time, and only the wise, faithful believers will be able to feast at the messianic banquet.

JESUS' REJECTION OF APOSTATE CHRISTIANS ON JUDGMENT DAY (25:1–46; CF. 13:24–30, 36–43, 47–50)

Apart from those who will be judged for not being prepared at the *parousia*, other parables and stories in Matthew unrelated to the "watch" motif likewise depict judgment on emerging Christians. The parable of Wheat and Tares and the parable of the Net share in common an eschatological bifurcation that will take place when the Son of Man returns. They refer to the mixed nature of God's kingdom. The parable of the Talents is similar in this regard, and the final story of the Sheep and Goats portrays judgment day for all humanity. *These stories seem to affirm that unrighteous Christians will be among those who are sentenced to final judgment.*

The Wheat and Tares parable relates to the coming harvest (13:24–30, 36–43). At the end of time the wheat or "sons of the kingdom" will be gathered and separated from the tares or "sons of the evil one"; the latter will burned in a fiery furnace. The parable seems to speak primarily against Israel's religious leaders and their followers who oppose Jesus' kingdom message and who see themselves as God's elect community. In the final harvest they represent the tares that will be "uprooted" and rejected by God (cf. 15:8–13).[182] These leaders also seem depicted in parables about servants who lose their original standing due to their own unfaithfulness or negligence; they are judged and their benefits given to another (21:33–46 esp. v. 43; 22:1–14; cf. 21:28–32). These apparently are the ones who will be replaced by Gentile believers and will experience eschatological punishment even though they were originally "sons of the kingdom" (13:38–39, 42; cf. 8:11–12).[183] Because they reject Jesus' message, they are replaced by the followers of Jesus who seem to be identified as the sons of the kingdom (13:38). Nevertheless, in a secondary sense, this parable relates to Christians. The Matthean community would have interpreted God's kingdom to include the church, and as such the parable reflects the mixed nature of the church.[184]

---

182. Cf. Jeremias, *Parables of Jesus*, 61–62.

183. Allison and Davies, *Matthew*, 2.27, make the point that those who come from the east and west in Matt 8:11–12 are not Gentiles but Jews of the Diaspora. This is possibly true of the original *logion* (so Gregg, *Final Judgment Sayings*, 229–32), but in its Matthean form Jesus contrasts the Gentile centurion's faith as exceeding the faith in Israel (8:10), making it quite clear that Gentiles are meant to be the ones who come from east and west in 8:11.

184. On the idea of a mixed church in Matthew, see Smith, "Mixed State," 149–68.

In the Footsteps of Judas and Other Defectors

For them, not everyone who is outwardly part of the Christ-community belongs to Jesus or continues with him. The parable of the Net (13:47–50) reiterates this point by focusing on missionary activities with fisherman catching both good and bad fish. The fish probably represent all humanity ("every kind," 13:47). It portrays a mixed church at the end of time, with the angels separating the righteous from unrighteous and the unrighteous being cast into a fiery furnace.

The parable of the Talents (25:14–30) presents a separation between two servants who are faithful and one who is wicked and lazy. When the master returns, the first two are rewarded for being resourceful with the talents their master had given them before he went on a long journey. The third man buried his talent and is punished when his master returns (25:28–29). His talent is given to another, and he is then cast into outer darkness, a description of eschatological punishment (25:30; cf. 8:12; 13:42, 50; 24:51). Some suggestions about what the talent represents in this parable include natural abilities, spiritual gifts, spiritual knowledge, good works, or simply money.[185] Perhaps the meaning should not be narrowed down to one choice because it may be intending to convey everything that God entrusts to his servants. The fact that these are servants, and the servant represents Christians in 24:45–51, suggests that the term represents Christians here also.

This parable could function as a warning against immoral living in the early church; the *Gospel of the Nazoreans* has the servant using his master's resources on "harlots and flute girls" (frag. 18).[186] It might recall the Wicked Servant in Matt 24 who beats other servants and drinks with drunkards. The meaning of the parable, however, may be broader than this. The lazy servant is not condemned for immoral living but for negligence; he buries that which is entrusted to him. It is assumed in the parable that the faithful servants have produced good fruit with what they have been given, and for Matthew such productivity would seem to involve doing righteous deeds motivated by love (25:34–40; cf. 3:8–19; 13:8, 23–24, 26; 21:19, 24, 43). The gospel's stress on the concept of "doing" is seen here,[187] and this aspect is further attested in the next pericope on the Sheep and Goats. In Matthew, the Christians are to demonstrate their righteousness by moral living and loving service. Failure to do so could result in dire consequences when Jesus returns, as seen by the fate of the servant who is cast out of his master's household for burying his talent.

The Lukan parable of the Minas is related to this one, but it probably comes from a separate source or oral tradition (Luke 19:11–27). It also may be discussing the delay of God's kingdom, and in this story ten servants are each entrusted with

---

185. See various interpretations in Chenoweth, "Identifying the Talents," 61–72.
186. Schneelmelcher, *New Testament Apocrypha*, 1.161.
187. Cf. 7:21, 24, 26; 13:41; 16:27; 6:6–10; 10:14–15, 41–42; 19:16–21.

a mina and told by their master to do business until he returns. When the master returns, one of the servants did not invest his money. Unlike Matthew's parable, this unproductive servant is not cast out even though he is called "wicked" (i.e., disobedient). His mina is given to a more productive servant. Some scholars consider this to be an indication that the servant represents a Christian who loses eschatological rewards but still remains in the Lord's kingdom (cf. 1 Cor. 3:10–15).[188] This is possible, but we are not told about his final destination, unless his master's judgment implies this. The point of his sin seems related to Jesus' exhortation to take heed how one hears: if one does not put to practice the word of God, this would amount to disobedience and spiritual dullness, which will generate more of the same (Luke 19:26; cf. 8:18–21).[189] Matthew's parable, then, announces a more severe judgment than Luke's. The servant is cast into "outer darkness" where there is "weeping and gnashing of teeth" (Matt 25:30). Both images in Matthew depict punishment in hell (cf. 8:12; 22:13; 13:40, 50; 24:50). Negligence and spiritual dullness parallel the backslidden conditions of some of the churches in Asia Minor at the end of the first century (cf. Rev 2–3).

The story of the Sheep and Goats also addresses the final judgment, with Jesus as the Son of Man judging all the nations (Matt 25:31–46).[190] In this case the bifurcation is universal in scope including all the Gentiles or nations (πάντα τὰ ἔθνη 25:32). If we suggest that 25:31–46 refers to judgment on corporate nations rather than individuals, this may be too sweeping, especially if "the least of these brothers and sisters of mine" that are to be helped presumably live in the very nations that are judged. Do "all the nations" refer to all non-Christian Gentiles, Christian Gentiles, or something else? Elsewhere in Matthew πάντα τὰ ἔθνη refers to non-Christians (24:9, 14; 28:19) and it seems to mean this primarily here also. Yet the proximity of this story with the other passages directly related to Christ's followers in Matt 24–25 would seem to imply that such might be included in this judgment. Moreover, "all the nations" is used of Christ-followers in other places of the New Testament (Acts 15:17; Rom 15:11; 16:26; Rev 7:9–10). Hence, while the judgment related to the sheep and goats centers primarily on non-Christians, it may not necessarily preclude Christians. At very least the Matthean listeners would need to compare the conduct mentioned in this passage with their own.

188. See Danker, *Luke*, 309–10.

189. Luke's audience may have been left wondering about this individual's outcome and perhaps pondered on whether they and their leaders were "listening" appropriately and remaining faithful stewards of all that God had entrusted to them.

190. Problems arise when we compare this passage with other prophetic/apocalyptic texts in early Christian literature. For instance, a millennium seems to be mentioned before similar judgment takes place in Rev 20:11–15 (cf. 20:1–10), but no such timetable is found in Matt 25.

In the Footsteps of Judas and Other Defectors

Eternal life for the sheep and eternal punishment for the goats is based on their respective good treatment or neglect of those who are considered Jesus' brothers and sisters. We should probably refrain from classifying the sheep as Christians and goats as non-Christians—their entrance into or exclusion from the heavenly kingdom does not rest on their personal beliefs, nor on their following Jesus, but on their good works, which seem to exemplify Jesus' command to love one's neighbor as oneself (cf. Matt 22:39).[191] They inherit the kingdom because they feed the hungry, give drink to the thirsty, show hospitality to the stranger, clothe the naked, and visit the sick and imprisoned. In doing these things for Jesus' brothers and sisters, they have done it for Jesus (25:40).[192] The story of the Sheep and Goats thus presents us with the possibility that some non-Christians will be allowed entrance into the kingdom of heaven. The "least of these . . . brothers (and sisters)" probably identifies Christ's followers: they are considered both "little" and Jesus' spiritual siblings (12:48–50; 18:6, 10, 14; cf. 11:11).[193] Although this phrase stresses the treatment of Christians, it does not necessarily preclude non-Christians.[194] Perhaps, in a secondary sense, all needy and disenfranchised people are in view because loving one's neighbor includes proper treatment of all people, including foreigners, widows, orphans, and the poor (Matt 6:1–4; cf. Lev 19:33–34; Isa 58:6–7; 4 *Ezra* 2:20–23; Jas 2:15–17; 1 John 3:17–18). We are reminded of Paul's exhortation to the Galatians: "So then, as we have opportunity, let us do good to all people, and especially to those who are of the household of faith" (Gal 6:10). If this is the proper meaning for Matt 25:31–46, then this passage universalizes Jesus' command to "love your neighbor as yourself" (Matt 22:37–42; cf. 7:12; 19:19b), and to mistreat or neglect one's neighbor, whether Christian or non-Christian, constitutes violating Jesus' law of love. *This story turns out to be an ethical responsibility for all people, Christians and non-Christians, to love their neighbors; failure to do so may constitute eternal punishment.*

Apart from the potential influence of false prophets within the group, perhaps the Matthean community also had some members who were not following the moral precepts of Jesus. Such parables about judgment day and future condemnation of what seem to be "insiders" may have been used to clean house within the

---

191. For judgment according to works in Matthew, see 7:24–27; 11:16–17; 12:43–45; 13:24–30, 37–43, 47–50; 18:23–35; 20:1–16; 22:11–14; 24:42—26:30.

192. That the kingdom "has been prepared for you from the foundation of the world" (Matt 25:34) is not a reference to the sheep's predestination but to the kingdom's establishment: cf. Hultgren, *Parables of Jesus*, 314.

193. Oddly, "brothers and sisters" is missing from the parallel Matt 25:45.

194. Allison and Davies, *Matthew*, 3.429, challenge this phrase as referring to Christians on the basis that it is unrealistic to expect "all the nations" to have the opportunity to help out Christians. Some will never get a chance to meet a Christian.

community. The vigilant would be comforted to know that their faithfulness will be rewarded, imposters would be warned of future judgment that awaited them if they refused to repent, and those who were failing to keep the law of Christ might be scared back to a right standing once again.

CONCLUSION

It has been suggested in this chapter that the Matthean community, or more precisely communities, are predominantly Jewish Christ-followers who live in the late first century CE between Antioch and Galilee. Their conflict is with the leaders of the local synagogues. Perhaps they have broken away from the synagogues (cf. Matt 4:23; 9:35; 10:17; 12:9; 13:54), but this is not entirely clear of all Matthean Christ-followers in the area (cf. 23:1–3). They may be in the process of breaking away. Jesus' words about God revealing spiritual knowledge to the disciples and ordinary people while hiding it from scribes and Pharisees has become for them an apologetic for why these leaders and their followers are rejecting the kingdom message of Jesus (cf. 11:27–30). Similar to demonized people who have been cleansed by exorcism but then fall back to become seven times worse, the religious leaders, especially the Pharisees, have hardened their hearts to the point blaspheming the Spirit (12:22–32, 43–45).

Similar to Mark's gospel, the crowd is obdurate also and must be taught in parables in Matthew; but unlike Mark, their callousness is more an effect of their *own* doing than a judgment from God (13:13–15). The disciples of Jesus, on the other hand, are blessed with spiritual insight and are given special authority from Jesus (13:16–17; 18:15–20). Their responsibility to both watch over the "sheep" of Israel and ostracize rebellious church members perhaps served as legitimation for the authority of the Matthean community's leaders as perpetrators of Jesus' teachings. They also have a responsibility to make sure they do not despise the weaker members of the church. A mindset of self-importance, exaltation, and neglect of members not only might cause a leader to be rejected from the heavenly kingdom, but such an attitude can cause "little ones" in the church to fall away (18:1–14). If parables such as those of the Wheat and Tares, the Net, the Wedding Banquet, and Talents speak to the community, they suggest that Matthew's group is a mixed church with faithful and unfaithful members (cf. 13; 22:1–14; 25). Unloving behavior and negligence are seen as dangers that can threaten the spiritual well-being of the members. As well, the community may have been influenced by false prophets who use Jesus' name but do not belong to him. They are antinomians and the community will again encounter an increasing amount of these imposters as the eschaton comes to a close (7:15–23; 24:11, 24).

In terms of beliefs and practices, it appears that the community honors Jesus as the messianic son of David and the fulfillment of the coming Isaianic Servant. The members see themselves as Jewish and interpret keeping the Torah as keeping Jesus' words, which involves, among many other things, keeping his teachings from the Sermon on the Mount and loving their neighbors as themselves (Matt 5–7). For the disciples of Jesus, doing righteous deeds involves doing God's will, which is inextricably bound up with following Jesus' teachings on the Law. To violate Jesus' commands is to be excluded from the heavenly kingdom (e.g., 5:17–20; cf. 7:12, 23; 22:36-40). The primary way to apostasy, then, is by violating Jesus' interpretation of the Law. The disciples are warned not to lose their "saltiness" or righteous deeds, which act as a witness to outsiders, or they will be punished. They are instructed that being angry at one's brother or sister is tantamount to murder, and lusting is equated with adultery. Both sins can lead to *Gehenna*. The way they judge others and withhold forgiveness will be reciprocated back to them on judgment day, and not bearing righteous fruit or doing God's will might lead to Jesus denying that he knows them. They must therefore put to practice the words of Jesus, pray to be spared from temptation, and they must strive to walk the narrow path of righteousness; the broad way leads to eschatological destruction. The false prophets who perform miracles in Jesus' name are prime examples of those who have chosen the wrong path.

In the Olivet Discourse, such prophets will lead astray many Christians, and lawlessness will abound with believers hating one another. God will spare the elect community from complete annihilation, but even so, many individuals will commit apostasy (24:10-13, 22-26). Their election as a community does not guarantee their final salvation as individuals. Likewise, vices such as drunkenness and adultery lead to condemnation, and so the Christ-followers must watch and be prepared for Jesus' return, lest they be caught doing lawless deeds (24:42–51; cf. 5:28-30; 18:8-9). Persecution can also lead to apostasy, and so it behooves the faithful to continue confessing Christ before others and be ready for martyrdom. To save one's mortal life is to lose eternal life, and to deny Christ will be reciprocated be Christ denying them on judgment day (10:32–39; 16:24–27). They must not be like a builder whose house is established on sand and is destroyed by winds and floods, and they must not resemble the second seed/soil in the parable of the Sower, which falls away in times of persecution (7:24–28; 13:5–6, 20–21).

The consequences for violating Jesus' law and committing apostasy are legion in Matthew, but most can be broken down to the apostate being rejected by Christ on judgment day and denied access to the fully realized heavenly kingdom. Apostates, false prophets, and the wicked world that creates stumbling blocks for believers will suffer in *Gehenna* and "outer darkness" (e.g., 5:19–20, 22, 29–30, 7:21–23; 10:28; 18:9; 22:12–13; 25:30). There is a possibility for restoration of the apostate, however, which is depicted by God compassion for the lost sheep that goes astray (18:12–14). As well, Peter and the disciples' restoration after forsaking Christ at his arrest is more pronounced in Matthew than in Mark. Even Judas shows remorse for betraying Christ, unlike the recalcitrant character we find in Mark (Matt 27:1–5; cf. 26:24). His final destiny, however, remains ambiguous in Matthew.

3

Luke-Acts

Perseverance and Temptation among Jews and Gentiles in the Plan of God

The author of the third gospel and Acts is not named in these writings, but the traditional view is that Luke, physician and companion of Paul, wrote the two volumes.[1] The "we" passages in Acts are said to affirm his travels with Paul.[2] These passages probably do suggest a first-person witness who travelled with Paul, and even though that person is not identified, the author may be including himself in the narrative. We notice also the "us" in the prologue of Luke (1:1–4). While scholars continue to debate the author's identity, there is no compelling reason for us to reject the author of the third gospel and Acts as Luke.[3] His authorship will be assumed here and also that his two-volume work can be read together as Luke-Acts.[4] Since he is not listed with Paul's colleagues who are circumcised (Col 4:11), some suggest that Luke is a non-Jew. It can be surmised, however, that as a companion of Paul in the

---

1. Muratorian Canon; P⁷⁵ [Luke 24:53: "ευαγγελιον κατα λουκαν"]; Irenaeus, *Haer.* 3.1.1; 3.14.1; Tertullian, *Marc.* 4; Eusebius, *Hist. eccl.* 5.8.3. Apart from the "we" passages in Acts, in the NT see Luke in Col 4:14; Phlm 24; 2 Tim 4:11. For references to the church fathers, see further Barrett, *Acts*, 1.30–48.

2. Acts 16:10–17; 20:5–15; 21:1–18; 27:1–28:16; cf. 11:28 (D, cop^G67, it^P); Irenaeus *Her* 3.14.1. Other suggestions for the "we" passages include that the author uses different source material at these points or the passages affirm typical sea voyage narratives. For various viewpoints see Wehnert, *Wir-Passagen*; Fitzmyer, *Acts*, 98–103; Schneider, *Apostelgeschichte*, 1.89–95.

3. For further support on the traditional authorship, see Fitzmyer, *Luke* 1.35–53. For problems with Lukan authorship, see e.g., Haenchen, *Acts*; Vielhauer, "Paulinism of Acts," 33–50.

4. A majority of scholars affirm some unity between Luke and Acts, but for dissenters, see esp. Parsons and Pervo, *Rethinking the Unity of Luke-Acts*. See scholarly discussion in Bird, "Unity of Luke-Acts," 425–48.

"we" narratives, he is to be included as one of the "Jews" who are reportedly causing trouble in Philippi (Acts 16:20). If a Gentile, he seems extremely competent in the Septuagint scriptures; if a Jew, he seems unfamiliar with some Jewish customs (e.g., Luke 2:22/Lev 12:6).[5] If the second-century document "Prologue to the Gospel" is correct in claiming Luke as a Syrian from Antioch (cf. also Jerome's preface to his *Commentary on Matthew*), then Joseph Fitzmyer would be on target by identifying this author as a non-Jewish Semite and native of Antioch.[6] In Acts, however, Luke appears to join Paul's team in Troas of Asia Minor (Acts 16:8, 10–11; cf. 20:5), not in Antioch of Syria, which is perhaps where we would expect him to join Paul, or at least return with Paul, since this is the city where the apostle begins and ends this mission (Acts 15:35–36; 18:22). Our tentative guess is that he is either a Gentile or Hellenistic Jew and wrote these volumes somewhere between 70 and 90 CE.[7]

A LUKAN COMMUNITY?

There is not much we can discover about a community behind Luke-Acts.[8] Luke does not address a provenance directly. He may have written his works somewhere in Achaia ("Prologue to the Gospel"), but there does not seem to be strong internal evidence that points to this option. Other possibilities raised by scholars include Rome, Caesarea, Decapolis, Ephesus, or a region of Asia Minor.[9] If Luke relies heavily on Q, should we not also attempt to determine the community behind this source? Such an endeavor may be too speculative for our purposes.[10] What can be affirmed more securely about Luke's volumes is that they are addressed to "Theophilus" (Luke 1:1–4; Acts 1:1–3), who is doubtless a historical rather than symbolic or abstract figure.[11] That Luke attributes to him the term "most excellent" (κράτιστος) suggests Theophilus is an official of some sort; the same word is used to honor Gentile gover-

---

5. On the latter point, see Shellard, *New Light on Luke*, 45–51.

6. Fitzmyer, *Luke*, 1.38–47.

7. Cf. Kümmel, *Introduction*, 151. Paul's death in the 60s CE may be hinted at in Acts 20:25 and the fall of Jerusalem in Luke 13:35; 19:41–44; 21:6, 20–24; 23:29–31. Likewise if Mark is one of Luke's sources (cf. Luke 1:1–2) and the former was written in the mid to late 60s, then Luke must have been written later.

8. For problems on determining the Lukan community, see further Allison, "Was There a 'Lukan Community?,'" 62–70; Johnson, "Finding the Lukan Community," 1.87–100; Bauckham, "For Whom Were Gospels Written?," 9–48.

9. See Kümmel, *Introduction*, 151, for scholars who support these views.

10. Some scholars nonetheless attempt such pursuits for the Q community. Prominent options include Galilee (Kloppenborg, *Excavating Q*, 214–61); Jerusalem (Frenschkowski, "Galiläa oder Jerusalem?," 535–59); and Antioch or Jerusalem (Pearson, "Q Community in Galilee?," 476–94).

11. See Bovon, *L'Évangile Luc* 1.28.

nors such as Felix and Festus (Luke 1:3; cf. Acts 23:26; 24:3; 26:25; Josephus, *Ag. Ap.* 1). It is not known whether this man was a Greek or Roman convert, non-Christian, Luke's patron for these books, or some prominent Gentile proselyte of Judaism who came out of the synagogue.[12] Perhaps he was an uncircumcised God-fearer[13] familiar with formative Judaism and was either falsely or insufficiently informed (κατηχέω) about the Christians (Luke 1:4).[14] If so, then possibly some Jewish opponents of the emergent Christian faith informed him that Christ-followers were apostates.[15] Luke's task may have been to provide him a more accurate account of Jesus and the earliest Christian movement (1:4; cf. Acts 18:25–26; 21:21, 24). Along these lines or in addition to them, Luke's writings might be an exercise in legitimation for a relatively new movement that claims ancient promises from Israel's scriptures.[16] In a broad sense Luke-Acts shows Theophilus how the gospel message spread from its Palestinian origins to other parts of the world and how the Christian mission spread from Jews to Gentiles (e.g., Acts 1:8).

Vernon Robbins correctly suggests that by addressing the inscribed reader (Theophilus) as "most excellent," the inscribed author (Luke) adopts a position subordinate to his communicant. The author is "near the artisan class" and takes on the "social posture of communicating upwards in the social order rather than downward to artisans or peasants."[17] What we can surmise, then, is that the designated reader of Luke-Acts is a socially upper-class Gentile. Beyond this, if Luke's gospel was circulated to various Christian communities,[18] then his audience would doubtless include Christian recipients and perhaps the God-fearers they wished to reach in their respective communities.

12. Cf. Kümmel, *Introduction*, 130.

13. Here I understand "God-fearer" or σεβόμενοι τὸν θεόν as "a term applied to former polytheists who accepted the ethical monotheism of Israel and attended the synagogue, but who did not obligate themselves to keep the whole Mosaic law; in particular, the males did not submit to circumcision" (BDAG, 918). Cf. Acts 10:22; 17:4, 17.

14. The word κατηχέω (to "sound over" or "sound through": LSJ, 927) may be understood in Luke 1:4 either as being informed/ receiving news about something or being taught, possibly in reference to elementary religious instruction such as baptism (cf. 1 Cor 14:19; Gal 6:6; *2 Clem.* 17.1; Schürmann, *Lukasevangelium*, 1.15). Its other occurrences in Luke-Acts suggest the persons are informed insufficiently (Acts 18:25–26) or falsely (Acts 21:21, 24) about Christians. In these cases, as well as in Luke 1:4, there may be a need to correct or provide additional information.

15. Cf. Nolland, *Luke* 1.xxxii–xxxiii, who considers Theophilus a God-fearer and "outsider" (contrast "us" in Luke 1:1, 2) who may have been informed that the emergent Christian faith was a "dangerous perversion" of the Jewish heritage.

16. On Luke and legitimization, see Esler, *Community and Gospel*, 16–23.

17. Robbins, "Social Location," 323 cf. 311, 321–22.

18. On early Christian circulation, see e.g., Col 4:16; *Herm. Vis.* 2.4.3; Burridge, "About People," 135; Talbert, *Reading Luke*, 3.

Luke adds to his narrative a surplus of passages favoring the poor over the rich. The inclusion of parables such as that of the Rich Fool (Luke 12:13–21; cf. 12:22–34), the Dinner Banquet (Luke 14:15–24; cf. 14:33), the Rich Man and Lazarus (Luke 16:19–31), as well as the story of the rich young ruler (Luke 18:18–29), the woe sayings against the rich (Luke 6:24–26), the condemnations of Ananias and Sapphira (Acts 5) and Simon Magus (Acts 8) all seem to function at least partially as warnings against the wealthier sectors of his audience. Fitzmyer is instructive here: "Obviously, he [Luke] is not satisfied with what he has seen of the Christian use of wealth in his ecclesial community and makes use of sayings of Jesus to correct attitudes within it."[19] The repetitive stories of rich people missing out on salvation may have shocked wealthy Christians (Luke 12:13–21; 16:19–31; 18:18–25).[20] To assist in countering a materialistic trend among the recipients, Luke includes stories about wealthy individuals who give away their possessions such as Zaccheus (Luke 19:1–10), Barnabbas, and believers in Jerusalem who share all things in common (Acts 2:44–45; 4:32–37). Moreover, the cost of discipleship in Luke's gospel includes not only placing Jesus and his kingdom before family and possessions but also selling all that one has and following him (Luke 14:25–33; cf. 3:11; 5:11, 28). The Lukan Paul cites a unique saying attributed to Jesus: "it is more blessed to give than to receive" (Acts 20:33–35). The personal message to Luke's audience behind these passages seems clear—they must give of their possessions generously for the sake of Christ and his church.

It is commonly suggested that the recipients of Luke's gospel are Gentiles rather than Jews; the latter might have considered Paul's turn to the Gentiles in Acts 28 to be quite unsettling, and Luke omits some Jewish elements included in the other gospels.[21] As well, Luke presents Rome and Romans in a somewhat irenic light. Paul claims Roman citizenship, for instance, and Romans deliver him from persecution (Acts 18:15; 19:37–41; 21:35; 23:16–31; 22:28; 25:16). The Romans, however, are not always portrayed favorably (cf. Luke 13:1; 23:12; Acts 4:27; 18:17; 24:26).[22] Luke's excessive use of Israel's scriptures (see below) would have to appeal to an audience familiar with such traditions, and so it cannot be ruled out that Jews or Jewish Christians from the Diaspora would have also read his works. The Lukan "community," then, is perhaps best described as an audience from a wide variety of

19. Fitzmyer, *Luke*, 1.247.

20. Cf. Pilgrim, *Good News to the Poor*; Horn, *Glaube und Handeln*; Rohrbaugh, "Pre-Industrial City," 137–47.

21. See lists of supporters in Schnelle, *Einleitung*, 244; Brown, *Introduction*, 269–71. Differently, a Jewish Christian community is proposed by Tiede, *Prophecy and History*.

22. For a pro-Roman position, see Shellard, *New Light on Luke*, 37–41. For the converse, see Cassidy, *Jesus, Politics and Society*.

communities and churches in the late first century that included people from the upper echelons, Gentiles, God-fearers, possibly Jews, and even some officials and former aristocrats like Theophilus, Manaen, and others (Luke 1:3; cf. Acts 13:1; 17:4, 12).[23] Indeed, Luke writes to mixed communities.[24] *If such wide readership is in view, then it may not be best for us to talk about a Lukan "community"; "audience" is a more appropriate term.* For Theophilus, and by extension a much larger audience, Luke validates the events and claims of Jesus and his followers by showing how they fulfill or relate to Israel's scriptural tradition (Luke 1:1: "the things that have been accomplished among us"), and such validation would not only confirm believers and refute the claims of opponents (apologetics) but would also serve to convert unbelievers (evangelistic).[25] If the inscribed reader is a God-fearer, and the extended audiences are primarily Christians, then Luke-Acts would seem to provide multiple functions including didactic, apologetic, and missionary-evangelistic purposes.[26] To this we may add even a pastoral purpose: in light of the many who reject the Christian message, Luke-Acts served to encourage its audience to persevere in faith.[27]

ECHOES OF THE PROPHETS AND THE GENTILE MISSION

Luke-Acts is filled with citations and allusions to Israel's scriptures. These scriptures inundate the two volumes and are assumed in the prologue by the "things accomplished" (Luke 1:1). The scripture are echoed in the infancy narratives (Luke 1–2), inform the audience about Jesus' calling (Luke 3–4), are interpreted to the disciples by the resurrected Jesus (Luke 24), cited by the early Christian witnesses (Acts 1–2), and used to justify the mission to Gentiles (Acts 13, 28). Luke uses the scripture not only with a christological focus, but also stresses theocentric, ecclesiocentric, and eschatological foci.[28] To be sure, the third gospel functions as a type of ancient biography about Jesus, and certain scriptures are intended to point to him; but as a whole, Luke-Acts also shows how God's people embrace not only repentant Israel but also believing Gentiles. Moreover, this inclusion of another people involves the

---

23. With Tannehill, *Luke*, 24.

24. On the mixed community in Luke-Acts, see Esler, *Community and Gospel in Luke-Acts*, esp. 220–23; Shellard, *New Light on Luke*, 55.

25. Talbert, *Reading Acts*, 224–25, 269, gives examples from the ancient Mediterranean world showing the common belief that prophetic fulfillment brings validation (e.g., Deut 28/2 Kings; Josephus, *Ant.* 2.16.5[333]; 10.11.7[278–81]; Lucian, *Alex.*; Apuleius, *Metam.* 11.7, 13).

26. For other interpretations, see in Powell, *Saying about Acts*, 13–20, 114.

27. See, e.g., Brown, *Apostasy and Perseverance*; Bock, "Luke," 351, 371.

28. E.g., Steyn, *Septuagint Quotations*, 237; Litwak, *Echoes of Scripture*, 34, 202; Brawley, *Text to Text*.

fulfillment of a salvific plan that God intended long ago when he spoke of it through the prophets.[29]

Similar to the other gospels, Luke-Acts most frequently cites or alludes to Isaiah. Luke cites Isaiah at key intervals throughout his two volumes, often using a text similar to the Septuagint.[30] In the synagogue Jesus quotes from Isaiah at the beginning of his ministry, affirming himself as the prophetic fulfillment of the "anointed" Servant of God (Luke 4:14–30/Isa 61:1–2; cf. Isa 42:1; 58:6; Ps 2:7).[31] In relation to this passage, major themes in Luke-Acts include endowment by God's Spirit, Jesus as the Christ or the "anointed" one, the preaching of the gospel, and the Christ's/Christian ministry of doing good and healing.[32] A mission to the Gentiles is also clearly implied here.[33] To this we might add that Jesus did not fulfill the mission to the Gentiles except through his followers in Acts,[34] and this argues rather pointedly that Luke 4:14–30 serves as a central pericope for the entire corpus of Luke-Acts.[35] Jesus, Peter, and Paul all exemplify a pattern of God's special servant who is full of the Spirit and proclaims the good news to God's people while releasing the oppressed from infirmities (Luke 5:17–19; 6:17–19; 9:11; Acts 5:14–15; Acts 14:8–11; 19:11–12). They declare God's appointed time of salvation has arrived,[36] and this time includes or implies the salvation of Gentiles (Luke 4:23–30 cf. 2:27–32; Acts 15:7; 13:46–48; 26:17, 20).[37]

Jesus mentions the prophets Elijah and Elisha as ministers to non-Israelites,[38] and throughout Luke-Acts both the Messiah and his followers continually mimic the Elijah/Elisha narratives.[39] What is significant for our purposes is that the ministry of these prophets point to God's turning away from Israel to other nations due to Northern Israel's apostasy, especially through the house of Ahab (e.g., 1 Kgs 18–19). As Israel has become apostate in the Elijah/Elisha narratives, so *Luke considers*

---

29. See further Bovon, *Luke the Theologian*, 87–121, 525–31.

30. See, e.g., Sawyer, *Fifth Gospel*, 26–28; Holz, *Untersuchungen*; Koet, "Isaiah in Luke-Acts," 79–100.

31. For the Messiah-Servant as Luke's christological emphasis, see Strauss, *Davidic Messiah*; Pao, *Isaianic New Exodus*.

32. Cf. Seccombe, "Luke and Isaiah," 252–59.

33. Even before this passage, however, this mission appears in Luke 1:78–79; 2:28–32; 3:6.

34. Acts 1:8; 2:39; 9:15; 11:18; 15:1–21; 22:15; 26:17–18.

35. In agreement with Cosgrove, "Divine DEI," 179; Tannehill, "Mission of Jesus," 72–73. On the Gentile mission related to Luke 4, see Tannehill, *Narrative Unity*, 1.71; Wilson, *Gentile Mission*, 40–41.

36. Luke 4:19; Acts 2:14–17; 3:19–21; 13:46–48 cf. Isa 49:6–8.

37. For the continuity of this salvific time between Luke and Acts, see in Talbert, "Shifting Sands," 381–95, esp. 386; *pace* Conzelmann, *Theology of St. Luke*.

38. Luke 4:24–27; cf. 1 Kgs 17—2 Kgs 13.

39. E.g., Luke 4:1–13/1 Kgs 19:8; Luke 9:10–17/1 Kgs 17:1–16; cf. 2 Kgs 4; Acts 8:5, 26–40; 9:29–30, 32; 16:6–8/1 Kgs 18:46; 19:4; 2 Kgs 2. See further Brodie, "Luke the Literary Interpreter."

In the Footsteps of Judas and Other Defectors

Israel's rejection of the message of Jesus and his followers to be an indication of its spiritual obduracy and grounds for why the Christian mission turned towards the Gentiles.

FULFILLMENT AND NECESSITY IN THE PLAN OF GOD (LUKE 1:1–4; ACTS 2:23; 4:28)

Luke writes that certain events (πρᾶγμα) had been accomplished among them (Luke 1:1–4). These events include the life, death, and resurrection of Jesus as well as the things recorded in Acts that are seen as fulfilling and relating to Israel's tradition-history. John Squires is correct in affirming that the key events related to God's plan (βουλή) in Luke-Acts focus on the passion of Christ and mission related to Gentiles (Luke 7:30; Acts 2:23; 4:28; 5:38; 13:36; 20:27).[40] This plan involves the things that "God has done" in relation to fulfilling his divine purpose,[41] taking initiative in saving those who believe or call on him,[42] calling and choosing various individuals to ministry,[43] and calling/choosing Israel and the Gentiles.[44] The Lukan concept of this divine plan may be traced back at least to Isaiah where the theme is prevalent in new exodus contexts.[45] The importance of prophetic fulfillment can be seen through the calling of Jesus based on Isa 61:1–2/Luke 4:21 and his suffering that is inadvertently fulfilled by those in Jerusalem who have him killed (Luke 9:31; Acts 3:18; 13:27–33). It was the purpose of God to have Jesus killed and raised from the dead, in accordance with prophetic tradition (Luke 22:22; 24:25–27; Acts 2:23–24; 3:17–21; 4:25–28; 10:36–43; cf. 17:30–31). The Isaianic Servant plays a prominent role in this regard.[46] The human figures in both Isa 40–55 and 61 possess God's Spirit and are sent by God to release captives and heal the blind,[47] but there are dissimilarities between these figures also.[48] Luke, in any case, understands both figures to be pointing to Jesus, perhaps with Isa 61 stressing Jesus' early ministry (Luke 4:14–30/Isa 61) and Isaiah 52–53 emphasizing his suffering and death. Both aspects were part of God's salvific plan that is carried on by those who follow Jesus and imitate his Spirit-anointed ministry and suffering. Squires adds that "Luke insists on the inevi-

---

40. Squires, *Plan of God*, 76–77, 186.
41. Acts 2:22–23, 33; 5:38–39; 15:4; cf. 18:21; 20:22–23; 21:14.
42. Acts 2:39, 47; 9:1–19; 10:1–6; 11:15–18; 16:14.
43. Acts 1:24; 9:15; 10:41; 15:7, 22, 25; 22:14; 26:17–18.
44. Acts 11:18; 13:17, 46–48; 15:4, 7.
45. Isa 40:5, 21; 44:26; 45:21; 46:10–11; 55:7–8; cf. 5:19; 14:26; 19:3–17; 25:1; 34:16–17.
46. Isa 52:13–53:12/cf. Acts 8:30–35; Luke 18:31–33; 22:37; Acts 3:14, 18, 26; 7:52; 10:43; 22:14. See further, Sawyer, *Fifth Gospel*, 23.
47. Isa 40:2; 42:1, 7; 48:16; 49:8; 61:1–2.
48. For both, see Beuken, "Servant and Herald," 411–41.

tability of Jesus' preaching, traveling, betrayal, suffering, death, resurrection, return and judgment, as necessary elements in the plan of God."[49]

A brief survey of divine necessity or "must," identified as δεῖ in Luke-Acts, renders further insight on God's plan. God's timing is fixed and requires the necessity of certain events to take place (Luke 21:9; Acts 1:7[τίθημι]; cf. 17:31), and Christ must remain in heaven until the restoration of the time announced by the prophets (Acts 3:21). Charles Cosgrove perceives that not only does God's plan accomplish what God wills but God also dynamically intervenes in history at appropriate times (e.g., Acts 4:28–30; 11:21).[50] Both Jesus' ministry and passion are portrayed as *necessary* events. Jesus needs to be in his father's house and proclaim the good news of the kingdom (Luke 2:49; 4:43), and it is imperative for him to suffer and be raised again (Luke 9:22; 13:33; 17:25; 22:7, 22[ὁρίζω], 37; 24:7, 26; Acts 17:3). The ideas of necessity and prophetic fulfillment play prominently in Luke 24 when Jesus meets his disciples after his resurrection. He expounds to them through Moses, the Prophets, and Psalms how it was necessary that everything written about him must be fulfilled (24:44), which would seem to include his suffering, resurrection, the forgiveness of sins, and proclamation to the nations/Gentiles (Luke 24:26, 44–47; cf. Acts 10:43; 26:22–23). The necessity of Christ's suffering is carried over into the proclamations of the early believers such as Peter and Paul.[51] Paul's own calling involves a necessary suffering for the sake of Christ (Acts 9:6, 16; 22:10[τάσσω]; cf. 14:22). This calling eventually results in his imprisonment, and yet it is divine necessity that allows Paul to reach Rome despite death threats, shipwreck, and a poisonous snakebite (Acts 19:21; 23:11–22; 25:10; 27:23–26). God wants him there and God will make sure he gets there!

For Luke, the major events related to Jesus and his early followers are ordained by God to take place, and they could be found beforehand in Israel's scriptures (e.g., Luke 4:17–21; 24:27, 44–48; Acts 2:17–23; 15:13–19). Divine purpose makes it inevitable that the Gentiles be included as God's people (Luke 24:47). Whether through prediction or intervention, God's saving purpose would seem to preclude ultimate failure. *Even apostasy, which might be seen as a foil to God's plan, is incorporated into it. The Lukan Jesus affirms that apostasy is inevitable—it must take place* (Luke 17:1a: ἀνένδεκτόν ἐστιν τοῦ τὰ σκάνδαλα μὴ ἐλθεῖν). *But this will not prevent God*

---

49. Squires, *Plan of God*, 173.

50. Cosgrove, "Divine DEI," 184–85. Talbert, *Reading Acts*, xv–xvi, 219, shows that in antiquity the idea of divine necessity controlling the path of human history was widely believed: e.g., Polybius, *Histories* 1.35–36; 1.4.1–2; Josephus, *Ant.* 10.8.2–3[142].

51. Acts 2:22–24 cf. 36 (ὁρίζω, πρόγνωσις); 3:18(προκαταγγέλλω); 4:28(προορίζω); 7:52 (προκαταγγέλλω); 10:38–42(ὁρίζω, προχειροτονέω); 17:3.

from spreading his word to the "end of the earth" through his saints. In fact, obduracy and apostasy ultimately help increase the word, whether through Peter's strengthened leadership after his denial of Christ, Matthias replacing Judas, persecution that forces believers to go to different cities, or the obduracy of Jews that paves the way for more Gentiles to hear the message. Even so, if apostasy is inevitable, this does not nullify human responsibility (Luke 17:1b). Those who cause others to fall away will be severely punished by God, and it behooves every disciple to take heed against σκάνδαλον, lest they become its prey (Luke 17:1b–3).

SPIRITUAL OBDURACY, UNBELIEVING JEWS, AND THE ACCEPTANCE OF GENTILES (LUKE 8:10; ACTS 28:17–23; CF. ACTS 13:14–50)

Luke cites Isa 6:10–11 twice, once in his gospel and again at the end of Acts. In Luke 8:10 spiritual obduracy is less prominent than in the parallels of Mark and Matthew. He has Jesus quoting a shorter rendition of Isaiah to his disciples regarding those who are not part of their group. The ambiguous "the rest" (τοῖς λοιποῖς) identifies those who cannot see or hear spiritually. Unlike Mark (cf. Mark 4:11), Luke may be playing down the contrast between insiders and outsiders at this point because such a thought stands in tension with the universality of his message that is to be proclaimed to all.[52] If so, this mood changes by the end of Acts. Luke has Paul cite a longer version of Isa 6:10–11 as the grand finale of his two volumes. As a prisoner Paul finally reaches Rome and states his innocence to the leaders from among his people (Acts 28:17–23).[53] He presents to them the good news of Jesus and the kingdom through Israel's scriptures (28:23; cf. Luke 24:27, 44), and some of them are persuaded by his message while others do not believe. In the end a division among the Jews in Rome breaks forth as a result of Paul's teaching (28:24).[54] Their unbelief prompts Paul to claim that "rightly the Holy Spirit spoke through Isaiah the prophet to your fathers" (28:25), and then he cites Isa 6:9–10 (LXX) in Acts 28:26–27.[55]

He then declares that salvation has been sent to the Gentiles, because they too will listen (Acts 28:28/Isa 40:5).[56] It becomes evident that spiritual callousness ac-

---

52. See Gnilka, *Verstockung Israels*, 124.

53. Cf. Jervell, "Paulus," 176–81.

54. The imperfect verbs in this passage may be read that some "were being persuaded" (ἐπείθοντο) while others "were disbelieving" (ἠπίστουν). Acts 5:36–37 uses the same imperfect construction to affirm true followers of Theudas and Judas.

55. His quote follows the Septuagint almost verbatim, but on the minor differences, see Steyn, *Septuagint*, 224–25. On differences between Luke's quote and parallels in Matthew and Mark, see Evans, *See and Not Perceive*, 115–16.

56. Litwak, *Echoes of Scripture*, 191–97, is probably correct when saying that "salvation of God" in

counts for the unbelief of these Jewish leaders and others who oppose the word of God.[57] In Luke-Acts, unlike Mark's gospel, spiritual blindness does not appear to be directly caused by God. In keeping with the Septuagint version, the Luke's citation of Isa 6 stresses personal responsibility of the hearers in relation to their own obduracy. The people are blind and dull of hearing, and they shut (ἐκάμμυσαν) their own eyes (or the eyes "shut themselves").[58] No doubt, the text is suggesting that the blindness of the Israelites mentioned in Isaiah correlate to the stubbornness of the Jews in Rome who reject Paul's message. A similar phenomenon occurs when Paul preaches in a synagogue in Ephesus. Some were hardening themselves and becoming disobedient, speaking against the Way (Acts 19:8–9). The imperfect middle voice of "harden" (ἐσκληρύνοντο) most likely refers to their responsibility of gradually hardening themselves.[59] Hence, in Luke-Acts responsibility for Israel's unbelief rests on the hearers who reject God's word; it does not appear to center on God's direct activity.

Even though the plan of God will not fail, and God initiates invitations to his kingdom, Israel and unbelievers are free to reject those invitations.[60] This perspective is confirmed by at least several other examples in Luke-Acts. In the parable of the Great Feast, those who were originally invited made up excuses not to come to the feast, and so new guests were invited instead (Luke 14:15–24). The parable seems directed primarily at Jewish leaders who were refusing Jesus' invitation of the kingdom (cf. 14:1, 15). They would not taste of the eschatological messianic banquet if they persisted in rejecting him. In the parable of the Prodigal Son, the older son

---

Acts 28:2 echoes Isa 40:5, which affirms that "all" (Gentiles included) will see the salvation of God (cf. Isa 49:6).

57. E.g., see the Jewish Hellenistic false prophet who opposes Paul in Acts 13:8–11. Here even though his blindness is physical, there may be a metaphorical meaning implied.

58. Cf. Barrett, *Acts*, 2.1245–46. Notice Evans, *See and Not Perceive*, 118, on Luke 8:"the disciples of Jesus receive full disclosure of the details pertaining to the kingdom of God, those who have not chosen to follow Jesus receive no more than parables. The implication is that not until one becomes a disciple of Jesus will one receive all the truth."

59. Räisänen, *Idea of Divine Hardening*, 92 writes that if it were referring to God initiating this hardening, one might expect an aorist tense. On the middle voice of ἐσκληρύνοντο, cf. Schneider, *Apostelgeschichte*, 2.268; Bock, *Acts*, 600. Even if the word is to be understood as a passive, Barrett, *Acts* 2.904, suggests, "Luke is not thinking of an extraneous hardening agent."

60. Even so, Satan is also viewed as a hardening agent. In the parable of the sower, Luke's version turns on calling the "seed" the word of God, which is central to the salvific plan of God in Luke-Acts (Luke 3:2; 5:1; 8:21; 11:28; Acts 4:31; 6:7; 8:14; 11:1; 13:5, 46; cf. 2:41). He adds that the devil takes away the word from their heart "so that they may not believe and be saved" (Luke 8:12c). The phrase is probably a Lukan redaction and it stresses his view that God's kingdom and salvific plan may be obstructed or confused by Satan and his minions. Part of Jesus' mission is to defeat the power of the devil (Luke 4:2, 13; 10:17–20; 11:18–22; 22:3, 31; Acts 5:3–4; 10:38; 13:10; 16:16–19; 26:18).

refuses to feast with the father and the younger son who was recently restored. The father leaves open an invitation for the older son, which implies a similar invitation is being given to the Pharisees and scribes: instead of criticizing Jesus for fellowshipping with tax collectors and sinners, they should rejoice and celebrate with him that such people are being restored to God's kingdom (Luke 15:1–2, 25–32). In the final lines of the parable of the Rich Man and Lazarus, the gist of the message is that no amount of persuasion will convince someone who will not "hear" God's word delivered through Moses and the Prophets (Luke 16:27–31). The parable of the Wicked Tenants implies that God (who is represented by the owner of the vineyard) is not the one who first rejects his tenants (represented by Jewish leaders); it is they who first reject him by refusing to listen to the messengers he sends them (cf. Luke 20:9–15, 19).

Moreover, Jesus desires to gather those from the Jerusalem, but they are "not willing" (οὐκ ἠθελήσατε: Luke 13:34–35; Matt 23:37), and human freedom is assumed when Jewish leaders refuse God's purpose for themselves by rejecting John's baptism (Luke 7:30–35). Stephen calls his accusers among the Sanhedrin stiff-necked, uncircumcised in heart, and resisting God's Spirit. When he claims to see Jesus standing at the right hand of God, they covered their ears from hearing (Acts 7:51–57), a gesture that hints at Luke's citations of Isa 6:9–10. Stephen's rebuke relates their stubbornness to following in the footsteps of their rebellious forefathers (Acts 7:51–52; cf. 28:25b). In his speech, Israel turns away from God, and so God hands them over to their own desires (Acts 7:39–42).[61] Spiritual obduracy in such cases happens as a result of God surrendering stubborn leaders over to their own desires, and only those who reject God and his word via his messengers, including Jesus and the apostles, are rejected by God. Such refusals must be factored into the reasoning behind why peace would be "hidden" from the resident's eyes in Jerusalem (Luke 19:41–44), and why God's plan in Luke 10:21–23 (cf. Matt 11:25–27) is kept hidden from wise (i.e., the proud religious leaders) and revealed instead to "infants" (i.e., Jesus' innocent followers: cf. Matt 11:25–27). Luke-Acts suggests to its ancient audience that God is entirely just to reject Israel's leaders—they spurned Jesus, falsely accused him at his trial, ridiculed him on the cross, and yet they were still shown mercy and given chances to repent (Acts 3:17–20; 4:5–12; 7:60; cf. Luke 23:34).[62]

---

61. Luke's view may be compared with Paul's. Both Acts 7 and Rom 1 have God handing over (παρέδωκεν) an idolatrous people to their own desires: compare ἔστρεψεν "δὲ ὁ θεὸς καὶ παρέδωκεν αὐτοὺς λατρεύειν" (Acts 7:42) with "διὸ παρέδωκεν αὐτοὺς ὁ θεὸς . . . ἐλάτρευσαν" (Rom 1:24–25). In Rom 1, however, the idolatrous people are Gentiles rather than ancient Israelites.

62. See Kingsbury, *Conflict in Luke*, 104–7, who lists a number of unjust and deceitful things done by the authorities.

The inclusion of Isa 6:10–11 in Acts 28 may serve as rhetoric to persuade Jews to repent *vis-à-vis* Paul's quote.[63] It thus has an evangelistic purpose. A call to repent is a call for God's people to turn back to God in faithfulness (cf. Luke 3:7–14; 15:17–21; 24:47; Acts 2:38).[64] It assumes an apostasy in Israel has taken place. Here again, as in other gospels, we are reminded of the apostasy of Israel in Isa 1–6. But Luke's reason for including the quote at the end of his two-volume work also serves an apologetic purpose. It helps explain to his audience why a number of Jews had not responded to Jesus and the apostles' messages. They follow their predecessors during Isaiah's time in shutting their eyes to God's word about Jesus and God's kingdom. This particular slant is put well by Evans: "According to Luke, Jewish unbelief does not mean that Christianity is wrong. Jewish unbelief, on the one hand, fulfills scripture (thus fending off the charge that Christian claims are false) and, on the other, justifies the Gentile mission."[65] Luke may be implying that *Paul is not an apostate despite the rumors Theophilus might have heard; he is a true teacher of Israel's traditions and his Jewish opponents are the real apostates for rejecting God's messenger.*[66]

Moreover, Jewish obduracy is not so much a detour in God's plan as a bridge—it paves the way for more Gentiles to be reached. The abrupt ending of Acts would seem to encourage Luke's audience to continue with the apostolic mission, especially to Gentiles. Daniel Marguerat suggests that the closing of Acts 28 is a case of the rhetoric of silence or "narrative suspension" used in the Greco-Roman world in order to get the reader to finish the story (e.g., Homer, *Illiad* 22.405–515; *Odyssey* 23.248–96; Herodotus, *Histories* 9.114–22).[67] In this framework, the text remains ambivalent, refusing to decide the outcome of the relationship between church and synagogue; it may also point to the readers' own mission to be witnesses to the "end of the earth" (Acts 1:8).[68] If this view is correct, then Luke's audience is encouraged to carry on Paul's mission while at the same time abandoning the original Pauline strategy to preach to the Jews *first*, and then the Gentiles (cf. Rom. 1:16). Nevertheless, Luke's audience is to welcome all people to receive the word, whether Jews or Gentiles, as

---

63. Along these lines, see Koet, "Paul in Rome (Acts 28,16–31)," 397–415.

64. Rightly here is Bock, "Luke," 363, who also highlights the importance of "turn" as referring to a change of direction in relation to repentance (Luke 1:17; 17:4; 22:32; Acts 3:19; 9:35; 11:21; 14:15; 15:19; 26:18–20; 28:27).

65. Evans, *See and Not Perceive*, 136.

66. Along the lines of Paul's role, see Jervell, "Paulus," 164–90. On the thought of Jewish apostasy here, see further, Maddox, *Purpose of Luke-Acts*; Powell, *Saying about Luke*, 51–52.

67. Marguerat, "Enigma," 284–304. On the virtues of not telling a reader everything, see Quintilian, *Inst.* 2.13.12–13; Ps.-Longinus, *Sub.* 9.2.

68. Cf. Marguerat, "Enigma," 300, 304. Marguerat thinks Acts 28 shows that a hope of a unified Jewish people "around Jesus" has been lost.

In the Footsteps of Judas and Other Defectors

Paul did (Acts 28:30–31). It might be said that the plan of God will prevail despite the unbelief and obduracy of those who oppose the plan, but more accurately God is able to use such unbelief to advance his purposes. The Jewish leaders' apostasy from God's message provides opportunity for Paul's mission to concentrate on saving Gentiles so that they could join God's people (Acts 28:24–28/Isa 6:10–11), and in this manner God is fulfilling his salvific plan. For Luke the apostolic mission will now center more on Gentiles.[69] By the end of Acts the Gentiles "listen" while the Jews fail to "hear" (Acts 28:26–28), and the city of Rome is the focus instead of Jerusalem.

At this juncture a strong qualification must be emphasized. Paul's rejection of the Jews neither suggests that Jewish people no longer belong to God's plan nor that Gentiles have replaced them as God's people (*contra* supersessionism). A significant tidbit at the end of Acts is Luke's inclusion of the word "also" (καὶ: 28:28). Paul tells the Jews in Rome that the plan of salvation is given to the Gentiles because "they *also* will listen." The word καὶ affirms that some Jews *do* listen to Paul's messages, and so the verse is not really a rejection of Jews but an inclusion of Gentiles.[70] While the purpose of Isa 6:9–10 in Acts 28 relates to the unbelieving Jews, Paul does not directly address this quote to them but to their Israelite "fathers" (Acts 28:25b; cf. 28:17; 3:25), namely, their Israelite ancestors in Isaiah's day who turned away from God's message. This manner of indirect address to the listeners perhaps functions as a rhetorical device with the intention of getting the hearers to make a connection between their attitude and the apostasy of their predecessors and therefore repent. The Lukan Paul in addition provokes the Israelites to jealousy in relation to the Gentiles who are receiving salvation (cf. Rom 11:13–14).[71] Also, those who reject the apostolic message are not entirely without hope. All along Luke has been dropping hints to his audience that in the future, Israel will be saved (Luke 13:34–35; 21:24; Acts 3:20–22; cf. Rom. 11:26), and this is possibly implied by the future tense "I will heal them" in Acts 28:27c.[72] Luke-Acts then ends with Paul welcoming *all* who came to him when he was under house arrest (28:30–31).

---

69. Isaiah begins with judgment on God's people (Isa 6) and ends with restoration and salvation (Isa 40). These roles are reversed in Luke-Acts, which begins with the hope of salvation of God's people (Isa 40/Luke 3) but ends with judgment coming on them (Isa 6/Acts 28): cf. Pao, *Isaianic New Exodus*, 105–9.

70. The Gentiles are stressed in 28:28 as "they" (αὐτοὶ here is emphatic).

71. See Pesch, *Apostelgeschichte*, 2.310; Lehnert, *Provokation Israels*; §G. In both Acts 28 and Rom 9–11, Jewish obduracy is partial, only taking place among Jews who reject Paul's message (cf. Rom 11:7, 25).

72. On the final verse, see Bovon, "Il a bien parlé à vos pères," 150. On the future salvation of Israel, see Fusco, "Luke-Acts and the Future," 1–17.

It might be suggested that Luke is anti-Semitic,[73] but there are problems with this perspective.[74] His negative language toward Jewish unbelievers hardly seems any different than what is found in Jewish communities that speak against other Jewish groups they oppose (e.g., Josephus, *Ant.* 18.1.4[16–17]; 20.9.1[199]; 1QS 1.9–10; *1 En.* 38.5; 95.3; *m. Yadayim* 4.7; *m. Sanhedrin* 10.1).[75] The early "Jesus as Messiah" movement, originally a sect of emergent Judaism, is no exception to this rule in its use of language against those whom they perceive as opponents. With such references in the New Testament, however, later Christian readers tragically ran in the direction of anti-Semitism. In some ways Luke's language on the opponents appears to be somewhat tame: he portrays Jesus and the disciples offering forgiveness to those who persecuted them and had Jesus crucified (Luke 23:34; Acts 2:38–39; 3:14–17; cf. 7:51–60), the songs related to the infancy narrative speak to Israelite nationalism (Luke 1:33, 54–55, 68–79; 2:25, 30–31), and the apostles call Jews "brothers and sisters" even when the latter are clearly non-Christian (Acts 3:17; 7:2; 13:26, 38; 22:1, 5; 23:1).[76] Interestingly also, through the apostles' speeches, those who seem to be responsible for the death of Jesus are Jerusalemites and their leaders who are called "you" (cf. Acts 2:23; 3:14; 4:10), but when the apostles speak to Diaspora Jews about the death of Jesus, those who are responsible are not the Diaspora people but "they," i.e., those from Jerusalem (cf. Acts 13:27–29).[77] A related observation is that in Luke-Acts the opponents of the divine commission to save Gentiles are not always identified as unbelieving Jews. The primary persecution Paul and his colleagues face in Philippi and Ephesus, for example, come from the local non-Jewish residents (Acts 16:16–24; 19:23—20:1).

If the salvific plan of God is offered first to the Jews and then gravitates toward the Gentiles, Acts 1:8 is programmatic for Acts.[78] The disciples are to receive the Spirit's power and be witnesses of Jesus in Jerusalem, Judea, Samaria, and the "end of the earth" (ἕως ἐσχάτου τῆς γῆς). The last of these might suggest Rome as the remotest part of the earth because this is where Paul is found at the end of the book (Acts 28). But given the echo of Isa 49:6 LXX in Acts 1:8 (both share the phrase: ἕως ἐσχάτου τῆς γῆς), we can suggest a viable alternative. In Isa 49:6 God through his

---

73. See e.g., Sanders, *Jews in Luke-Acts*; Sandmel, *Anti-Semitism in the NT?*, 77–89.

74. For critiques see, e. g., Brawley, *Luke-Acts*; Seccombe, "New People of God," 349–72. On the debate see further, Tyson, *Luke-Acts*.

75. In Israel's scriptures we see the Hebrew prophets condemning their own so as to depict their cities as harlots (Ezek 16, 23), Sodom (Isa 1), and not God's people (Hos 1–2). Within such traditions, we find a pattern of "in-house" denouncements and condemnations.

76. Cf. Evans, "Jewish Rejection," 29–56.

77. Cf. Walton, "Acts: Many Questions," 248; Weatherly, *Jewish Responsibility*.

78. E.g., Witherington, *Acts*, 110–11; Conzelmann, *Acts*, 7.

In the Footsteps of Judas and Other Defectors

chosen Servant will restore the remnant of Israel and include the Gentiles/nations; "light" will be given to them. The Isaianic passage appears elsewhere; in Luke 2:32; Acts 13:47; and 26:18, where it refers specifically to Gentiles.[79] The Gentile mission does not stop at Rome but is intended to extend worldwide or wherever Gentiles and nations might exist.[80] Given this perspective of "the end of the earth," we find its primary fulfillment in Acts 13, when Paul and Barnabas turn their mission to Gentiles, providing "light" to the nations as stand-ins for God's Isaianic Servant (13:47–48).[81] Acts 28:28, then, is not the primary fulfillment of 1:8 in terms of Christ's witnesses reaching the remote part of the earth; rather, the ending of Acts 28 is simply a reaffirmation of Acts 13:47–48.[82]

If Acts 13 marks the beginning of the "end" and references the Isaianic tradition (Acts 13:34/Isa 55:3; Acts 13:47/Isa 49:6), then it may be important for our study on Gentile missions in the plan of God. Paul and Barnabas are called and sent out by God's Spirit to preach primarily in Asia Minor. In a synagogue of Antioch of Pisidia, Paul addresses Jews and God-fearers (Gentiles) about the good news of salvation, associating it with the tradition-history of Israel. Jesus is said to bring to fruition a promise that a descendant of David would become Israel's savior (13:15–33; esp. 23, 32).[83] As a result many Jews and Gentiles begin to follow Paul and Barnabbas, but other Jews and some prominent Gentiles oppose them (13:43–45, 50). In this speech the Lukan Paul combines a Septuagint reading of Isa 55:3 with Pss 2:7 and 15[16]:10 to affirm God's choice of Jesus and his resurrection from the dead (Acts 13:32–38). At the end of his speech Paul cites Hab 1:5 not as fulfilled but as hypothetical; it is used as a warning against the scoffers (Acts 13:40–41).[84] The Isaianic phrase in Acts 13:34 "the assured holy things of David" (τὰ ὅσια Δαυὶδ τὰ πιστά: Isa 55:3) is understood here to be confirming Christ's resurrection, and the Psalms are used as further verification of this. Several significant points relevant to Acts 13:32–48 are often missed in relation to the larger context of Isa 55:3 (Isa 55:1—56:11).

---

79. On Luke-Acts connections with Isaiah 49:6 see further, Pao, *Isaianic New Exodus*, 84–101. On the Gentiles in Isaiah, see also Isa 2:2; 40:5; 42:6, 16; 46:13; 52:10; 56:7.

80. Cf. Witherington, *Acts*, 111. On this reading, Rome might be the center of the earth but not the "end."

81. Cf. Grelot, "Note sur Actes," 368–72; Polhill, *Acts*, 308.

82. If Acts 1:8 finds its fulfillment in Acts 13, why does Luke continue writing another 15 chapters up to Acts 28? Perhaps the simplest answer is that Theophilus needed further essential information about the Christian movement. Another explanation is that he demonstrates Paul's innocence and thus validates Paul's message as coming from God.

83. Cf. Jervell, *Apostelgeschichte*, 355; Fitzmyer, *Acts*, 516.

84. Paul's speech ends at this point, and so the next Isaianic reference in Acts 13:47 should not be included as the same speech. Cf. Porter, *Paul in Acts*, 136.

First, the audience in Isa 55:1 are addressed as "all those" or "those" (ὅσοι: cf. Acts 13:48) in which an open invitation is given to them to eat "good things" and pay attention with their ears, following the Lord's ways in order to prosper (Isa 55:1–3a; contrast 6:9–10). Second, the holy things of David include God establishing an "eternal" covenant (αἰώνιος cf. Acts 13:46, 48/Isa 55:3) with those who obey him just as he did for David (Isa 55:3b, 13; cf. 2 Sam 23:5; Pss 88[89]:3–4, 33–37; cf. 131[132]:11–12). Third, this invitation includes the ἔθνη or nations/Gentiles (Isa 55:4–5 LXX; cf. Acts 13:47–48a). Fourth, it includes salvation (Isa 56:1; cf. Acts 13:26, 46–48) involving people calling on the Lord (Isa 55:6; cf. Acts 2:21, 39; 22:16), repentance (Isa 55:7a; Acts 13:24; 2:38), and forgiveness of sins (Isa 55:7b; cf. Acts 13:38). Fifth, Isa 55:8–11 assures those invited that God fulfills what he sets out to do via the inevitable accomplishment of God's plans (βουλαί) and God's word (cf. Acts 13:26, 32f, 36, 44, 46). Perhaps it is not too much of an exaggeration to say that Isa 55–56 contains some major themes in Paul's speech in Acts 13 and in Luke-Acts as a whole.

In Acts 13:47 Paul quotes from Isa 49:6 to justify his turning away from the Jews to the Gentiles. Isaiah 49:3–8 agrees with Isa 55 in referring to God's establishment of a covenant with the Gentiles, and this covenant looks forward to a set eschatological time of salvation.[85] Clearly Acts 13:47–48 is intended to be read in terms of a divinely appointed salvation coming to the Gentiles, who are identified in 13:48 not only as τὰ ἔθνη but also as ὅσοι. These Gentiles are appointed to "eternal life" (13:48; cf. 11:18). Conversely, the Jews who oppose Paul judge themselves unworthy of such life (13:46), as did presumably those Gentiles who opposed the apostles (13:50). The term "eternal life" is rare in Luke-Acts (Luke 10:25; 18:18; Acts 13:46, 48) though it is implied in other passages that mention "life" (Luke 9:24; 15:32; 17:33; Acts 5:20; 11:18).[86] Luke's preferred concept is "salvation" (Luke 1:77; 2:30; 3:6; 19:9; Acts 2:21, 40, 47; 4:12; 11:19; 13:26, 47; 15:1; 16:17, 31; 28:28), and eternal life, no doubt, functions as sort of a synonym for the salvation that is mentioned in Acts 13:47b/Isa 49:6.[87]

In a nutshell, we have in Paul's speech of Acts 13 a significant turning point in the Luke-Acts narrative. Because the Jews of Antioch Pisidia reject Paul's message, he will now turn to the Gentiles and thus salvation will come to them in fulfillment

---

85. In Isaiah this salvation has been set for an appointed time, intimating the age to come (cf. Acts 1:7; 2:17; 17:26; cf. Luke 4:13; 21:24; 22:53).

86. The idea of receiving eternal life was already being used in Jewish traditions earlier than or contemporaneous with the NT era (4Q418 fr.69.13; CD 3.20; Dan 12:2; 4 Macc 15:3; *1 En.* 40.9; *Pss. Sol.* 3.16; 14.10; *T. Job* 18; Pesch, *Apostelgeschichte*, 2.46).

87. Luke understands eternal life in terms of the resurrection of Jesus, and perhaps by implication the resurrection of the righteous (cf. Bock, *Luke*, 2.1023).

In the Footsteps of Judas and Other Defectors

of the Isaianic prophecies and plan of God (13:46; cf. 18:6; 28:28). That Paul is justified by Luke for this decision is evident because of the unbelieving Jews' rejection of salvation, not to mention that it will be discovered later on that, via Paul's Damascus experience, Jesus already called him to preach to the Gentiles (e.g. 22:21; 26:20; cf. Acts 9). For Theophilus and the majority of Luke's audience, Acts 13 confirms *them* as a legitimate community of God's people. They are included in God's salvific plan that was predicted in Israel's scriptures and brought to pass through Paul and Barnabbas's mission. Tremors of this change may have been felt by the conversions of the Samaritans, the Ethiopian eunuch, and Cornelius (Act 8, 10), but now a specific God-ordained mission to all Gentiles is established by the Christ-followers and confirmed through Israel's scriptures. Nevertheless, the audience's privileged status gives them no ground for boasting. The warnings and stories about unbelief and apostasy in Luke-Acts would help them realize the importance of perseverance and the possibility of losing salvation. Likewise, we will see below that the apostolic message creates divisions among God's people, and sometimes even among the Christ-followers themselves.

Excursus: Determinism, Freedom, or Both? Acts 13:48

In Acts 13:48 the Gentiles' divine appointment precedes even their belief. We may wish to ask how this verse plays into God's plan and in what sense Luke holds humans responsible for divine acceptance and rejection. Several interpretations are possible.

Our first option interprets the appointment to eternal life in an inclusive sense and assumes these Gentiles have already been predisposed to salvation. Most, if not all, those who receive eternal life in 13:48 are already God-fearers and proselytes to emergent Judaism before Paul preaches to them, and along with the Jews who follow Paul they continue "in the grace of God" even prior to 13:48 (Acts 13:43 cf. 16, 26).[88] They already know the God whom Paul proclaims. Prior to the apostle's message, however, they did not know about the forgiveness of sins made possible through Jesus and his resurrection (Acts 13:37–39). The idea behind this verse may be simply that they were *predisposed* to believe in the message about Jesus.

A second option centers on how the verb τάσσω is translated. It has a range of meanings including "ordain," "arrange," and "determine," depending on the context.

---

88. Cf. Marshall, *Kept by the Power*, 93–94, who compares their disposition to that of Cornelius (Acts 10) and the Ethiopian eunuch (Acts 8) prior to their full conversion. He qualifies that 13:44 introduces a different group than 13:43 (238). Nevertheless 13:48 would seem to include those in 13:43 if Paul is still in Antioch of Pisidia. Bock, *Acts*, 421–22 agrees that God-fearers and proselytes are two distinct groups in 13:43 that are being combined.

It is sometimes related to time references, which is relevant for our text (e.g., 2 Macc 6:21; *1 Clem.* 40:1f). In 13:48 it can be translated either in the middle or passive voice (τεταγμένοι). If the passive is preferred, the meaning could be that they had been appointed or ordained by God, or it can be defined as "belong to, be classed among those possessing."[89] If the middle voice is accepted, the meaning could be that these Gentiles had appointed or "set themselves" for eternal life. This would make good symmetry with 13:46, where the Jews judge *themselves* unworthy of eternal life.[90] If nothing else, 13:46 suggests that the Gentiles who receive salvation in 13:48 should be juxtaposed with the Jews who reject God's salvation in 13:46.

A third option suggests that Acts 13:48 is still influenced by the Isaianic tradition cited in 13:47. God's appointed time of salvation will come when the Gentiles/nations join the people of God (Israel). The Gentiles' salvation in Acts signals that this anticipated era, predetermined by God and written long ago by the prophet, has finally arrived. Luke may have adopted ὅσοι from Isa 55:1, in which an open invitation is given to "those" or "all those" who are thirsty to come and drink freely, listen, live, and participate in God's everlasting covenant (Isa 55:1–3).[91] The intertextual backdrop of 13:48 may suggest that the people are offered salvation through invitation; what is predetermined is God's appointment of his Servant-Messenger and the time for the Gentiles/nations to come to salvation (Isa 49:8; cf. 42:6). Their salvation was inevitable because God promised such a time would arrive, and God will accomplish the word God has spoken (Isa 55:10–11).

The appointment to salvation in Acts 13:48, then, may be understood in terms of the divine and prophetic purpose that finds fulfillment on the targeted people group called the Gentiles. With this view in mind, there is no contextual sense of divine coercion or arbitrary selection of individual Gentiles. Now that the salvific era finally arrived through Jesus and the apostolic message, the Gentiles could accept God's invitation, and those who do so find themselves belonging to the Servant's community that had been destined by God through the prophetic word.

---

89. BDAG, 991. See further, Delling, "τάσσω," 8.27–31.

90. In 13:46 κρίνετε is in the active voice but is joined with the reflexive pronoun ἑαυτοὺς and thus it parallels the meaning of the middle voice in 13:48. Special thanks to Bart Buhler for drawing this to my attention. Notice also that the Jews in Ephesus hardened *themselves* (19:9) and there ἐσκληρύνοντο is in the middle voice or at least conveying some sense of self-hardening.

91. The meaning of the correlative pronoun ὅσοι may be rendered "all those who" or all those Gentiles/God-fearers appointed to eternal life (cf. Acts 4:6, 34; 14:27; 15:4). See ὅσοι in Isa 43:7/Acts 2:39; Isa 56:4; 66:10. In Acts 13:48 "those"/"all those who" is preferred over "as many as" (NASB) because the former highlights the plural and corporate sense of the context. Moreover, as BDAG, 729 affirms, πάντες/πάντα ("all") is used with the plural ὅσοι/ὅσα to mean "all who" or "all that" (e.g., Acts 3:24; 5:36, 37). Even when πάντες is not used with ὅσοι, the meaning of the latter can still be "all who" or "all that" (Acts 4:6, 34; 10:45; 13:48; cf. Gal 3:10, 26–27; Rev 3:19; Ign. *Phld.* 3.2; *Herm. Vis.* 2.2.7).

A fourth option understands τάσσω as "enrollment."[92] On this interpretation the Gentiles are "enrolled" in the heavenly records (cf. Luke 10:20). In this light the passage may be referring to something similar to having one's name recorded in a book of God's people or book of life (Exod 32:32; Phil 4:3; Rev 13:8).

A final option is to suggest God's predetermination of individuals or the Gentiles to salvation, whether arbitrary or based on some sort of foreknowledge.[93] Such a view may be possible given Luke's fondness for divine necessity. If so, then Luke does not bother to sort out for us the ramifications of such wording, nor does he attempt to reconcile such a thought with the type of human freedom he assumes in other passages.

Regardless of which interpretation we choose for 13:48, they do not eliminate all tensions between the divine plan and human freedom and responsibility in Luke-Acts. The Gentiles who turn to God do so as a result of God's prophetic word realized in the Acts narrative (Acts 13:47–48; 14:15; 15:17–19; 26:17f; 28:28; cf. Isa 44:28–45:6, 45:14–26; 51:4–5; 55:10–11). Moreover, if Isa 52–53 predicted that the Servant-Messiah had to be killed, this plan is still determined by God (Luke 22:22; Acts 2:23; 4:26–28), and if God's word necessarily accomplishes God's purposes, it is still in some sense inevitable (Isa 55:3–11; Luke 1:1–4; Acts 6:7; 12:24; 19:20). God takes initiative in saving humans, and they cannot be saved without divine grace (Acts 11:23; 13:43; 14:3; 20:24; cf. 2:39, 47; 15:11; Luke 19:10).

On the other hand, as we observed earlier, God's word and purpose can be rejected by human choices (e.g., Luke 7:30; 13:34; Acts 3:26; 7:51, 57; 13:46; 17:30; 19:9).[94] God "opened the heart" of Lydia to understand the scriptures and believe Paul's message (Acts 16:14), and yet Lydia is already a believer in the one God and this verse refers to God giving her understanding in the word (cf. Luke 24:45). The choice still remains hers to accept or reject the word—there is no indication that she cannot refuse to believe.[95] The Lukan Peter's invitation for the Jews to receive salvation on the Day of Pentecost mentions God's sovereignty in selecting Jesus and calling people via apostolic proclamations (Acts 2:23, 39), and Luke claims that the Lord was adding to his church those who were being saved (Acts 2:47). Nevertheless, Peter declares to his

---

92. Cf. Dan 6:12(Theodotian); *1 Clem.* 58.2; Bruce, *Acts*, 283–84.

93. Compare *m. Abot* 3.15A: "Everything is foreseen, and free choice is given."

94. George, "Conversion," 351–68, is helpful in seeing God's initiative and human acts related to conversion. Cosgrove, "Divine DEI," 186, rightly understands "each one" in Acts 3:26 not as individual election, but rather "God's very individualistic purpose for each Israelite is presented as frustrated by Jewish unrepentance."

95. The words of Manson, *Sayings of Jesus*, 130, are apropos here: "Man [sic] cannot save himself; but he can damn himself."

listeners their own responsibility in receiving salvation. Among other things, they must repent and call upon the name of the Lord (Acts 2:37–40; cf. v. 21).

The tensions between divine determinism and human freedom are likewise found in Israel's scriptures (e.g., Prov 16:1, 4, 9, 33; 19:21; 20:24; 21:30–31; cf. Gen 50:20). Humans can choose their own paths, either serving God or not (Deut 11:26; 26:17–19; 30:11–20; Jer 21:8; Prov 11:19; 14:27; 18:21). A preliminary observation of such sources seems to imply that these ancient writers did not consider it necessary to resolve the tension between the two categories. Luke-Acts seems to function in a similar way. For Luke, the ultimate plan of God cannot be frustrated despite human freedom. Moreover, the wisdom of God can outsmart mere mortals, and God can always intervene in miraculous ways to ensure that God's word is accomplished.[96]

Thus, even though the inclusion of the nations/Gentiles is predicted long ago through God's inevitable plan, and God takes initiative to save humanity, Luke maintains human freedom to receive or reject the purposes of God, and he holds responsible those who refuse to believe. Both human freedom and God's inevitable plan are affirmed.[97] Squires considers Luke to be similar to Josephus and certain Stoic writers on fate, especially Dionysius of Halicarnassus and Diodorus Siculus.[98] Along these lines Josephus claims that the Essenes believe fate governs "all things, and that nothing befalls men [sic] but what is according to its determination,"[99] while the Sadducees do away with fate. The Pharisees believe that fate governs some actions but not others: "and some of them are in our own power, and that they are liable to fate, but are not caused by fate" (Josephus, Ant. 13.172–73). Josephus tends to hold to a position similar to the Pharisees (Ant. 16.397–98; cf. 10:142; J.W. 2.119–66).[100] Luke's view would appear to be similar to this. Such a paradox does not seem to mitigate the reality of apostasy in Luke-Acts.

---

96. See Cosgrove, "Divine DEI," 190.

97. Cosgrove, ibid., maintains that divine coercion was used on Zechariah's naming his son John the Baptist and Paul's commission (187). Zechariah's salvation, however, is not directly at stake (Luke 1:5–66). On the sovereign will of God in Luke-Acts, see further, Marshall, *Luke: Historian and Theologian*, 103–11.

98. Squires, *Plan of God*, 156–62; 177–78, 180, 184, 189.

99. Whiston, *Works of Josephus*, [AQ page, orig. sec.].

100. Cf. Squires, *Plan of God*, 161–66; Carson, *Divine Sovereignty*, 115–19.

In the Footsteps of Judas and Other Defectors

JESUS AS PROPHET OR APOSTATE? BELIEVERS AND UNBELIEVERS AMONG THE JEWS (LUKE 24:3, 14; CF. LUKE 15:1–32)

If the flow of Luke-Acts favors a Gentile mission, this needs to be tempered with the fact that the narrative also affirms that many Jews accepted the message of Christ and the apostles. At the beginning of Luke-Acts the angel predicts that Jesus' forerunner, John the Baptist, will turn "many" in Israel to the Lord (Luke 1:16), and Jesus himself teaches and performs miracles with the result that "many" Jews follow him during his ministry (Luke 5:15; 7:21; 8:3; 12:1). After his resurrection his disciples who remain in Jerusalem until Pentecost are numbered at 120 (Acts 1:5). On the Day of Pentecost Luke claims that 3,000 Jews and proselytes believe the apostolic message (Acts 2:41) and soon the amount increases to 5,000 and "great numbers" (4:4; 5:14; 6:7). Even more follow the Way as the apostles begin to preach in other cities (Acts 9:35, 42; cf. 11:19).[101] Likewise, in the narrative "many" priests come to the faith (6:7) and some of the Pharisees believe (15:5). In the early chapters of Acts the disciples fulfill the commission of Jesus to be witnesses in "Jerusalem and Judea" before going to the "end of the earth" where the Gentiles live (cf. Acts 1:8). The gospel eventually spreads to Asia Minor, Macedonia, and Rome, and, while many Gentiles come to believe Paul's message, there are still great numbers of Jews who also believe (Acts 13:43; 14:1; 17:1–4, 11–12; cf. 18:8). There are "many thousands of believers" among the Jews that are reportedly in Jerusalem for Pentecost when Paul is arrested (21:20). Hence, the total number Jewish converts to the Way increases rather than diminishes by the end of Acts.

The great number of Jews following Jesus and the apostles almost runs counter to passages, such as Acts 28:23–28, that confirm Jewish unbelief. The narrative of Luke-Acts, it seems, presents a consistent pattern of presenting Jesus and the apostolic witness as the basis for a division among Jews. When Jesus is still an infant, Simeon predicts the child would be set for the "fall and rise" of many in Israel (Luke 2:34). This thought associates Jesus with the chief stone of the Isaianic tradition that becomes a stumbling block for some Israelites but an object of trust for others (Isa 8:14–15; 28:16; cf. Luke 20:17–18). The concept of the chief cornerstone as a point of division is also used by other early Christian writers (e.g., Isa 28:16 in Rom 9:31–33; cf. 9:6–8, 24; 1 Pet 2:6–8). As played out through the rest of Luke-Acts, the message of Jesus creates division among Jews and members of one's own household so that some believe and others do not (Luke 4:29; 6:22; 12:51–53; 13:28f; 14:26; 16:25; 19:44–48; 21:16–17; cf. 10:13–15; 11:31–32).[102] This phenomenon of a mixed

---

101. Cf. Jervell, *Apostelgeschichte*, 195–97.

102. See Neyrey, "Symbolic Universe," 299–300. Gregg, *Final Judgment Sayings*, 273 (cf. 73), ob-

response is seen repeatedly in Acts also when the Jewish people hear the apostolic messages (Acts 4:1–4; 5:16–17; 13:43–45; 14:1–2; 17:4–5, 11–12; 23:6–10), and this continues up to the final message given by Paul to the Jews in Rome (Acts 28:24–25, 29): some believe his teachings while others do not (28:24).

A thorough exploration on why this division takes place in Luke-Acts is beyond the scope of our study, but perhaps one thought relevant here happens on a social level. In the narrative the upper echelons refuse to acknowledge the lower classes as their equals, and because the message of Jesus targeted the latter, conflicts with the former were bound to arise. The prophetic restoration among Jews focused on those who seem to be the most unlikely candidates in Israel, such as sinners, women, tax collectors, the sickly, and the poor. Such people are precisely those whom the coming Messiah would be called to reach. Jesus' proclamation of the good news to the marginalized is central to Luke, who considers such activity to be fulfilling the role of God's Servant in Isaiah.[103] The wealthy, proud, and religiously self-righteous in Israel, on the other hand, typically reject the message of Jesus (e.g., Luke 7:29–30, 39; 10:25; 11:14–19, 37–54; 12:13–34; 13:10–17; 16:19–31; 18:9–25). Essentially Luke portrays a division among two classes of Israelites: the outcasts and poor, over against the religious and wealthy who neglected and despised the former group (e.g., 15:1–2). The former group is more prone to accept Jesus and his message than the latter group.

The concept of apostasy interacts with this division and may be seen through the way Luke reverses the social order. The marginalized Jews are granted salvation while the more prestigious Jews, often identified by their religious leaders, become recalcitrant and reject the salvation that Christ offers (e.g., 11:37–54).[104] A glimpse of this reversal may be viewed in the context of the "lost" parables, which primarily refer to sinners and outcasts among Israel. They are compared with a lost sheep, a lost coin, and a lost son (15:1–32). In the parable of the Prodigal Son, for example, the younger son disowns his father and spends his inheritance on immoral living (15:13, 30) and then returns in humility confessing his unworthiness before his father. The father claims that his son was "dead" but is alive again (15:24). The meaning most naturally refers to the son living with Gentiles and never intending to come back, hence being "dead" in a practical sense to his father. On another level, the thought may refer to being dead to God or spiritually dead as an apostate. Even though the stress on this parable emphasizes restoration and celebration, the restoration is from

---

serves a similar pattern of separation within Israel in both Q and late Second Temple sources.

103. Luke 4:14–31/Isa 61:1–2; Luke 6:20–23; 7:20–23, 36–50; 8:26–39; 10:25–37; 14:1–2, 12–14, 16–24; 15; 16:19–31; 17:11–19; 18:9–14; 19:1–10; 23:39–43.

104. For passages in Luke related to reversal, see York, *Last Shall Be First*.

being "lost" and so some sense of apostasy may be assumed. In relation to Jesus' ministry, the "sinners" and tax collectors are those among the Jews whose immoral lifestyle made them violators of the Torah, covenant breakers. Jesus' ministry is to reach such people as these (Luke 19:10; cf. Matt 10:6; 15:24). They were despised in the eyes of religious leaders (cf. Luke 15:1), but now, *by following Jesus, the marginalized are being restored to God, and the scribes and Pharisees who criticize Jesus for associating with them are becoming apostates for rejecting God's appointed Messiah.*

Another kind of reversal takes place between the religious leaders' perception of Jesus in the narrative and the perception of Luke's audience. When Jesus is finally arrested, the religious leaders' charge before Pilate is that Jesus perverts (διαστρέφω: Luke 23:2) the people and misleads them (ἀποστρέφω: Luke 23:14). These accusations may be seen in a twofold manner. Most obviously the charges are intended to get Pilate to pronounce a guilty verdict on Jesus as a political revolutionist inciting the people to revolt against Rome (cf. 23:5)—he is teaching disloyalty to Caesar.[105] Beyond this, it is apparent throughout the narrative that the elders, scribes, and chief priests in Jerusalem are not devoted to Caesar but are concerned with Jesus' messianic claims and how they might use those claims as ground for accusations against him before Pilate (cf. 22:66–71).[106] Their accusations against Jesus in 23:2 and 14 betray a secondary meaning—he is not only an insurrectionist but also a false prophet who teaches and leads astray the Jewish people from God (cf. Deut 13).[107] Διαστρέφω is the same word the Lukan Paul uses to denounce Elymas or "Bar Jesus," the false prophet and magician who attempts to lead astray the proconsul, Sergius Paulus, from the faith (Acts 13:10 cf. 13:6–8). He uses the same word again to warn the Ephesians about false and apostate teachers who will arise from among them and lead astray followers after them (Acts 20:30).[108] Likewise ἀποστρέφω is frequently used for the thought of leading or being led astray into apostasy (cf. Acts 7:39; 2 Tim 4:4; Heb 12:25; Num 32:15; Deut 31:18; Josh 22:16–18; Judge 2:19; 3 Kgs 9:6; 2 Chr 7:19). *Despite the opponents' belief that Jesus is a false prophet and apostate, Jesus is affirmed in Luke-Acts as a true prophet God* (Luke 4:29, 32; 7:16; 24:19; Acts 3:22–23), and even Pilate finds him innocent of the opponents' charges (23:4, 14, 20).

---

105. See, e.g., Nolland, *Luke* 3.1117.

106. Ibid., 3.1106, 1111–12, among other things, suggests their indictment centers on Jesus' royal messianic claim (cf. Ps 110); they are primarily interested in using the aspect of his kingship against him before Pilate (cf. 23:2b).

107. We notice Bovon, *Evangelium Lukas* 4.383, regarding διαστρέφω: "In den Augen der Juden bringt Jesus das Volk vom Weg zu Gott ab und verdirbt es."

108. Marcion adds to Luke 23:2 that Jesus "causes women and children to fall away": see Bertram, "στρέφω," 7.718. On διαστρέφω and apostasy see further Num 15:39; Prov 10:9; *1 Clem.* 46.8–9.

In Luke a divine reversal has taken place through the coming of Jesus in which the lowly and sinners among the Jews find salvation, but the powerful and religious become estranged to Jesus, the latter accusing him of being a false prophet and apostate. Luke's gospel plays on a movement that favors the marginalized Jews over the religious Jews, and this pattern can be traced back to the plan of God imbedded in the Isaianic prophetic tradition that would be actualized by the messianic servant.

PAUL AS MESSENGER OR APOSTATE? DIVISIONS AMONG CHRISTIANS (ACTS 6–7; 15:1–29; 21:20–21)

If Jesus and his salvific message bring about a bifurcation among Jews in Luke, then the apostolic witness to Gentiles would seem to be the main cause for divisions among the Christians in Acts. The unified view among the early Christ-followers in Jerusalem soon gives way to a conflict over widows among the Hellenists who are being neglected of daily necessities (Acts 6). Seven Hellenistic leaders are selected to serve the widows. Stephen, the first Christian martyr, is included among them. The Hellenists here are probably not Greeks but Greek-speaking Jews.[109] They most likely come from the Diaspora and stayed in Jerusalem after the Pentecost event (Acts 2).

Beyond the problem with the widows, it is possible that the Hellenistic Christ-followers held to a less stringent view of the Law, being more acculturated to Greek thought. Although Luke does not address the issue, their Greek influence possibly became a source of irritation with the Aramaic-speaking majority of Christian Jews in Jerusalem. Many priests were coming to the faith (6:7) and so it could be surmised that frictions existed over purity rituals or similar issues with the priests, so to speak, on the traditional end, and Jewish Hellenists on the progressive end. However, the appropriate question we must ask is not whether tensions between the two groups were possible, but whether conflicts between the groups escalated to a level that made it impossible for them to have fellowship anymore. To what extent are these Hellenistic Jews assimilated into Greek culture? Complete assimilation to Greek ways would be considered apostasy,[110] but there is no hint from this passage or elsewhere in Acts that the Aramaic Christ-followers thought the Hellenistic members had stepped over such a boundary. It is simply not a good idea for us to stress an irreparable division between the two groups where none is clearly evident.[111]

109. See Gaventa, *Acts*, 111–12.

110. See Barclay, "Who Was Considered an Apostate," 80–98. But more precisely in Acts 6 the question we raise would be to what extent Aramaic-speaking Jews might consider Jews from the Diaspora as apostate in relation to assimilation.

111. Along this path, Hill, *Hellenists and Hebrews*; idem, "Jerusalem Church," 39–56, argues persuasively against F. C. Bauer and others who overemphasize the differences between the Hellenist and

In the Footsteps of Judas and Other Defectors

The accusations raised against Stephen before the Sanhedrin are first instigated by Jews from the Diaspora, not Jews from Jerusalem (6:9–12). The various charges against him that he speaks against the holy place and the Law, and that Jesus would destroy the temple and change the customs of Moses, are false according to the narrator (6:13–14). In essence Stephen is accused by his Jewish opponents of blaspheming Moses and the temple (Acts 6:11–13).[112] The nature of his blasphemy does not seem to be a direct profanation of the Name, which was the official ground for blasphemy in the Mishnah (*m. Sanhedrin* 7.5; cf. *m. Keritot* 1.1). Perhaps he is stoned by his opponents mainly for associating Jesus with the exalted "Son of Man," who is the eschatological judge and by implication will judge those who judge Stephen (Acts 7:55–60; cf. Dan 7:13–14).[113] In any case, Stephen's speech in Acts 7 does not confirm that their accusations against him in 6:13–14 are true; rather, his speech denounces the Jewish leaders. It seems that they are acting similar to their apostate forefathers who rejected God's message through Moses (7:39–43). In this manner Stephen is accusing them of being obdurate towards the plan of God, who through Moses predicted the coming Messiah, Jesus the righteous one (Acts 7:37, 52; cf. Deut 18:15, 18; Acts 3:14, 22). Regarding accusations against the temple, Craig Hill's words are apropos: "Assuming a post-70 dating of Acts, the inaccuracy and irony of this accusation would be obvious to readers: Jesus himself did not destroy the temple."[114] Nevertheless, a discrimination against the Hellenistic Christians is evident after Stephen's death when the Jewish Christ-followers are persecuted and driven out of Jerusalem. The apostles could remain in Jerusalem (8:1), suggesting perhaps that this persecution was leveled against the Hellenistic Christians only, not the Aramaic-speaking Christians.[115] After Paul's conversion, divisions among emerging Christian groups are more evident, especially between the Christian Jews from Jerusalem and Paul's churches and his law-free gospel.[116]

Hebrew groups.

112. On accusations made against the apostles, see Malina and Neyrey, "Conflict in Luke-Acts," 121.

113. So Polhill, *Acts*, 206–7.

114. Hill, "Jerusalem Church," 50.

115. Incidentally, Saul the Pharisee (Paul) is portrayed as a primary leader of this assault (8:3; 9:1–2; 22:4) and we discover that he is actually a Jew from Tarsus, a city of the Diaspora, and claims Roman citizenship (9:11; 21:39; 22:3; cf. 16:37–38; 22:25–29; 23:27).

116. Hints of a similar tension may be implied with the Matthean community's stress on keeping the entire Law (Matt 5:17–20) in comparison to the Markan community, which does not consider dietary laws to be important (Mark 7:1–23). Luke-Acts leans in the Markan direction with its stress on Gentile mission, but even so, Luke must consider both the Law and the Prophets to be divinely authoritative if he grounds his perspective of the divine plan on Israel's scripture. He also demonstrates that Jesus is a true prophet of God, and as such, Jesus affirms the authority of the Law (Luke 16:17), but

Early opposition to the Gentile mission comes from the Jewish Christians in Jerusalem who criticize Peter for eating with Cornelius, an uncircumcised Gentile (Acts 11:1–3).[117] The conflict centers on table fellowship with Gentiles, which is seen as a violation of Jewish customs, perhaps primarily because Gentiles have contact with unclean foods (cf. Acts 10:28–29; John 18:28; *Jub.* 22.16).[118] The complaints are assuaged in our narrative when Peter reiterates how God spoke to him in a vision and how Cornelius was converted by receiving the Spirit (11:4–18). If there is a historical element to this story, this criticism by the Jerusalem Christ-followers in 11:1–3 may have had a lasting impact on Peter—after eating with uncircumcised Gentile believers in Antioch, he refuses to do so again when certain men from James in Jerusalem visit Antioch. Paul interprets Peter's act as hypocrisy and rebukes him before others who were present (cf. Gal 2:11–15).

Rising tensions among the Judean Christ-followers regarding the admittance of uncircumcised Gentiles into the church reaches a boiling point when certain Pharisees who believe in Christ come to Antioch and insist that the Gentiles must be circumcised according to Jewish customs if they are to be saved. It is quite evident that they oppose the Gentile mission of Paul and Barnabas (cf. Acts 15:1–5). Paul's experience in Jerusalem that he mentions in Gal 2 may reflect a conflict with these Pharisees or a similar group as the "false brothers" (Gal 2:4). Paul and Barnabbas's meeting with James, Peter, and John in Gal 2:1–10 probably recalls the Jerusalem meeting in Acts 15, with Paul's confrontation with Peter in Antioch (Gal 2:11–15) taking place sometime after the meeting in Jerusalem. At the meeting James decides that Gentiles do not need to be circumcised to belong the emergent Christians, but in keeping with the Levitical code to aliens living among the Israelites they are to refrain from idol meats, fornication, and consuming blood and things strangled (Acts 15:19–29; cf. Lev 17–18).[119]

It seems that the decision did not make much of an impact on Paul, who fails to cite the verdict against his opponents who are influencing the Galatians: Gentile believers do not need to be circumcised. If Paul follows the Jerusalem meeting's

---

the Law is reinterpreted by Jesus in light of the new epoch of God's kingdom (16:16). See Banks, *Jesus and the Law*, 218.

117. In 11:2 οἱ ἐκ περιτομῆς can refer to all the circumcised believers in the church; hence, basically everyone (Conzelmann, *Acts*, 86; cf. 10:45; Gal 2:12; Rom 4:12), or a smaller, more conscientious group within the church (Bock, *Acts*, 406). Given that Cornelius is supposed to be the first officially uncircumcised Gentile to become a Christ-follower, and Peter is very reluctant to have fellowship with him at first (Acts 10), we prefer the former.

118. Cf. Bock, *Acts*, 406.

119. On the relationship of Acts 15:20, 29 with Lev 17–18 and Targums, see further Wehnert, *Reinheit des 'christlichen Gottesvolkes.'*

In the Footsteps of Judas and Other Defectors

verdict regarding fornication (see 1 Thess 4:3–7), he does not seem to adhere to its call for Gentile Christians to abstain from idol meats and certain other foods (see 1 Cor 8–10; Rom 14). Moreover, the decision at this meeting seems to have no effect on Paul's opponents, some of which maintain a strict adherence to the Law and threaten his congregants to get circumcised (Gal 5–6; Phil 3:2–8). Jewish Christians of the Diaspora who are zealous for the Law become Paul's opponents in Acts 21:21–25 and may have even been among the hostile multitude demanding Paul's death (21:26–36; 22:22–23).[120]

Interestingly, however, Luke's final narrative of Paul in Jerusalem shows no conflict between James and Paul. In fact James and the elders of the Jerusalem church glorify God when they hear of Paul's missionary activities to the Gentiles (21:19–20a). Moreover, Paul is assured that his Gentile colleagues who are with him have no need to fear the Jewish Christians in Jerusalem: those in Jerusalem are aware of James's decision regarding Gentiles abstaining only from fornication, idol meats, things strangled, and blood, and they will not insist that Paul's colleagues be circumcised, make offerings, or perform other observances related to the Law (21:25).

Along with this assurance, however, James wants Paul to make a sacrifice at the temple so that accusations of his forsaking the Law might be quelled (21:22–24). Thousands of Jews have believed the Christ message and yet are zealous for the Law, sort of like Paul before he became a Christian (cf. Gal 1:14; Phil 3:6). They have heard that Paul teaches the Jews from the Diaspora "apostasy (ἀποστασία) from Moses," allegedly telling them not to circumcise their children or walk in Jewish customs (Acts 21:21; cf. 21:28).[121] Conceptually close to the assumption in this verse is *Mishnah Abot* 3.11A–B, in which the person who removes "the signs of the covenant of Abraham" (circumcision) and teaches "aspects of the Torah not in accord with the Law" has "no share in life to come."[122] The rumor about Paul is false so far as the Acts narrative is concerned, which never discloses Paul doing such things and in fact portrays Paul as following Jewish practices related to the Law (Acts 16:3; 18:18; 20:5, 17).

A deeper question is for us to ask whether this accusation in 21:21 can be adduced as true in Paul's letters. Paul does not teach *Jews* not to circumcise their children (1 Cor 7:18); albeit, perhaps his maxim "neither circumcision nor uncir-

---

120. On the Christian opposition to God's plan, see Rapske, "Opposition," 239–45.

121. On ἀποστασία cf. 2 Thess 2:3; Jer 2:19; 1 Macc 2:15; Josh 22:22; *Jub.* 10.21; *Mart. Ascen. Isa.* 2.4; 2 Chr 29:19. Some closely related terms could mean abandonment of marriage (Deut 24:1, 3), political rebellion (Neh 2:19; 6:6), and apostasy/forsaking God (Num 14:19; Josh 22:16, 19; 2 Macc 5:8; Sg Three, 1:9; Josephus, *Ant.* 11.8.6–7[340, 346]).

122. Neusner, *Mishnah*.

cumcision matters" could be easily interpreted this way (Gal 5:6; 6:15; 1 Cor 7:19; Col 3:11). His teaching on the Law being fulfilled in Christ (e.g., Gal 3:10–25; Rom 10:4; 2 Cor 3) certainly may have been misunderstood by some as an abandonment of Moses. More than this, Barrett raises the issue that circumcision is mentioned in 21:21 only "as the outstanding example of practising the customs generally, and it is undoubtedly true that Paul taught his fellow Jews to sit loose to legal regulations."[123] Luke does not bother to resolve such tensions for us, let alone explain how Paul would submit to James and make a token offering in the temple to appease his accusers (21:22–24; contrast Gal 2:3–6).[124] Perhaps Paul would obey James for the sake of maintaining unity with the Jerusalem church, and his own maxim of becoming a Jew under the Law for the sake of those under the Law might alleviate his conscience somewhat (cf. 1 Cor 9:20). Then again he becomes all things to all people for the sake of winning them to salvation (1 Cor 9:19, 22), and here James and the elders do not need to be saved. From the Jewish Christians' perspective in Acts 21:21, at any rate, Paul is considered an apostate, or more precisely, teaching apostasy.

Paul is almost killed in Jerusalem before his arrest; he is protected from harm because God's plan includes getting him Rome. By the end of Acts, Luke's audience finds that a reversal has taken place similar to the end of Luke's gospel. Instead of Jesus being vindicated as a true prophet of God, Paul is affirmed as a faithful messenger of God and his opponents who tried to kill him in Jerusalem, implicitly represented by the Jewish leaders in Rome, are viewed as the apostates (Acts 28:23–31). *As Jesus is vindicated of the charge of apostasy in Luke's gospel, so also Paul is vindicated of a similar accusation in Acts.* Luke wants to make a close connection between Jesus and Paul.

We notice a clear distinction between Paul and his Christian opponents, whether Pharisaic believers or the many Jewish believers who think he teaches apostasy. In Paul's own writings it is also evident that his view on the Law in relation to Gentiles is different than that of Peter and James (Gal 2:1–16); moreover, Paul does not seem to agree entirely with James's decision at the Jerusalem meeting in Acts 15 (e.g., 1 Cor 8–10). *What we are seeing here in Acts is that not all the Christians thought or believed alike, including those who may have penned some of the letters of the New Testament.* If Acts portrays actual events related to the earliest Christians, we already see competing communities among them: the Pharisaic believers do not consider uncircumcised Gentile believers to be saved, but Paul does. Followers of Christ from among the Jews think Paul is apostate, but Luke believes him to be a true messenger of God. *In these instances apostasy centers primarily on issues related*

---

123. Barrett, *Acts* 2.1009.
124. Johnson, *Acts*, 377–80, highlights the tensions.

to the Law and Jewish customs, and it seems to be relative to whoever is making the claim that the other is apostate. But there are other types of apostasy in Luke-Acts, as we will observe below.

TEMPTATION AND THE NEED FOR PERSEVERANCE (LUKE 8:4–15; 18:8; 21:18–19, 36; ACTS 11:23; 13:43; 14:22; 20:24)

Luke's version of Jesus' parable of the Sower follows the general structure of Matthew and Mark by describing four kinds of soils where seeds are sown and then providing an interpretation of the parable's meaning (Luke 8:4–15). The most immediate application of the first seed on the wayside that is taken by the devil would seem to recall the closed hearts of the Pharisees, scribes, and other Jewish leaders. Their followers would also seem to be included here, as well as all those who do not respond to the "word of God."

The second seed in Luke 8:6, 13 grows on rocky ground, i.e., "rock lightly covered with the earth."[125] The Lukan version of this parable has some interesting nuances. The seed/soil represents those who "receive" the word and "believe" for a time but then "fall away" (ἀφίστημι) in a time of testing or "temptation." The seed does sprout and grow, but it does not survive because it lacks roots in the soil and does not receive proper moisture because the ground is shallow. Instructive in this regard is Jesus' call for a radical commitment to discipleship in Luke (e.g., 9:23–26, 57–62; 14:25–35). The reality of trials his followers would face requires their absolute loyalty and obedience. The saying in Luke 9:62 captures this attitude: "no one after putting his hand to the plow and looking back is fit for the kingdom of God." The ploughman with divided loyalties is unfit for God's kingdom.[126] The saying recalls Elisha plowing his ground when Elijah calls him to be his follower (1 Kgs 19:19–21). The echo relevant in this case is that Elisha resolves to follow Elijah; there is no second-guessing about his calling.[127] Jesus is requesting a steadfast commitment from those who choose to follow him. Shallow would-be followers should not enlist in his service; they will likely become a liability when times get tough. Those who are not fully committed are like tasteless salt, which the possessors throw out (Luke 14:33–35; cf. Matt 5:13; 10:34–39).[128] Unfortunately, the meaning behind the second

---

125. Easton, *Luke*, 110.

126. A practical aspect of this saying imagines a ploughman furrowing a crooked path if he is not paying attention to what he is doing: cf. Jeremias, *Parables*, 195.

127. See Brodie, "Luke 9:57–62," 237–45.

128. Cf. Manson, *Sayings of Jesus*, 132–33. On the use of βάλλω in this verse, compare Matt 5:29; 18:9; Luke 3:6.

seed implies that many do enlist without embracing radical discipleship, and then they fall away after a period of time.

Luke's use of the terms "believe" (πιστεύω) and "receive" (δέχομαι) suggest a typical response hearers make to apostolic preaching that leads them to salvation.[129] In fact belief is directly associated with salvation in this parable (cf. 8:12).[130] In Luke's redaction we perceive a sharp contrast between the second individuals that "fall away" and the fourth individuals that "persevere" and bear fruit (8:15). We can assume, then, that those sown on the rocky ground are people who believe. From the Luke-Acts perspective they are Christian converts who are initially saved but do *not* persevere through temptations or times of testing.[131]

In 8:13 Luke uses ἀφίστημι instead of σκανδαλίζω to describe their falling away (the latter is used by Mark and Matthew in this parable). The former word in Luke-Acts normally means "to turn away" or "depart," but elsewhere in the narrative it does not mean to apostatize in a religious sense (cf. Luke 2:37; Acts 5:37–38; 12:10; 19:9; 22:29); albeit, Luke 4:13 and 13:27 and Acts 15:38 come close to such a meaning. In other ancient Jewish and Christian traditions the word is used frequently for apostasy (e.g., Deut 13:10, 13; Josh 22:18; Jer 3:14; Dan 9:9; 1 Tim 4:1; Heb 3:12; *Herm. Vis.* 2.3.2; *Herm. Sim.* 8.9.1).[132]

The "temptation" (πειρασμός) mentioned in Luke 8:13 does not seem to be related to one particular event. The word has special relevance for the concept of failing morally through enticement (Luke 4:2, 13; cf. 1 Tim 6:9; 1 Cor 10:13–14; Jas 1:12–14).[133] The parallel in Mark 4:17 stresses external suffering by using θλῖψις (affliction/tribulation) and διωγμός (persecution) instead of πειρασμός, in keeping with this gospel's emphasis on apostasy through persecution.[134] In Luke-Acts, we

---

129. πιστεύω: Acts 2:44; 4:4; 8:12, 37–38; 13:12, 48; 16:30–31/ δέχομαι: Acts 8:14; 11:1; 17:11f cf. Luke 9:48; 18:17.

130. The alternative is to suggest that this seed represents "ungenuine" or unsaved people: cf. Schreiner and Caneday, *Race*, 219–21. A weakness with this position is that these people do believe. Contrast Luke 8:12 with 8:13. The assumption is that if they believed, they would be saved. Moreover, the nature of falling away in 8:13 involves temptations, which is a type of testing authentic believers face in Luke-Acts.

131. Cerfaux, "Fructifiez en Supportant," 485–89, rightly observes a connection between 8:13 and 8:15 in terms of perseverance and temptation/testing. See further studies of these concepts in Bovon, *Luke the Theologian*, 436–42.

132. For other instances, see Bauder, "Fall, Fall Away," 1.606–8. Luke 8:13 is the only NT instance of the word as a present middle/passive indicative verb. See Sir 10:12 and 1 Macc 6:10 for the same nuance in the LXX.

133. Bovon, *L'Évangile Luc* 1.400, views the word here as "un terme éthique."

134. Cunningham, *Through Many Tribulations*, 76–77, maintains that Luke has no eschatological preference in using θλῖψις or πειρασμός. Both words are virtually synonymous in Acts 20:19, 23.

In the Footsteps of Judas and Other Defectors

discover that defection through persecution is rare, and this may be why πειρασμός is used instead of διωγμός and θλῖψις. At the same time, persecution and other trials are still evident by the use of this term (Luke 22:28, 40, 46; Acts 20:19; cf. Gal 4:14; Rev 3:10).[135] In Luke-Acts πειρασμός, then, most likely refers to allurement and testing the Christ-followers might face until the second coming (Luke 4:13; 11:4; Acts 15:26 [D, *Syr.*]; cf. Jas 1:2–4; 1 Pet 1:6). Moreover, there is no indication that the apostasy in Luke 8:13 is only temporary so that, like Peter, the second seeds are eventually restored after they have been withered. The final impression we are left with is that *those represented by the second seed are believers who depart from their faith when facing a temptation or trial. They fall away primarily because of ethical failure.* Although persecution or other threats are not necessarily precluded as possibilities that undermine their salvation, they are not emphasized here. Perhaps Luke prefers the word ἀφίστημι over σκανδαλίζω in 8:13 because he has in mind Theophilus and the socially prominent readers of his work.[136] Falling away to enticement would seem to be a more relevant issue for them than denying Christ because of being oppressed or persecuted. It also prepares the auditors for the allurement discussed in the third seed.

The third class of people fail to bear fruit because wealth and the anxieties and pleasures of life prevent them from bearing fruit to maturity (Luke 8:7, 14). The "pleasures" (ἡδονή) of life is found only here in Luke-Acts; elsewhere in the New Testament the term is associated with lust (Jas 4:1–3), the practices of non-believers (Titus 3:3), and apostates (2 Pet 2:13). The combination of this word with "riches" in Luke 8:14 recalls the images of those who trust in their wealth rather than God and are excluded from God's kingdom (e.g., Luke 16:19–31; 18:18–25; cf. 6:24–26; 19:22–26). The anxieties, pleasures, and riches of this life may be viewed as things that lead a person away from God and from the needs of others.[137] Elsewhere in Luke-Acts, the word "anxieties" (μέριμνα) is found in 21:34 where it applies to Jesus' followers.[138] They are not to get caught up with the cares of life before the eschaton takes place. If they are not alert, that final day will come upon them suddenly like a

---

135. Tannehill, *Luke*, 142, is correct here by maintaining that "Although testing may cover more than persecution, persecution is included, and Jesus will repeatedly seek to prepare his disciples for it (cf. [Luke] 9:23–26; 12:4–12; 21:12–19)."

136. Brown, *Apostasy and Perseverance*, 31, suggests the shift in this language in Luke might have to do with "an ecclesialization of the notion of apostasy." We do find σκανδαλίζω in Luke 7:23, however, and the noun form takes on the meaning of apostasy in 17:1–4.

137. So Green, *Luke*, 328.

138. In Luke 21 the disciples are not mentioned, but a vague "some" (21:5). Nevertheless it is assumed that these are followers of Jesus in 21:13–19, 36.

"trap" (παγίς), perhaps suggesting a type of divine destruction in which such followers will suffer the fate of immoral outsiders (cf. 1 Thess 5:3-10).¹³⁹

The fate of those representing the third seed is not mentioned in the parable. We could surmise that like a number of rich people in Luke-Acts they are excluded from God's kingdom, but there are quite a number of exceptions such as the centurion (Luke 7:1-10), Zaccheus (Luke 19:1-10), Barnabbas (Acts 4:36-37), Sergius Paulus (Acts 13:7-12), and others, Theophilus included. The issue of wealth does not seem to center on whether a person possesses riches but what a person *does* with those riches. Greed would seem to be involves as a negative factor. Clearly a warning against high living may be derived from this message, but categorical apostasy in relation to the third seed is not clear unless Luke has a later teaching on wealth and preoccupation in mind, such as in 17:32-33. In any case, *the wealthy from among Luke's audience would be instructed by the second and third seeds/soils not to abandon faith or be lead astray because of the allurement towards worldly pleasures and riches, or conversely, the potential anxieties they bring.*

Similar to the other gospels, Luke has the fourth seed/people sown in good soil bearing fruit, but he adds that this is eventually accomplished by their having an honest and good heart, holding fast (κατέχω), and having "perseverance" (8:15).¹⁴⁰ Namely, the Christ-followers are to possess moral qualities, persist in faith, and never give up. The same word for perseverance (ὑπομονή) is found again in 21:5-37 where Jesus affirms to his disciples that, despite upcoming persecutions, "not a hair on your head will perish, for by your perseverance you will gain your souls" (21:18-19; cf. 21:36). This is not a promise that they will be physically protected; he had just mentioned that some of them would be killed (21:16-17). Rather, those who endure the upcoming trial related to the end times may lose their physical life through martyrdom, but they will be spiritually unharmed. Those who lose their physical life for the sake of Jesus will save it for life eternal. Conversely, and similar to Mark and Matthew, those who attempt to save their physical life at the cost of denying Jesus will lose eternal life (cf. Luke 9:24; 12:5-9). Whatever physical harm might occur to Christ's followers during times of persecution, if they persevere in faith and do not deny Christ, when the future resurrection of believers takes place, they could expect a complete recompense.¹⁴¹ The type of endurance needed here requires persistence

---

139. Löverstam, *Spiritual Wakefulness*, 123-24, considers Luke 21:34-36 to be an allusion to Isa 24:17-20, in which a trap is set for the earth dwellers who will fall and never rise again. The faithful disciple will "stand before the Son of Man" in contrast to those of the earth who will fall by destruction. Cf. also *1 En.* 62.8-13; 1QH 4.21-22; 7.29-31; 18.10; 1QS 11.16-17.

140. On the terms in 8:15 see further, Bock, *Luke* 1.738-39.

141. The element of the physical would seem to be included with respect to eternal life in Luke-Acts. The author considers the resurrection of Jesus to be physical (e.g., Luke 24:36-43) and this resurrection

in faith and prayer (Luke 18:1–8). The parable of the Persistent Widow is given to encourage the "elect" (i.e., Jesus' followers) to pray, trusting that God will bring justice to their situation. The question of whether the Son of Man will find faithfulness when he returns assumes his followers would face temptations and persecutions in which they might apostatize, especially if they get discouraged in thinking that God is not answering their prayers.[142] Schrenk adds that, "The possibility of falling away is not suppressed; otherwise the final question [in Luke 18:8] would be pointless."[143] At Gethsemane Jesus' warning to the disciples that they must pray lest they enter into temptation confirms the importance of prayer as a spiritual weapon against temptation and apostasy (22:40, 46; cf. 11:4c).

Another term related to perseverance is the concept of believers remaining or continuing (μένω and variants) in the Lord (Acts 11:23; cf. Luke 22:28), in the grace of God (Acts 13:43), and in the faith (Acts 14:22; cf. 27:31). With such terms the Christ-followers in Acts are encouraged to persevere. They must continue in the gospel message as preached by the apostles and given by God's grace (Acts 13:43; 14:22; cf. 6:7; 13:8; 14:3; 20:32).[144] The Lukan Paul also hoped to finish his own "course" (Acts 20:24 cf. 13:25), which seems to convey language similar to Paul's own thought that he must endure a metaphoric footrace related to his life's journey in order to arrive at final salvation (1 Cor 9:24–27; Phil 3:14; cf. 2 Tim 4:7). In Acts, Paul's course is related to his desire to continue in the "way" of the new exodus or God's plan, even if that means his physical death. As the children of Israel were set free from their bondage to Pharaoh to travel through the desert, and as a remnant are restored to make a new trek through the wilderness in Isaiah, so the "way" or "course" in Acts involves a journey from Jerusalem to the end of the earth. And as the goal for the community is the "promised land" (Exodus–Deuteronomy) or "Zion" (Isaiah), so the community of Christians, comprised of Jews and Gentiles, must persevere until they enter their place of rest at the second coming. Failure to do so would seem to constitute apostasy.

Through the parable of the Sower in Luke we find that despite the reality of apostasy that might overtake Christ-followers because of various temptations, the way to resist is through perseverance, along with faith and prayer. The disciples are devoted to such things in Acts as they bear much fruit by reproducing other disciples as they preach the word of God. If the parable of the Sower is paradigmatic for what

---

guarantees a future resurrection of the righteous (cf. Luke 14:14; Acts 23:6; 24:15; 26:23).

142. Cf. Marshall, *Luke*, 676.

143. Schrenk, "ἐκλεκτός," 4.187–88.

144. Johnson, *Acts*, 254, rightly emphasizes this as a community affair.

follows, then his audience is prepared to encounter more examples of perseverance and falling away.

FAILURE AND DEFECTION AMONG CHRIST'S FOLLOWERS (LUKE 22:31-34, 54-62; ACTS 26:11)

In common with Synoptic parallels, fearfulness prevents the disciples from meeting the standards Jesus requires of them.[145] One example of the disciples' fear is seen when they are afraid of dying with Jesus onboard a ship during a wind storm (Luke 8:22–25). Here J. D. Kingsbury rightly notices that Jesus' question to the disciples, "Where is your faith?," alludes back to the parable of the Sower (8:4–15). If the disciples are to be among the seed sown in good soil, they must receive God's word "with a faith that holds firm and brings forth fruit with endurance, or perseverance (8:15)." Instead they perform poorly during their test when confronted by a storm at sea—they do not exercise "persevering faith."[146]

More directly relevant to persecution, and unlike the Synoptic parallels, Luke minimizes the disciples' failures. Apart from Peter's denials, Luke does not mention the disciples' abandonment of Jesus during his arrest. There is no prediction from Zech 13:7 that the disciples would fall away from him (cf. Mark 14:27; Matt 26:31); at very best their defection is only implied in 22:45–46. Some refer to 22:32b as indicating the disciples' failure,[147] but this verse may not be referring to the Twelve in relation to Christ's passion. The "brothers" whom Peter is called to strengthen in the future probably points to Christian disciples in general (e.g., Acts 6:3; 9:17; 10:23; 15:1; 17:6; 21:7) and has special relevance for Peter's commission to "strengthen" the

---

145. Although they are blessed with spiritual insight (Luke 8:10; 10:23–24), they are unable to grasp Jesus' teachings until after his resurrection (Luke 9:13, 32–33, 40–41, 44–45; 18:31–34; 19:11; cf. 24:16, 31). A full comprehension of Jesus' words are "hidden" or "concealed" from them until after his resurrection, and then their minds are "opened" to understand the scriptures as interpreted by Jesus (Luke 24:44–45). In this manner their lack of spiritual insight is associated with God's desire to bring about God's purposes at appropriately appointed times (Luke 12:42, 56; 13:35; 19:44; 21:8, 24; Acts 1:6–7; 3:19; 17:26; cf. Luke 4:13). In Acts, on the other hand, the disciples are among the eyewitnesses who have "seen and heard" the events of God's actions in Jesus (Acts 2:33; 4:20; 22:15; cf. Luke 1:2; 2:20; 7:22), and oftentimes those in the narrative who are receptive to the word of God "see" or "hear" it, whether Jews or Gentiles (Jews: Luke 5:15, 20; 6:18; 19:3–4; Acts 2:33; 17:11; cf. Luke 8:21; 11:28; 14:35; Gentiles: Acts 11:18; 13:47–48; Acts 26:17–18, 23; 28:24–28; cf. Luke 3:6). Contrast the Jewish crowd who "see" and predict weather but cannot comprehend the time of the present events related to Jesus (Luke 12:54–56). Also see Gentile opponents who have seen and heard about Paul persuading people to turn from idols (Acts 19:26). See further on the crowd in Luke in Tannehill, *Narrative Unity*, 1.158–66.

146. Kingsbury, *Conflict in Luke*, 117.

147. E.g., Manson, *Sayings of Jesus*, 340.

In the Footsteps of Judas and Other Defectors

Christ community in Acts (cf. στηρίζω in Acts 14:22; 15:32, 41; 16:5; 18:23).[148] In Luke's narrative the other disciples do not need any strengthening immediately after the passion events; no restoration is necessary because they did not abandon Jesus (cf. Luke 22:28). Luke seems to have a somewhat idealized picture of the disciples as examples of perseverance that his audience should emulate; they faithfully remain with Jesus during his temptations (Luke 22:32; cf. 21:8–9). In Luke's resurrection narrative they do have doubts and slowness to believe the scriptures (Luke 24:25–26, 38) but not to the point of defection.[149]

The same perseverance cannot be said, however, about Peter when facing potential persecution during Jesus' arrest. Perhaps Luke's audience was already familiar with the story about Peter's denials (cf. Matt 25:34–35, 69–75; Mark 14:66–72; John 13:37–38; 18:15–18, 25–27), and this might be one reason why Luke does not attempt to omit this tradition even though it might be interpreted as a foil to his generally positive portrayal of the disciples' fidelity (Luke 22:54–62). Even so, Peter's failure is played down. Satan seems partially to blame for his meltdown (22:31). Schuyler Brown asserts that Peter's denials do not constitute a loss of faith—Peter never denies that Jesus is the Messiah; he only claims that he does not know Jesus. His denial amounts to "a sin of cowardice but not a loss of faith."[150] However, Brown's distinction between Peter denying that he knows Jesus as opposed to denying Jesus as Christ does not mitigate Peter's failure. Jesus' warnings in 12:8–9, relevant in Peter's case, refers to denying Jesus "before others" (12:8: ἔμπροσθεν τῶν ἀνθρώπων; 12:9: ἐνώπιον τῶν ἀνθρώπων). Such a person will be denied by the Son of Man at the eschaton (cf. 9:26). Here it makes no difference whether a person publically denies Jesus as the Messiah or whether that person publicly denies any knowledge of Jesus. *In Luke-Acts, it would seem that any public denial of Jesus is tantamount to apostasy and places a believer at eternal risk.* Brown nonetheless discerns that Peter's faith did not completely fail. Before Peter's denial, when Jesus tells him that Satan has desired to sift him as wheat, Jesus says that he has prayed that Peter's faith "fail not," and when he is restored he is to strengthen others believers (Luke 22:31–32). That Peter's faith would not "fail" (ἐκλείπω) means that it would not be destroyed or "drained away to nothing" (22:32; cf. 16:9; 23:45).[151]

---

148. See Brown, *Apostasy and Perseverance*, 71–74.

149. Brown, 76–77, however, considers the two disciples on the road to Emmaus as examples of believers who were committing apostasy (Luke 24:12–35; cf. John 20:10). Among potential shortcomings related to this view, we question whether such weight should be given to their departing from Jerusalem when this event happened before Jesus appeared to the Twelve and charged them to stay in Jerusalem (Luke 24:49; Acts 1:8).

150. Brown, 70–71.

151. Nolland, *Luke*, 3.1072.

It is evident that Luke assumes Peter's denial is some sort of soft and temporary defection: Jesus tells Peter, "when you are returned [ἐπιστρέψας] strengthen your brothers" (22:32b). The meaning of ἐπιστρέφω conveys a return after a lapse into moral or spiritual failure, as it does in similar cases in Luke-Acts (Luke 1:16; Acts 3:19; 26:20; 28:27).[152] It could be argued hypothetically that if Peter had not repented after denying Jesus, his fate would have been similar to that of Judas, which has eternal consequences (Luke 22:22; see below). The point, however, is that Peter is assured beforehand that his faith will not be destroyed totally. Peter's mitigated lapse will take place, and when he is over his brief period of failure he will strengthen other Christ-followers. The story of Peter's denial would seem to function for the Lukan audience as an incentive to pray diligently when facing temptations, lest they fail to pray like Peter at Gethsemane and deny Christ (Luke 22:39-46; cf. Matt 26:36-46; Mark 14:32-42). On a positive note, they would also learn from Peter's remorse and subsequent leadership in Acts that those who defect for fear of persecution can be restored and greatly used in the plan of God.

Falling away as a result of persecution is almost non-existent in Acts. Witnesses such as Peter, John and his brother James (Acts 4-5, 12), Stephen (chs. 6-7), and Paul (e.g., chs. 14, 16, 18, 21-28) all stand before authorities, suffer physical harm, and yet are unafraid to proclaim Christ before hostile listeners. Paul's words seem to resonate faithfulness to Jesus' saying that the one who loses his life saves it (Acts 20:24; 21:13; cf. Luke 9:24; 17:33). For Luke's audience and Theophilus, such witnesses are bastions of perseverance; none of them falls away. As Jesus perseveres through his suffering and death in volume one, so his closest followers imitate the pattern of Jesus' perseverance in volume two of Luke-Acts. The affects of persecution, in fact, only serve to bear more fruit for the Christian witness: it helps spread the word of God to other regions including Rome at the end of the narrative,[153] it results in producing more piety and prayer among believers (e.g., 4:23-31), and it helps Luke correlate Jesus' final months with the last years of Paul (e.g., Luke 9:22, 24; 22:15-16/Acts 20:22-25, 38; 21:13, 14; Luke 9:51/Acts 19:21).[154] This all happens because the plan of God must prevail against all opposition, and Paul's message of salvation needs to reach Rome (cf. Acts 19:21; 23:11). Beyond his own agendas in the narrative, Luke's view of persecution may have been influenced by his colleague

---

152. cf. Mark 4:12; Matt 13:15; Jas 5:20; 2 Cor 3:16; Sir 48:10; 2 Kngdms[Sam] 15:20 LXX; Josephus, *Ant.* 10:53; oppositely Gal 4:9); and Fitzmyer, *Luke*, 2.1425-26, for a further range of meanings and references. Jeremias, *Parables of Jesus*, 216, goes so far as to interpret the "turn" as "be converted."

153. E.g., Acts 8:3-4; 11:19; 13:50-51; 14:5-6, 19-21; chs. 21-28.

154. On these points, see further Killgallen, "Persecution," 155-60.

In the Footsteps of Judas and Other Defectors

Paul, who rarely admits failure when it comes to being persecuted (see volume 2 of this work).

We do find one possible counterexample of believers denying Christ as a result of Paul's persecution. At Paul's defense before Herod Agrippa II, the apostle mentions his earlier days as Saul the Pharisee when he persecuted the Hellenistic-Jewish sector of the church (Acts 26:11; cf. 8:1–3; 9:1–2). His goal was to compel them to "blaspheme" (βλασφημέω), in other words, deny or curse Jesus. More specifically A. E. Harvey suggests that Paul forced them to renounce what they believed about Jesus: that he is exalted at the right hand of God as the Christ even though sentenced to death under Jewish law.[155] This would be similar to a reversal of Stephen's claim (Acts 7:54–60) and what Jesus affirmed about himself at his trial (Luke 22:66–71). This claim suggests that Jesus possessed both exalted authority and the ability to judge the Sanhedrin; and, incidentally, it is considered by the high priest as "blasphemy" in Mark 14:60–64 and Matt 26:63–65.[156]

The manner in which Paul, prior to knowing Christ, would accomplish this end may have been by torture or lashes (cf. Josephus, *J.W.* 2.8.10[152]; m. *Makkot* 3.10–15; Pliny, *Epistulae* 10.96.1–5). It could be surmised that Paul was unsuccessful in his attempt at compelling (ἀναγκάζω) the Christians to apostatize.[157] Barrett, however, is probably more accurate by saying, "we have no right to suppose that Saul was never successful in compelling Christians to blaspheme."[158] The many examples of apostasy during the Roman persecutions of the church would tend to support this claim (e.g., Pliny, *Epistulae* 10.96; Eusebius, *Hist. eccl.* 4.15; 5.1; 6:41; 8.2; Cyprian, *Laps.*).[159] There is hardly any doubt on historical ground that Paul persecuted the church in his pre-Christian days. Apart from the evidence in Acts, Paul makes such claims several times in his letters (Gal 1:13; 1 Cor 15:9; Phil 3:6; cf. 1 Tim 1:13). Paul's persecution of the Way, then, may be viewed as the first of many persecutions that would cause faithful Christians to commit apostasy. His ultimate mission of eradicating the Jewish-Hellenistic church was unsuccessful, but this does not mean that he never succeeded at getting individual Christians to renounce Jesus. Even so, *despite the historical plausibility that some of the Christians persecuted by Paul defected, Luke's idealization of Christians persevering through persecutions makes it*

---

155. Harvey, "Forty Strokes Save One," 84.

156. See Evans, *Mark*, 450–57.

157. E.g., Bruce, *Acts*, 490. The imperfect ἠνάγκαζον in Acts 26:11 could be understood as conative (attempted): e.g., Wallace, *Greek Grammar*, 550; though BDF, 169, claims it is both conative and repetitive. Notice that the imperfect ἐδίωκον in the same verse means repetitive and cannot be conative.

158. Barrett, *Acts*, 2.1156.

159. See further examples in Wilson, *Leaving the Fold*, 74–99; Oropeza, *Paul and Apostasy*, 8–9.

difficult for us to affirm that this is how Luke intended Acts 26:11 to be read. Hence, the only person who in some sense defects because of persecution in Luke-Acts is Peter. On the other hand, Luke's retention of certain Jesus' sayings makes clear that the reality of apostasy through persecution is being warned against, as we notice below.

WARNINGS OF APOSTASY RELATED TO PERSECUTION AND BLASPHEMING THE SPIRIT (LUKE 12:4-10; CF. 9:23-26; 21:12-19)

The possibility of falling away to persecution is found more clearly in the Synoptic sayings of Jesus related to discipleship (Luke 9:23-26; 12:8-9; cf. Mark 8:34-38; Matt 10:32-33, 39; 16:24-26). In Luke's version of such sayings, Jesus tells "all," not merely disciples, to take up their crosses if they wish to follow him (9:23; cf. 14:27), for whoever saves their mortal life will lose eternal life (9:24).[160] Moreover, gaining the whole world is not worth losing one's eternal life (9:25; cf. 4:5-8). We can suggest that 9:23-26 refers primarily to persecution because, similar to the Synoptic parallels, the speech is prompted by Jesus' upcoming suffering and death in Jerusalem (9:21-22), and we also read that, when Christ returns, those who are ashamed of him or have denied him before others will be disowned by him and excluded from his kingdom (9:26-27; 12:8-9). Moreover, in the coming days before the temple's destruction, the disciples would experience betrayals even from family members as a result of persecutions (21:12-19). Hence, it is quite evident that persecutions could undermine the faith of believers in the Gospel of Luke.

A significant distinction from the Synoptic parallels involves Jesus' warning against anyone who blasphemes the Holy Spirit, which in Luke's gospel is set in the context of persecution (12:10; cf. 12:4-9).[161] Unlike the other Synoptic writers, Luke does not relate this sin to an accusation made by religious leaders that Jesus casts out devils by the power of Beelzebul (cf. Matt 12:22-32; Mark 3:19-30). That story is included in Luke 11:14-22 but without the warning related to their blaspheming the Spirit. In 12:4-12 Jesus' warning is addressed to his disciples, who in the impending future will be brought before rulers and authorities.[162] As this passage

---

160. Luke has two variants of the save life/lose life saying of Jesus. Luke 9:24 follows Mark 8:35, but Luke 17:33 is sometimes said to be derived from Q: cf. Schmidt, "Zum Paradox," 332; Bovon, *Evangelium Lukas* 3.175-76. One the other hand, oral traditions might help explain the variations, especially if we accept that the historical Jesus uttered a variation or variations of the saying. See further Matt 10:39/16:25 and Mark 8:35 above.

161. Luke has probably relocated the saying from its original context. See further, Menzies, *Empowered for Witness*, 164-67.

162. The disciples are described in 12:4 as "friends" (φίλοι), which is unprecedented in the Synoptics (but see John 15:13-15). It is used here "to express the close relationship between Jesus and those who do his will and are entrusted with his secrets" (Marshall, *Luke*, 513).

In the Footsteps of Judas and Other Defectors

might imply, such events will take place in the era of the Spirit, which would come about as a result of Pentecost in Acts 2.[163] Acts lists numerous occasions in which the Christ-followers stand before such authorities (4:3-23; 5:17-40; 6:9-7:58; 16:19-36; 17:5-9; 18:12-17; 23:1-11; 24-26). The disciples must not fear persecution from such authorities who can kill the body only; they should fear instead God who has power to cast them into *Gehenna* (Luke 12:5). No doubt, if the disciples were to deny Christ before others during such times, they would also be denied by him and suffer eschatological punishment (12:8-9). Hence, in Luke the notion of blaspheming the Spirit cannot be properly understood as a temporary phenomenon relevant only to the pre-Easter blasphemy of his opponents.[164]

A case could be made that Luke 12:8-9 exhorts the disciples and their followers not to fall away during coming persecutions, while 12:10 is directed against the persecutors instead of the disciples. This interpretation would seem to flow with 12:11-12, in which "they" (the opponents) will confront and persecute the disciples while at the same time the Holy Spirit will give the disciples the right words to say when standing before their accusers. This perspective complements the account of the authorities resisting the Spirit when Stephen preached to them and his face shined as an angel (Acts 7:51; cf. 6:15). But this interpretation is far from certain. A person cannot be forgiven for blaspheming the Spirit; that individual has committed the unpardonable sin (Luke 12:10). We would need to explain, then, how the Apostle Paul, a persecutor of Christians at that time, was consenting with the stoning of Stephen at the event and yet obviously did not blaspheme the Spirit if later he was able to convert, be filled with the Spirit, and apparently be forgiven of his previous mistreatment of Christians (Acts 7:58; cf. 9:17). Moreover, the conjunction καί opening 12:10 would seem to connect well with the preceding verses 8-9, and this may suggest that the disciples are the ones who are in danger of blaspheming the Spirit. Such an interpretation of the unpardonable sin was adopted by early Christians (e.g., *Did.* 11.7; Origen, *Princ.* 1.3). For them, the *logion* was a warning for insiders instead of outsiders.

We suggest, then, that uniquely in Luke *blaspheming the Holy Spirit is something Christians can commit, as the context in 12:4-10 implies.* If persecution is being highlighted here, then in some sense it would seem to be associated with the unpar-

---

163. Cf. Gregg, *Final Judgment Sayings*, 197.

164. Incidentally, blasphemies against Jesus as the Son of Man that occurred during the time of his earthly ministry could be forgiven (cf. Luke 2:34; 23:34; Acts 3:17-19; 13:27). Brown, *Apostasy and Perseverance*, 107-8, suggests that during the future ministry of the apostles, however, blasphemies against their work will not be forgiven because such blasphemies are directed against manifestations of the Holy Spirit (Acts 13:45; 18:6). Problematic with this view is the assumption that it is once again the opponents who are blaspheming the Spirit during the apostolic age (see below).

donable sin. The notion of committing apostasy may be related to blaspheming the Spirit, but if so, then not all forms of the former amount to the latter. In particular, those who deny Jesus but afterward repent can be forgiven (12:9–10a). This shows that restoration is possible for defectors who deny Christ, and a similar case might be said for Peter (22:54–62). Blaspheming the Holy Spirit, on the other hand, cannot be forgiven (12:10b). Perhaps the missing premise is that blaspheming the Spirit involves not only denying Jesus but doing so at a time when the Spirit is being manifested in an extraordinary way. This act is something hardened apostates might do. They could experience the power of the Spirit when they were believers but then deny Jesus when facing trials and never feel the need to repent afterward. A more precise nuance in this context may suggest that this is a sin committed by Christians who resist the Holy Spirit during the time in which the Spirit is giving them correct words to say before their accusers (12:11–12). Rather than trust God's Spirit at such times, they deny Christ. It is evident that the Spirit manifests in extraordinary ways at such moments of persecution (cf. Acts 4:8, 31; 6:10, 15), and rejection of the Spirit in the face of sublime visions or spiritual manifestations may amount to final apostasy.[165]

Along these lines we seldom explore questions such as these: What if Stephen, being filled with the Spirit, had denied Jesus rather than be stoned in Acts 7:51–57? What if Paul would have rejected Christ immediately after he revealed himself to Paul and filled him with the Spirit in Acts 9? Tannehill seems to be in agreement with us: "Luke 12:10 is speaking of a disloyal disciple who, in the threatening situation where the Spirit will be most active (cf. vv. 11–12), refuses to be led by the Spirit and instead publicly reviles the Spirit given through Jesus."[166] This interpretation also provides us with one more reason why we must strain at finding any Christians falling away through persecution in Acts. To do so in view of the powerful moving of the Spirit would be equated with blaspheming the Spirit. If Christians are able to commit the unpardonable sin according to Luke 12:10, they would be denied by Christ at his second coming and presumably cast into *Gehenna* (12:5, 9).[167]

---

165. Menzies, *Empowered for Witness*, 166, seems to agree when he writes that blaspheming the Spirit "is committed by the believer who rejects the inspiration of the Spirit and denies Christ in the face of persecution."

166. Tannehill, *Luke*, 203.

167. Luke's picture of judgment, however, is not always related to the eschaton. At least sometimes he seems to suggest that punishment and rewards take place immediately after death (cf. 16:19–31; 23:43).

In the Footsteps of Judas and Other Defectors

DIVINE JUDGMENT AGAINST IMMORAL LIVING, DECEIVERS, AND THOSE WHO CAUSE OTHERS TO FALL AWAY (LUKE 12:35–48; 17:1–4, 32–33; 21:8, 34–36; ACTS 20:17–35)

Jesus' exhortations for the disciples include their being prepared for times of testing and the upcoming *parousia* (Luke 12:35–48; cf. 21:8, 34–36). In this context Peter asks Jesus, "Are you saying this parable to us or also to all?" (12:41). Given its present context, Peter would be making a distinction between the disciples and others. His "us" refers to the disciples and "all" refers to everyone, including the crowd. Peter's question seems to be a redaction included for the sake of Luke's contemporary audience. Christian leaders in particular might apply the warnings in 12:35–48 to themselves.[168] Jesus does not immediately answer Peter's question but tells another story, this time about the faithful and wise steward who is blessed when his master returns (12:42–44). We notice among Lukan alterations of this text how this version omits the Matthean "hypocrites" (Matt 24:51) to include instead "unbelievers," coinciding with his emphasis on belief/fidelity in relation to salvation. The faithful steward hints back at those disciples who will gain heavenly treasure for their faithfulness (Luke 12:33, 41–44). If the servant, thinking the master is delayed, begins to beat fellow household servants and engages in eating, drinking, and drunkenness, his master will return when he does not expect him, and will "cut him in two" and assign him with the unbelievers (12:45–46). He will be punished for his immoral living, and the judgment most likely refers to punishment in the afterlife (cf. Matt 24:51). The message is clear enough: Christians who behave like the unfaithful servant can expect to be excluded from the Lord's household and suffer the same fate as unbelievers. In essence *this servant's hatred toward fellow servants shows him to be ashamed of the "words" of Christ* (Luke 9:26), who taught his followers to love their neighbors as themselves (10:25–37; cf. 6:27, 35–37, 11:42). That servant is shown to be an apostate through his deeds.

The passage continues that the servant who knows the master's will but does not do it will be beaten with many stripes, but the one who did not know his will, will be beaten with few (12:47–48). This saying may have been originally an independent *logion* that Luke added to the preceding verses in order to elaborate on punishment awaiting unfaithful servants.[169] The text would seem to imply either that there are various degrees of punishment in the afterlife or that a stricter judgment awaits

---

168. More precisely than me, Bovon, *L'Évangile Luc* 2.297, interprets 12:41 in a binary way related to the church. Although the word "parable" is singular in 12:41, it most likely refers to 12:35–40 rather than only 12:39–40. If 12:41 is not entirely created by Luke, an alternative explanation is that he may have heavily edited Mark 13:37.

169. On its possible Aramaic origin, see Black, *Aramaic*, 256–57.

those who know the word of God and teachings of Christ (cf. Luke 10:14; 20:47; cf. Jas 3:1; 4:17). In this thought we find similarities with the ancient dichotomy of a person sinning ignorantly and a person sinning with a high hand (Num 15:30; Deut 17:12; *m. Shabbat* 7.1; CD 8.8; cf. 2 Pet 2:21).[170] The servant is placed in authority over others and supposed to be morally prepared (cf. Luke 12:42); instead, he does not do what he is supposed to do and is thus punished more severely than the one who does not know the Lord's will. The implication is that disciples have a higher degree of responsibility than the ignorant. In effect 12:47–48 is a roundabout answer to Peter's question in 12:41. The "parable" is for "all," both disciples and the crowd, but the disciples and Christian leaders will be punished more severely or with greater strictness than other individuals if they are not prepared for the *parousia* of the Son of Man (12:40). Their responsibility is proportional to what they are given (12:48b cf. 16:10–12; 19:26). In 12:35–46 all the hearers of Jesus' words are warned of dire eschatological consequences that await them if they are unfaithful to the Lord, and *apostate Christian leaders would seem to face a more rigorous standard of punishment than typical apostates or non-Christians.*

The Lukan exhortation to "remember Lot's wife" is also instructive in relation to Christ's *parousia* and eschatological judgment (17:32). The disciples are warned not to look back as Lot's wife did at the destruction of Sodom when she turned into a pillar of salt (cf. Gen 19:17). In early Jewish and Christian traditions the story of Lot's wife is often used as an example of apostasy.[171] Looking back is dangerous because it marks the first step toward *turning back*, and turning back is one Lukan way of expressing a departure from the way of salvation (Luke 22:32; Acts 7:39; cf. Heb 10:38; 2 Pet 2:2). The error in 17:32 probably has to do with believers holding on to the material concerns and pleasures of this life (cf. 17:26–30) and so it may recall the Christians represented by the third seed in the parable of the Sower (cf. Luke 8:14). Luke combines the warning about Lot's wife with a common Jesus *logion*, "the one who seeks to keep his life will lose it," in 17:33.[172] That is, *the disciples are warned that looking back and self-preservation can lead to apostasy that will result in their losing eternal life at the second coming.* Unlike the parallel in 9:24, the prominent saying of Jesus in 17:33 has been removed from the matrix of persecution and cross-bearing to a new setting related to the temptation of worldly pleasures and preoccupations

---

170. Cf. Culpepper, *Luke*, 264–65.

171. E.g., Wis 10:7; Josephus, *Ant* 1.11.4[203]; Philo, *Alleg.* 3.75[213]; *Dreams* 1.247–48[42]; *Flight* 22[121]; *Virtues* 181[34]; *1 Clem.* 11:1–2; 23:9; Tertullian, *Marc.* 4.35.

172. Here the nuance of the saying contrasts the idea of keeping/preserving life (περιποιέω, ζωογονέω) and losing it.

of life as the end the age approaches.[173] To hold on to such things constitutes saving one's mortal life, but letting go of such things (i.e., lose one's mortal life) will gain one eternal life.

Similar to the other Synoptic parallels, the Lukan Jesus states consequences worse than death by drowning for the one who causes "little ones" to fall away (σκανδαλίζω), intimating eschatological condemnation for such a person (Luke 17:1–2; cf. Mark 9:42–48; Matt 18:6–9).[174] Again, as in the Synoptic parallels, the little ones are believers, but the context of children and imagery of sheep does not seem to be present in Luke's case. Since he highlights the marginalized, such as the poor, weak, and outcasts, these type of believers may be primarily in view. Apostasies are inevitable, but a woe is given to the one by whom they come (Luke 17:1; cf. Matt 18:7). The woe here is properly understood as an "expression of pity for those who stand under divine judgment" (Luke 6:24–26; 10:13; 11:42–47, 52; 22:22).[175] In this setting Jesus speaks directly to his disciples (17:1) and relates falling away to internal struggles among fellow believers in the area of forgiving the ones who sin against them (17:3–4). It becomes evident, then, that 17:1–2 does not center on outsiders causing Christians to fall away, but on Christians causing other Christians to fall away. An unmerciful and unforgiving attitude among fellow believers might become the cause of a person abandoning Christ and his church (cf. 6:36–37). Unloving behavior or divisions may play major factors in this type of falling away.

For Luke's audience, 17:1–4 would be entirely relevant to problems arising from within the congregation. The difficult task of forgiving a repentant Christian "seven times" a day would prompt both believers and leaders alike to request Jesus to "increase our faith!" (17:5). Luke's version of this teaching omits Jesus' exhortation to cut off body parts rather than be cast into hell. This omission is probably not because Luke wanted to play down a fiery judgment against sinning congregation members; immediately prior to this teaching, he inserts a vivid picture of what the punishment

---

173. Schmidt, "Zum Paradox," 332, likewise argues that Luke 17:33 is not directly related to martyrdom. Gregg, *Final Judgment Sayings*, 261, suggests from 17:33 the meaning that one must forsake the world to preserve one's life.

174. Brown, *Apostasy and Perseverance*, 29, associates Luke 17:1–2 with the parable of Lazarus and the rich man (Luke 16:19–31) to affirm Lazarus as a "type" representing the "little ones." For Brown, the "scandals" in 17:1 are related to those who inflict offenses on the Christian community from the outside. The comparison of 17:1–2 with this parable is quite interesting, but much depends on whether the one who is causing the stumbling in 17:1–2 is an insider or outsider. In the story involving Lazarus the rich man does not represent a Christ-follower but an outsider whose disposition resembles King Herod.

175. Marshall, *Luke*, 255. Contrast Nolland, *Luke*, 2.837, who writes regarding 17:1, "We need not think that some extreme form of sin or apostasy is in view here." But his mitigation is unlikely given the severe judgment in 17:2, which has eternal consequences.

in 17:1–2 would look like by describing a rich man burning in Hades (cf. 16:19–31). In 17:1–4, then, both the inevitability of apostasy among Christians and divine judgment on the congregation members who cause it are affirmed.

One further venue for apostasy in Luke-Acts comes through deception by false teachers. Luke's version of the coming eschatological crisis follows Mark 13 and Matt 24 by warning that Jesus' followers must not be misled by false messiahs (cf. Luke 17:21–23; 21:8/Matt 24:11, 23–24; Mark 13:22). Luke seems concerned about his audience behaving like false teachers. In his version of the Beatitudes, Jesus warns his hearers that if all speak well of them, so did their ancestors speak of the false prophets. Together with the rich and those who live at ease, a warning of divine judgment, or woe, is given to such individuals (Luke 6:25–26). Moreover, Jesus not only warns his followers against the hypocrisy of the Pharisees (12:1) but also against false teaching that could arise from among their very ranks. Jesus' saying about the blind leading the blind in 6:39–40 is here a warning addressed to his followers; it does not seem to be directed against the Pharisees as in Matt 15:12–14. Luke has in mind the thought that Christians must not only avoid false teachers, but also they must not become false teachers themselves.[176] But the context is difficult, and we must admit that this is only one of many interpretations. Another possibility is that 6:39–40 is related to the notion of wrongly attempting to correct the faults of others (6:41–42).[177] Certainly, for Luke's audience there is a warning that misguided Christian leadership has negative consequences for both the leaders and followers. The "pit" (βόθυνος) refers to a deep, gaping hole.[178] The idea here may recall sheep falling into a pit (cf. Matt 12:11) and suggests a terrible end that includes divine judgment (cf. Isa 24:17–23).

The power of deception is a grave concern for the Lukan Paul when he gives his farewell speech to the church leaders of Ephesus at Miletus (Acts 20:17–35). It is evident that this group was comprised of both Jews and Gentiles (19:8–10),[179] but Gentiles eventually seem to predominate.[180] Paul exhorts their leaders to "take heed" (προσέχετε: 20:28) and "be alert" (γρηγορεῖτε: 20:31) in relation to themselves and their congregation. Elsewhere in Luke-Acts, being alert and watching is tantamount to staying morally faithful (γρηγορεῖτε: Luke 12:37–39; προσέχετε: Luke 21:34) and

176. Along these lines is Schürmann, "Warnung des Lukas," 57–81.

177. Nolland, *Luke*, 1.306, raises a list of competing viewpoints.

178. Cf. Bock, *Luke*, 1.611.

179. On diversity in the ancient church in Ephesus, see further Trebilco, *Early Christians*, ch. 3, esp. 152–53.

180. Many of the idolaters were being persuaded by Paul to abandon their gods (19:21–41). The Ephesians also practiced magic, even as Christians, before finally destroying their books on magic (19:18–20).

In the Footsteps of Judas and Other Defectors

avoiding the influence of false teachers (βλέπετε: Luke 21:8), Pharisees (προσέχετε: Luke 12:1), and scribes (προσέχετε: Luke 20:46). The reason for this warning in Acts 20:31 is that Paul predicts "fierce wolves" will come in and not spare the community (20:28-29). The "wolves," in contrast to shepherds, appear to be false teachers who would infiltrate the group and have the potential to lead astray many followers, causing them to pervert their faith.[181] The Lukan Paul's use of the phrase "I am innocent of the blood of all of you" (20:26) is a declaration that is featured in farewell discourses, and as Paul Trebilco affirms regarding this instance, it is "a Lucan expression, which implicitly envisages the defection of some of the Ephesian Christians" (cf. Acts 5:28; 18:6).[182] Farewell speeches frequently include predictions about apostasy or calamity (cf. 2 Tim 3:1-5; 4:3-4; 2 Pet 2:1-3; *T. Levi* 4.1; 10.2-5; *T. Jud.* 18.1-6; *T. Isaac* 6.1-4; *T. Naph.* 4.1-5).[183]

More than this, some of their leaders (καὶ ἐξ ὑμῶν αὐτῶν) will become apostate and seduce their congregation members away from the Christian message (Acts 20:30-31).[184] *In Ephesus it is some of the seasoned elders, once tried and true, who will become false teachers.* They will draw away members to themselves presumably to start a rival church that corrupts the gospel message.[185] Since Acts 20 is addressed to the Ephesian Christians in the late first century, it is significant that other early church writings addressed to this community likewise identify false teachings at this location (cf. 1 Tim 1:3, 19-20; 4:1-3; Rev 2:2, 6; 1 John 2:18; Ign. *Eph.* 7-9, 16). The Pastoral Letters, Rev 2:2, and Acts 20 might be suggesting the same group, but other accounts in this location describe the false teachings and opponents differently. Beyond the prediction of false teachers, it may be that magicians and sorcerers are inferentially warned against (cf. Acts 8:9-24; 13:6-11; 16:16-18). Apostolic encounters with such people always have the Christians triumph over the deceivers. Theophilus and other readers would affirm through such narratives that God's Spirit is more powerful than magical forces and evil spirits. *The inclusion of the warning*

---

181. Cf. Matt 7:15; *Did.* 16.3; Ign. *Phld.* 2.1-2; 2 *Clem.* 5.2-4; Justin, *Apology* 1.16.13; Gen 49:27; Prov 28:15; Ezek 22:27; Zeph 3:3; 4 *Ezra* 5.18; 1 *En* 89.13-27. For early Christian references to false prophets and teachers, see Lampe, "Grievous Wolves," 254-55, 268.

182. Trebilco, *Early Christians*, 189.

183. Cf. ibid., 189n144.

184. Walton, *Leadership and Lifestyle*, 82, seems to agree. Although Codex Vaticanus (B) omits αὐτῶν in Acts 20:30a, multiple attestations of other ancient witnesses support its inclusion.

185. In agreement with Trebilco, *Early Christians*, 191. The nuance "draw out" (ἀποσπάω) may not be strong enough, a more violent "tear away" might convey the sense, according to Schneider, *Apostelgeschichte*, 2.364. BDAG, 120, has the meaning of the present active infinitive in 20:30 as "draw away, attract, proselyte," and reserves the passive/middle voice for "tear oneself away" (cf. Acts 21:1; *Herm. Sim.* 6.2.3).

in Acts 20 nonetheless would alert the Lukan audience of dangerous teachers situated within the Christian community that lead believers away from apostolic faith.

JUDAS' BETRAYAL AND DEATH
(LUKE 6:16; 22:4, 6, 21–22; ACTS 1:15–26)

Multiple accounts from Luke and the other gospels identify Judas as the one who delivered Jesus over to the authorities, and he was numbered among twelve disciples.[186] William Klassen argues that παραδίδωμι, which is normally used in the gospels to describe the act, should be interpreted as "hand over" rather than "betray" (e.g., Mark 3:19; cf. Luke 9:44; 18:32; 20:20; 22:4, 6, 21–22, 48; 24:7, 20). Klassen maintains that Judas's act was not a betrayal; in fact, "we have no reason to believe that Jesus considered the act of Judas sinful or wrong."[187] F. A. Gosling, however, surveys the word παραδίδωμι in classic literature, the LXX, and Josephus, and shows many instances in which "betray" is the appropriate meaning.[188] We are on safe ground to determine that Judas is viewed as a "traitor" for handing over Jesus to the authorities (cf. Luke 6:16). His motive for betrayal is the same as in the Synoptics: he is tempted by money and so succumbs to greed. Luke adds, however, that he was also possessed by Satan at this time, and so the devil becomes a type of co-conspirator who influences Judas to betray Jesus (Luke 22:2–6).

A comparative survey of the early stories about Judas' death reveals conflicting reports. What seems to stand out as a common thread between these different accounts is that Judas' death conveys an end that is negative.[189] Judas hangs himself in Matthew (27:1–3), he falls down and explodes in Acts (1:15–19), he swells up or is crushed by a wagon in Papias traditions (*frags.* Papias 18),[190] and he is stoned in a vision in the *Gospel of Judas* (44.23—45.2, 11–12). It is not entirely clear, however, that Judas actually dies from the stoning, and we do not know if his vision comes to pass. The author apparently knew about Judas' replacement by Matthias from Acts 1:15–26 or a tradition similar to it. Jesus says to Judas that someone will replace him,

---

186. Mark 3:19; 14:10–11, 18–21; Matt 10:4; 26:21–25; 27:3; Luke 6:16; 22:3–6, 22, 47–48; Acts 1:15–26; John 6:71; 12:4; 13:2, 21–30; 18:2–5.

187. Klassen, "Authenticity of Judas' Participation," 409; cf. idem, *Judas*, 47–58.

188. Gosling, "Oh Judas!" 117–25. The issue of exonerating Judas seems motivated in part by the tragic stereotype he has played throughout history as an alleged representative for the Jewish people: cf. Maccoby, *Judas*. Anti-Semitic interpretations of Judas in church history should be rightly condemned. For literary sources in church history associating Judas and anti-Semitism, see in Zwiep, "Judas and the Jews," 72–82; Burnet, *L'évangile de la trahison*, 230–52.

189. See fuller treatment in Oropeza, "Judas' Death."

190. See further elaboration of Papias in Zwiep, *Choice of Matthias*, 112–15.

In the Footsteps of Judas and Other Defectors

and Judas is associated with the number thirteen (*Gos. Jud.* 35.27–36.4; cf. 44.21; 46.19–20). This gospel possibly expands on Judas' death from Acts 1:18. His "falling headlong" and being "burst open in the middle" (Acts 1:18) may have been understood as a result of falling down a cliff while being chased by the other disciples. This would be similar to Luke mentioning a hostile crowd at Nazareth unsuccessfully attempting to throw Jesus off a cliff (cf. Luke 4:29). The purpose of doing so may be related to an ancient procedure of casting down a victim before stoning the person (*m. Sanhedrin* 6.4; Eusebius, *Hist. eccl.* 2.23.16).[191] If so, then the *Gospel of Judas* cloaks a possible scenario that takes into account Judas' death and reads a plausible meaning into Acts 1:18. This interpretation of his death raises a new speculation on how the historical Judas may have died: an angry crowd of Jesus sympathizers chased Judas, intending to stone him in a lynch-mob manner, and he died either by falling or being thrown off a cliff.

Some interpreters synthesize Matthew and Acts to read that Judas hung himself, then the branch or rope upon which his body suspended broke, plunging Judas to the ground so that his entrails burst out.[192] This synthesis of stories, however, is not very convincing and does not explain why Acts would omit details as important as Judas' repentance and subsequent suicide by hanging. Both Matthew and Acts mention money, a Field of Blood, and the fulfillment of scripture, but there are major differences: 1) in Matthew the priests buy the field, while in Acts Judas buys it; 2) the field is called Akeldama (Field of Blood) in Matthew due to blood money, while in Acts it is called this because of what happens there (Judas' entrails burst out); 3) in reference to Judas, Matthew cites Zech 11:12–13 (Matt 27:9–10; cf. Jer 39:7–9 LXX; 18:2; 19:1), whereas Luke cites Pss 68[69]:26 and 108[109]:8 (Acts 1:20); and finally 4) in Acts there is no mention of the Potter's Field, thirty pieces of silver, or the field's use as a cemetery.[193] In all likelihood the two versions come from different sources that have different endings: Matthew claims Judas died by hanging; Luke writes he died by falling. Both deaths suggest a tragic ending for this disciple, but a harmonization of the two seems artificial.

The historical reason for these contrasting stories about Judas' death remains a mystery. One possibility is that Judas' death stems from an original community that was embarrassed to speak about him and reluctant to remember what happened to him once he defected from their group. The apostasy of Judas was a bad memory the earliest followers of Christ would have liked to forget. Most of the original disciples

---

191. For other sources see Blinzler, "Jewish Punishment," 147–61.
192. E.g., Augustine, *Fel.* 1.4; Vulgate of Acts 1:18: "being hanged, he burst asunder..."
193. Cf. Zwiep, *Choice of Matthias*, 106–8.

probably did not know firsthand what happened to Judas after he defected.[194] Then years after the betrayal took place conflicting stories and rumors began to develop about his end, some of them resembling the death of apostates and betrayers in earlier traditions.

In Israel's scriptures and ancient Jewish traditions, parallels to Judas' death include suicidal hangings, stonings, spilling of entrails, bursting asunder, and destruction.[195] Acts records similar tragedies: Ananias and Sapphira drop dead after holding back possessions and lying to God's Spirit (Acts 5:1-11), Herod Agrippa suffers a belly disorder and is eaten by worms for dishonoring God (12:21-25; cf. Josephus, *Ant*. 19.8.2 § 343-50), and Elymas the sorcerer is struck blind when opposing Paul (13:9-11). The resemblance between these stories with the death of Judas in earliest Christian sources lead us to suspect that his end may have happened as a result of divine curse or punishment. It is quite plausible that *the early auditors of these stories would have concluded that Judas' life was cut short because this is typical of what happens to apostates, traitors, and people who commit terrible acts*. For the most part this suspicion is confirmed by implications related to Judas' final destiny after death in these sources, which may have been developed through early pronouncements about Judas attributed to Jesus.

JUDAS' REPLACEMENT AND ETERNAL DESTINY
(LUKE 22:22; ACTS 1:20-26; CF. MARK 14:21; MATT 26:24)

If there remains ambiguity in early Christian sources about how Judas died, the oldest record of his end in the Synoptic Gospels is univocal in attaching condemnation to Judas (Luke 22:22; Mark 14:21; Matt 26:24). Mark's version is perhaps the earliest: "For the Son of Man goes according as it is written concerning him, but woe to that man through whom the Son of Man is betrayed; better for him if that man had not been born!"[196] The saying probably originates with Jesus: its language is primitive, there is multiple attestation of the saying, and it reveals the discomfiting aspect of a traitor in the midst of Jesus' most esteemed followers.[197] Whether we translate παραδίδοται here as "betrayed" or "handed over" makes relatively no

---

194. Interestingly Zwiep, *Choice of Matthias*, 47-48, 53, compares psychoanalytic collective repression (Freud and Fromm) with the community's shame in relation to Judas.

195. E.g., Josh 7:22-26 LXX; 2 Sam 17:23-24; 20:9-10; Josephu,s *Ant*. 7.9.8 § 228-32; *J.W*. 7.11.1-4 § 441-53; *Ahiqar*; cf. Tob 14:10-11; 4Q198 2. For other parallels, see Paffenroth, "Stories of Judas," 80; Zwiep, *Choice of Matthias*, 63-72.

196. Mark 14:21 and Matthew 26:24 are almost alike, but Luke 22:22 has more significant differences. On possible redactions, see discussion in Fitzmyer, *Luke* 1.95-96, 166-69.

197. On possible Semitic aspects see, e.g., Black, *Aramaic*, 117-18.

difference in the context; the pronouncement clearly suggests Judas is guilty for participating in Jesus' arrest.

The first sentence of the saying is repeated in variations by Jesus who speaks of his upcoming suffering and death in accordance with God's plan or Israel's scriptures (Mark 14:21a/Matt 26:24a/Luke 22:22a cf. Mark 9:31, 44; 13:33; Matt 17:12; 20:18; Luke 9:44; 18:31–32). Luke's version omits "as it is written" and inserts "as it has been determined" (ὡρισμένον) to stress Jesus' upcoming death as a divine necessity in keeping with God's overall plan of salvation (cf. ὁρίζω in Acts 2:22–24; 10:42; 17:26, 31). Even so, this necessity seems related to the fulfillment of scripture (cf. Luke 18:31; 24:25–27, 44–47).[198]

Despite Jesus' death being determined by God, there remains a responsibility Judas must bear for delivering up his teacher, even if he is the instrument "through" (διά) whom this divine plan takes place (Luke 22:22; cf. Mark 14:21; Matt 26:24). There is no evidence in the gospels or Acts that Judas knowingly cooperated with God in betraying Jesus or was coerced to do so. It would be inappropriate, then, to claim that Judas' fulfilling of scriptures or God's purposes in having Jesus arrested somehow suggests Judas' innocence. The phrase "woe to that man" recalls the numerous woe oracles of impending divine judgment prominent in prophetic literature (e.g., Isa 30:1; 31:1; Hos 7:13; 9:12; Amos 6:1; Mic 2:1–3).[199] The six woes addressed to the wicked in Isa 5:8–22, for example, which immediately precedes the Isaianic curse of spiritual blindness on apostates from among God's people (6:9–10), includes the houses of these apostates being left desolate (5:9; cf. 6:11). This thought perhaps recalls Ps 68[69]:26, which is cited in reference to Judas's habitation left desolate (Acts 1:20).[200] Perhaps Ps 68[69]:26 echoes Isa 5:9 or vice versa. Similar to Judas' death in Acts 1, the woes in Isa 5 continue by saying that the wicked among God's people will face the consequences of God's wrath and their dead bodies will be exposed like refuse (Isa 5:25).

---

198. Exactly what scripture is being echoed in Mark 14:21 and the parallels is a matter of guesswork—the list of candidates is fairly long (cf. Isa 52:13–53:12; Zech 9–14, esp. 13:7; Dan 9:24–27; Ps 22; 34:19; 41:9; Wis 2:10–20; 3:1–9). The aspect of his upcoming suffering would seem to favor the Isaianic "servant" motif (Isa 52–53), which the gospels recognize as having special relevance to Jesus' death (e.g., Mark 10:45; 14:24; Matt 20:28; 26:28; Luke 22:37; Acts 8:30–35); but perhaps most likely of all is the perspective that Jesus is referring to the scriptures in a general way without having any particular passage in view.

199. Similar woe imagery is adapted by apocalyptic writers in reference to God's eschatological wrath upon the wicked (e.g., Rev 9:12; 11:14; 18:10–19; *1 En.* 38.2; 95.4–7; 99.11–16; *2 Bar.* 10.6–7; *Sib. Or.* 3.310).

200. Steyn, *Septuagint Quotations*, 54, recognizes the comparison between Isa 6:11 and Acts 1:20/Ps 68[69] but without connecting these to the woe motif.

Luke and Matthew commonly use the word "woe" (οὐαί) to express impending divine judgment,[201] and evidently from these gospels Jesus' woe suggests divine judgment against Judas (Matt 26:24; Luke 22:22). Differently, Mark does not use "woe" elsewhere except when expressing deep emotion for pregnant and nursing women who will face tribulation during the end times (Mark 13:17). Comparable with this nuance Klassen argues that Jesus' woe to Judas in Mark 14:21a conveys sorrow rather than a curse or condemnation.[202] This woe, however, does not *merely* express great sorrow or compassion for Judas; it also declares impending divine judgment, as the following phrase in Mark 14:21b (cf. Matt 26:24b) reveals: "better for him if that man had not been born." The woe against Judas in all three Synoptics, then, suggests an impending judgment or destruction awaits the betrayer. Luke 22:22 notably omits "better for him if that man had not been born," which is probably for simplification's sake; it might have seemed somewhat redundant for him to add it given that elsewhere in this gospel the notion of woe is clearly related to divine judgment (e.g., 6:24–26; 17:1–2). The woe in 17:1–2, for example, implies eschatological punishment—a fate far worse than drowning awaits the person who causes one of Jesus' followers to stumble. It is also possible that the woe and comparative sayings in Mark 14:21 were originally separate *logia*. "That man" may recall a curse formula from Israel's scriptures (cf. Lev 17:4, 9; 20:3–5; Deut 17:5),[203] and the thought of being better off not born evokes from other traditions those who undergo great judgment, curse, or suffering.[204] In *1 En.* 38:2–3 the concept involves the eschatological destruction of those who are separated from God's elect and have denied the Lord.

The comparative "better" in Mark 14:21b parallels well with Mark 9:42–47, in which Jesus warns against the person who causes followers of Jesus to fall away: it would be "better" for that person if a millstone were fastened to his neck and he was drowned in the depth of the sea (9:42). It is also "better" to cut off an offensive member of one's body than to be cast into the fires of hell or *Gehenna* (9:43–47). Jesus gives these warnings to his disciples, suggesting their own potential to commit apostasy and suffer damnation at the eschaton. Matthew 18:6–9 reads similar to Mark 9:42–47, sentencing the wrongdoer to "eternal fire," but among other nuances it adds "woe to that man," the phrase used to refer to Judas in Mark 14:21/Luke 22:22/Matthew 26:24. The connection between Matt 18:6–9 and 26:24 became evident enough for Clement of Rome to conflate the two sayings and announce a woe

---

201. Matt 11:21; 18:7; 23:13, 15, 16, 23, 25, 27, 29; Luke 6:24–26; 10:13; 11:42–47; 17:1–2.

202. Klassen, *Judas*, 81–84.

203. So Allison and Davies, *Matthew*, 3463.

204. Cf. Job 3:1–12; Sir 23:14; *2 Bar.* 10.6–7; *2 En.* 41.2; *4 Ezra* 4.12; *m. Hagigah* 2.1; *Sib. Or.* 3.310; *1 Clem.* 46:8; *Herm. Vis.* 4.1.2; 4.2.6; Irenaeus, *Haer.* 2.20.5; 4.28.1–2.

In the Footsteps of Judas and Other Defectors

on the man who causes one of the elect to fall away: it would be better for him "if he had not been born" and better also "to have been tied to a millstone and cast into the sea" (1 *Clem.* 46:8).

The judgment on Judas, then, in Luke 22:22/Mark 14:21/Matt 26:24 addresses more than Judas' physical death and loss of property; it seems to suggest his final condemnation. The early hearers of this denunciation from the gospels would have most likely come to this conclusion when recalling the parallel sayings of Jesus in Luke 17:1–2, Mark 9:42–47, and Matt 18:6–9. Perhaps the saying also gave rise to diverse speculations about how Judas died, as evinced by the later stories of his death. His fate was perceived negatively by Jesus as a result of his betrayal and apostasy, and so the early Christian writers may have imagined that, apart from any punishment Judas would face on judgment day, his physical death must have also been horrible. Judas' negative fate seems sealed in Mark, but Matthew leaves open the possibility of Judas' exoneration due to his remorse (see above). In Luke-Acts, however, there is no evidence of Judas' remorse before his death. His eternal fate is viewed most clearly in this account.

In Luke's gospel Judas enjoys having authority over demons and ability to heal diseases (9:1). He also partakes of the Lord's Supper (22:17–23). Yet he becomes a traitor possessed by Satan and is promised money when collaborating with the authorities about Jesus' arrest (Luke 6:16; 22:2–6; Acts 1:16b). Schuyler Brown correctly observes that discipleship in Luke involves a journey with Jesus leading the way, and perseverance is necessary for those who stand by Jesus. Judas' act is viewed as apostasy, a "departure" from Jesus (Luke 22:4).[205] Judas is therefore a traitor and apostate, and severe judgment awaits those followers of Christ who turn out of the way, especially those who were once leaders (12:4–10; 17:1–2, 32–33). As we have observed already, a greater punishment occurs to those who know the Lord's will and do not do it than for those who do not know the Lord's will (12:46–48). Judas would appear to be an example of the first case. The fate of Judas in Luke 22:22 seems associated with final judgment when we compare it with Luke's version of Judas' end in Acts 1:15–26. At least three observations from Acts suggest Judas' punishment involves more than losing his physical life.

First, the citations in Acts 1:20 from Pss 68[69]:25–26 and 108[109]:8 are imprecatory, related to cursing one's enemies. The latter involves sending an accuser (διάβολος) to stand at the right hand of the Davidic enemy, who is judged guilty and his name "blotted out" (Ps 108[109]:6–8, 13; cf. v. 17). The former psalm includes a prayer for the enemies' life to be cut short, their food to become a poisonous snare

---

205. Brown, *Apostasy and Perseverance*, 82.

and stumbling block, and their name to be blotted out of the book of the righteous (Ps 68[69]:22–29). The motif of God having a heavenly book wherein the righteous are listed and the wicked are not follows early Jewish and Christian traditions, often in reference to eternal destinations.[206] The choice of these psalms would seem to favor a reading in which Judas' end involves something more than physical death.

Second, Jesus promised the Twelve they would sit with him on thrones "judging the twelve tribes of Israel" (Luke 22:30/Matt 19:28). The apostasy of Judas reduced the number of disciples to eleven (Acts 1:26; cf. Luke 24:9, 33) and left a vacant seat that needed to be filled if twelve disciples were to reign in the future kingdom, and so Luke includes the replacement of Judas by Matthias in the Acts narrative.[207] Significantly no replacement is needed for James, another member of the Twelve, when he dies later on in Acts 12:1–2. His eschatological place is secure because he died a martyr. He will sit on one of the twelve thrones judging the tribes of Israel. The same could not be said of Judas; another must take his place because he will not participate in the future kingdom of God.

Third and finally, Judas went to his own "place" (Acts 1:25–26). This could be referring to his death in the field that he purchased, but when combined with the implied curse from the Psalms and the reason for his replacement, Judas' "place" (τόπος) more likely refers to a transcendent region related to one's final destiny, a sense τόπος connotes on a number of occasions.[208] In this case the term probably refers to hell (cf. Luke 16:28; *T. Ab.* A13; B10; *Tg. Eccl.* 6.6; *Herm. Sim.* 9.4.7; Ign. *Magn.* 5.1). Judas died an apostate and apostates will not be with Christ; their lot is with the wicked.

Thus, in Luke-Acts *Judas' end is portrayed as a form of divine punishment that leads to loss of eternal life, and this lends to an implication that his betrayal was seen as a wrongful act and apostasy.* Unlike Peter, however, he falls away not because of persecution but because of succumbing to Satan and the temptation of greed (cf. Luke 22:2–6). To be sure, there are probably other motives behind this great betrayal, but we will probably never know them. Judas' betrayal of Jesus over a sum of money

---

206. E.g., *Jub.* 30:20–23; 36:9–10; *4 Ezra* 14:50; *1 En.* 81:4; 12:3; Rev 3:5; 22:18–19; cf. Luke 10:17.

207. Interestingly, Basil (*Hom.* 19) relates a legend about forty Christian soldiers of Sebaste who became martyrs after refusing to sacrifice to idols. They are forced by Licinius' officers to spend a night naked in a frozen pond in the sight of a hot bath. Under this torture one man apostatized, jumped into the hot bath, and died immediately. One of his tormentors, saw a vision of angels carrying rewards for the thirty-nine, but a fortieth angel had no one left to whom he could give a reward. The man threw off his clothes and jumped into the pond claiming to be a Christian, and so the number forty was maintained in relation to these martyrs.

208. Conversely, τόπος is also used of the place of salvation (e.g., Tob 3:6; *T. Job* 49.2). See examples of both in BDAG, 1011.

EXPULSION FROM THE WAY: THE SIN OF ANANIAS AND SAPPHIRA (ACTS 5:1-10)

In the early days of the Way, when believers held all things in common, Ananias and Sapphira's death took place because they held back some of their possessions while pretending to lay down everything before the apostles (5:1–11; cf. 2:44–45; 4:32–37). Ananias is struck dead when Peter exposes his duplicity, and later Sapphira dies when confronted by Peter. In both cases they fall dead on the spot, leaving the reader with a strong impression that their death has resulted from divine punishment, as was the case with Judas (cf. 1:15–20).

This couple's conversion probably took place either at Pentecost (Acts 2) or with the added number of Jews who believed afterward (4:4). If so, they believed, were baptized, and received the Holy Spirit (2:38–39; 4:31). Most likely, then, Ananias and Sapphira are seen as authentic believers whom Satan influences to commit a gross sin. Their being "filled" with Satan (5:3) may be set over against being filled with the Spirit of God (2:4; 4:31).[209] Whereas Satan enters into Judas (Luke 22:3), he fills or incapacitates the "heart" of Ananias to lie to the Holy Spirit (Acts 5:3).[210] This probably is not intended to suggest Ananias is demon-possessed; the emphasis instead seems related to Satan's influence on the hidden motives, thoughts, or plans of Ananias (cf. Luke 5:22; 9:47; 24:38).[211]

Ananias and Sapphira's failure turns on covetousness and duplicity rather than their inability to give all they have. To be sure, Jesus had taught his disciples to give up everything for his sake (Luke 12:33; 14:33; 18:22, 28; cf. 5:11, 28), but we also see salvation extended to the house of Zaccheus even though he did not give up all his possessions (Luke 19:1–10). Moreover, Peter affirms that Ananias and Sapphira have authority over their own property, and so their condemnation does not appear to be centered on the amount they gave or withheld (Acts 5:4). Instead Ananias

---

209. Brown, *Apostasy and Perseverance*, 113–14, notices this contrast between the Holy Spirit and Satan but cites the Lukan version of the return of the unclean spirit (Luke 11:24–26) to argue that Luke omits the word "vacant" (Matt 12:44) after the demons are cast out because in Luke-Acts humans are "either the dwelling-place of demons or the house of the holy spirit." But this is not entirely correct. Acts 8 has the Samaritans believing but not receiving the Spirit until Peter and John laid hands on them; they obviously were not possessed by demons in the transition, and neither were the disciples of pre-Pentecost.

210. The latter meaning comes out clearer in the alternative reading of Acts 5:3 from the Sinaiticus text.

211. We notice Johnson, *Acts*, 88.

and Sapphira's vice seems to be greed and serving unrighteous "mammon" (cf. Luke 16:1–13). A comparison with Judas is helpful here. Both Judas and Ananias function as examples of demon-influenced Christ-followers who betray Jesus for "mammon." Both owned property and were punished by death (Luke 22:3; Acts 1:18; 5:1, 3, 5, 10). We also find the corrupting effects of money in other passages in Luke-Acts,[212] which can be set in contrast with the generous and sacrificial giving of believers (Acts 2:44–45; 4:32–37; 9:36–39; 11:27–30; 20:33–35).[213] This passage in Acts 5, similar to others, may have functioned as a warning to wealthy Christians not to be covetous.

Even though the couple is motivated by greed, their punishment results from the act of lying to the Spirit. Schuyler Brown argues that lying to the Holy Spirit relates to Jesus' warnings about blaspheming the Spirit, a sin that could never be forgiven (cf. Luke 12:10). To lie to the apostles is to lie to the Spirit by which the apostles operate during the post-resurrection age.[214] If this perspective is correct, it would explain the severity of Ananias and Sapphira's punishment. Their sin in this case would be unpardonable. We have argued from Luke, however, that the sin of blaspheming the Spirit occurs in the context of persecution when a believer rejects the Spirit's guidance at such times and proceeds to deny Christ. A more plausible viewpoint regarding Ananias and Sapphira's sin is that the early church community in Jerusalem recognized the phenomenon of radical giving as a work of the Spirit. Hence Luke Timothy Johnson may be correct in saying that the couple's lying to the Spirit involves making "counterfeit the actions generated by the Spirit."[215]

The couple's death may appear to be rather harsh from our perspective, especially given that many Christian parishioners and leaders throughout the centuries have coveted possessions or acted with duplicity without being zapped dead! Moreover, when Simon Magus attempts to buy the power of God's Spirit from Peter he is severely rebuked, but he does not die (see on Acts 8 below). A plausible justification regarding the severity of this judgment may be related to the plan of God in advancing the early Christian movement. First, if the couple were successful with this façade influenced by Satan, the genuine unity of the movement, as well as its spiritual authority, holiness, and integrity, would have been compromised.[216] Second, the result of this particular "curse" miracle produced positive fruit. No half-hearted persons joined the believers at this time (5:13a), and yet many more people believed as the

---

212. E.g., Acts 8:18–24; 16:16–19; 19:23–28; 24:26.
213. Cf. Tannehill, "Ethics of Acts," 116–20.
214. Brown, *Apostasy and Perseverance*, 107–9.
215. Johnson, *Acts*, 88.
216. See Dunn, *Acts*, 63.

In the Footsteps of Judas and Other Defectors

disciples gained respect (5:13b–14). Third, this event established both the authority of Peter and the "church"; the ἐκκλησία is first mentioned in 5:11. More astounding miracles would follow from this event, including Peter's "shadow" healing of the sick (5:14–15), his healing and exorcism ministry that resembles Jesus' miracles (Acts 5:16; 9:32–35; cf. Luke 4:38–41; 5:17–26; 8:40–56; 9:1; Mark 6:53–5), and his raising Tabitha from the dead, which mimics Jesus bringing Jairus's daughter back to life (Acts 9:36–42/Luke 8:40–56).

Relevant to Acts 5:1–11 is the manner in which Jesus and his followers, most notably Peter in this case, echo curse narratives from Israel's scriptures. Ananias and Sapphira's death recalls the "curse" miracles of Elijah and Elisha (e.g., 2 Kgs 1: 9–12; 2:23–24). Peter does not announce a curse, but he does predict that Sapphira would join her husband in death (Acts 5:9–10). In this manner the story resembles the prediction of death that Elijah pronounces on King Ahaziah (2 Kgs 1:4–6) and that Elisha declares on Jehoram's captain and King Ben-Hadad (2 Kgs 7:2, 19; 8:10–15). Elisha, like Peter, discerns the motives of the captain supernaturally and mentions the presence of "feet" at the "door" (Acts 5:2–3, 9/2 Kgs 6:32).[217] Another possible allusion in Acts 5 recalls Elisha's supernatural knowledge that his servant Gehazi had become unfaithful by coveting the silver and clothes offered to Elisha by Naaman, captain of Aram, after the prophet heals the captain from leprosy. Gehazi is struck with leprosy as a result of his greed (2 Kgs 5). Luke clearly knows the story; allusions to it appear again when the Lukan Paul claims to the Ephesians that he has coveted no one's silver, gold, or clothes (Acts 20:33). The curse motif in the stories of Elijah and Elisha probably find their origin in the idea of expulsion or "cutting off" from the community via premature death or calamity. This motif is frequently mentioned in Deuteronomy (e.g., Deut 28–30) and is exemplified in Aaron's sons being killed by God for offering "strange fire" (Lev 10) and Achan being stoned for coveting items from the city of Ai (Josh 7).[218] Prior to the couple's death in Acts 5, when the Lukan Peter refers to Jesus as a prophet like Moses, he also mentions a curse related to those who refuse to listen to this prophet: they will be destroyed or "rooted out" (ἐξολεθρευθήσεται) from among God's people (Acts 3:22–23; 7:37/Deut 18:15–20; Lev 23:29).[219]

---

217. Here "feet" may indicate an omen (cf. Ezek 24:23). Derrett, "Right of Property," 198, adds the interesting but speculative observation that the "feet" of the young men approaching could have been heard if "wearing sandals," but not barefoot, as would be typical if they were mourning over Ananias' death.

218. Some in fact, have argued the story of Achan as Luke's source, e.g., Johnson, *Acts*, 92. For a summary of various possible sources behind this text, see Marguerat, "Mort d'Ananias," 210–11; O'Toole, "You Did Not Lie," 201–2.

219. The word ἐξολεθρεύω is unique in the NT, but the LXX often mentions it in relation to some-

Hence, the sudden death of Ananias and Sapphira is perhaps another example of a long tradition related to Deuteronomic curses and premature deaths found in both the exodus-wilderness stories and Elijah/Elisha narratives. Whereas Acts 5:3 identifies the sin as lying to the Spirit, 5:9 identifies it as *testing* the Spirit of the Lord.[220] The latter idea recalls the children of Israel testing God's spirit in the wilderness (Deut 6:16; Exod 17:2; Num 14:22; Ps 77[78]:41, 56; Isa 63:9–14).[221] The result of such disobedience was that many were killed without entering the Promised Land (e.g., Num 14:35–37; 16:41–49; 21:6; 25:9). Ananias and Sapphira's deaths come by way of their testing the Spirit during the new exodus-wilderness journey of the Way.[222] They are killed so as to be physically "cut off" from God's community.

Does their physical death suggest their eternal punishment? One option for us is to hold that their quick burial without ceremony or mourning is the manner in which deviants, rebels, and apostates are buried (cf. Lev 10:6; Ezek 24:21–23).[223] In this case we might expect them to be eternally condemned just like Judas. Some would add that if their sin is similar to blaspheming the Spirit it might not be pardonable. But lying to the Spirit and blaspheming the Spirit may not be the same thing in Luke-Acts, and while the couple's quick burial might confirm them as deviants of some sort, this says nothing explicitly about their eternal destiny.

A second option is that they will be saved but with a "loss of reward." This view is similar to the notion of people receiving different rewards and punishments in the afterlife (Luke 12:47–48; cf. 19:11–27; 1 Cor 3:10–15).

A third option is for us to regard their death as the full extent of their punishment. J. D. M. Derrett compares the Acts 5 story with Achan's confession of guilt and the *Mishnah*'s interpretation that his confession provides him a share in the "world to come" (Josh 7:19; *m. Sanhedrin* 6.2). He considers premature death as atonement according to Jewish thinking, and Ananias's silence and Sapphira's reply, he suggests, are confessions (Acts 5:5, 8).[224] But there is no clear indication of their confession of

---

one or something being utterly destroyed from the land; cf. BDAG, 351.

220. The "Lord" in Acts 5:9 probably refers to Jesus (cf. Acts 4:33; 16:7; 20:22–24; cf. Luke 12:11–12 with 21:12–15). See O'Toole, "'You Did Not Lie,'" 193–94. Instructive in the thought of testing the Lord is Paul's account of Israel's wilderness generation being destroyed by the Destroyer (compare Acts 3:23, ἐξολεθρευθήσεται, with 1 Cor 10:9, ὀλοθρευτοῦ). Here Paul mentions the Israelites testing the "Lord" or "Christ." Those who did so in the wilderness were destroyed (1 Cor 10:9–10).

221. In agreement with Johnson, *Acts*, 89; Marshall, *Kept by the Power*, 96.

222. On the Way and new exodus, see Pao, *Isaianic New Exodus*, 60–69.

223. Cf. Derrett, "Right of Property," 198, 200–201, who cites Josephus, *J.W.* 4.5.3; Philo, *Spec.* 2.27; and the Jewish document *Shemahot/The Tractate 'Mourning.'*

224. Derrett, "Right of Property," 199.

In the Footsteps of Judas and Other Defectors

wrongdoing in the passage, and this omission seems rather odd if Luke wanted to suggest to his readers that their death atoned for their sin.

A final option, and perhaps the best, is to let the question remain unknown. Luke probably did not know their eternal fate, or if he did he was not interested in letting his audience know. *Perhaps Luke withheld such information as a way of getting his audience to ponder the question in relation to their own potential to fall away through greed and acting with duplicity.* If so, this passage may be another example of a narrative of suspension similar to the ending of Acts 28.[225]

THE CASE OF SIMON MAGUS: APOSTATE, FALSE BELIEVER, OR SOMETHING ELSE? (ACTS 8:9–24)

When Philip preaches in Samaria, the Samaritans and Simon Magus, a local magician, believe and are baptized (8:9–24).[226] The Spirit of God, however, did not fall on the believers, and so Peter and John are sent from Jerusalem to lay hands on the Samaritans to receive the Spirit. When Simon observes the manifestation of the Spirit, he attempts to buy the power from them and receives a swift rebuke from Peter: "May your money be destroyed with you . . . you have no part or portion in this word, for your heart is not right before God. Repent therefore of this wickedness and beg the Lord, if possible, the intent of your heart may be forgiven you. For I see that you are in the gall of bitterness and bound by unrighteousness" (8:20–23). The story ends with Simon requesting the disciples pray for him so that none of the things Peter mentioned would happen to him (8:24). Is Simon the magician an apostate or something else? A number of scholars question Simon's conversion or consider it to be a counterfeit faith.[227] If Simon were a genuine disciple, he would need to become, as Brown suggests, "the special object of Satan's activity," as was the case for Judas (Luke 22:3) and Ananias (Acts 5:3). Simon's "heart has never ceased to be under Satan's influence, so that there is no need for Satan to 'fill' it."[228] Indeed Luke-Acts does seem to indicate that those who are not God's people are under Satan's dominion (Acts 26:18). On the other hand, there is no distinction between Simon's belief and that of the other Samaritans. James Dunn suggests, "the impression is given that he [Simon] was a whole-hearted convert, devoted to Philip" (8:13).[229]

---

225. On the narrative of suspension, see Marguerat, "Enigma," 284–304; and Acts 28 above.
226. On the Samaritans as apostates from Judaism, see Josephus, *Ant.* 11.8.6[340].
227. E.g., Witherington, *Acts*, 288.
228. Brown, *Apostasy and Perseverance*, 113.
229. Dunn, *Acts*, 110.

It is almost impossible for us to discern Simon's faith in this episode given the atypical situation of the Samaritans believing and yet not receiving the Spirit. If the believers in Samaria are in the process of being saved (cf. Acts 2:47), it may be a moot point to discern whether or not Simon was a truly saved prior to his failure. Simon is certainly not a complete convert, but neither are the other Samaritans until they received the Spirit—and this is perhaps the key. The reception of the Spirit is normally what identifies true repentance that leads to salvific life (Acts 11:15–18; cf. 2:38; Rom 8:9). We are never told in the narrative that Simon received the Spirit and possibly, if he did receive it, he would not have attempted to "buy" its power.

Whether Simon is originally in the process of salvation or not, Peter rebukes Simon and claims that he possesses no share in the "word," here representing the apostolic proclamation of God's word or the ministry related to it (Acts 8:21).[230] A background to Elijah/Elisha narratives seems present in Acts 8 with Philip being granted divine assistance in his travels similar to Elijah (Acts 8:39–40/1 Kgs 18:45–46). The Ethiopian eunuch's baptism imitates Naaman's washing and renewal in the Jordan at Elisha's instruction (Acts 8:26–38/1 Kgs 5:1–14), and Simon's attempt to exchange money for spiritual power is similar to Gehazi's desiring Naaman's gift (Acts 8:9–24/1 Kgs 5:15–24).[231] Gehazi's role as Elisha's servant is forever altered as he becomes leprous. A reversal in judgment is implied here: Naaman is cleansed of his leprosy and now Gehazi is plagued with it. The presupposition here may be related to the *lex talionis* pattern and blessing/cursing of Deuteronomy (e.g., Deut 19:16–21).[232] We might suggest that if Simon's judgment coincides with the Elisha narrative at this point, Simon's "cleansing" or baptism and its effects are reversed by Peter's rebuke. If so, Simon is "out"; he does not participate in the blessings of the God's people[233] and is in danger of eschatological destruction.[234] This reading, however, remains tentative—we should recall that Peter grants Simon the possibility of repentance.

Simon does show remorse, suggesting a willingness to repent (Acts 8:24), and the Western tradition (D) sharpens this aspect: Simon "did not stop weeping copiously."[235] Moreover, the second-person plurals Luke places in the mouth of

230. Alternatively, if the word λόγος in 8:21 can be translated as "matter," then it would seem to refer to receiving the Spirit by the laying on of hands. For other options, see Barrett, *Acts*, 1.414–15.

231. On the last points, see further Brodie, "Unraveling the Rhetorical Imitation," 41–67. Although the Gehazi narrative fits well with Acts 5:1–11, it is certainly not impossible that Luke is alluding to this story again in Acts 8.

232. Wenkel, "Imprecatory Speech-Acts," 85, raises this possibility as a "faint echo" in Acts 8.

233. Cf. Deut 12:12; 14:27, 29; Ps 78:37.

234. Cf. Matt 7:13; Rom 9:22; 1 Tim 6:9; Heb 10:39; Dan 2:5 (Theodotion).

235. Metzger, *Textual Commentary*, 358–59.

Simon when he is requesting prayer (δεήθητε ὑμεῖς) is somewhat unexpected given that Peter alone rebukes him. The language may be emphatic, stressing Simon's repentance and strong desire for the entire *community*, or at least Peter and John, to pray for him. The Western text again stresses this aspect further: Simon said "to them," "please" pray for me to "God" that none of "these evils" come upon me. The text may point to genuine repentance or at least a sincere desire for it.[236]

Luke, however, drops the story without mentioning whether or not Simon is restored and continues with the Samaritan converts. It is possible that this ending of the story is deliberate and another example of his narrative of suspension. Two goals may arise from this reading of the text. First, *Luke leaves Simon's fate in the hands of the readers, inviting the Christian audience to participate in praying for Simon and others like him who need repentance and restoration.* Second, the passage would also serve as an implicit warning to the audience to question themselves about their own potential to act like Simon, attempting to exploit the Spirit through material substance.[237] In subsequent generations, his repentance is often overlooked as well as the need to pray for him.[238] When Christian readers came across Simon and Luke's silent ending of the story, they speculated on Simon's fate and often arrived at negative conclusions—in their elaborations of this magician, Simon becomes a heretic venerated as deity and a founder of Gnosticism (e.g., Justin, *Dial.* 120.6; *Apology* 1.26; 1.56; Irenaeus, *Haer.* 1.23; Hippolytus, *Haer.* 6.2–15).[239]

We may never know whether or not Simon Magus was restored to the early Christian church in Samaria; at best *he is a convert in process* with no indication that he received the Spirit. Whatever identity we may wish to give him, "apostate" might be too premature. He functions better as a misguided individual from within the ranks of the church, or given his magician background, possibly a proto-false prophet.

CONCLUSION

Our study of Luke-Acts drives us to several important observations related to apostasy. First, Luke shows Theophilus and by extension a larger Christian audience, many of which seem to be socially prominent, that salvation has come about as a

---

236. Differently, Witherington, *Acts*, 288, writes that Simon is only frightened instead of remorseful, and cites *Ps.-Clem.*, which claims that Simon's tears are of disappointment and rage (*Homilies* 20.21; *Recognitions* 10.63).

237. On magicians as having "money hungry" reputations among Greco-Romans, see Talbert, *Reading Acts*, 70.

238. If so, then the Western tradition (D) of this story would be an exception, not the rule.

239. On Simon in later traditions, see Haar, *Simon Magus*, ch. 2; Meeks, "Simon Magus," 137–42.

result of God's salvific plan that fulfills Israel's scriptures, and this plan includes joining the Gentiles with God's people Israel (cf. Luke 4:14–30; Acts 2:22–24; 4:28–30). In this plan, unbelief and apostasy are inevitable (Luke 17:1; 22:22), but God uses such things to advance his purposes. Jewish rejection of the apostolic message provides an open door for the disciples to reach Gentiles without abandoning the Jewish people. By the end of Acts, the apostolic mission no longer grants priority to the Jew *first*, then the Gentile (Acts 28:24–28; cf. 13:46–48). Even so, many Jews come to believe (e.g., Acts 2:41; 21:20), primarily those among the outcasts and marginalized.

The divine plan, however, has brought about conflicts among Jews, Gentiles, and Christians. Jesus is accused by the leaders in Jerusalem of teaching apostasy (Luke 23:2, 5, 14), and Paul is likewise accused by Jewish Christians of teaching apostasy (Act 21:21). Both, however, are vindicated of such charges by the Lukan narrative—Jesus is seen as a true prophet of God and Paul a true messenger of God and Christ. Among the emerging Christians there is evidence of conflicts between Palestinian and Hellenistic Jews (Acts 6–7) and between Pharisaic Christ-followers and the Pauline mission (Acts 15:1–5). The latter centers on issues related to the Law, especially circumcision and table fellowship with Gentiles (cf. Gal 2). In Luke's version, the Jerusalem meeting in Acts 15 attempted to turn this tide. But later on in the narrative we find that zealous keepers of the Law among Jewish Christians interpret Paul's version of the gospel as apostasy from Moses. Such divisions have ramifications for our study because, among other things, they show diversity in the earliest Christian communities. The communities and their leaders did not all believe and practice the same things, and their perception of what constitutes apostasy varied depending on *who* identified *the other* as apostate. We see differences of beliefs among emergent Christian communities in Acts. They all seem to affirm the salvation that God brings through Jesus, but they do not all agree on exactly what the divine plan might say regarding the interpretation of the Law and solidarity with the Gentile believers. Diversity such as this is reflected in other New Testament writings in relation to apostasy, as we will continue to discover.

The opponents of Jesus and the Way, however, are not the only ones who reject God's salvific plan. Jesus warns his followers that temptation can cause them to fall away. As the parable of the Sower suggests, Jesus' followers must persevere through temptations (Luke 8:6, 13; cf. 11:4; 18:8; 22:40, 46). If the central thought of apostasy in Mark's gospel is persecution and in Matthew it is violation of the Law, Luke centers on the aspect of perseverance over temptations, and these enticements frequently come in the form of wealth and greed. Judas betrays Jesus over a sum of money, Ananias and Sapphira fall because of holding back possessions, Simon the magician tries to bribe Peter, and Christ's followers must be diligent not to be caught up with the cares of living so as to lose eternal life (Luke 22:2–6; Acts 5:1–10; 8:4–24; cf. Luke 8:7, 14; 17:27–33). Such an emphasis might reflect indirectly Theophilus' social prominence and wealth and thus function as an incentive for him to give to the poor and store up treasure in heaven rather than earth. The various stories of wealth and poverty may have also impacted the original audience beside Theophilus.

The phenomenon of falling away also occurs through immoral living and deceptive teachings; hence, the believers must be watchful at all times (Luke 12:40–48; 21:34–36). Likewise faulty leadership can be the cause of apostasy and deception, as exemplified by Jesus' warning against disciples causing marginalized believers to fall and Paul's warning of deceptive leaders that will arise from among the ranks of Ephesian Christians (Luke 17:1–4; Acts 20:28–31). Defection through persecution, unlike in Mark and Matthew, is played down by Luke in an effort to portray Jesus and his apostles as exemplars of perseverance. Likewise his narrative shows that opposition to God's plan cannot prevail. The exceptions are Peter's denial of Jesus and the possibility of Christians blaspheming the Spirit. Unlike the other Synoptic Gospels, the unpardonable sin in Luke can be committed by Christians rather than their opponents (12:5–12). A few of the Synoptic sayings of Jesus are repeated in Luke's gospel; these sayings warn against the possibility of falling away through persecution (9:23–26; 12:8–10). In Acts there is only one possible example of defection related to persecution: Paul persecuting Hellenistic Christians to the point of making them blaspheme Christ (26:11). His success at getting them to fall away is not presented very clearly by Luke.

The consequences of apostasy include divine punishment, loss of eternal life, and suffering in *Gehenna* (Luke 9:24; 12:5, 9; 17:33). It is not clear in Luke, however, that such punishment is reserved for a time when Christ returns. Judgment can take place immediately after death (e.g., 16:19–31; 23:43). Even disciples could suffer such judgment if they commit apostasy. In fact Christian leaders who become apostates are "beaten with many stripes," that is, punished more strictly or severely than others (12:47–48). Judas' apostasy becomes a prime example of eternal judgment on a leader and Christ-follower. He is neither the remorseful sinner that Matthew portrays him to be nor does he meet his death by suicide. In Luke, Judas is a bona fide Christ-follower who turns apostate, becomes possessed by Satan, and whose body is destroyed in a field as a consequence of his betrayal (Acts 1:15–25; cf. 22:22). He is replaced by Matthias after his death because it is not expected that he will reign with the Twelve in the future kingdom. He goes to his own "place," which is presumably hell (Acts 1:25).

Similarly, Ananias and Sapphira are killed by God for their sin of lying to the Spirit of God (5:1–10). They exemplify a divine style of expulsion from the community of God. Nevertheless the Christ-followers are assured that repentance, along with Christ's intervention, makes possible the complete restoration of lapsed individuals. Peter and the Prodigal Son are two such examples (Luke 15; 22:55–62; cf. 22:31–32). Theophilus and the rest of Luke's audience would have been instructed well by these warnings and examples related to perseverance and apostasy. The rhetoric of suspension at the end of Acts 28 would encourage Luke's Gentile audience that they are now included as God's people; at the same time this rhetoric challenges them to continue the apostolic mission of Paul. It would likewise exhort Jewish hearers to believe and not behave like their forefathers who became apostates and spiritually blind according to the Isaianic tradition. Finally, Simon Magus's fate and the eternal fate of Ananias and Sapphira would leave the Lukan Christ-followers, especially wealthy ones, pondering on their own potential to covet after material things or attempt to manipulate God's Spirit. They would also be encouraged to pray for Simon's restoration.

4

The Gospel of John and the Epistles of John

Defectors from the Johannine Community

Traditionally the fourth gospel is attributed to John the son of Zebedee, one of the twelve initial disciples of Jesus, but early Christian sources are not always clear when identifying which John is the author.[1] Contemporary scholars suggest that this gospel went through stages of redaction by multiple authors, which can be detected in the writing itself (e.g., John 19:35; 21:24);[2] it was perhaps shaped into its final form somewhere between 90–110 CE.[3] While questions remain on whether the author of John's gospel is the same as the author(s) of the three letters of John, it is perhaps correct to suggest that the similarities between the letters and the gospel warrant that both came from the same community.[4] The authorship of these writings will not be finally decided here, but we will use the term "Johannine" to identify the writer of the fourth gospel and 1–3 John. We do agree with the majority of scholars that the original recipients of the Johannine writings appear to be from Asia Minor, Ephesus in particular, and that the date of these writings seems to be toward the end of the first century.[5] The many similarities between John's gospel and epistles are well

---

1. Eusebius, *Hist. eccl.* 3.23; 5.8; Irenaeus, *Haer.* 2.22.5; 3.1.1; Tertullian, *Praescr.* 22; *Marc.* 4.2; see further sources in Haenchen, *John*, 1.7–19.

2. For further discussion on authorship see Culpepper, *Son of Zebedee*.

3. See, e.g., Brown, *Introduction*, 334 (c. 80–110 CE); on 1 John, see Klauck, *Johannesbriefe*, 48–49 (c. 100–110 CE).

4. See Hengel, *Johannine Question*, 48; Kümmel, *Introduction*, 234–46, 442–45; Ehrman, *New Testament*, 178–80. For discussion of authorship of the epistles, see Brown, *Epistles of John*, 14–35; Harner, *About the Catholic Epistles*, 59–63, 81–83.

5. On the community's location, see Painter, *John*, 51–57; Tilborg, *Reading John*.

recognized.⁶ We will proceed with the perspective that the Johannine gospel and epistles could be studied together with mutual benefits.

Various proposals suggest that the fourth gospel be read on two levels, both in terms of Jesus' episodes and those experienced by the Johannine community years later.⁷ In essence, this view teaches that the community emerged from or near Palestine and developed a high view of Christ that created a rift with other members who interpreted this as abandonment of monotheism. The Johannine group was then banished from the synagogue. The group moved away from Palestine and taught Greeks, and then another schism arose over Christology, which resulted in some members leaving the community (1 John 2:19).

In agreement with the two-level perspective, we believe that John's gospel assumes an expulsion from a synagogue that is difficult to explain sufficiently if it were to take place during the life and times of Jesus (c. 30 CE). Passages such as John 9:22, 34; 12:42; and 16:2 reflect a process of redaction that took place many years after the events they record. They may reflect a time in the late first century when a Jewish Christian community was set at odds with a local Jewish synagogue, perhaps primarily because the Christian group claimed the preexistence of the Christ and that God dwelt uniquely in him (e.g., 5:18; 10:30–33; 14:7–11; 20:28; cf. 1:1, 14, 18; 8:58–59).⁸ It is unlikely, however, or at best it is not known, whether the blessing on heretics in the Eighteen Benedictions (*Birkat ha-minim*, Benediction 12) was ever used against the Jewish Christians of the Johannine community.⁹ Nevertheless, scholars have *not* refuted a two-level reading of John simply by refuting *Birkat ha-minim* as the basis for the expulsion of the Johannine community.¹⁰ As Paul Anderson rightly points out, "it cannot be claimed that there were *no* pressures against the Jesus movement within middle-to-late first-century Judaism."¹¹ We may find glimpses of such pressures in John 9:22, 12:42, and 16:2 even if they are not related to the *Birkat ha-minim*.

To be sure, we may never know the precise history behind the Johannine community's early conflicts, and we are less confident than some two-level advocates who assign certain motifs to specific phases of the community's development. This being

---

6. See examples in Schnelle, *Einleitung*, 434–35.

7. E.g., Brown, *Community*; Martyn, *History and Theology*; Ashton, *Understanding the Fourth Gospel*; Painter, *Quest for the Messiah*; Anderson, "Antichristic Errors: Proselytization," 217–40.

8. On Jesus' messianic claims and synagogue expulsion, see recently, Hirschberg, "Jewish Believers in Asia Minor," 230–34.

9. Contra Martyn, *History and Theology*, 50–62. For criticisms of the *Birkat ha-minim* as indicating exclusion of Johannine or emergent Christians see, e.g., Kimelman, "*Birkat Ha-Minim*," 226–44; Horbury, "Benediction of the *minim*," 19–61; Reinhartz, "Johannine Community," 115–17.

10. Similarly, another misperception arises if we think that by refuting Martyn we have dismissed everyone else who holds to a two-level reading of John.

11. Anderson, "Antichristic Errors: Proselytization," 219.

said, a *two-level reading of John does seem to provide helpful clues on the disruptions that took place within the community*. Such experiences would have no doubt played on the sociological identity of the group, making it rather easy for it to denounce outsiders as "them" rather than "us."[12]

PURPOSES AND COMMUNITIES IN JOHANNINE WRITINGS

The author claims that the signs in John's gospel are written so that the auditors may believe Jesus is the Christ, the Son of God, and by believing they might have eternal life (John 20:31). Was this verse assigned to believers in order to strengthen their faith in the midst of hostilities they encountered, or was it directed at non-believers so that they might come to believe? The accurate nuance of πιστεύω ("to believe") in this verse is almost equally divided among ancient text witnesses: the present subjunctive (πιστεύητε: e.g., p[66vid], ℵ, B) tends to support a continuation in faith that is more relevant to believers, but in the aorist subjunctive (πιστεύσητε: e.g., ℵ[2], A, C, D, TR) it may mean "come to believe" and would be more relevant for non-believers.[13]

Perhaps the gospel's purpose is discerned well when we consider broader issues. Alan Culpepper contemplates the plot of this gospel as being propelled by conflicts in relation to various responses to Jesus in an attempt to "enclose the reader in the company of faith. The gospel's plot, therefore, is controlled by thematic development and a strategy for wooing readers to accept its interpretation of Jesus."[14] It is only when the readers consider Jesus as the divine *logos* and the "exalted Son of Man" that they will understand his ministry.[15] Nevertheless, the wording of this gospel assumes familiarity with concepts related to believers and Israel's scriptures.[16] Its ambiguities and double meanings (e.g., "glory," "lifted up," "born anew/again") would have made it far more accessible to Johannine insiders familiar with the "jargon" than outsiders, who would mostly find themselves perplexed by the gospel's "closed metaphorical system."[17] It is probably the case, then, that *John's gospel was written for the benefit of*

---

12. See Kysar, *Maverick Gospel*, 63–64, who has a brief but lucid section on this kind of social reorientation the Johannine community experienced.

13. See discussion in Witherington, *John's Wisdom*, 30–31, who points out the distinction is not always the case in John and cites John 6:29–30 and 17:21 as examples of present subjunctives of "to believe" that are used in reference to the unbelievers.

14. Culpepper, *Anatomy*, 98.

15. Ibid., 232.

16. Cf. ibid., 225.

17. Phrase from Meeks, "Man from Heaven," 70, who claims this gospel "could hardly be regarded as a missionary tract." Bauckham, "Audience of the Fourth Gospel," contends against the "in-group" view, arguing among other things that Jesus often spoke in riddles and such language may be intended to "tease initially uncomprehending readers into theological enlightenment" (109). However, the

believers, but this does not preclude that the author may have assumed the possibility that non-believers would also read or hear it.

The Johannine epistles are more clearly addressed to believers (cf. 2 John 1:1–2, 13; 3 John 1–4). The three writings deal with internal problems. The first opposes false teachings in the aftermath of a schism in the community. Its ultimate purpose is to provide encouragement to believers by assuring them of eternal life (1 John 5:13), and this seems to interact with a pastoral concern that aims at preventing further apostasy from the community by strengthening the cohesion of the group.[18] The other two, 2 and 3 John, focus on itinerate false teachers and an abusive leader, respectively. *The community was an emerging Jewish Christian group in its earlier years, but after it relocated to Ephesus, Gentiles and Hellenized Jews probably began to join the group.*[19] We can adduce from the first epistle that assimilation with outsiders may have been a problem for the members (1 John 2:15–17).

Johannine literature mentions several other communities. First and foremost are "the Jews," who are the opponents of Jesus throughout John's gospel, including but not limited to the Pharisees, chief priests, and officers of the Sanhedrin (John 7:32, 45; 8:3; 18:3). The chief priests and officers pertain to Jerusalem in the pre-70 CE era, and it is doubtful that such groups were a concern for John's own community. The scribes are mentioned only once in a passage without strong textual support (8:3) and the Sadducees are not directly mentioned at all. On a second-level reading, John's negative attitude towards "the Jews" may reflect the later expulsion of the Johannine community from a synagogue in Palestine (9:22; 16:2). John's group then met in house churches (2 John 10) and remained separated from the synagogue in its new location.

A second community comprises those who believe but choose to remain in the synagogue (12:42–43; cf. 3:2; 7:50; 19:38). On a secondary level these might refer to Jewish Christians who worshipped in the synagogue. A third group is identified as the "world" that is hostile to the Johannine community (1 John 2:13–15). Fourth, there are Christian apostates or secessionists who once belonged to the Johannine church but left it (1 John 2:19). Fifth, there exists a sect belonging to John the Baptist that may have interacted with the Johannine community (John 3:22–26). They do

---

Johannine letters, unlike the fourth gospel, do not intend to communicate Jesus' direct sayings, and they are clearly addressed to believers rather than unbelievers, and yet similar ambiguous terms such as "light," "darkness," "truth," and so on, remain in these writings akin with John's gospel. The enigmatic language seems best explained not by its inclusive but exclusive readership. Those who belong to this Christian community would seem to understand the authors' language far better than non-members.

18. On a pastoral emphasis for the first epistle, see Griffith, *Keep Yourselves from Idols*, 1, 146; Lieu, *Johannine Epistles*, 41.

19. On Greek names in the letters, see Smalley, *John*, 344, 360.

not follow Jesus, and this may account for the gospel's somewhat low estimation of the Baptist (John 1:9, 15, 19–24, 30; 3:29–30; 10:41). Interestingly Luke records that Paul encounters such a group in Ephesus, and their faith is insufficient; they need to receive the Holy Spirit and get baptized in the name of Jesus (Acts 19:1–7). These disciples of John the Baptist are converted in Acts, but even if the historicity of such an encounter were accepted, there still remains a strong possibility that other disciples of this sect were not converted to Christian message.[20]

We can identify a sixth community as the "other sheep" (John 10:16) and Greeks that Jesus encounters in Jerusalem (12:20–22). This group intimates the inclusion of believing Gentiles into the Johannine community (cf. 7:35; 11:32; 17:20).[21]

Seventh and finally, Jesus' restoration and commissioning of Peter after his denial of Jesus probably functions as an appendix intended by the Johannine redactor as a way to join the Johannine and Petrine Christian communities (John 21).[22] The necessity of such a union was perhaps needed due to the community's estranged relationship with the local synagogues and internal schisms with other professing Christians that had affected the group. Nothing is mentioned in John about a Pauline church in Ephesus, and there is no evidence that this group simply merged with John's assembly. Trebilco may be correct by suggesting that the two groups knew each other and were not hostile towards one another but chose to remain separate entities.[23]

Another significant community might be present if Raymond Brown is correct in identifying a group of Jewish Christians who left the synagogue but were not part of the Johannine group due to irreconcilable differences related to beliefs about the Eucharist (John 6; esp. vv. 59–66) and Christology (8:31–58).[24] The groups in John 6 and 8 seem to reflect apostate Christ-followers (see below).

THE "JEWS" IN JOHN'S GOSPEL

John's gospel frequently uses the term "the Jews" in a negative way, and this has led to the question of whether the fourth gospel should be considered as anti-Semitic.[25] We

---

20. Brown, *Community*, 70, refers to the third-century Pseudo-Clementine *Recog.* 1.54, 60 as an example of Baptist sectarians who consider their master, John, to be the messiah.

21. The alternative is to understand the "other sheep" as Diaspora Jews. To support this view, the "Greeks" in 12:20 would need to be Greek-speaking Jews. On this view see, e.g., Robinson, "Destination and Purpose," 117–31.

22. Cf. Brown, *Community*, 161–62; Borchart, *John*, 1.335.

23. Trebilco, *Early Christians*, 626–27.

24. See further Brown, *Community*, 73–81.

25. See discussions in, e.g., Bieringer et al., *Anti-Judaism*; Rensberger, "Anti-Judaism," 120–57.

should read John through post-Holocaust lenses, and yet at the same time we should attempt to read it as would a first-century reader, some of which were themselves Jewish. In Johannine thought, careful distinctions would not be made between racial, cultural, ethnic, and religious boundaries. Be that as it may, the negative Johannine texts are primarily concerned with Jewish unbelief in Jesus as the Christ. As such the gospel's harsh language rests in the religious spectrum. Explanations for such language are as follows.

First, the Johannine community itself seems to be originally Jewish. Its many references and allusions to Israel's scriptures, feasts, and practices make this point rather clear. The author himself is almost certainly Jewish and he uses language typical of Jewish polemic.[26] He could not have envisaged how in later centuries a predominantly Gentile church would become the dominant religious and political power that would misconstrue such language.[27] In essence what we have in John's gospel is one group with Jewish origins denouncing another Jewish group, which would be similar to the Qumran community denouncing the priesthood in Jerusalem, or Pharisees and Sadducees contending against each other (e.g., 1QH 10.22–29; Josephus, *Ant.* 18:17; m. *Yadayim* 4.7). *In John's gospel we are only getting this information from the Johannine writer's perspective, not from the opponents in the text* who allegedly think Jesus to be an opponent—they perceive Jesus to be leading people astray (7:12, 47), possessed of demons (7:19; 8:48; 10:20), and a blasphemer (10:31–36).[28] On a secondary level, the Johannine community may have thought that leaders from the synagogue of their day considered them to be apostate deceivers who, among other things, violate Sabbath protocols and blaspheme by making Jesus the embodiment of God (John 1:1, 14, 18; 5:17–18; 10:30–33; 20:28; cf. Deut 13:1–18; m. *Sanhedrin* 7.4–5, 10–11).

Second, the Johannine passages that refer polemically to "the Jews" mostly seem to be ascribed to the religious leaders whether high priest, chief priests, Pharisees, or those who follow them (cf. John 1:19–27; 7:32, 45; 11:47, 57; 18:3, 12). Not all "Jews" are presented as unbelievers and hostile toward Jesus and his followers (e.g., 4:22; 11:45). In fact many do believe (2:23; 7:31; 8:30–31; 10:42; 11:45, 48; 12:11; 12:42). Third, the most vituperative language against "the Jews" in John's gospel—"you are of

---

26. Scott, "Jews or Christians?," 94–95, draws our attention to "we" in John 4:22 to affirm Jesus identifying himself as Jewish. In Scott's view the Johannine author is dealing with inter- and innergroup struggles, and the ideal reader of John's gospel may understand "the language of exclusion as marking out boundaries in an inter-Christian dispute."

27. Special thanks to James McGrath for this point and sharpening my thoughts elsewhere in John.

28. On these charges see further Pancaro, *Law*; Sloyan, *Saying about John*, 74–75. In the view of Klink, "Expulsion from the Synagogue," 47, Jesus is considered a *mesith* or *min* in what might be considered "intra-Jewish familial turmoil."

In the Footsteps of Judas and Other Defectors

your father the devil" (8:44)—is reserved for those who once believed Jesus but were now rejecting his claims (8:31–32). In other words, for the Johannine author, they represent apostate Jewish Christians rather than non-Christian Jews. Their association with "the devil" seems foremost to be intended to denounce their apostasy[29] and their plot to "kill" Jesus in the narrative (8:37, 44b).[30] Using a literary-critical method adopted by Northrop Frye, Mark Stibbe posits 8:31–59 as an informal satire of the "snarling rather than smiling kind" to suggest John is satirizing apostasy with lapsed Jewish disciples of Jesus as the "worst of all sinners."[31] Finally, scholars have noticed that the unbelieving Jews are almost always Judeans rather than Galileans; the latter are put down by the former, and the former provide the place of origin for Jesus and his immediate disciples (e.g., 7:1, 52; cf. 1:46). Some argue that in all but two references (6:41, 52) the term "Jew" is used of authorities and those from the region of Judea (e.g., 18:3, 12–13, 18).[32] The basic meaning for Ἰουδαῖος is in fact "Judean."[33]

The contemporary mind stumbles over why the negative instances of "the Jews" are not qualified in John's gospel. Some explanations are as follows: 1) The Johannine group had been excluded from a local synagogue and this is why the author writes with bitter and antagonistic tones.[34] 2) It should be noted that the author is not encouraging the persecution of others but is reacting against being persecuted *by* others. 3) The author may be using the term "Jew" ironically—the Judean authorities claim to be Jews but this is not how authentic Jews are supposed to act (cf. Rev 2:9; 3:9). Perhaps the Johannine community thought themselves to be true Israelites by affirming Jesus as the Son of God (cf. John 1:47–49). 4) Robert Kysar suggests that the term "Jews" has become a symbol or "stylized type" of people and individuals who fail to believe or accept Jesus as the Christ, much the same way as the "official police" are characterized as bumbling fools in detective plots.[35] In this way, as Kysar

---

29. This would be similar to the reason why Judas is called a "devil" in the Johannine gospel (6:70–71; cf. 13:2): he represents foremost an apostate Christ-follower. Tragically, later Christian writers interpreted Judas as representing the Jewish people.

30. Jesus' opponents in the narrative essentially call *him* a devil, too, by thinking he is demon-possessed (8:48, 52). For the Johannine Jesus, however, the devil plays a murderous role "from the beginning," which may suggest the devil's deception of the original couple in Genesis that led to their death, or perhaps more likely, he may be assumed by the Johannine group to have instigated Cain to kill his brother Abel (cf. 1 John 3:10–12, 15). Interestingly, Cain may have been considered an apostate in certain Jewish Christian circles (cf. Jude 11). Also, the one who commits "sin" is of the devil (1 John 3:8), and this sin in 1 John may be referring to apostasy (cf. 1 John 5:16–17).

31. Stibbe, *John's Gospel*, 115, 123–25.

32. So Von Wahlde, "Johannine 'Jews,'" 44, who attributes the two verses to a redactor. See also Bassler, "Galileans," 243–57.

33. Cf. Chilton, "Jews in the NT," 3.845; BDAG, 478.

34. Cf. Brown, *Community*, 42–43.

35. Kysar, *Maverick Gospel*, 57–58.

argues, "the Jews" represent a "stereotype of rejection. Any person who refuses to accept the human identity proposed by Christ in the gospel is for the evangelist a 'Jew' . . . [an] Israelite is the one who accepts the revelation (1:31)."[36] These explanations do not necessarily justify the harsh and unqualified language related to "the Jews" in John. Tragically, Christians in later centuries read hatred into these passages and exploited them as grounds for mistreating and persecuting Jewish people. The reasons above, anyway, should deter individuals from exploiting John's literature as justification for prejudice and hate crimes.

MURMURERS IN THE WILDERNESS AND THE ISAIANIC "WORD" OF GOD (JOHN 6)

Jesus' feeding of the five thousand and the bread of life discourse in John 6 compiles echoes from Israel's wilderness traditions.[37] It is significant that the setting begins in the wilderness during Passover and that Jesus goes up to a mountain. This recalls the Israelites being fed with manna in the wilderness with Moses who ascends to Mount Sinai, and the twelve baskets recall the twelve tribes of Israel (John 6:1–14/Exod 13–19; Num 13–14; Ps 77[78]:23–31).[38] After seeing the sign of miraculous food, the people believe Jesus to be the "prophet" who was to come according to the prediction in Deut 18:15 that God would raise up "another prophet" like Moses (John 6:14; cf. 1:21, 45; 5:36–47; 6:32; 7:40). Although Jesus is said to fulfill scripture written by Moses and the prophets (1:16, 21–23, 45; 3:14–15; 5:39, 45; 6:14, 45; 7:19–23, 40), he is not, technically speaking, the *new* Moses in John's gospel (cf. John 1:17). Jesus functions as the word from heaven "above" rather than merely the predicted prophet who is like Moses. He is "the Holy One of God" who has the words of eternal life (John 6:68–69).

Similar to the Israelites rebelling against Moses in the wilderness after seeing the miracles God performed through him, "the Jews" begin to murmur against Jesus' claims (John 6:41–45, 52, 61; cf. Exod 16:2–12; Num 14; Pss 77[78]:17–20; 105[106]:25). Their obduracy is seen in their failing to discern the work of God in Jesus' actions and asking for a sign after Jesus had already provided them with the miracle of multiplied loaves (John 6:30; cf. vv. 1–16).[39] At the end of the narra-

---

36. Ibid., 58. Similarly, Keener, *John*, 1.216–17, suggests the "Jews" in John are portrayed as "flat" rather than "round" characters, in keeping with ancient biography.

37. See Borgen, *Bread from Heaven*.

38. On fish in the wilderness, see Num 11:22; *Sifre Num.* 11.22; cf. Wis 19:10–12. On the significance of Ps 78 (John 6:31/Ps 78:24) in John 6, see Köstenberger, "John," 445–46.

39. Cf. Köstenberger, "John," 445.

tive, a great defection of believers who once followed Jesus takes place, similar to the apostasy of the generation that rejected the word of God through Moses (6:66). Conversely, and much like Joshua, Caleb, and the younger Israelites who make it to God's promised land of rest, the Twelve are the only remnant who spiritually survives the wilderness episode in John 6. They affirm through Peter that Jesus has the words of eternal life (6:67–69).

The only passage the Johannine Jesus directly cites in the discourse is Isa 54:13 (cf. John 6:45): "they all shall be taught by God."[40] The prominence of Isaianic tradition is evident with over thirty allusions in the fourth gospel.[41] In the context of Isa 54, Zion is the locus rather than Sinai, and David rather than Moses comes to the foreground. The city is depicted as an afflicted and vacillating individual who is assured restoration and will soon be granted stability, security, and establishment in righteousness (Isa 54:11–14; cf. 54:1—56:8). The pericope continues with a call going out to a crowd, including the "nations" and "peoples" (ἔθνεσιν . . . καὶ λαοί), and this call invites everyone who is hungry and thirsts to "come" and partake of a feast. To those who listen, God, the Holy One of Israel, will make an everlasting covenant related to the assurances of David (Isa 55:1–5; cf. 25:6). In this passage God's "word" is said to be like rain and snow that saturates the earth to give "bread for food" (ἄρτον εἰς βρῶσιν). The word comes down from heaven (καταβῇ . . . ἐκ τοῦ οὐρανοῦ) and will not return again (i.e., ascend to heaven) until it accomplishes what God wills. Because of the word that comes down as rain, the desert thorns and briers will be turned into fertile vegetation, indicating a new and everlasting era of salvation (Isa 55:10—56:1).

Significant ideas in Isa 54–56 correlate with the bread of life discourse in John 6.[42] First, it is noteworthy that the only time the Isaianic referent to "the Holy One" of Israel (cf. Isa 55:5) appears in John's gospel, it is here in John 6:69 when Peter attributes the title to Jesus. In this manner the title suggests Jesus is distinctively the word of God. William Domeris rightly suggests that true confession of Jesus as the Holy One here centers on knowing him as God's unique representative and agent bringing God's revelation to humanity.[43] In light of Isaiah, God's revelation would seem to be associated with God's word, which is in some sense an extension of God.

40. It is not clear whether the Isaianic tradition in John 6:45 is Greek or Hebrew; it does appear to be a text citation or accurate memory of a text. Cf. Witmer, "Overlooked Evidence," 134–38. The text's omission of "your sons" widens the Johannine application to include Gentiles; cf. Menken, "Old Testament Quotation," 170–71.

41. See lists in Reim, *Studien zum alttestamentlichen*, 162–83; Hanson, *Prophetic Gospel*, 381–83.

42. Elsewhere it is evident that the Johannine author is quite familiar with Isa 54–56 (cf. John 3:8/ Isa 55:9–13; John 7:33–34/Isa 55:6; John 10:16/Isa 56:8–11; John 12:28/Isa55:5; John 16:20–22/54:11).

43. Domeris, "Confession of Peter," 165, 167.

This particular facet of God's revelation recalls the Johannine Prologue (1:1–18), in which the "word" or λόγος is God, and this "word" descends from heaven and is made manifest to humans by the incarnation of Jesus. It ascends to heaven again when the gospel reaches its revelatory climax in Thomas' confession of the risen Jesus as Lord and "God" (20:28).

Second, if Jesus is considered God's word in the Johannine foreground and through the Isaianic background, this thought carries with it a particular nuance to 6:45b, which claims that all those who have learned and heard from the Father come to Jesus. Isaiah 54:13 intimates the manner in which all Israel's children were educated (i.e., "learned and heard") in the Torah. The inhabitants of the new era would be taught by God himself (cf. Isa 2:3; Jer 31:33; Ezek 36:26–27; *Pss. Sol.* 17.32; CD[B] 20.4; *b. Berakot* 64A).[44] It would seem that John's gospel equates Jesus with the living word taught by the Father in the new era, yet a Johannine double entendre may be at play here, and if so, the "word" may likewise suggest the word of God as revealed in Israel's scriptures. The people who respond positively to Israel's scriptures will also respond to Jesus; the people who murmur show they have not understood the scriptures and will reject the message of Jesus.

Third, the imagery of Zion/Jerusalem's instability in Isa 54 may be echoed in the sign of Jesus walking on water when the strong sea winds were blowing on his disciples in the boat (John 6:16–21). The MT of Isa 54:11 is illuminating in this case,[45] which claims that prior to God's restoration of Zion the city was afflicted, not comforted, and "storm-tossed" (סֹעֲרָה).[46] This language from Isaiah may have influenced the Johannine writer to include the story of Jesus walking on the raging sea. As the Isaianic new era of restoration marks the settlement and security of God's people in Zion, so Jesus as God's word brings about security in a new era. Moreover, Jesus' "It is I" (ἐγώ εἰμι) reflects God's self-reference in the Isaianic new exodus, when the desert will be changed into a fertile place (Isa 41:4; 43:10; 48:12; 51:12; cf. 55:12-13).[47]

Fourth, in John 6:45 "all" is included from the citation of Isa 54:13. The Isaianic text is inclusive and brings in the nations and peoples to God's restored city and buildings; both Jews and Gentiles will feast during the restoration (Isa 55:1–5; 56:7–

---

44. Cf. Watts, *Isaiah 34–66*, 239; Schnackenburg, *John*, 2.51, 451. On rabbinic sources making this connection directly to Isa 54:13, see Borgen, *Bread from Heaven*, 150.

45. While the actual quote from Isa 54:13 in John 6:45 has more in common with the LXX (Menken, *Old Testament Quotations*, 71–77), similar to John 12, the Isaianic source of John's gospel is not quite the same as the LXX or MT versions we currently possess. See Freed, *Old Testament Quotations*, 18–19.

46. Cf. BDB, 701 (pual perfect of סער).

47. The narrative of Jesus walking on the sea also bears similarities to Job 9:8 and Ps 106:30 LXX, which may also suggest Jesus as deity. Notice also the murmuring in Ps 105[106]:25 and John 6:41, 51.

8; cf. John 10:16; 11:51–52). The "all" in John 6:45 likewise may be hinting at "all" peoples coming to Jesus. We notice perhaps a similar use of "all" in 1:7; 5:23; and 12:32. It does not seem to be referring to every individual; otherwise the text would appear to be espousing universalism, which is contradicted by the fact that many do *not* believe Jesus in the narrative and throughout the fourth gospel.

Finally, the Isaianic text refers to God's word that descends from heaven and provides "bread" to the peoples in the era of restoration and salvation.[48] All the people may come to eat bread and drink wine and milk (Isa 55:1–3). The food is associated with an eternal or "everlasting covenant" (διαθήκην αἰώνιον) of salvation given to those who listen to and obey the Holy One. This implies a comparison between the Mosaic covenant as God's word (Deut 30) and the Davidic covenant of the new era, the "assurances of David" with its future blessings of salvation, a perpetual kingdom, and new life (Isa 54:14; 55:3–56:8; cf. 2 Sam 7:12–16; Pss 16:9–10; 89:2–37; Acts 13:32–38). The Johannine writer associates these covenantal thoughts with the eschatological resurrection and one's abiding in Jesus as the "bread of life." Christ has descended from heaven and abiding in him comes about by a person "eating and drinking" of him (John 6:35, 39–40, 44, 54–57). In John 6 the consumption of God's word/Jesus may bring about a covenant related to communion with him, eternal life, and the assurance of a future resurrection (6:48–59).

As we have noticed through the Isaianic backdrop to John 6, this passage suggests that *Jesus and scriptures are the word of God, and a new era of restoration has come about in which God himself teaches his people the true meaning of Torah. Jesus also provides security for his followers, which seems to include "all" peoples.* When a person eats and drinks of Jesus, the bread or manna that has come down from heaven, that person enters into a new life and covenant related to eschatological salvation. If there emerges in John 6 an allusion to God teaching Israel at Sinai in which God's word or Law comes down from heaven as a gift,[49] the Johannine Jesus seems to redirect the crowd to himself as the embodiment of the word/Law, and instead of coming to Sinai the people must come to Jesus (cf. 12:32).

To this we may add that the Johannine community probably alludes to the celebration of the Eucharist/Lord's Supper in this text.[50] If so, it may be considered a

---

48. On manna or heavenly bread given to God's people in the future, see Wis 16:20; *2 Bar.* 29.8; *Sib. Or.* 3.46–49; Philo, *Alleg.* 3.169–176; *Mut.* 259–60; Rev 2:17; Köstenberger, "John," 446.

49. E.g., Exod 19:11–20; Deut 30:11–14; *m. Sanhedrin* 10.1; *Exod. Rabbah* 28.1–3; Philo, *Spec.* 3; cf. Rom 10:4–10; Maloney, *John*, 215, 220.

50. Jesus as God's "word" is virtually synonymous with the notions of "manna" and "bread" (John 6:47–51). While certain Jewish traditions have bread (Isa 55:1–3) or manna (e.g., *2 Bar.* 29.8) being eaten in the eschaton, John 6 turns on Jesus bidding the "Jews" to come and eat *him* (6:35, 47–59). Nevertheless traditions about "eating" God's word were not unknown in ancient Judaism (Deut 8:3; Jer

form of mystical communion or "abiding" in Jesus that the believers were to continually practice in the present age until Christ returns again at the resurrection of the righteous (John 6:50–54; cf. 1 Cor 10:15–20; 11:26). More than this, Jesus' followers were to "consume" his blood, which has intimations related to his suffering on the cross and relates to his atoning death (cf. 1 John 1:7). The stress throughout John, however, is that believing in Jesus brings about eternal life (John 6:40, 47; cf. 3:15–16, 36; 5:24, 38; 11:25; 20:31; 1 John 5:12–13), and so participating in the Lord's Supper is not the primary point; coming to Jesus and having spiritual communion with him seems to be the main point. *The grumblers in the wilderness (and synagogue: John 6:59), like their apostate predecessors who traveled with Moses, do not partake of the blessings of eternal life because they do not believe or remain with Jesus* (John 6:36, 41, 66). It is interesting to compare the Johannine text with Paul's warning to the Corinthians. Even though they partake of Christ via the Lord's Supper, they are in danger of falling away because of their murmurings and other vices, much like the Israelites who were destroyed in the wilderness after partaking of miraculous food (1 Cor 10:3–12).

The upshot of the Johannine interpretation of Isa 54–56 is that *the word of God and covenantal life are seen as providing salvation and security for all peoples who abide in Christ* (John 6:35–58). It becomes evident that in John 6:45/Isa 54:13 being "taught by God" means that in the new era, which is now breaking forth through the incarnation of Christ, Jesus is the word taught by God (the Father) to the peoples, and it is through believing in him that they participate in God's everlasting covenant. Elsewhere in the Johannine gospel Jesus declares that the Law points to him (5:39–47), the Law/scripture is understood as God's word (10:34–35; cf. 3:34), and God's word is embodied and realized through Jesus (1:14; cf. 3:34).[51] In typical Johannine fashion the "word" has polyvalent meaning: both Jesus and the scriptures/Law embody divine revelation, so that receiving God's "word" is equated with receiving Jesus. This becomes important for our interpretation of John 6:35–47 below.

GIVEN, DRAWN, AND TAUGHT BY GOD (JOHN 6:35–47)

In John 6:37 Jesus affirms that "all" which the Father "gives" to him will come to him, and the one coming to him he will never cast out. Here the concept of coming to Jesus is virtually synonymous with believing in him as evinced by parallel word-

---

15:16; cf. Ezek 3:1–3; Rev 10:9–11).

51. On the christological emphasis of the embodiment of God's word in John, see Obermann, *Christologische Erfüllung*, 426–27.

ing in 6:35 (cf. 1:39; 3:21; 5:40; 6:45; 7:37-38).[52] The "all" in this verse is a neuter singular, stressing a collective aspect about those who are given.[53] This aspect probably recalls the Isaianic backdrop in which all people come to the Lord's rebuilt city of Zion/Jerusalem (Isa 55:4; 56:7 cf. 54:13/John 6:45).[54] Foreigners, eunuchs, and Israelite outcasts are to come.[55] God is the one who takes initiative by gathering and bringing in the peoples to this center of worship that has a restored temple (Isa 56:5, 7; cf. 44:28; 63:18; 64:11), and if they hold fast to his covenant their names will not fail or be "cut off" (cf. Isa 55:13–56:8; cf. 54:7, 10).[56] In this eschatological restoration God calls the people groups, bids them to come to him, and asks them to seek him (Isa 55:1-3, 6).[57] Through the lens of Isaiah, Zion/Jerusalem possibly symbolizes the kingdom of God for John (cf. John 3:3, 5; 18:36), and Jesus represents the new temple (2:19-21); hence the people now must "come" to Jesus. In any case, Zion may be viewed by John as the place where God draws his people to worship God "in spirit and truth" (4:24; cf. 6:63).

What is emphasized in 6:37a, at least, is not the individual; neither individualistic election nor individualistic universalism is the central point in this particular thought. *The passage recalls a prophetic Isaianic promise: God gives the Son a collective people comprising of various people groups.* All people—Jewish outcasts, foreigners, and eunuchs in Isaiah; Greeks, Samaritans, Galileans in John—will come to Jesus. What is inevitable is the collective whole made up of various people groups coming to Jesus. These groups are destined for salvation, rather than every individual or a preselected number within these groups. They are predetermined in the sense that God, through his prophet, promised that such an event would take place—i.e., that the various peoples would all be saved in the new era—and God's word would accomplish that what it sets out to do (Isa 55:1-11).

Notwithstanding, 6:37b *does* center on the individual. In light of the Isaianic backdrop to 6:35-47, the Father "gives" the peoples to Jesus, gathering and drawing them to him, and Jesus' proclaims, "the one who comes to me I will never cast out" (6:37b; cf. 10:28-30; 17:12; 18:9; 1 John 5:18). To be "cast out" (ἐκβάλλω) anticipates the cured blind man expelled from the synagogue (John 9:34-35). The true house of

---

52. Cf. Barrett, *John*, 293; Brown, *John*, 1.79, 269.

53. Zerwick, *Grammatical Analysis*, 305, suggests "generality rather than individuals is envisaged." Witherington, *John's Wisdom*, suggests 6:37 refers to an "elect group" rather than "elect individuals" (158). But neither ἐκλεκτός nor ἐκλέγομαι is used here.

54. On the city as New Jerusalem and having God's presence, see Childs, *Isaiah*, 429-30.

55. In Isa 56:7 the neuter is used (πᾶσιν τοῖς ἔθνεσιν), but here it is plural.

56. The LXX stresses "fail" (ἐκλείπω) and MT "cut off" (בָּרַת).

57. The aspect of coming/proceeding in Isa 55:1 is marked by הָלַךְ (MT) and πορεύω; βαδίζω (LXX).

God has become Jesus in Johannine thought. He is the word of God made flesh that "tabernacled" (σκηνόω) among humans and becomes the place of worship among people who have intimate communion with him (John 1:14; cf. 2:13–22; Rev 3:20; 21:2–3, 22). An everlasting covenant has been given to all peoples through Jesus: those who come to him and abide in him will have eternal life, eat, and be spiritually satisfied. Jesus' words have great significance for the Johannine community. *Unlike the Pharisees, who expel Jesus' followers from the synagogue, Jesus promises that he will never cast out from his own presence those who continue to believe in him.*[58] It is quite possible in 6:37b that the Johannine redactor is reflecting on his own community that was ostracized by religious leaders of a local synagogue (cf. 16:2), and this may be the reason why the location of Jesus' message in 6:22–59 has somehow segued from the fertile wilderness to a synagogue in Capernaum (6:59).[59] Jesus will never forsake the Johannine community and its members who trust him. At the same time, according to Raymond Brown, these scriptures provided the community with "ammunition" in winning over the "Crypto-Christians" who believed but feared leaving the synagogues.[60]

The will of God is that Jesus would lose none of the collective peoples or "all" but raise "it" up in the last day (6:39–40; cf. 6:12). Likewise, the will of God is that individuals who see and believe Jesus should have eternal life and be raised up in the last day.[61] Here the "will of God" is being contrasted with Jesus working on his own initiative rather than the Father's. The Son's desire is to do the Father's will, which reinforces the surety on Jesus' words (cf. 4:24; 5:30; 8:29). Thus the collective "all" is given to Jesus by God, and Jesus will never reject individuals who believe in him, and it is God's desire that both the "all" and every individual from the "all" be kept by Jesus until the completion of the eschaton. Both collective and individualistic perseverance are taught here. Even so, these promises seem to assume human responsibility because final perseverance applies to those individuals who continue believing (notice the present participles of "come" and "believe" in 6:35, 37, 40), and Johannine thought assumes humans are presumably free enough to either do or not

---

58. Cf. Gnilka, *Johannes Evangelium*, 51. In light of the Johannine synagogue situation, the explanation that "I will never cast out" is a *litotes* ("I will certainly welcome/preserve") is not needed. Carson, *Divine Sovereignty*, 184, suggests for most references in John, to "cast out" presupposes someone already "in" (John 2:15; 9:34–35; 10:4; 12:31).

59. The murmurers appear in 6:41, 52, 61, but the location changes from the wilderness to a synagogue in Capernaum (6:59). The segue takes place, it seems, either in 6:41 or 6:52. Alternatively, the Johannine author may be fusing together two or more stories with similar discourse(s).

60. Brown, *Community*, 67–68. Brown argues that the Jews who rejected the message of Jesus and expelled the Johannine community from the synagogues are perceived as having no hope.

61. Whereas the "it" in 6:39 refers back to the collective "all" in 6:37a, the "one/he" in 6:40 refers back to "the one/he" in 6:37b.

do God's will (John 7:17; 9:31; 1 John 2:17; cf. John 5:34–47).⁶² A final assurance of perseverance independent of human responsibility to believe does not seem to be what is claimed here.

Since one of the functions of 6:37 is to provide assurance for the Johannine community, we are not told in the context what happens to a person who does not *continue* "coming" in or believing. Elsewhere in John's gospel, we find that believers who do not continue abiding in Christ are cast away from him and forfeit eternal life (e.g., John 15:6; cf. 12:25). When the contexts of 6:37 and 15:6 are read together we either have an irreconcilable tension on our hands or perhaps a fuller picture on Johannine perseverance and apostasy in relation to abiding in Christ. *God initiates salvation by giving and drawing people to Jesus; thus "getting in" Christ and the eternal life that he brings is an explicit act of divine grace.* The one who continues to "come" to Christ, that is believe in Jesus, will never be rejected by him but will be raised to new life in the last days. But the one who does not remain in Christ will be cut off from Christ (see 15:6 below). If *John 6:37b and 6:44 support the notion of individualistic predestination, which is certainly a possibility in Johannine thought, the predestination seems to find its end at one's entrance into an abiding relationship with Christ and the Christ community. Once "in" this relationship, oddly enough, it is still possible to find oneself eventually "out" of this relationship and forfeit eternal life.* When 6:37 and 15:6 are heard together, and related Johannine passages on both sides of the conundrum, Johannine predestination does not ultimately secure one's final perseverance. If such a person falls away, that person is held responsible for his or her own failure, and Christ is not to be blamed for that person's apostasy.⁶³

The previous episode in John 5:31–47 provide further insight on 6:34–47. Jesus proclaims that "the Jews" are to hear and learn from the Father through their scriptures/Law, which testify of Jesus.⁶⁴ But they are rejecting the scriptures (cf. 5:45–47), or in other words, the predicted salvation in these scriptures that God brings their way through Jesus.⁶⁵ If they would hear the Father speak to them through the scrip-

---

62. It would seem to be a misconception to assume that people are innocent prior to encountering Jesus. Carson, *Divine Sovereignty*, 165, when interpreting John 15:21–24, correctly asserts that the passage is not stating the world's innocence prior to Jesus' coming, as though those who are in the world were sinless before he spoke to them; rather, "they would not be guilty of the sin in question, viz. persecuting Jesus and his disciples."

63. In agreement with Wikenhauser, *Evangelium nach Johannes*, 127, on this final point.

64. That John 5 takes place in Jerusalem and John 6 takes place in Galilee and a synagogue in Capernaum does not disrupt this argument. Both passages are addressed to "Jews," who are stylized as unbelievers (5:1, 18; 6:41).

65. Compare Ridderbos, *Gospel of John*, 233: "What prevents 'the Jews' from coming to Jesus and believing in him, therefore is not that salvation is not intended for them but that they do not want to receive it in the manner in which God would give it to them, namely by their coming to Jesus."

The Gospel of John and the Epistles of John

tures they would come to Jesus because Moses spoke about Jesus (5:37, 45–47). This notion more than merely alludes to Deut 18:15–18; Jesus is more than another prophet like Moses (cf. John 6:14 with 6:50–59, 68–69; cf. 9:17 with 9:35–38). For the Johannine author, the true believers receive Jesus as the *logos*, agent of creation, the "word" who has been around before the beginning of Israel's tradition history. Moses saw the glory of this *logos* at Sinai when receiving the Torah (John 1:14–18/ Exod 33–34) and Isaiah also saw the same glory (John 12:41/Isa 6).[66] Culpepper's insight is instructive here:

> During the historical past, the history of Israel, he [Christ] came into the world and enlightened those who had eyes to see him (1:9). Moses and the prophets wrote about him (1:45; 5:46), and Abraham saw his "day" (8:56). Isaiah, presumably in his heavenly vision (Isaiah 6), saw "his glory" (12:41) . . . there is little doubt that for John the *logos* was the inspiration of the prophets and Jesus was the fulfillment to which they pointed.[67]

With these thoughts in view, we interpret the Father's "drawing" (ἕλκω) in John 6:44–45 in terms of his teaching "the Jews" the scriptures, and these scriptures testify of Jesus.[68] Similar thoughts are found in the *Mishna* in which disciples of Aaron are to draw people to the Torah (*m. Pirke Abot* 1:12). God also draws his people Israel with love (Hos 11:4MT; Jer 31:3 [38:3 LXX]).[69] In John 6 God draws people to his "word" (i.e., the scriptures and Jesus); the people who come to Jesus are those who have heard and learned the scriptures from the Father, and it is Jesus who makes the unseen Father fully known (6:45b–46; cf. 1:18; 3:33–34; 12:45; 14:7–10). This language comes close to a saying of Jesus denoting a mutual relationship between Father and Son in revealing divine teaching to humans: "no one knows the Son except the Father; nor does anyone know the Father except the Son" (Matt 11:27a/Luke 10:22a).[70] It is the Son who reveals the Father to whom he wills (Matt 11:27/Luke

---

66. In agreement with Keener, *John*, 1.662. Schnackenburg, *John*, 2.125, brings out, "The word of Scripture and his [Jesus'] own word form a unity (cf. 2:22), and in light of his glorification the Scripture finally discloses its hidden meaning (cf. 12:16; 20:9)."

67. Culpepper, *Anatomy*, 106.

68. The "given" in 6:37 and "draw" in 6:44 are not synonymous: the former is corporate and guarantees belief of the "all" that are given to Jesus; the latter is individualistic. On the other hand, 12:32 is a corporate "draw," and faith would seem to be a condition related to this salvation: cf. Schnackenburg, *John* 2. 393.

69. On these and further sources on ἕλκω see, Theobald, "Gezogen von Gottes Liebe," 323–36.

70. Schnackenburg, *John*, 2.51, explains this mutual working as an inward attraction related to the Father and external hearing related to the Son; hence, "No one can come to the Son without having received the teaching of the Father; no one can hear the Father and learn from him except through the Son." In John, the Son also gives life to whom he wills (John 5:21), which is not intended to express his arbitrary choice but authority.

10:22b); in John 6:44, 65 it is the Father who wills. *In John, the Father takes the initiative to draw people, apparently teaching and enlightening them through the scriptures, and these scripture testify of Jesus. The unbelieving crowd, however, fail to understand what the Father has spoken through the scriptures and Jesus.*

In a related passage to 6:44 we read that "all" are drawn to Jesus once he is lifted up on the cross (12:32). The uplifted Jesus shows God's love, which in turn draws all people to him (cf. 3:16; 1 John 3:16; 4:10).[71] They will believe, whether Jews, Samaritans, or Greeks. The passage, however, is not espousing universalism on an individualistic level; it affirms instead that various collective groups of people will come to Jesus. This "post-Easter" perspective of the divine "draw" may help enlighten our understanding of 6:44. In the narrative neither the crowd, nor "the Jews," nor yet Jesus' disciples could have possibly understood the eucharistic aspects of Jesus' sermon without understanding the upcoming crucifixion. It would take the work of the Spirit of Truth in a post-Easter setting to enlighten people and convict the world of sin (16:7–15; cf. 12:16; 20:9). The Spirit, then, will also be involved in drawing people and is perhaps the instrument by which the Father draws (cf. 6:63), but the Spirit had not yet been given because Jesus still needed to be "glorified" through his death and resurrection (14:26; 15:26–27; 16:7–15). *Part of the mystery of divine drawing in 6:44 is thus centered on Jesus' crucifixion,* without which neither the crowds nor Jesus' disciples could fully comprehend what he was saying, anymore than Nicodemus was able to understand Jesus' teaching about the Spirit and being "lifted up" prior to Christ's crucifixion (3:1–14). They could not be "drawn" to Jesus fully until Jesus' death and resurrection took place and the Spirit was given. *The appointed time of the Father to draw all peoples to Christ according to Isaianic prophecy had not completely arrived in John 6.* Jesus speaks about upcoming events, and as to be expected those who listen to him do not comprehend him (3:13–14; 6:62–64; 8:28; 12:32–34).

We are not told in 6:44 to what extent the Father is responsible for the people's failure to understand and to what extent the people are responsible.[72] In some sense God does allow blindness to engulf the unbelieving "Jews" (cf. 12:37–41 below), and

---

71. Cf. Painter, "Monotheism," 129. The witnesses, however, are divided between the masculine plural πάντας ("all people" or "everyone": B, A, P[75], *TR*) and the neuter plural πάντα ("all things," "all," "everyone": P[66], ℵ, D, syr, vg). "All people" would seem to be a good translation given the Jewish/Gentile context of John 12.

72. Is redaction at fault here? It is possible to surmise two layers: the first layer reflected earlier Johannine teaching or traditions that emphasized human responsibility; the second or later layer added to the gospel shows that faith was a gift given by the Father to some but not all: cf. Fuller, "Son of Man," 193–98. Even with this explanation, however, our problem today is that we have a Johannine text that affirms both.

if the divine drawing is connected with God's appointed time for Christ to be crucified that had not yet arrived in John 6, they could not be "drawn" in the full sense of the word. Gerald Borchert, in any case, correctly maintains the tension between divine initiative and human responsibility here: "Salvation is never achieved apart from the drawing power of God, and it is never consummated apart from the willingness of humans to hear and learn from God."[73] Divine drawing, at any rate, does not seem to nullify the responsibility of the crowd to hear and be taught by God.

This gospel's view of faith involves an abandonment of human confidence or self-effort; one must approach God humbly and submit to his will and word.[74] To listen to God and walk humbly before him and not rebel against him is something "the Jews" would be expected to know.[75] Instead they do not accept the one whom the Father sent (5:38), and they refuse to come to him (5:40), receive him (5:43), or believe him (6:36).[76] Divine drawing, then, does not seem to be entirely irresistible; there appears to be some sense of mutual attraction.[77] If this is the case, then the Father's "drawing" is not entirely one-sided in 6:44, and presumably neither is his "giving" in 6:37a. In light of the passage's intertextual background, one may interpret 6:37 as: "All the people groups that the Father gives to me on the basis of his word in the scriptures being fulfilled will believe in me, and the individual who continues believing in me will never be cast out." Thus it is quite possible for us to suggest that what is being taught from the pericope is neither individualistic predestination to salvation nor individualistic final perseverance independent of one's responsibility to believe. The thought against individualistic predestination, however, may be weakened by the role of Judas (see below), but the limited role of perseverance in view of apostasy is definitely supported elsewhere in Johannine thought. The upshot of the latter thought is that 6:37–45 does not nullify the possibility that individuals who believe in Christ can fall away from Christ.

---

73. Borchert, *John*, 1.268. On John and predestination see further in Schnackenburg, *John*, 2.265–70; Schnelle, *Evangelium nach Johannes*, 141–43.

74. Cf. Bultmann, *Gospel of John*, 231–32, 443, who emphasizes the necessity of humans to abandon their own judgment to hear God and so allow him to speak to them: "The 'drawing' by the Father occurs not, as it were, *behind* man's decision of faith, but in it."

75. On a secondary level would the Johannine community be overconfident in their own ability to save themselves? A better case could be made for their *lack* of confidence (cf. 20:31; 1 John 5:13).

76. Although Peter on behalf of the Twelve may confess a different attitude, one that believes God by affirming Jesus as the Holy One and possessor of the words to eternal life (6:68–69), the confession may still be tarnished somewhat with human confidence. This is perhaps why Jesus informs them that even among his chosen disciples, one of them is a devil (6:70–71).

77. So even Trumbower, *Born from Above*, 85.

In the Footsteps of Judas and Other Defectors

DEFECTORS FROM JESUS AND THE JOHANNINE COMMUNITY (JOHN 6:60–66; 8:31–59; CF. 1 JOHN 2:19)

In the final section of John 6 we read that "many disciples" of Jesus turned away from following him after they could not fathom his teachings (6:60–66).[78] His discourse on the bread of life had become for them a point of murmuring and ground for σκανδαλίζω (6:60–61; cf. 16:1), the same term that often refers to apostasy in the gospels and here refers to their stumbling over the words of Jesus (cf. 16:1; Matt 11:6; 13:57; Luke 7:27; Mark 6:3). The force of the phrase "they turned back" in 6:66 (ἀπῆλθον εἰς τὰ ὀπίσω) means to abandon an association with someone.[79] Significantly εἰς τὰ ὀπίσω in the LXX, among other meanings, is used to refer to Lot's wife looking back at the destruction of Sodom (Gen 19:17, 26), a story referenced by Jesus in Luke as a warning for the disciples not to fall away (Luke 17:31–32; cf. 9:62). The phrase also appears in contexts related to Israel's spiritual blindness and apostasy in Isaiah (Isa 28:13; 42:17; 44:25; cf. Ps 43[44]:18–19). It is used in John 6:66 to describe the apostasy of many Galilean disciples who professed some belief in Jesus and followed him. The Twelve stay with Jesus, but other followers depart.

On a second level the passage may reflect a later Johannine situation in which many Christ-followers defected. We notice that the location of "Jews" murmuring in the wilderness has changed; they are now murmuring in a synagogue in Capernaum (John 6:52, 59). The narrative possibly recollects the Johannine community's expulsion from the synagogue and Jewish "Crypto-Christians" parting company with them by remaining in the synagogue. If this were the case, however, we might expect the Twelve to break away from *them* rather than vice versa, or better yet we might expect officials to banish Jesus from the synagogue in Capernaum. *The narrative more likely reflects the schism between the emergent Christians that took place within the Johannine community in Ephesus* (cf. 1 John 2:19).[80] This defection probably took place, among other reasons, because certain members denied Jesus as the Messiah (e.g., 1 John 2:22–23; see below).

If the many disciples who fall away in John 6:66 reflect the Johannine community's later schism, this may tend to support an idea that they were never genuine followers of Jesus in the first place. In 1 John 2:19 the secessionists that went out from

---

78. "As a result of this" (ἐκ τούτου) in 6:66 probably refers to the hard teaching related to the bread of life discourse rather than referring only to 6:65. Already in 6:60 they are questioning Jesus' earlier teaching.

79. Cf. BDAG, 102. Literally, they "went away to the things they had left behind" (Köstenberger, *John*, 220).

80. Kim, *Apostasy Embedded*, 24–25, 304–5, rightly argues for the association of the schisms in John 6:66 and 1 John 2:19.

The Gospel of John and the Epistles of John

the Johannine community did not really belong to the community; the Johannine author writes that if they had been authentic members of Christ's community, they would have remained with the community.[81] It became clearly evident that none of them really belonged to the community.[82] The party probably left voluntarily rather than being expelled or excommunicated; otherwise, the author's argument that they would have "remained" would seem awkward. The Johannine writer claims that the members of the departed group were inauthentic Christians and "antichrists" bringing about division in the community (1 John 2:18–19).[83] *It is reasonable to assume, then, that the Johannine author considered the defecting disciples in John 6:60-66 as inauthentic followers of Jesus.* Although we are not told in 6:60–71 whether the defecting disciples were ever true believers at one time, the assumption in the text seems to be that they were not. They were not granted enlightenment to understand the true meaning behind Jesus' words, which seems to indicate they were not "drawn" by the Father or had no real interest in spiritual things (6:64–65; cf. 6:44).[84] They followed Jesus presumably for wrong reasons, much like the people who followed Jesus in the wilderness and desired to make him an earthly king and craved food more than his words (6:15, 26–27).

What is difficult to ascertain is how many of these wrong motives reflect the attitudes of the people or "Jews" rather than Jesus' disciples. Carson claims some possibilities that resulted in their departure included an interest in food, political perspective on messianism, manipulation of miracles more than spiritual realities to which the eating pointed, inability to relinquish their own authority, and Jesus' claim

---

81. The Qumran community describes in CD-B 19.5–21 the faithful of the covenant who stand in contrast to covenant breakers. We notice the similarity of these apostates with the Johannine community—they seem to have never left the path of traitors even though entering God's covenant (19.16–17).

82. The final phrase of 2:19 (οὐκ εἰσὶν πάντες ἐξ ἡμῶν) conceivably means, "not all of them belong to us"; e.g., Bultmann, *Johannesbriefe*, 42: "nicht alle (die den Anspruch darauf erheben) gehören zu uns." This reading would tend to support the idea that the Johannine community was mixed: some believers, some not. Brown, *Epistles of John*, 341, however, refers to Rom 9:6 to show an example of a negative placed before the "all," and argues that "Paul did exactly what the author of 1 John would have done if he wanted to say, 'Not all from us belong to us.'" The literal reading from the Greek is "not they are all from us." The "all" is probably understood collectively, as in "none [are from us] . . ."

83. Strecker, *Johannine Letters*, 64, correctly maintains that their "antichrist" nature is evident by their disruption of church unity.

84. John 6:65 has more in common with 6:44 than 6:37. In 6:65 the individual is granted something by the Father: spiritual insight to come to (i.e., believe) Jesus. In both 6:44 and 6:65 the language refers to what the Father initiates for individuals, whereas 6:37 is a corporate giving of peoples to the Son. The stress on Judas in 6:64–65 is exemplified in p[66] and other witnesses that omit τίνες εἰσὶν οἱ μὴ πιστεύοντες καὶ. Though the wording in 3:27 is similar to 6:65, the former relates to the ministry of Jesus eclipsing John the Baptist's. See also 19:11 for a somewhat similar meaning to 3:27.

In the Footsteps of Judas and Other Defectors

to be greater than Moses (6:15, 26, 30–34, 41–46, 58).[85] They also found it difficult to fathom the words of Jesus about his heavenly origin and the necessity for them to eat his flesh and drink his blood.[86] In the narrative belief also must be accompanied with endurance (6:27).[87] In the end, they rejected Jesus and no longer followed him. He was not the Messiah they had expected.[88]

In John 8:31–59 we find a group of "Jews" who believe in Jesus. In his dialogue with them Jesus affirms his preexistence and reveals them as sinners contradicting the works of Abraham whom they claim as their forefather. By the end of Jesus' dialogue with them they attempt to stone him as a blasphemer. For the Johannine community this group would doubtless be considered an apostate Jewish-Christian group. It is possibly the same one mentioned in 6:66 if the perfect participle πεπιστευκότας in 8:31 conveys a pluperfect meaning that this group had believed in Jesus but no longer did so.[89] This would help explain why in the course of one dialogue with Jesus they could devolve into murderers and be called the devil's children by Jesus. They were already apostates at the beginning of the dialogue. On this reading of the passage, rather than confirming them in their belief in 8:31–32, Jesus is actually extending to them the possibility of their restoration to his teachings, and their return will be contingent on how they respond to his dialogue with them.[90] It is not impossible that a number of believers during Jesus' earthly ministry would have fallen away and become hostile towards him, but given the Johannine situation and two-level reading of the text we must press further and surmise who these apostates in 8:31–58 might be. If this group refers to those who had already defected in 6:66, then we have our answer. These apostates represent those who left the Johannine community in 1 John 2:19.

One weakness with this view is that Jesus says to these apostates that they must abide/remain (μένω) in his teaching if they are truly to be considered his disciples (8:31; cf. 13:35; 15:8). Elsewhere besides 8:31, ἐάν + the aorist subjunctive μείνητε is addressed to the Twelve who (apart from Judas) are not apostates (15:7). In 1 John 2:24 a similar construction is addressed to the believers, as is the notion of abiding/remaining in the word or truth (1 John 2:14; 2 John 2; cf. 1 John 3:9). Apostates and unbelievers are not invited to abide/remain in the truth (John 5:38; 2 John 9; cf.

---

85. Carson, *John*, 300.

86. Notice Harrill, "Cannibalistic Language," 158: Jesus' "cannibalistic" language "functions to divide insiders from outsiders."

87. Cf. Harrill, "Cannibalistic Language," 153.

88. Cf. Köstenberger, *John*, 220.

89. See argument in Griffith, "Jews Who Had Believed," 183–92; Swetnam, "Meaning of πεπιστευκότας," 106–9.

90. Cf. Griffith, "Jews Who Had Believed," 188.

John 15:6; 1 John 2:19; 3:14–15), unless here in John 8:31. Moreover, if the perfect participle of πιστεύω refers to believers as it does elsewhere in the New Testament (Acts 15:5; 18:27; 19:18; 21:20, 25; Titus 3:8), then the Jewish believers in 8:31 could be understood quite easily as those who had just believed the previous message of Jesus in 8:30.[91] If so, then the reason why they could believe and yet quickly fall away is not necessarily because they have spurious faith,[92] or that their belief was limited to Jesus as the prophet who was to come,[93] but as new believers they represent a phenomenon similar to the second seed of Jesus' parable of the Sower, which has little or no depth in the word of God and so quickly falls away (cf. Mark 4:16–17; Matt 13:20–21; Luke 8:13). This resembles the phenomenon of "precipitate" defection common also in modern apostasies. But more than this, in the narrative they quickly become antagonistic defectors who attempt to kill Jesus.[94]

This option veers us away from equating the defectors of 8:31–59 with those who seem to be ungenuine in 6:66, and so once again we must ask which community is the author referring to that would be relevant to the Johannine *Sitz im Leben*. One possibility is for us to concede with Schnackenburg that the text betrays a polemic against (emergent) Judaism: "the attempt to confirm Jews who had become believers in loyalty to Jesus combines with the polemic against the Judaism of John's time, which was mounting violent attacks on the Messiahship of Jesus. The polemical aspect predominates in the rest of the section [of 8:31–59] because a rebuttal of the Jewish counter-arguments had become a necessity for the sake of the Jewish Christians, who had become insecure."[95] Another possibility is for us to notice that Jesus departs from the temple away from the apostates in the narrative (8:59); they do not depart from him as in 6:66. Perhaps these defectors represent pre-70 CE Christians from Jerusalem or Palestine who had earlier been hostile to the Johannine group and in some way may have even helped expel them from the synagogue. Along these lines the next story depicts the Pharisees expelling Jesus-followers from the synagogue (John 9).

---

91. Nonetheless, Griffith (ibid., 184) does bring out two examples of the perfect particle of πιστεύω that are related to apostasy in *Herm. Vis* 3.6.4 and 3.7.1. He also raises other reasons why 8:31 should not be read with 8:30 (see his article on 186), but they seem insufficient to affirm two distinct groups in 8:30 and 31.

92. E.g., Carson, *John*, 345, 347–48; Haenchen, *John*, 2.20.

93. E.g., Motyer, *Your Father the Devil?*, 163, 166.

94. On precipitate and antagonistic defectors from a social perspective, see Wilson, *Leaving the Fold*, 124–25. The alternative for their quick desertion would be along the lines of a poor redaction by the final editor who decided to copy the aspect of believers in 8:30 to 8:31 (see Brown, *John*, 1.354–55).

95. Schnackenburg, *John*, 2.205; Beasley-Murray, *John*, 132–33.

In the Footsteps of Judas and Other Defectors

JUDAS AS THE REPRESENTATIVE DEFECTOR AND PREDICTED BETRAYER (JOHN 6:64–71; 12:4–6; 13:2, 10–11, 19–30; 17:12; 19:11)

Judas is among the Twelve who did not defect with the other disciples in John 6:66. Jesus nevertheless says that one of the Twelve he had elected is a devil. The Johannine commentator adds that he was speaking about Judas, who was going to betray him (6:70–71). We also notice that in John 6:68–69 Peter makes a confession about Christ somewhat similar to Mark 8:29 and Matt 16:16, but in John's version Judas is associated with the devil rather than Peter (cf. Mark 8:32–33; Matt 16:22–23). Jesus' revelation about one them being a devil, in any case, may be read as an implicit warning against any overconfidence the Twelve may have felt for not leaving with the defectors.[96]

Judas is a recalcitrant betrayer in Mark's gospel, a remorseful disciple in Matthew, and a genuine disciple turned apostate and traitor in Luke-Acts. In John's rendition of this disciple, Judas is a "devil," thief, betrayer, and is vilified more than the other gospels (John 13:2, 10–11, 19, 21–30; cf. 21:30).[97] He is also motivated by the vice of greed, and similar to Luke, he becomes possessed by Satan (6:70–71; 12:4–6). In essence he personifies evil, and in keeping with those who do evil deeds and fall away in "night" or "darkness" (cf. 3:19–20; 11:9–10; 12:35) Judas leaves the dinner table after being exposed as the betrayer, "and it was night" (13:30).[98] In terms of Judas' fate, the Johannine Jesus considers him "the son of destruction" (ὁ υἱὸς τῆς ἀπωλείας), the one destined to be destroyed (John 17:12; cf. 2 Thess 2:3, 8–12; Isa 34:5; 57:4; 2 Sam 12:5; *Apoc. Pet.* 1.2). The scripture being fulfilled in 17:12 refers back to 13:18 citing Ps 40[41]:9–10; thus the scripture in 17:12 is not related directly to the phrase "son of perdition" but to the role of Judas as betrayer.[99] He will be punished because of his betrayal, not because the scripture predicted his destruction.

Even so, the Johannine Judas seems predestined or at least foreknown for his role as betrayer according to John 13:18/Ps 40[41]:9–10: "the one who is eating my bread has lifted his heel against me."[100] The Greek word for eating that appears in the

---

96. In a similar manner, Xavier, "Judas Iscariot in the Fourth Gospel," 250–58, posits that the author uses Judas in the text to warn the community.

97. John 21:20 is not referring to a new betrayer among the Twelve but refers back to Judas' betrayal in 13:25.

98. The aspect of falling away is implied not only when a person loses his/her way in darkness (12:35) but also "stumbles" (προσκόπτω) without light in the night (11:9–10; cf. Rom 9:32; 14:21; Jer 13:16; Prov 3:23).

99. Van Wahlde, "Judas," 167–81, argues (unconvincingly in my opinion) for Prov 24:22a as the passage behind this phrase.

100. The quote seems to be closer to the MT than LXX: cf. Daly-Denton, "Psalms in John's Gospel," 129. Menken, *Old Testament Quotations*, 138, argues that the author used his "own translation from the Hebrew."

passage (τρώγω) is also found in Jesus' bread of life discourse four times in 6:54–58, the same context in which Judas' betrayal is mentioned for the first time.[101] In Ps 40[41]:9–10 Judas' betrayal is what fulfills the passage, and the prophecy is given *post-facto*, after Judas had already decided to betray Jesus. The psalm originally recalls Ahitophel betraying David during Absalom's rebellion (cf. Ps 54[55]:13–15; 2 Sam 15:12, 31, 34; 16:15, 20–23; 18:28).[102] If the Johannine author understood Jesus as the Davidic Messiah (e.g., John 1:41, 49; 7:26–27, 41–42; 9:22), then perhaps he, like other early Christian interpreters, reconfigured David's enemies as Christ's. The betrayal in the psalm portrays an event in David's life; only later and on a different level would it be considered a phenomenon occurring in the Messiah's career.[103] The Johannine community read Ps 40[41] as rationale for the betrayal long after it had taken place. This does not necessarily preclude the possibility that Jesus originally made the connection between Judas' betrayal and Ps 40[41] (e.g., Mark 14:18; Luke 24:44–45), but it does suggest that the necessity clause "so that the scripture might be fulfilled" (John 13:18; 17:12) is a Johannine formula rather than Jesus' actual words (cf. 12:28; 15:25; 19:24, 28, 36–37).[104] It functioned as a type of apologetic to show that the events in Jesus' life, even negative ones, were all foreknown by God and Jesus, who are able to bring good out of evil.[105]

Whereas election in John relates to the task of Jesus' disciples abiding in him and bearing fruit (15:16–19), Jesus' choice of Judas seems to be for the purpose of the betrayal (13:10–11, 18; cf. 6:70–71). John 13:18a is not a denial of Jesus choosing Judas (cf. 6:70); it affirms that he knows Judas is a traitor and has chosen him for the purpose of fulfilling Ps 40[41]:9–10. It does not appear to be the case that another individual in Johannine tradition is chosen and predicted by Jesus for such an unpleasant role; if Judas is an example of individualistic predestination in a negative sense, he seems to be the exception, not the rule. For the Johannine author, Jesus knows all things (13:18a; cf. 1:47–48; 2:24–25; 8:14; 10:27; 21:12–17); thus he knows

---

101. Cf. Daly-Denton, "Psalms in John's Gospel," 130.

102. Menken, *Old Testament Quotations*, 132–36, makes a case that 2 Sam 18:28 is echoed in Ps 41:10. Daly-Denton, "Psalms in John's Gospel," 129, suggests that Ps 41:10 and 55:13–14 are sufficient to explain John's quote.

103. In other words, if Judas' betrayal had never taken place, no early interpreter would have pointed out a betrayal from Ps 40[41] still needed fulfillment. The name "Judas" is not tagged onto Ps 40[41]:9–10.

104. Contrast the possibility of the same Psalm reference without a citation formula in Mark 14:18.

105. In agreement with Painter, "Monotheism," 128–29. The reason why the author has this perspective of the betrayal may also be related to an accusation made by the Johannine community's opponents that Jesus could not be God if he made a mistake in choosing Judas (Menken, *Old Testament Quotations*, 137). This line of reasoning seems to be strangely similar to Celsus' accusation against Jesus according the Origen (Origen, *Cels.* 2.11, 12).

Judas would betray him when he first chose him. We notice that Judas becomes the treasurer of the group (12:6) even though presumably in John it would have been foreknown that Judas was a thief! What the Johannine writer does not tell us is how Jesus could use such a person for betrayal having full knowledge of the terrible perdition apparently awaiting Judas. Given the dualistic nature of this gospel and that Judas is reprobate even prior to his plans of betrayal, we can surmise from the Johannine author's perspective that Judas would have been damned anyway.[106] The fourth gospel at any rate does not seem to be concerned about psychological implications behind the betrayal.

The Synoptic Gospels do not run into this problem because in them Jesus does not know everything (e.g., Matt 24:36; Mark 13:32; Luke 8:45–47). As such, he could select Judas to be one of his closest disciples without knowing about his future betrayal. Unlike John, there is no hint in these gospels that Jesus chose Judas with foreknowledge about his future role or apostasy. Moreover, in the other gospels and especially Luke, Jesus' stress on radical discipleship would seem to make it difficult for an insincere follower to become part of Jesus' core group (e.g., Luke 9:23, 57–62; 12:33; 14:25–33; cf. Matt 16:24; Mark 8:34).[107] Judas may have been a treacherous disciple during Jesus' final days, but he did not start out following Jesus as one. On a historical note the real Jesus chose Judas to be with the Twelve presumably because he was a promising and exemplary disciple.

It is significant that Judas is first mentioned in John's gospel immediately after an apostasy of Jesus' disciples takes place in 6:66. Culpepper rightly considers Judas as the representative defector.[108] He models the many antichrists that threatened the Johannine community (1 John 2:18–19; cf. 2 Thess 2:3–4). Given dualistic meanings inundating this gospel, it is just possible that Jesus' words to Pilate veil a reference to Judas even though they are primarily targeting Caiaphas: "he who delivered me to you has greater sin" (John 19:11).[109] *John portrays Judas as a defector within Jesus' community of disciples similar to those who left the Johannine community years later (e.g., 1 John 2:18–19; cf. John 6:66–71). He is portrayed as an inauthentic believer*

---

106. Paradoxically he is given opportunity to repent, at least on one interpretation of John 13:27.

107. It is also interesting that the standards for discipleship in the Synoptic texts, such as taking up one's cross daily and giving up all that one has, are not as explicitly mentioned in John (see John 12:26 and compare Matt 16:24; Mark 8:34; Luke 9:23; 14:27). On discipleship in relation to Johannine abiding, see Winbery, "Abiding in Christ," 104–20.

108. Culpepper, *Anatomy*, 125. Kim, *Apostasy Embedded*, 213, considers the Johannine Judas as the "quintessential apostate," representing the "believing Jews" who become apostate in John 6 and 8 (cf. 25, 151–214). Judas' connection with apostasy is valid, but an association between Judas and the "Jews" sounds too similar to later church fathers who made horrible accusations of anti-Semitism based on this alleged connection.

109. Keener, *John*, 2.1127, likewise mentions Judas as another possible link in this verse.

who follows Jesus. Although he remains with Jesus after the great defection in John 6:66, he is immediately identified as a devil after this event and then later revealed by the Johannine author to be a thief even prior to his betrayal. His external defection is made clear by being influenced by the devil to betray Jesus, and when his treachery is exposed he vanishes into the darkness (13:2, 30). Yet even though Judas' betrayal seems inevitable, he is still held responsible for his act, and there is no indication that he was coerced to do it (John 12:4-6; 18:2-5). For the Johannine community, he receives eternal "destruction" rather than eternal life along with unbelievers and other defectors from the community (John 17:12; cf. 3:16-17, 36; 5:29; 15:6; 1 John 3:14; 5:16).

DIVINE PROTECTION OF DISCIPLES AND SHEEP (JOHN 10:1-31)

Jesus' speech on the Good Shepherd enlists a number of images including a shepherd, sheep, thieves and robbers, a porter, wolf, hireling, and "other sheep." Given the complex nature of this proverbial message or "figure of speech" (παροιμία: 10:6), which functions similar to a riddle or parable,[110] we find difficulties in determining whether all the characters are intended to represent something or someone else or whether some are mentioned simply to enrich the teaching and buttress the main point of Jesus' message. Central to the message, which follows on the heels of Jesus' encounter with "blind" Pharisees (John 9), is its emphasis on Jesus as the true shepherd of God's people as opposed to the Pharisees and other Jewish leaders that harm or neglect the flock of God. The Johannine tendency for polyvalent meanings of words and a two-level reading of the text further complicates our interpretation. If this message was mostly directed against the religious leaders of Jesus' day, what would that mean to the Johannine community? We can affirm some tentative possibilities.[111]

The robbers and thieves (10:1, 5, 10) are outsiders who enter into the fold and do not use the front "gate" (Jesus) to get in. Such individuals climb into the sheepfold some other way (10:9). The thief's purpose is to steal sheep from the fold. For the Johannine community, such persons would probably be interpreted as imposters, deceivers, or false prophets who enter the congregation illegitimately, do not know Jesus, and disrupt the congregation by leading astray its members (cf. 1 John 4:1-6;

---

110. On the term see further Smith, *John*, 204; Lincoln, *John*, 294; Hauck, "παροιμία," 5.854-56.

111. Kowalski, *Hirtenrede*, addresses a two-level reading of this text: the external threats represent Jewish opposition to the Johannine community, and the indecisions of community leadership results in membership fallout.

2 John 7–9).¹¹² Apostates such as those who had left the congregation in 1 John 2:19 might also be implied if they were attempting to draw others away from the community (cf. 1 John 2:26).¹¹³ The leaders of the community should only let Jesus and the Spirit into their church homes, not other spirits or false prophets. Jesus' explanation of the thief stealing, killing, and destroying sheep gives us a rare glimpse of the possibility that the Johannine author is aware that *genuine "sheep" or believers who have entered through the gate (Jesus) could be destroyed potentially*, and here their physical death seems insufficient. If Jesus gives them "life," which no doubt refers to eternal life, then their death or destruction means loss of eternal life (10:10).¹¹⁴ Here, as in many other cases in the scriptures, ἀπόλλυμι probably refers to final destruction that could happen to Christ-followers or God's people (e.g., Matt 10:28; Rom 14:15; 1 Cor 8:11; Heb 10:39; 2 Pet 2:1, 3; 3:16; Jude 5).¹¹⁵ More specifically in John's gospel it functions as the antipode of eternal life (cf. 3:16; 10:28), hence, loss of eternal life and the fate of those who commit apostasy (12:25; 17:12). To be sure, no one is powerful or cunning enough to snatch the sheep away from Jesus, the sacrificial and model shepherd (10:27–30; cf. 10:11),¹¹⁶ but there are prerequisites: the sheep hear his "voice" and follow him (10:27). That is, they are responsible to obey his teachings and continue in them.¹¹⁷ Otherwise they *could* be lead astray by other voices into eternal doom (10:5, 8b).

The identity of the "hired hand" likely refers to some leaders within the church.¹¹⁸ Well known in ancient Jewish sources is the aspect of leaders failing to fulfill their duties and so leaving those they are responsible for open to attack (Jer 23:1–4; Ezek 34; Zech 11:4–17; *4 Ezra* 5.18; *1 En.* 89.12–76; *T. Gad* 1.2–4).¹¹⁹ The hirelings probably represent for the Johannine community Christian leaders who are negligent or

---

112. The identity of those who came before Jesus (10:5) probably refers to false prophets or messianic pretenders, or possibly the Pharisees and other religious groups who later became Jesus' opponents.

113. Cf. Trebilco, *Early Christians*, 292.

114. Explanations that "to kill" in this verse refers to sacrifice and "a sly reference to priestly authority" and may also refer to the devil as a murderer (Brown, *John*, 1.386, 394) or that this verse functions as a "foil to Jesus' own mission statement" (Lincoln, *John*, 296) may be correct, but such reasons in themselves are insufficient to account for the aspect of destruction mentioned in 10:10.

115. See further examples in Oepke, "ἀπόλλυμι, ἀπώλεια, Ἀπολλύων," 1.394–97; BDAG, 115–16.

116. Cf. Brown, *John* 1.386. Lindars, *John*, 361: "ideal shepherd."

117. Köstenberger, *John*, 310, is instructive on the "voice" by affirming that in the past, "People listened to God's voice by living in conformity with his revealed will. At the present (from the perspective of the earthly Jesus), those who desire to follow God should do so by listening to Jesus' words and obeying his commandments (e.g., 15:10)."

118 See Brown, *Community*, 178. Keener, *John*, 1.814–17, thinks them to be "irresponsible shepherds of Israel (Ezek 34:10)."

119. See further, Köstenberger, "John," 463.

fear persecution at the price of leaving their flocks unprotected against outsiders. This second-level meaning seems insinuated in John's gospel.

On the primary level, however, the hirelings may refer to the twelve disciples. The scattering of the sheep alludes to Zech 13:7 (John 10:11–12; cf. 16:32).[120] This lends credibility to an implication that the hirelings might be Peter or the disciples who were scattered when Jesus was arrested (16:32; cf. 13:33, 36–38). If so, their connection with the hirelings is not that they are paid to watch over Jesus' sheep, but that they are not ready to lay down their lives for the sake of Jesus and fellow believers (cf. 12:25; 15:13).[121] When Jesus predicts Peter's denials, Peter mimics Jesus' words in 10:11 by saying that he is willing to "lay down" his "life" for Jesus (13:37).[122] As in the other gospels, the Johannine author has Peter denying Christ three times (18:17, 25–27). In this version of the disciple's failure, we notice a contrast between Jesus, who claims "I am" at his arrest (18:6, 8), and Peter, who denies Christ by saying, "I am not" (18:17, 25). Perhaps this is a Johannine hint that a denial of Christ takes place not only by church members who publically deny Jesus before others, but also by their denying him as the "I am" or the preexistent person in whom God uniquely dwells (cf. 8:23–24, 28, 58). Peter's defection, however, is somewhat minimized by his bravery at Jesus' arrest—he uses a sword to cut off the ear of the high priest's servant (18:10).[123] If Peter is considered a hireling in John 10, then his restoration in John 21 takes on a further nuance: Peter is finally commissioned to watch over Jesus' sheep, now as a shepherd rather than a hireling (21:15–17). But Peter's denials, at best, should be seen as only a temporary defection; Jesus knows beforehand that

---

120. In this passage it is assumed that Jesus is the shepherd; this shepherd may be contrasted with the bad shepherd in Zech 11:17 (cf. NET). Another significant echo in this passage may be Ezek 34, which contrasts bad shepherds as Israel's leaders and God as shepherding his own flock as well as "David" as Israel's shepherd during their restoration.

121. Presumably, then, the "wolf" in the narrative represents religious leaders who had arrested Jesus. For the Johannine community, it probably represents their opponents. It is not clear if the community would equate these with the thieves and robbers. The hirelings "abandon" (10:12: ἀφίημι) the flock when the "wolf" comes. In Matthew and Mark, ἀφίημι is used to describe the defection of the Twelve the night that Jesus was arrested (Mark 14:50; Matt 26:56). Significant for the Johannine community, the word is used to depict the apostasy of those in Ephesus who departed from their first love in Rev 2:4.

122. The Johannine version of this exchange provides another example of Jesus' omniscience in "knowing all things" (13:36–38; cf. 1:47–49; 2:24–25; 5:42; 6:70–71; 21:17).

123. Differently, Kim, *Apostasy Embedded*, among other things, notices that the Johannine Peter never actually denies Jesus' self-revelation nor uses words such as "oath" and "curse," used as litmus tests before Roman magistrates in discerning authentic Christians. He thus claims that Peter's denial is not to be equated with an apostate's denial in John's gospel (29–150). This viewpoint is difficult to reconcile with the warning related to persecution in John 12:25, but Kim rightly notices that John may have softened Peter's denials in comparison with Mark and Matthew.

Peter will be restored after his denials (13:36), and so ultimately he also is kept safe. Judas is the real exception as the representative defector.

Peter aside, the disciples' abandonment of Jesus at his arrest is played down as a defection in John's gospel. It is implied elsewhere but viewed in terms of the disciples being scattered and having sorrow rather than their forsaking Jesus (13:33; 16:20–22, 31–32).[124] Although they are not commended by Jesus as stalwarts of perseverance as in Luke, neither are they portrayed as defectors as in Mark and Matthew. Instead of predicting their apostasy (cf. Mark 14:27; Matt 26:31), the Johannine Jesus instructs them about things to come and forewarns them of persecution and expulsion so that they would *not* fall away: ταῦτα λελάληκα ὑμῖν ἵνα μὴ σκανδαλισθῆτε (16:1; cf. vv. 2–4).[125] They are in fact protected from physical harm and apostasy on the night Jesus is arrested (18:8–9; cf. 17:12). Hence, if there are hints that the disciples and Peter represent the hirelings in 10:11, then it should be added that any thought of abandonment here does not seem to be interpreted as apostasy.

The second discourse related to sheep is set in Jerusalem during the Feast of Dedication (10:22–39). It turns out that the audience in this narrative are the apostate "Jews" who once believed in Jesus. After his speech we read that "again" they picked up rocks to stone him (10:31). The only other instance where Jesus is threatened to be stoned is when he speaks to the apostate Christ-followers in Jerusalem (8:59; cf. 8:31).[126] In the later narrative they demand that Jesus tell them once and for all whether he is the Christ. Jesus responds by saying that he already told them this and they do not believe (10:25). This previous assertion about Jesus' messianic claim makes proper sense if the inquirers are former believers who once accepted him as Messiah; otherwise, one searches in vain to find an actual reference in John's gospel where Jesus tells his audience in Jerusalem point blank that he is the Christ, unless he is doing this by saying "I am he."[127] One might understand 10:26 not as "you are

---

124. Interestingly, and unlike Matt 27:46 and Mark 15:34 (cf. Ps 22), Jesus also is portrayed as not being abandoned by the Father in John's gospel (cf. John 8:29; 16:32); see discussion in Borchert, *John*, 2.181–83.

125. Cf. σκανδαλίζω: John 6:61; σκάνδαλον: 1 John 2:10. Lincoln, *John*, 413, suggests that the source for John 16:1 is Mark 14:27.

126. The word "again" does not refer back to 5:18 because no attempt to stone Jesus took place in that context. In 10:39 "again" may refer back to 10:31. If so, then here it is possible that they wished to "seize" (πιάζω) him in order to stone him (cf. NET notes ad loc.). But since πιάζω more generally refers to "arrest" elsewhere in John 7:30, 32, 44; 8:20; 11:57 (in 21:3, 10 it refers to fishes that are caught), this event might refer to some later time during the same feast in Jerusalem (i.e., sometime after Jesus' speech in 10:22–38) at which they sought to arrest Jesus. Either this, or in 10:39 "they" refers to a different group of opponents who had previously attempted to arrest Jesus.

127. The mysterious "I am" saying probably has messianic implications (8:23–24, 58); in fact, Freed, "*Ego Eimi* in John 1:20," 288–91, argues this term as referring to Messiah. If we accept that the term suggests Jesus as Messiah in John 8, the audience is generally the same audience as here in 10:31 (see

not my sheep because you do not believe," but as "you do not believe because you are not my sheep."[128] But it is perhaps reading too much into this verse to suggest that unbelief always happens as a *result* of not being Jesus' sheep, which runs counter to human responsibility implied in 10:37–38. More importantly, since these "Jews" are the same ones that became apostates (cf. 8:30–59), they *did* believe at one time and heard his "voice" but failed to continue hearing it. Now that they have already become apostates, they are not recognized as Jesus' sheep (10:27). The point of not belonging to Jesus seems to be one of verification rather than predestined origin. In the current narrative they remain in a state of unbelief and are obdurate to the point of attempting to kill Jesus once again for what they perceive as blasphemy (10:30–33).

It is in this particular situation that Jesus gives assurance to those who are among his sheep (10:27–29). In 6:37 the individual who comes to Jesus will never be cast away from him; in 10:27–29 the metaphoric flock of sheep who follow Jesus will never be destroyed or taken from him. They are "given" by the Father to Jesus (cf. 6:37), and they know, follow, and hear Jesus' voice (10:4, 14, 16, 27). They will not be "snatched out" (ἁρπάζειν ἐκ) of the Father's hand (10:28–29). The passage points back to 10:12, in which the wolf "snatches" and scatters the sheep that are under the care of a hireling instead of Jesus.[129] The believers cannot be snatched away because they have Jesus as their shepherd and remain part of his fold. No "wolf" or opponent of Jesus and his followers is powerful enough to pry them away from his grip. The "sheep" are assured that they will not lose eternal life. *The passage thus provides a sense of assurance for the Johannine community. Nonetheless, for the Johannine community, the notion of following Jesus means something more than simply acknowledging him as their leader; they are to obey his teachings, continue following him, and believe that he and the Father are "one"*—the last of which to the ears of his audience suggests that Jesus is making himself out to be God (10:30–33). The passage stresses the perseverance of the collective group or "flock" of believers.[130] If the individual continues in Jesus' teachings, then no doubt that person can rely also on such assurance.

In certain ways the message in John 10 is reflected in the prayer of Jesus in John 17. The group whom the Father has "given" to the Son are the collective group of disciples and those who will believe through their word (17:20; cf. 17:2, 6, 9, 12, 24), the

---

8:30–31 above). Hence, whether by being once insiders or by hearing "I am," the same audience seems to be addressed in both John 8 and 10.

128. Cf. Trumbower, *Born from Above*, 104.

129. In agreement with Borchert, *Assurance and Warning*, 121–22.

130. The word "sheep" is always plural in John 10 (πρόβατα; contrast the singular πρόβατον in Luke 15:6).

Christians or Johannine community. The language is still emphasizing a community rather than individuals, and the fact that Jesus is praying for the Father to "keep" and protect this group (17:11, 15) probably assumes that individuals within the group may be tempted in the future to fall away or betray Jesus, as was the case with Judas (17:12). Jesus protects the disciples,[131] and he intercedes for them so that they be kept in and by the Father's name as his own possession (17:11). The final ἐν in 17:11 may be understood as instrumental, "*by* your name," to mean that the Father protects the disciples by the power of his person or character. Or it may be locative, "*in* your name," namely that they are to be kept in the Father's name, kept loyal to the Father as "a place of security, i.e., keep them safe in their profession of faith in the revelation which they have received" (cf. 17:17).[132] Brown may be correct in affirming both meanings here,[133] which is certainly consistent with Johannine texts that have both Jesus and the Father keeping the believers (John 17:12, 15; 1 John 5:18), and the believers keeping the word of Jesus and the Father (John 8:51–55; 15:10, 20; cf. 14:21–24; 1 John 2:3–5; 3:22–24; Rev 3:3, 8). We notice a similar reciprocating relationship in Rev3:10: "because you have kept the word of my perseverance, I will also keep you . . ."[134] In John 17 a blend of God's keeping power on the one hand, and the believers' keeping God's word on the other, may be in view. The reciprocating relationship between divine protection and human responsibility should not be missed. The idea in this context relates to their becoming a unity or "one" in purpose, love, and communion with the Father and Son. External forces such as the world or the Evil One's hostility against them attempt to disrupt that unity (17:12, 14–15).[135]

ISAIANIC OBDURACY AND HUMAN RESPONSIBILITY (JOHN 12:37–41; CF. 9:39–41)

Unlike the other gospels, John's adaptation of spiritual blindness from Isa 6 is not related to parables about the kingdom of God, and the Johannine author is the one who cites the passage, not Jesus. The quote occurs at a significant juncture in this gospel (12:37–41)—immediately after Jesus had performed all of his miraculous signs in John 2–11. In the first half of the gospel "it is written" (ἐστιν γεγραμμένον) is the common introductory formula used for scripture citation. This formula changes

---

131. 17:11–23; cf. 6:37–39; 10:28–30; 13:36b; 14:3; 18:8–9; 1 John 4:4; 5:18.

132. Lindars, *John*, 524.

133. Brown, *John*, 2.759.

134. Keener, *John*, 2.1058, is a recent scholar who notices the relevance of Rev 3:10 for John 17.

135. This group is selected out of the "world," implying that the world itself is not given to Jesus by the Father (17:6, 9). In Johannine literature the world is seen as hostile to God even though individuals may believe and, as it were, come out of the world (John 3:16–17; 1 John 2:15–17).

in 12:38 to "that it might be fulfilled" (ἵνα ... πληρωθῇ), suggesting a shift from scripture assisting as a way of understanding the Christ event to the Christ event as fulfilling scripture (12:28; 13:18; 15:25; 17:12; 19:24, 36–37).[136] The Johannine alteration of formulas assists in demarcating a transition from the Book of Signs (chs. 2–12) to the Farewell Discourses (chs. 13–17).

At this pivotal moment a sign comes from heaven: God the Father speaks to Jesus in the presence of the crowd in Jerusalem during Jesus' final week. Jesus claims the voice was for their sake and urges them to walk and believe in the light, or else darkness will overtake them (12:27–36). The narrator then adds that although Jesus performed many signs before them, the crowd in Jerusalem kept on refusing to believe in him.[137] Their unbelief is connected with scripture from Isaiah being fulfilled: "Lord, who has believed our report, and to whom has the arm of the Lord been revealed?" (John 12:37–38/Isa 53:1).[138] The narrator then claims that they could not believe because of the words in Isa 6:10: "He has blinded their eyes and incapacitated their heart, lest they see with the eyes and understand with the heart and turn and I will heal them" (John 12:39–40).[139] The source of the quote does not seem to come directly from the MT, LXX, or Targums. The author may be paraphrasing from oral memory with words similar to both the LXX and MT.[140]

In the Johannine rendition of Isa 6, the unnamed third-person "he" who does the blinding in 12:40 is typically interpreted by scholars as God the Father, and the person who would heal them is identified as Jesus.[141] That God spiritually blinds and hardens people is not very unusual (e.g., Exod 4–14; Isa 63:17; cf. Deut 29:3–4; 1 Sam 24:1–10; 1 Kgs 22:19–23; Ezek 25:26–27). [142] If this meaning is followed, then John's interpretation of Isa 6 resembles the harsh language in Mark 4:11–12. What

---

136. Cf. Obermann, *Christologische Erfüllung*, esp. 426. The formulas are combined in John 19:28.

137. The imperfect οὐκ ἐπίστευον in John 12:37 suggests their unbelief was continual, perhaps implying that God gave them numerous opportunities to believe through the signs. We are not able to make too much of this tense, however, because the imperfect ἠδύναντο follows in 12:39 (albeit, the latter is connected with an infinitive and is similar to Mark 4:33).

138. In John 12:38 ἵνα can either refer to purpose or result (cf. John 6:7; 9:2; Roberston, *Word Pictures*, ad loc.).

139. In John's gospel διὰ τοῦτο ("therefore" or "for this reason"), when coupled with ὅτι, primarily seems to point to what follows in the narrative (cf. 5:16, 18; 8:47; 10:17; 12:18; 1 John 3:1 NET; Lindars, *John*, 438). This is most likely the case in John 12:39.

140. The phrase "and I will heal them" is found in the LXX. Most Johannine references follow the LXX with modifications. Cf. Schuchard, *Scripture within Scripture*, 152–53, who prefers the term "Old Greek" over LXX.

141. See Obermann, *Christologische Erfüllung*, 244; Kühschelm, *Verstockung*, 188–92, 200–202; Williams, "Testimony of Isaiah," 114–15.

142. Cf. Kühschelm, *Verstockung*, 188–92. See further sources in Räisänen, *Idea of Divine Hardening*. On sin as causing spiritual blindness, see *T. Dan.* 2.2–4; *T. Jos.* 7.5; Keener, *John* 2.883nn149–50.

In the Footsteps of Judas and Other Defectors

is awkward about the Johannine version is that, if God is the blinder and Jesus the healer, this almost seems to pit Son against Father or imply that they are not working with the same purpose in mind, a thought foreign to the rest of John's gospel (e.g., John 5:17–19; 10:28–30; 14:6–11; 17:11, 21–23).

John Painter argues that the one who blinds in 12:40 and prevents the people from believing is the power of darkness or the devil (cf. 12:31, 35, 40). The unbelievers have an attraction or inclination to the things of darkness (cf. 3:19–21), and spiritual blindness is not referring to predestination but judgment: "Choosing the darkness rather than the light involves consignment to the darkness and all that it brings. This is the judgment."[143] The signs of Jesus were intended to make insiders out of outsiders, but instead they became "instruments of judgment."[144] If this reading of the passage is correct, then "he" in 12:40 may refer to the devil rather than God. At first glance this connection appears to be tenuous: we must go back nine verses to 12:31 in order to find a direct reference to the devil. But there are several points that make this interpretation more credible.

First, the devil can be viewed as the instigator of darkness 12:35, and a parallel connection could be made between the thought of darkness in 12:35 and blindness in 12:40. An echo of Isa 6:10 in 1 John 2:11 indicates that it is not God but "darkness" that blinds the one who hates his brother, and darkness here seems associated with the "evil one," namely the devil (1 John 2:13–14; cf. 3:10–15).[145] Second, the idea of the devil or Satan causing people to become spiritually blind is not unique in early Christian literature: it is found in Paul (2 Cor 4:3–4) as well as later authors such as Origen and Cyril of Alexandria.[146] Third, if the "he" in John 12:40 is doing the blinding and the first-person "I" is doing the healing, then it seems difficult to maintain that both persons are working on the same side. How is that God, or Jesus, who is himself portrayed as divine in John, could be involved in the contradictory role of both blinding and healing the people? One person is blinding the people while the other intends to give their sight back. If the devil is blinding and God or Jesus is healing, this awkwardness is removed. Fourth and finally, in the Bodmer and Sinaiticus texts, "incapacitated" (ἐπήρωσεν) replaces "hardened" (ἐπώρωσεν) in 12:40.[147] The former verb (πηρόω) is found only in variant manuscripts of the New Testament and

---

143. Painter, "Monotheism," 125; Blank, *Krisis*, 301–5.

144. Painter, "Monotheism," 121.

145. On Isa 6:10 in 1 John see Lieu, "What Was," 472–75.

146. Cf. Painter, "Monotheism," 136–37, who also notes that the rare usage of the LXX τυφλόω is found only in John 12:40, 1 John 2:11, and 2 Cor 4:4.

147. Menken, *Old Testament Quotations*, 101–4, interprets the former as "he maimed" (ἐπήρωσεν), which is found in p$^{66, 75}$, ℵ, and other witnesses. Metzger, *Commentary*, 238, opts with the majority for ἐπώρωσεν. The antiquity of the Bodmer witness has me tentatively agreeing with the former.

rarely in the LXX.¹⁴⁸ What is hardly recognized is that πηρόω is also found in the Sinaiticus manuscript of Acts 5:3, where Satan incapacitates the heart of Ananias to lie to the Holy Spirit (Acts 5:3 א).¹⁴⁹ If the Sinaiticus version of John 12:40 and Acts 5:3 are the accepted reading and then paralleled, then another supporting argument may be added to the case that the devil is the one who incapacitates the human heart in John. This final point is admittedly a bit weak; but together all these points make for an alternative interpretation that the one who spiritually blinds people is the devil.

Ultimately, whether God or Satan is the one who is identified as "he" in 12:40, *the "crowd" from Jerusalem are blinded and not able to believe "because" (ὅτι) Isaiah's prophecy says that "he" blinded them* (12:39–40). This prompts us to question whether they were able to believe *any* signs if they had already been blinded. If God is directly responsible for their spiritual blindness and they have always been blind, it might be assumed that a rather severe form of predestination is taking place in which God has decided to damn the crowd arbitrarily or for reasons unclear to us—they could not believe *because* God blinded them. If the devil is the one who blinds them, this interpretation does not explain why, prior to any human ability to believe, Satan is able to blind human hearts or how the believers were presumably able to overcome their inability. If the crowd in Jerusalem is already blinded prior to belief, perhaps we should inquire further on whether they were *always* blind. Is it possible that there was a time when God became displeased with them and as a result of this handed them over to Satan or blinded them himself?¹⁵⁰

Jeffrey Trumbower writes that John's gospel conveys a "fixed origins" predestination similar to Valentinian Gnosticism, in which the destinies of individuals are fixed from the beginning, some are predetermined to believe and others not.¹⁵¹ A noteworthy conclusion he presents is that the concept of "born from above" in John 3 affirms two peoples with fixed destinies: unbelievers who come from "below" and

---

148. The verb πηρόω is found in the Western (D) witness of Mark 8:17 and poorly attested in Rom 11:7. The blindness in these passages is both contextually partial and temporal. In the LXX see 4 Macc 18:21; Job 17:7[variant], and for further sources outside the NT/LXX, see BDAG 802; LSJ, 1401.

149. For discussion on this variant reading of Acts 5:3, see Metzger, *Textual Commentary*, 327–28, whose committee finally opts for πληρόω, but only with "considerable doubt" {C}.

150. This subject interacts with predestination similar to the Qumran community (e.g., 1QH 1.19–31; 9.1–10.4; 15.12–22; CD 2.2–13; 4Q180.1). Even so, Schnackenburg, *John*, 2.266–70, concludes that "it is impossible to assume a direct influence of the view of Qumran on John, though contact with ideas of this sort is very likely." On Qumran and predestination see further, e.g., Lange, *Weisheit und Prädestination*; Merrill, *Qumran and Predestination*.

151. Turmbower, *Born from Above*, 3–30, 52, 140–45. See, e.g. Origen against Heracleon in *Comm. Jo.* 2.14.100–1010; 3.15.91–97; *Gospel of Truth* 21.11–14; 22:2–20.

believers born "from above" (3:1–14, 19–21; cf. 1:13; 6:64; 8:44–47; 10:26; 11:32).[152] Then again, the term "from above" (ἄνωθεν) in 3:3–5 may be understood as having dual meaning—born "from above" and born "again." This would be in keeping with the immediate context of multi-faceted meanings of terms in Johannine literature.[153] It appears that Jesus alone is viewed as "from above" in the sense of preexistence (1:1, 14; 3:13, 31; 16:28; 17:5; cf. 1:15). The concept of being born from above/born of God does not seem to refer consistently to fixed origins if 3:5 hints not only at a supernatural origin but also at human conversion-initiation taking place through water- or Spirit-baptism, or both.[154] Even though such a thought may be rare in John, this verse seems to speak of conversion.[155] Such initiation involves human volition and perhaps a transfer (μεταβαίνω) or crossing over from death to life (John 5:24; 1 John 3:14; cf. Col 1:13; 2:13; Eph 2:1, 5; 5:8; 1 Pet 2:9).[156] The conversion of those who were once lost is made possible by Jesus' vicarious death (e.g., John 10:11, 15–18; 1 John 2:2).

Wayne Meeks suggests that the Johannine author's dualistic picture of humans involves a conferred rather than ontological status (cf. John 15:9; 17:6a, 14) with the disciples as "not of this world" and the "world" as belonging to darkness and "things below."[157] John's gospel "is content to leave unanswered the question how there could exist in 'this world' some persons who, by some pre-established harmony, could respond to the Stranger from the world above and thus become, like him, men 'not of this world.'"[158] If we apply Meeks's words to 12:37–40, then perhaps we are at an impasse in John's gospel and must admit a mystery or tension remains regarding how believers are distinguished from unbelievers. I am not satisfied with this explanation, and so we will probe further.

---

152. Trumbower, *Born from Above*, 72–74.

153. It is possible that Jesus intends it to be understood one way and Nicodemus misunderstands him by hearing it another way. On potential misunderstanding caused by the ambiguity, see Brown, *John*, 1.130.

154. On baptism as intimated here see, e.g., Barrett, *John*, 208–9; Brown, *John*, 1.141–42. Beasley-Murray, *John*, 49, references instructive sources: "The conjunction of water and Spirit in eschatological hope is deeply rooted in the Jewish consciousness, as is attested by Ezek 36:25–27 and various apocalyptic writings (e.g., *Jub.* 1.23; *Pss. Sol.* 18.6; *T. Jud.* 24.3), but above all the literature and practices of the Qumran sectaries, who sought to unite cleansing and the hope of the Spirit with actual immersions and repentance in a community beginning to 'see' the kingdom of God (cf. 1QS 3:6–9; 1QH 11:12–14)."

155. See *b. Yebamote* 48b, which originates from an earlier saying (c. 130–160 CE): "One who has become a proselyte is like a child newly born" (Köstenberger, *John*, 124).

156. On μεταβαίνω, see Brown, *Epistles*, 445–46.

157. Meeks, "Man From Heaven," 68.

158. Ibid., 71. Meeks continues that there is no grand myth to explain this. The Gnostics, however, later used Sophia for their projection of the myth.

We do read in John that humans are constantly challenged to believe and are held responsible for their choices (e.g., John 1:7; 3:15-18, 36; 5:24, 40; 7:17; 20:21; 1 John 2:2; 5:1, 10, 13). While the requirements related to moral obligation seem to center on belief and love, they still require human decision.[159] Scott Celsor would add to this list John 21:18 as an example of human freedom in determining one's "walk" or way of life.[160] On the other hand, passages such as 6:37-44 and 12:37-40 tend to undermine any overconfidence in human ability alone to make appropriate spiritual decisions.[161] There seems to be a pattern in John's gospel that wherever divine sovereignty might be suggested to control the believer's salvation or the unbeliever's condemnation, human freedom and responsibility is not far behind. In 1:13, for example, although being a child of God involves divine rather than human agency,[162] and points to the incarnation (1:14), the verse is tempered by a human act in 1:12—"as many as received him" became sons of God. Thus believing and being born of God are juxtaposed in 1:12-13.[163] God sends and gives to humanity (1:4, 6, 12-14), but the world does not know him and his own people do not receive what is sent to them (1:10-11). They reject God's gift. People of the world choose to stay in darkness rather than come to the light because their deeds are evil (3:17-20). Differently, the disciples believe Jesus, but they belonged to the Father before they belonged to Jesus (17:6b). This might imply their predestination, but more likely it suggests that the disciples have already belonged to the Father because they believed Moses (5:46), were taught by God (6:45), and were receptive to the teachings pointing to Jesus as fulfilling prophetic tradition prior to Jesus' ministry (cf. 1:35-41). Hence, they believe what is true and come to the "light" (3:21). What we do *not* find in 12:40 is that the crowd was blinded *from the beginning of creation* so that they would not believe the signs. It is not clear in John's gospel that the salvific status of every human being is fixed from the beginning of time.[164]

---

159. E.g., John 1:12; 3:15-18, 36; 5:24; 6:29, 35; 8:31f; 10:37-38; 12:36; 13:33-34; 1 John 3:16-23. Instructive on this point is Schnackenburg, *John* 2.259-74.

160. Celsor, "Human Response," 125-27.

161. Cf. Kysar, "Dismantling of Decisional Faith," 161-81.

162. E.g., whether through parents ("bloods") or sexual desire ("flesh") or a husband's desire ("will of man").

163. Cf. Smith, *Theology of John*, 94.

164. Although Jesus knew "from the beginning" those who did not believe (John 6:64), divine foreknowledge may not necessarily be the same thing as salvific pre-determinism. John 6:64 may not be referring to predestination but stressing Jesus' omniscience by showing that even though many of his disciples defected and Judas betrayed him (see above), these things did not take Jesus by surprise nor call into question his choice of disciples: he knew all along those who were true believers and those who were not.

In the Footsteps of Judas and Other Defectors

We do find in both John and in ancient Jewish thinking that humans are held responsible for their actions even though spiritual powers might influence their decisions. This perspective is woven into the very fabric of the story of original sin (Gen 1–3), which is implied in Johannine literature.[165] In the Adam and Eve story, although the serpent influences the couple to eat the forbidden fruit, the couple is still held responsible for their own choices even when Eve places blame on the serpent.

How then, should the obduracy of "the Jews" from Jerusalem be interpreted in 12:37–40? A couple of suggestions might be helpful in our attempt to find an answer. First, the spiritual blindness examined in John 12:40/Isa 6:10 seems related to various Johannine passages that depict "the Jews" (and sometimes disciples) misunderstanding what Jesus says.[166] Such verses give evidence to the claim that Jesus' words in John are marked by figurative meaning, ambiguity, and double entendre. No doubt the misunderstandings help separate insiders from outsiders. The insiders gain further spiritual knowledge after the misunderstanding in the text is fleshed out, and the outsiders get more confounded if they do not proceed beyond superficial, external, and worldly meanings. In this sense John's gospel relates to the Synoptic saying, "To the one who has shall more be given, and to the one who has not, that which this person has shall be taken away" (Mark 4:23–25; Matt 13:12; 25:29; Luke 8:18; 19:26). *The audience of John's gospel is thus left with a challenge not to misunderstand the words of Jesus as did "the Jews" and others in the text.* Culpepper lucidly points out that if the listeners fail to understand the riddles of Jesus (John 10:6, 16:25, 29) they "will eventually be 'scattered' (16:31–32). The *dramatis personae* do not offer a model of how one is to understand. They serve rather as representatives of the consequences of failure to do so."[167]

Second, as we have already suggested, the Johannine author is Jewish and his repetitive citations of Israel's scriptures probably assume that his audience understands these scriptures. In 12:37–41 it would seem that John and his audience would already be familiar with the Isaianic backdrop to Isa 6.[168] If so, then they probably

---

165. John 1:1–4; 8:44; 1 John 2:16; 3:8; Rev 12:9; 20:2; cf. Wis 2:23–24; Rom 5:12; *3 Bar.* 9:7. On this connection see Strecker, *Johannine Letters*, 100; Keener, *John*, 1.760–61. If Satan "was not standing" (imperfect ἕστηκεν) in the truth (John 8:44), might not this imply his fall from the truth (cf. Barrett, *John*, 349) in the "beginning," whether in the Genesis story or before it? And if so, is it possible that the Johannine author believes Satan's own destiny was not "fixed" but that he too fell away? Compare Wis 2:23–24 with Adam and Eve *Vita* 12–16; *2 En.* 29.4–5; 31.3. The other way to understand the meaning is that Satan was never standing in the truth.

166. E.g. John 2:19–22; 3:1–15; 4:10–15, 31–34; 6:32–35, 60–66; 7:33–36; 8:21–27, 31–33, 51–53, 56–58; 11:11–16, 23–25; 12:32–34; 13:36–38; 14:8–9; 16:16–19. See Culpepper, *Anatomy*, 152–65; Leroy, *Rätsel und Missverständnis*.

167. Culpepper, *Anatomy*, 165.

168. Interestingly, in the epistles of John, where a number of Gentiles might be among the audience,

knew that Israel's apostasy (Isa 1–5) preceded their obduracy (Isa 6).[169] Prior to God allowing blindness on the rebellious Israelites in Isa 6, Isa 5 claims that they substituted darkness for light and light for darkness (5:20); hence, God would bring judgment on them and make their light grow dark with clouds (5:30; cf. 13:9–11). Because the Israelites were committing immoral deeds of "darkness" and justifying this behavior, God would punish them with calamity and darkness, and thus confirm them in their own spiritual blindness (6:9–10; cf. 29:9; 42:18–19; 56:10; 59:10).

It would take the light of a new era led by a messianic figure to deliver them from such blindness and give them "light" (29:18; 35:5; 42:7; 43:8). In Isaianic literature "light" represents various things such as a new era, righteous living, spiritual life and insight, and God's very presence (e.g., 60:19–22). In this new era all peoples would follow the ways of God, both the Gentiles and remnant of Israel (9:2–6; 42:1–9; 49:6–9; 60:1–3; cf. 8:16–22; 45:3–7). The Johannine metaphor of "light" is also multifaceted, combining and colliding with imagery related to creation, life, God's presence, insight related to Torah, moral living, giving sight to the blind, and of course Jesus (John 1:1–14, 29–34; 3:18–20; 8:12; 9:5–34; 12:35–36). There is also certainly an association between wickedness and darkness in Johannine literature. Darkness is related to the personification of evil, sin, and apostasy,[170] and dualism between seeing/light and blindness/darkness is part of a larger framework in which John perceives two realms: one is God/truth/light and being "from above," and the other is the devil/falsehood/darkness and being "from below."[171] *If the people reject Jesus and his teachings, they reject the "light" that God is bringing into the world; all that is left for them, then, is "darkness."*[172]

With the Isaianic tradition in mind, then, spiritual blindness may be seen by the Johannine author not only as a precondition upon the Jewish crowd, but also as a judgment resulting from their unbelief at the signs Jesus performed. And similar to the Isaianic tradition, it would seem that God has reciprocated the people's own obduracy with more obduracy. They show themselves to be aligned with darkness, and so God judges them with more darkness. Perhaps this is similar to what is done in Mark's gospel; it is a type of *lex talionis* punishment.[173] God may be punishing them with this blindness directly himself, or maybe, as we have suggested, *the devil brings it on them* and God allows this to happen because they have rebelled against him. A view

---

much fewer scriptures from Israel are echoed.

169. On the backdrop to Isa 1–5 see above Mark 4.
170. 1 John 2:8–14; cf. John 1:4–5; 3:19–21; 8:12; 11:9–10; 12:35–36; 13:25–30; 1 John 1:5–7.
171. In particular, Kysar, *Maverick Gospel*, 47–64, brings out this dualism in a perceptive manner.
172. Along these lines, see Celsor, "Human Response," 115–35.
173. See Mark 4 above and Rom 1:25–32.

somewhere in between is that God delivers them over to the Prince of Darkness because they have insisted on darkness instead of light.

The entire trajectory of Israel's tradition-history often shows that human rebellion is first the cause rather than the result of divine judgment (e.g., Gen 3; Deut 28–32). In John's gospel, human beliefs and deeds, rather than divinely fixed origins, account for the divine hardening (cf. 1:11; 3:19–21; 5:46). The Judean crowds in Jerusalem are held responsible for their own unbelief, which resulted in God punishing them by confirming them in their own unbelief or handing them over to the power of darkness, and now they are spiritually blind as a result of divine punishment (12:39–40).[174] The Isaianic backdrop seems to provide a rationale for this way of understanding the situation. It may also provide an apology for the Johannine community that even though many Jerusalemites did not believe, this does not mean that Jesus is not Lord. Their unbelief "fulfilled" Isaianic scripture (12:37–38).[175] The community may have gravitated from an earlier "believe in Jesus" perspective related to human decision to the later realization that many did not believe, or continue to believe, in Jesus. Maybe unlike the earliest days when the community was welcomed by the synagogue, their later years were met with what they perceived as recalcitrant leaders. Perhaps this led to the author's perspective that God must be involved somehow with the people's unbelief. It is not because the message of Jesus or the Johannine community was misguided; it was rather that higher powers along with unbelief prevented certain people from believing.

Jesus' healing of the blind man in John 9 has close connections with John 12 because both mention spiritual blindness that comes on unbelievers in the context of expelling followers of Jesus from the synagogues (9:22, 34; 12:42). Also, the adaptation of τετύφλωκεν in 12:40 may have been derived from 9:39.[176] Moreover, John 9 also derives spiritual blindness from the Isaianic tradition (9:39–41/Isa 29:18;

---

174. Notice Ridderbos, *Gospel of John*, 444–45: "Unbelief is not thereby blamed on God in a predestinarian sense, but is rather described as a punishment from God: he abandons unbelieving people to themselves, thus confirming them in their evil, blinding their eyes and hardening their hearts, as a result of which whatever God gives them to see and hear can no longer lead to salvation, that is, to repentance and healing." Carson, *John*, 448–49 is similar: "God's judicial hardening is not presented as the capricious manipulation of an arbitrary potentate cursing morally neutral or even morally pure beings, but as a holy condemnation of a guilty people who are condemned to do and be what they themselves have chosen." The thought is captured by the biblical paraphrase: "first they wouldn't believe, then they couldn't . . ." (*The Message*, John 12:36–40).

175. Presumably, this would also be the case with passages such as John 8:47 and 10:26. See further the perspective of McGrath, *John's Apologetic Christology*, 199–202.

176. While the Greek word for blindness in John 12:40 is not used in Isa 6:10 LXX, it does appear in Isa 42:18–19; 43:8; 56:10. See Kühschelm, *Verstockung*, 129, 193. On connections between John 9 and 12, see Lieu, "Blindness," 83–95.

42:19), but in this case it is attributed to the Pharisees instead of the Judean crowd. John 9:41 probably means that those who do not claim to see are open to the light that Jesus brings. They can admit their ignorance and spiritual poverty, as did the blind man who is healed and comes to believe in the Son of Man. Such a person experiences the forgiveness of sin (9:25, 36–38). The proud Pharisees, on the other hand, claim to "see" or have what they think is spiritual knowledge from their traditions, and yet they refuse to accept Jesus; therefore, their sin continually remains (9:16, 22, 24, 29; 39–41 cf. 3:36; 15:22–24). C. K. Barrett considers this kind of blindness to be incurable and with this thought he cross-references the unpardonable sin (cf. Mark 3:29).[177] The Pharisees have in essence fulfilled the reversal that Isa 5:20 mentions—they, like the apostate Israelites before them, essentially call good "evil" and evil "good," exchanging light for darkness and darkness light. From Johannine perspective their spiritual blindness is well deserved.

Even so, the fate of these Pharisees would not appear to be the fate of all "Jews." John 9 and 12 probably reflect the Johannine community's experience with a local synagogue, and spiritual obduracy in these passages may have special reference to those who expelled them. The Johannine author did not consider all Jews to be blind; some of the Jewish authorities believed even though they were afraid to confess Jesus and be expelled from the synagogues (12:41–42). In the Book of Signs we detect a pattern of Jews who believe in Jesus (2:23; 7:31; 8:30–31; 10:42; 11:45, 48; 12:11; 12:42) and others who do not (5:38–47; 6:36; 7:48; 8:45–46; 10:25–26; 12:37–40). Apparently more Jews would come to faith after Jesus was crucified (8:28).[178] Interestingly the spiritual blindness/hardness in Paul (Rom 11), Luke (Acts 28), and the Johannine tradition (John 12) all relate the notion to unbelieving Jews in contrast with believing Gentiles. No doubt the concept served an apologetic function for many ancient churches.

NOT ABIDING IN JESUS (JOHN 15:1–6; CF. 12:25; 16:1)

In the vineyard pericope of John 15:1–17 Jesus claims himself as the true vine, the Father as the vine grower and pruner, and the disciples as the branches. Those disciples who abide (μένω) in Jesus will bear much fruit. Whereas in ancient Israel vineyard illustrations often represent the nation in terms of its unfaithfulness to God and his covenant (e.g., Isa 5; Ezek 15), the Johannine Jesus and his disciples represent

---

177. Barrett, *John*, 366.

178. On obduracy as partial or temporary, see Lincoln, *John*, 357–58; Schnackenburg, *John*, 2.417; pace Menken, *Old Testament Quotations*, 111.

a vine and branches that point to a restored Isaianic eschatological covenant with God's people.[179]

Those individuals who do not bear fruit and abide in the vine are cast off as a branch, dried up, and tossed into the fire for burning (John 15:6). The fruitless branches that God the Father cuts off in 15:2 and the ones that do not abide in 15:6 are probably the same.[180] Presumably it is the Father who casts out the worthless branches in 15:6 also. *The reason they are cast away is because they do not abide or remain "in" Jesus* (15:2). *Likewise, Johannine thought does not allow for fruitless disciples to continue in the vine because bearing "fruit" in this context is directly related to loving one another and keeping Jesus' commandments* (John 15:7–17; cf. 1 John 2:3–5; 3:17–24; 4:21). Both of these ethical precepts are essential for true believers. These branches refer to Jesus' followers, not the unbelieving "Jews." John 15:2 presupposes that the branches belong to Jesus and abide "in" him; namely, these are believers who have an authentic relationship with Christ. This relationship involves believing in Jesus and having some sort of a mystical union with him, that is, an actual inward and "enduring personal communion" with the Son.[181] *Such a relationship reflects the later Christian communion typified by the Johannine community, who had spiritual fellowship with the Father, Son, and Holy Spirit* (cf. 14:10, 17–23; 15:4–5, 10; 1 John 1:3; 2:24).

More than this, *abiding in Jesus seems related to abiding in a covenant with him*. As we noticed in John 6, abiding is associated with Jesus in terms of eating and life, and these are directly informed by the "everlasting covenant" mentioned in Isa 54–56. To abide in Jesus and his words is to have eternal life and remain in a perpetual covenant related to loving one another and keeping his commandments. The influence of the covenant motif on the Johannine concept "to abide in" (μένω ἐν) is verified by Edward Malatesta, who examines the related Septuagint term ἐμμένω ἐν to affirm that contexts using this term in the Septuagint are similar to the "Johannine formulae"—they are related to keeping God's covenant, observing commandments, "fraternal" union, and divine mercy and love (Deut 27:26; Isa 30:18; Sir 6:20; 28:6; cf. Isa 5:1–11).[182] Rekha Chennattu adds that the covenantal motif may be seen as

---

179. See Segovia, *Farewell of the Word*, 136; Borig, *Wahre Weinstock*, 192–94, 252. On sources in Israel's scriptures related to vine imagery, see Jaubert, "L'image de la Vigne," 93–96.

180. On this connection see, e.g., Wengst, *Johannesevangelium*, 2.142. In 15:2 αἴρω is not stressing a viticultural practice of "lifting up" unfruitful branches; instead it means "cut off" or "take away"; see BDAG, 28; Rosscup, *Abiding in Christ*, 213–14. Rosscup, however, views such branches as never truly "saved." This view seems contradicted by the fact that the branches were once abiding "in" Jesus (15:2).

181. Cf. Malatesta, *Interiority and Covenant*, 25.

182. Cf. ibid., 58–64. Relevant to Deuteronomic connections, Glasson, *Moses in the Fourth Gospel*, 76, notices a union with God in John 15:6 concomitant with the notion of cleaving to the LORD in

an undercurrent for John 15–16. He sums up important covenant elements from the Hebrew and Septuagint scriptures in terms of: 1) loving God and keeping his commands, 2) the community of God's public declaration of commitment to God, 3) God's promise of abiding presence, and 4) election and knowledge of God (e.g., Exod 19–24; Deut 26–32; Josh 24; Hos 2–6; Jer 4, 9, 31–33).[183] Several aspects derived from earlier covenantal language are identified in John 15–16, including abiding in Jesus/God (John 15:4–10/LXX Deut 27:26; 30:18), keeping his commandments and bearing fruit (John 15:9–17/Exod 19:5; Josh 7:11; Jer 2:21; 3:13), and being God's chosen people (John 15:16–19/Duet 7:6; 14:2; Exod 19:5).

Severe judgment awaits the people of God who fail to remain in God's covenant. *As failure to live up to keeping God's commandments resulted in Israel's destruction—often by fire—so the disciples failure to keep Jesus' commandments would result in eschatological destruction* (John 15:6/ Ezek 15:1–8; Isa 1:3–7, 31; 4:4; 5:1–6, 24; 6:13; Deut 29:10–28).[184] The believers, if they do not continue to abide in Jesus, wither or "dry up" (ξηραίνω), are cast off from Jesus, and burned (John 15:6). The term ξηραίνω often appears in agricultural contexts,[185] and perhaps significantly for our purposes it is found in Jesus' parable of the Sower where it refers to the drying up of the second seed sown on rocky soil, which refers to apostates (Mark 4:6; Matt 13:6; Luke 8:6; cf. *Herm. Sim.* 9.21.1–3).[186] It is clearly evident that the person who is cut off like a branch in 15:6 was once part of the metaphoric vine. He once belonged to God's covenant people who, for John, are the community of Christ-followers. More specifically this individual represents a genuine believer who becomes apostate. The possibility of bona fide disciples committing apostasy makes necessary Jesus' instruction in 16:1–4. This type of apostasy in addition is not the temporal sort comparable with Peter denying Christ. The severed "branch" is not restored or engrafted back into the vine; it is thrown with other branches into the fire to be burned (15:6b).[187]

John 15:6 does not seem to be recollecting the quasi-disciples' departure in 6:66 or those who departed from the Johannine community in 1 John 2:19. The defector in 15:1–6 is someone who truly abides in Jesus (cf. 15:2: ἐν ἐμοί), which could hardly be case with the spurious followers in 1 John 2:19 and John 6:64–66. This person

---

Deut 10:20; 11:22; 30:20, and related passages.

183. Chennattu, "Covenant Motif," 141–43.

184. Cf. ibid., 143–50.

185. See BDAG, 684–85.

186. Moreover if John 16:1–4 is associated with 15:1–6 (see below), then apostasy in both the second seed of the parable of the sower and John 15–16 is identified by σκανδαλίζω and persecution.

187. Even Carson, *Divine Sovereignty*, 192–93, while suggesting it is conceivable that the falling away is temporal in 16:1, and possibly inauthentic branches are represented in ch. 15, admits that despite qualifications, "both 16.1 and 15.1ff sound like warnings of potentially real dangers."

also does not seem to represent Judas;[188] the betrayer never abided in Christ and is portrayed as a fake disciple throughout the fourth gospel (e.g., 6:64–65).[189] The third person singulars in 15:6a are not referring specifically to Judas but generally to any individual who abides in Christ and then is cast away (cf. the indefinite singular pronoun "anyone": τὶς). The passage has special relevance to the later Johannine community who are to have a spiritual and personal union with the Son as well as the Father and Holy Spirit (John 14:10, 17–23; 15:4–5, 10; 1 John 2:24). The Twelve, including Judas, could not have had such a complete relationship with Jesus because Jesus was still physically with them, and the Spirit had not yet been given to them (cf. John 16:7; 20:22). The full meaning of an intimate relationship with him in 15:1–7 would become a reality for the disciples only after Jesus ascended to heaven and they, along with those who would be saved by them (the Johannine community), received the Spirit. Although the singular language in 15:6a focuses on an individual being cast away, such a person would seem to be joined by others, for in 15:6b the branches become plural with the neuter αὐτὰ: "they gather *them*" (i.e., the branches) to be cast into the fire and be burned. Borchert's comment is instructive here: "The early Christians could hardly not have thought of Judas when reviewing this verse. But the application is hardly to be restricted only to Judas."[190] More accurately, *the individuals who face a danger of being cut off from Christ are those who already abide in him, which means that the apostasy described in 15:6 refers to authentic believers.* Beyond the first disciples and Johannine community, Maloney may be correct when he writes that the gnomic aorist of the branch being cast away and withering suggests a "truth valid for all time and all potential disciples."[191]

The severity of these former believers being "burned" in fire in 15:6 has often been played down to the point of denying it has anything to do with eternal judgment.[192] The identity of "they," the ones who gather the broken branches and toss them into the fire, seems deliberately ambiguous in John 15:6b. It probably alludes not only to farm helpers but also to the task of angels gathering up a final harvest of people at the culmination of the eschaton (Rev 14:14–20; Matt 13:36–43; cf. 24:31; 25:31–32). In agricultural imagery the wicked are occasionally represented as chaff and tares that are burned in eschatological fire (Matt 3:10, 12; 13:30, 39–42; Luke 3:17; cf. Matt 25:31–32, 41, 46; Rev 14:10–11; 20:10–15; 21:8). The picture we find

---

188. Contrast Köstenberger, *John*, 452, 454.

189. Incidentally, in this narrative Judas had already departed from the Twelve (ch. 13) when Jesus exhorts the remaining disciples about the importance of abiding in him in 15:1–7.

190. Borchert, *John*, 2.144.

191. Maloney, *John*, 423; cf. BDF, 171.

192. See, e.g., Lindars, *John*, 489; Schnackenburg, *John*, 3.101; Maloney, *John*, 423.

in 15:6 may resemble the fiery imagery of *Gehenna* found in the Synoptic Gospels (e.g., Mark 9:42–47).[193] In any case, whether by "fire" or some other means, elsewhere Johannine literature affirms that defectors will face eschatological destruction (10:10; 12:25; 17:12; 1 John 5:16). John 15:6 is another example of this.

The reason why these disciples do not remain in Jesus is not explicitly mentioned, but the context may suggest that persecution is a potential threat to falling away. Chettannu detects a structure similar to a chiasm in 15:18—16:24:[194]

A: Persecution caused by the world (15:18–20)

  B: Reason for the persecution: the persecutors do not know God (15:21–25)

    C: Assurance through the giving of the *paraclete* (Holy Spirit) (15:26–27)

      D: Purpose of the message: to prevent the disciples from falling away (16:1)

    C¹: Assurance through the giving of the *paraclete* (Holy Spirit) (16:4–24)

  B¹: Reason for the persecution: the persecutors do not know God (16:3)

A¹: Persecution in relation to expulsion from the synagogue (16:2)

The center of the structure stresses the relevance of the entire pericope to a potential for the disciples to commit apostasy because of expulsion and persecution. Jesus claims, "These things I write to you so that you may not fall away" (16:1). The word for committing apostasy here is σκανδαλίζω, which refers to giving up one's faith in Jesus.[195] In this case hardships and conflicts related to opponents from the synagogue are what can cause apostasy. "These things I have spoken to you" refers back to Jesus' entire message beginning in 15:18, but it may also be inclusive of 15:1–17 given that the previous discourse concludes at 14:25 with the same phrase (ταῦτα λελάληκα ὑμῖν) found in 16:1.[196] The saying anticipates both the immediate trial the disciples would face during the Passion of Jesus (John 16:32; cf. Matt 26:31) and the Johannine community's eventual expulsion from the synagogue (John 16:2–4). The foretelling of this information to the disciples was given as a way to assuage the

---

193. On eschatological punishment here, see Schnelle, *Evangelium nach Johannes*, 266; Barrett, *John*, 475.

194. Cf. Chennattu, "Covenant Motif," 150–58.

195. Compare the Greek verb in John 6:61; Matt 13:41; 24:10; Mark 9:42–49; 14:27; Luke 17:1–2; 1 Cor 8:13; 2 Cor 11:29; *Did.* 16.5; *Herm. Vis* 4.1.3; *Herm. Mand.* 8.10. See also 1 John 2:10 (noun), and for further Johannine words on apostasy, see Kim, *Apostasy Embedded*, 365–74.

196. On the close relationship between 15:1–17 and 15:18–27, see Schnackenburg, *John*, 3.92.

initial shock of such opposition once it comes.[197] This passage would also comfort the Johannine community to know that Jesus is aware of their hardships.

In light of John 15:6 it seems that the most plausible explanation for Jesus giving such a warning is because such danger of falling away was a real possibility for the disciples.[198] Naturally this perspective creates tensions with 6:37, in which the Johannine Jesus promises that he will never cast out anyone who comes to him—a view that, along with 10:27–29, has been associated with the perseverance of the saints.[199] But this view does not address in an adequate manner how John 15–16 can function as a warning to the disciples and how a branch that was once abiding in Jesus could be broken off and face eschatological judgment.[200] This tension may be alleviated if we suggest that both 6:37 and 15:1–6 assume that *Jesus' followers must continually "come" to Jesus in faith. Their being cast away from Christ becomes a possibility when they fail to do this. Perseverance in faith is necessary.* The tension may be further alleviated in other ways also.

First, the vine illustration in John 15 comes from a different source than John 6; perhaps the saying reflects a tradition in common with the Synoptic Gospels. In this case we may be dealing with an authentic Jesus saying reworked by redactors but still sounding terribly un-Johannine in 15:6 because the verse allows for the possibility of genuine disciples committing final apostasy and seems to depict their fate as destruction by fire.[201]

Second, the basis for falling away in John 15 relates to persecution and is addressed to his immediate disciples; apostasy in John 6 reflects false believers who defected because of misconceptions about Jesus. The message is addressed to both the disciples and crowd. Likewise, in John 8 the new believers who immediately fall away do so because of distorted beliefs about the person of Jesus. The distinction of motifs in these early chapters (false beliefs) and John 15 (persecution), however, is not black and white. The concept of abiding/continuing in all these cases, for example, relates to communion with Jesus and holding on to his words; albeit, in John

---

197. Cf. Segovia, *Farewell of the Word*, 206–7.

198. Contrast Carson, "Reflections on Christian Assurance," 17: "genuine faith, by definition, perseveres: where there is no perseverance, by definition the faith cannot be genuine." This may be true of those involved in the schism of 1 John 2:19, but it does not seem to be case for those who fail to persevere in John 15–16.

199. See, e.g., Hofius, "Erwählung und Bewahrung," 81–86.

200. It is also noteworthy that the Father is the one who casts out the useless branches (15:2; cf. 15:6).

201. On the non-Johannine words in 15:6, see Heise, *Bleiben*, 87. On the possibility of an authentic parable of Jesus behind John 15, see Bauckham, "Parable of the Vine," 97: The *logia* of Jesus rests behind the Johannine text but essentially "vanished behind its interpretation."

15 ethical aspects of keeping Christ's commandments and loving one another are added.[202] Be that as it may, the nature of apostasy in John 6 and 15–16 is not entirely the same. There also appears to be different consequences, some more severe than others, depending on which sin is committed in the Johannine community (cf. 1 John 5:16–18).

Third, the notion of fake believers dominates the Johannine texts: Judas is viewed as the representative defector in John's gospel, and the apostates in John 6:66 and 1 John 2:19 were never genuine followers of Jesus. The Johannine community's own negative experiences with those who left their community shaped significantly the way they perceive apostates (cf. 1 John 2:19). They came to view the exemplar apostate as never being a true believer. Why would the Johannine author perceive former congregation members who defected as being imposters? It is quite possible that they always exemplified beliefs, actions, and character at variance with the other community members so that the author could confidently claim them as never really belonging to the community. Perhaps the author knew the secessionists firsthand when they were still members of the community. If we assume that they frequently showed signs of bad character and errant beliefs, the author perhaps always questioned whether these individuals were genuinely converted. Equally, he could affirm the genuineness of the conversion of many in his house church whom he had personally seen come to faith and be transformed in both character and beliefs. Assuming this scenario, when the secessionists broke away from the community, the Johannine author would probably have no problem affirming them as having always been counterfeit believers. But if some of the other members he could vouch for as genuine believers were to fall away, he might easily affirm that this latter set of individuals were in fact true believers who turned apostate.

Hence, while the Johannine author and his community might normally perceive apostates as spurious, they recognize that there could be exceptions to the rule. Not every defection is alike—most involve ungenuine believers in the community, but some may involve genuine believers. Verses such as 10:10, 12:25, and 15:6 are evidence of this. In this respect, the Johannine community would not be much different than the Matthean community, which warns genuine believers against apostasy[203] yet considers the faith of certain Christian prophets to be a sham (e.g., Matt 7:21–23). Later Hermas portrays apostasy, repentance, and restoration in complex ways; some apostates were genuine Christians but others received their faith in hypocrisy (e.g., *Herm. Vis.* 3.6–7; cf. 2.2).

---

202. Cf. the moral aspect of this fruit in Borig, *Weinstock*, 238–39; Keener, *John*, 2.997.

203. E.g., Matt 10:28, 32–33, 38–39; 13:20–21; 16:24–27; 24:10–12.

In the Footsteps of Judas and Other Defectors

Another possibility, this one quite different than John maintaining two distinct phenomena of apostasy, rests with the perspective of deviance and labeling theory posited by Lloyd Pietersen. In his view an individual or party that is denounced for deviating from the standards of a community is "categorized, stereotyped, and thereby depersonalized. Very often people will then engage in a process of retrospective interpretation through which the previous history of the offending person is reread and thus reinterpreted in the light of the newly perceived deviant status."[204] An example of this involves "status degradation" ceremonies in which, among other things, denounced individuals are identified as outsiders and their previous participation in the community "counts for nothing," existing "in appearance" only. Through a process of "retrospective interpretation," they are "now perceived as always having been deviants."[205] The labeling of deviant persons or groups is well attested in early Christian and Jewish circles (e.g., Phil 3:2; Jude 4–19; Qumran). Likewise, the aspect of forgetting an apostate's former status is found in passages such as Ezek 18. Here, if a righteous person turns away from his righteousness and does evil, none of his righteousness will be remembered but he will die in his sin and unfaithfulness (Ezek 18:21–31; cf. 3:20; 33:9–19). Incidentally, the Johannine author seems to be quite familiar with this tradition.[206] If such a perspective relates to the defectors from the Johannine community, then these former congregants may have once been productive members of that community, perhaps even having real faith before being labeled as "deceivers" and "antichrists" (e.g., 1 John 2:18, 26).

In any case, it is not that the *Johannine author* necessarily believes that every person who falls away was never a true Christ-follower, but *he interprets defection via the community's personal experiences with its own apostates.* The rare passages that convey the potential for genuine apostasy, such as 15:6, remind us that the author has not totally conformed the real voice of Jesus into that of the Johannine community's voice. As we have clearly seen in the Synoptic Gospels, Jesus taught that genuine disciples could fall away. John's gospel likewise retains vestiges of this fact despite the way the community's own encounters with apostasy have shaped their experiences differently.

A good example of this phenomenon may be observed not only in 15:6 but also in 12:25, which records another variant of a saying that almost certainly originates with the historic Jesus (see Mark 8:35; Matt 10:39; 16:25; Luke 9:24; 17:33 above). After Jesus speaks about his upcoming death (12:23–24) he proclaims in 12:25, "the

---

204. Pietersen, "Despicable Deviants," 347.

205. Ibid., 347–50, who examines the Pauline author's possible use of "status degradation ceremony" against opponents in the Pastoral letters.

206. E.g., John 3:3–7/Ezek 36:25–27; 10:1–16/Ezek 34; 15:1–6/Ezek 15.

one who loves his life loses it; the one who hates his life in this world will keep it for life eternal." In this variant, unlike any of its predecessors in the Synoptic texts, loving (φιλέω) and hating (μισέω) life are contrasted. And to love one's life is to lose it, and to hate it is to keep or protect (φυλάσσω) it.[207] The contrast between love and hate may be borrowed from a Semitic idiom of preferring one thing over the other, and the idea is found in other Jesus sayings (Luke 14:26; Matt 10:37; cf. Matt 6:24; Gen 29:31–33; Deut 21:15).[208] Compatible with Johannine themes, the redactor of this saying includes the words "this world" and life as "eternal" (εἰς ζωὴν αἰώνιον φυλάξει αὐτήν). Eternal life involves salvation pertaining to the eschatological age to come, which is given to those who believe in Jesus (e.g., John 3:16). *This brings into sharper relief what is already found in the Synoptic parallels: this saying warns against falling away and losing eternal life.*

Elsewhere in Johannine thought the "world" (κόσμος) is blind, unregenerate, and often hostile toward Jesus and believers (1:10, 29; 3:17; 6:51; 8:12; 9:39; 12:47; 15:18–20; 16:33; 17:13–16). Unbelievers live in this realm, and its destiny ends in destruction (John 3:16–18; 8:23–26; 12:31; 14:30; 16:11; 1 John 2:15–17; 1 John 5:19). The Johannine believers are not to "love" the world, that is, be assimilated to its attitudes and values of lust, fleshly desires, and pride (cf. 1 John 2:15–16). The disciples of Jesus are not of the world, and the world hates them (John 17:14–16); the world exemplifies loveless behavior opposite of what the believers are to practice (1 John 3:10–13). The nuance of loving one's life in John 12:25, then, may be related to the notion of conforming to the world. Possibly this passage functioned as a warning for the Johannine community not to be conformed to the "world." More pointedly, however, love is contrasted with hate, and the followers of Jesus who "hate" their life keep it for eternal life. In the Johannine context Jesus declares this saying in relation to his upcoming death on the cross. As in the Synoptic texts, then, the saying is relevant to persecution and martyrdom, and a true disciple of Jesus must be willing to "hate" his/her life in the sense of be willing to lose it for the sake of Jesus (12:23–26). In the narrative the disciples would soon be tempted to abandon Jesus instead of follow him to his death. Peter, unwilling to lay down his life for Jesus at his arrest, denies him three times (13:36–38; 18:15–18, 25–27). But his restoration is predicted and takes place after Jesus' resurrection (21:15–19; cf. 13:36), and so the effects of losing eternal life are not quite applicable in his case.

207. In John 12:25a the thought of losing/destroying one's life is marked by the present tense (ἀπολλύει) in contrast with all the Synoptic variants that have ἀπόλλυμι as a future tense (ἀπολέσει). John's version may imply judgment in the "now," but the future tense φυλάξει in relation to eternal life suggests that the latter is futuristic. The distinction between present and future, then, probably should not be stressed (Barrett, *John*, 424). Compare John 3:18; 10:10.

208. Cf. Köstenberger, *John*, 379.

In the Footsteps of Judas and Other Defectors

In 12:25, at any rate, we see another glimpse of a Johannine warning against apostasy directed at authentic believers. Apparently the Johannine redactor did not make this saying conform to the Johannine norm of apostates being inauthentic followers of Jesus. *John 12:25 and 15:6 both seem to be actual warnings in which the authentic voice of Jesus can still be heard through the Johannine narrative, and Jesus warns his faithful followers against committing apostasy.* Both passages likewise are set in a larger framework related to persecution. It is not clear that the Johannine community was currently experiencing persecution, but in the past they had faced faced suffering and hardships caused by their expulsion from a synagogue. Such texts would still seem to be relevant, though, as warnings to the so-called Crypto-Christians mentioned earlier, who believed Jesus but were not willing to suffer expulsion from the synagogue for his sake (12:42-43; cf. 5:44).

SECESSIONISTS FROM THE JOHANNINE COMMUNITY (1 JOHN 2:18-19; CF. 4:1-6; 2 JOHN 7-11)

In the Johannine Epistles the assurances of abiding in the Father and Son are related to the believer having the Spirit, confessing Jesus as Son of God, walking in the teaching and ways of Jesus, and loving others (1 John 2:6, 24; 3:24; 4:12-17). The person who does not love fellow Christians ("brothers and sisters") abides in death and lacks eternal life (1 John 3:10-17; cf. 1 John 2:10-11; John 3:36). Those who abide in Jesus hold to correct beliefs about him and keep his words (2 John 1-2, 9-10; cf. John 6:56, 63; 8:31, 35; 14:22-23). The opponents in 1 John 2:19, on the other hand, did not abide with the Johannine community (see above). They lacked the "anointing" (χρῖσμα) or the Spirit of truth that abides with the members who have the assurance of eternal life.[209] Although the concept of abiding is viewed in 1 John as a source of assurance, it functions also as an imperative. The believers are commanded to take on the responsibility of abiding in Jesus or God (cf. 1 John 2:27-28; 2:24). I. Howard Marshall is probably correct in his observation that John's use of abiding in Jesus is similar to the notion of persevering (cf. John 14:10; 15:4-6; 1 John 2:28; 2 John 7-11).[210] Malatesta adds that 1 John 2:12-28 helps distinguish "Christians from antichrists (see 4:1-6), in a predominately positive and encourag-

---

209. E.g., 1 John 2:18-20, 24, 27; 3:24; 4:2, 6; 5:12-13, 19-20; cf. John 14:17, 26; 15:26; 16:13; 20:22. See Strecker, *Johannine Letters*, 64-65.

210. Marshall, *Kept by the Power*, 171-86. For Marshall, not abiding therefore results in being cast out.

ing tone, but with the preoccupation of exhorting the community to perseverance by helping them to become more aware of their vocation of faith."[211]

The First Epistle of John automatically excludes secessionists as inauthentic believers even though they were once part of the community (cf. 1 John 2:19 see above). They are called antichrists (2:18–20), and it seems hard to imagine that the author would consider the proper "anointing" as ever abiding in such individuals (2:27). They apparently deny Jesus as the Christ (1 John 2:22–23; cf. 4:1–6; 2 John 7) and some of them may be influencing members of the Johannine community with their deception (1 John 2:26–27). The historic background behind the false teachings that this community faced has often centered on the interpretation of Jesus having "come in the flesh" (1 John 4:2–3; 2 John 7; see below), and the opponents are examined in light of three groups: proto-Gnosticism (emphasizing spirit over matter/flesh; denial of sin), proto-Docetism (denying Jesus' true humanity), or the doctrine of Cerinthus (Christ descended on Jesus after baptism and departed before crucifixion).[212] But if the opponents' denial that Jesus has "come in the flesh" is simply another denial of Jesus as the Christ, then the opponents may be quite different than these three standard proposals. The precise identity of the opponents will not be finally decided here, but it is noteworthy to mention that the Christians in Ephesus and western Asia in the late first century seem to have been repeatedly hammered by different sorts of false teachers that can be ascertained through the texts of Acts 20, Revelation, and the Pauline and Deutero-Pauline letters to the Ephesians, Colossians, and Timothy (see volumes 2 and 3 of this work).

With a second-level reading of John's gospel in mind, it can be surmised that the defector in John 6:66 may represent this group. Likewise, Judas seems to represent these defectors;[213] he is a fake disciple and personification of evil. He goes "out" into darkness away from Jesus and the disciples (13:29–30; see above). It could also be surmised that the primary reason they broke away from the Johannine community had to do with their beliefs about Jesus. It is not clear whether the defectors in Ephesus were Jews, Gentiles, or both. That they reject Jesus as Messiah may suggest this group as mostly Jewish, but the negative language against "the Jews" so prevalent in the gospel is not present in the epistles. They rejected belief in Jesus as Messiah, or at least the Johannine version of this claim, which includes Jesus as a preexistent be-

---

211. Malatesta, *Interiority and Covenant*, 197.

212. Cf. Brown, *Introduction*, 391. On the Gnostic view, see Meeks, "Man from Heaven"; Trumbower, *Born from Above*. On Cerinthus, see Irenaeus, *Haer.* 1.26; 3.3.4; 3.11.1.

213. Klauck, *Erste Johannesbrief*, 154, agrees.

ing and deity (1 John 5:20; cf. John 6).[214] Perhaps external influence or pressure from a neighboring synagogue or sect influenced them to abandon the Johannine group.

These apostates, as perceived by the Johannine author, are considered antagonists. They have left the group, but rather than ignoring the group they once belonged to, they are attempting to deceive others in the group. Of course, *we are not told the story from the perspective of the defectors*. One question that is left unanswered is whether they still affirm Jesus as the Christ but just not to the extent of claiming him as deity, as the Johannine group teaches. In other words they may still hold to an allegiance to Jesus. What is more, they might believe their perspective is so right that they are willing to talk to Johannine members in an attempt to persuade them to join another group without altogether abandoning Jesus. The deceivers in 2 John 7–9 are almost certainly Christians, or at least pretend to be, if they are entering into the Johannine house churches. This suggests to us that more is at stake than merely a confession of Jesus as the messianic deliverer foretold in the writings of the prophets. For the Johannine group, one's confession of Jesus as the Christ includes belief in his preexistence. He is God manifest in flesh (1 John 5:20; cf. John 1:1, 14, 18).

We do well not to go much beyond this portfolio of the secessionists. To be sure, a close parallel may be drawn between three passages that all label the opponent as "antichrist" and are described as going "out" from either the Johannine community (1 John 2:19) or into the world (1 John 4:1; 2 John 7–9). It is not clear, however, that the "many false prophets" with the spirit of antichrist in 1 John 4:1–6 and itinerate deceivers in 2 John 7–11 should be fully equated with the group in 1 John 2:18–19. They may represent other threats and opponents the community faces or will face.[215]

SHAME AT THE SECOND COMING (1 JOHN 2:28; CF. 2 JOHN 8)

The potential outcome of Johannine members who do not remain in Jesus may be implied in 1 John 2:28. The converse of abiding in Christ and having confidence is to experience shame when Jesus appears at his second coming (1 John 2:28; 2 John 8; cf. 1 John 3:19–21; 4:17).[216] Here the concept of being ashamed (αἰσχύνω) is

---

214. Schenke, "Johanneische Schisma," 105–21, for example, argues against the view that the schism involved merely a denying of Jesus as the Christ or Jesus as a real human (105–7). For Schenke, the schismatics are Jewish Christians who probably denied Christ's preexistence.

215. Anderson, "Antichristic Errors: Flawed Interpretation," 209–16, not only argues for a distinction in terms and timeframes between the various "antichrists," but also claims there are spatial, theological, ethnic-religious, and redactional differences between them. He believes the Johannine material unearths several different crises.

216. However, some interpret 1 John 3:19–21 not as assurance but as a warning. For this possibility see Jung, "Main Thrust," 97–111.

represented by the aorist subjunctive αἰσχυνθῶμεν, which could be understood in the middle voice as those who do not abide in Jesus but shrink back or turn away from him in shame at his *parousia*. But if the word is to be understood in the passive voice, it may suggest that it is Jesus who will put to shame the person who does not abide in him. Stephen Smalley writes that both meanings are suggested in 1 John 2:28: "the person who has been faithful to the truth of Jesus need not, at the end, be ashamed in the presence of Christ, and (furthermore) will not be 'disgraced' by him. . . . Those who deny Jesus (see vv. 22-23) now can expect to be denied by him eventually."[217] The author includes himself in the exhortation by using "we" in 2:28.[218] It seems questionable that the author is concerned about his own apostasy. More plausibly, *the author includes himself in this verse because as a leader in this community he would feel ashamed at the coming of Christ if some of them did not continue to abide in Christ.* This would be similar to Paul's sentiments in which the apostle hopes that his converts would not fall away so that he would be able to rejoice at the at the *parousia* that he did not labor in vain among them (Phil 2:14-16; cf. 1 Thess 2:19). In other words, the Johannine author (and perhaps his colleagues), though remaining in Christ and receiving eternal life, would nevertheless feel ashamed at the *parousia* that members of the Johannine community that he worked with did not continue in Christ. These former members, it seems, would be shamed by Christ and suffer eternal punishment (cf. John 3:36; 5:28-29; 15:6).

A parallel thought that might be echoed in 2:28 is found in a saying of Jesus from the Synoptic Gospels. The disciples are warned that if they are ashamed of Jesus and his words, he will be ashamed of them when he returns; in other words, he will reject the disciple who denies him before others (Mark 8:38; Matt 10:38-42; Luke 9:26 see above). In these passages the notions of divine judgment and exclusion at Christ's return are related to being put to shame. The apostasy implied in the context of these passages, however, relates to persecution, and this is not the case with the Johannine text where the problem centers on righteous living (1 John 2:29–3:3) and not being led astray into false beliefs about Jesus (2:18-27). Nevertheless, and despite the context of persecution in the Synoptic texts, the Johannine author may have known his own set of written and oral traditions of similar Jesus sayings and interpreted them in light of members of the Johannine community. If they deny Jesus as the Christ in this life (cf. 2:22-23), they will be denied eternal life at Christ's coming. Moreover, one could be ashamed of the "words" of Jesus also, that is, deny or reject

---

217. Smalley, *1,2,3 John*, 131. Notice Ign. *Smyrn.* 10.2: the Smyrnaeans have not been ashamed of Ignatius' bonds, and neither will Jesus, "our perfect hope, be ashamed of you."

218. On the various functions of "we" in the Johannine epistles, see e.g., Brown, *Epistles of John*, 158-61.

his teachings (Mark 8:38; Luke 9:26)—a thought that would certainly resonate with what the Johannine author is writing here.

The idea, notwithstanding, seems to run counter to the Johannine stress on those who abide in Christ having the assurance of eternal life (e.g., 1 John 5:13).[219] The exhortation on abiding in 1 John 2:28 might be a corporate affair, involving the entire Johannine community and the author.[220] But the language centers on individuals in 3:2–3, which necessitates that every believer needs to purify himself or herself (i.e., make oneself pure from sin: 3:2–9; 1:9) in preparation for the *parousia*.[221] The exhortation in 2:28, then, suggests that both the collective community as well as every individual member of it must continue to abide in Christ and be ethically prepared so that they are not put to shame at the second coming. Despite assurance claims to the contrary, certain members might be rejected or shamed by Christ when he returns for not continuing to abide in him. How does this take place? There are at least three options: 1) they could be exposed as having invalid faith either at the *parousia* or prior to it, and in either case they will be punished at the *parousia*; 2) they could lose the valid faith they have some time prior to the *parousia* and therefore be judged at the event; or 3) they could be shamed at the *parousia* despite having valid faith: they lose only their eschatological reward. We will explore these options further below.

The first option is preferred if we read 2:19 with 2:28. In favor of this meaning is that 2:28 stands in close proximity with the secessionists in 2:18–19. In this case the problem of being ashamed may be associated with those who have misperceptions about Jesus, which for the Johannine community typically identifies false believers (cf. John 6:64–66, 70–71). But if this were the case, why does the author address his audience as authentic believers or "little children," and states this emphatically in 1 John 3:1? This identity is attributed to those who belong to Jesus and whose sins are forgiven (1 John 2:28; cf. 2:1, 12; 3:7, 18; 4:4; 5:21).[222] It is occasionally argued that

219. Brown, *Epistles of John*, suggests the secessationists may have held to the view that only non-believers would be judged at the *parousia*; this text would counter such a belief. The Johannine author may also be applying the notion of bearing fruit from John 15:1–6 here (421). The first point seems to mirror-read the text. The second is more plausible, but if correct this fruit-bearing would seem to include the principle of abiding in Christ.

220. Similarly, Lieu, *Johannine Epistles*, 43, notes that the notions of abiding in 1 John 2:24–28 and 4:13 involve "a community rather than an individual experience" (cf. 1:3; 3:24). Contrast abiding as individualistic in 3:6; 4:15–16.

221. Cf. Strecker, *Johannine Letters*, 91–92, for the imperatival and ethical facets of purifying in 1 John 3:3. The individual aspect in 3:3 makes it unlikely that being put to shame in 2:28 is entirely corporate (contrast 2 John 8).

222. Is the believers' final perseverance viewed simply as a gift irrespective of human faith, obedience, and/or effort, and hence failing to abide in Christ disproves a person as an authentic believer?

the thought of "some" of the community's children walk in truth (2 John 4) implies that certain members are not genuinely part of the group. Georg Strecker suggests that 2 John 4 may hint at 2 John 9, in which the "elect lady" is told not to receive a person who does not abide in the Johannine teaching about Christ but goes beyond it.[223] But more likely is the view that the elder is recalling his own personal encounter with some of the congregants of the "elect lady" in verse 4.[224] The second approach is preferred because 2 John 4 includes a thanksgiving, which would hardly be the place to take an indirect jab at the church's fake members. The author treats all the members of the community as believers and they are assured of eternal life (1 John 5:13).

It could be argued that in 1 John 2:28, as well as in other exhortations such as 2:15, 24, 26–27, 3:7; 4:1; 5:21, the author does not expect the believers he addresses to actually fall away. If they are truly born of God they will take heed to the warnings and exhortations and thus persevere.[225] But this explanation often assumes that only a certain amount of hearers are chosen by God and will necessarily persevere on account of their election. With this theological presupposition in place, such a formula is used to interpret the various warning passages which then conform to the presupposition. It is highly questionable, to say the least, that the Johannine author (not to mention his redactors!), would have been armed with this systematic-theological grid as he repeatedly warns his audience against various sins and deception.

Option number two interprets 2:28 as addressing genuine believers and members of the Johannine community who must continue to abide in Christ or else they might fall away and be judged at his second coming. This interpretation would resemble the potential punishment on disciples who do not abide in the metaphoric vine in John 15:6. In 1 John 2:28, if some believers were to fall away the author would be shamed by the judgment on them even though he himself would not lose eternal life. If this view is correct, then 2:18–19 does not necessarily contradict 2:28; rather, the author may believe in two distinct phenomena related to apostasy. Some who fall away are genuine believers and others who fall away are not. But we will have to be content with the Johannine author's wisdom as a leader that he is able to determine by the actions and characters of his congregation members which ones show signs

---

This view is severely weakened by the fact that the recipients are *already* identified as God's children and promised eternal life (e.g., 1 John 5:13). Also, the author assumes that his hearers must obey his exhortations to persevere, and obedience seems to require human responsibility; as such, anything left to human responsibility would appear to involve the possibility of choosing wrongly and the real potential for turning one's back on God.

223. Strecker, *Johannine Letters*, 228

224. Cf. Marshall, *Epistles of John*, 65.

225. On this perspective see, e.g., Bass, *That You May Know*, 3, 177. Unfortunately, Bass does not examine 1 John 2:28 in any detail.

of being true believers and which ones do not. He *does* affirm the members of his audience in 1 John as authentic (2:13–15; 3:1; 5:13), and yet such members could potentially fall away through deception and leave the church in much the same way the inauthentic believers once did.

Another possible tact related to option two might be to consider 2:28 to be the beginning of a new pericope that is related more to what follows it contextually (2:29—3:10) than what precedes it (2:18–27).[226] With this break in mind, the potential for a person being ashamed at the appearance of Jesus may not necessarily involve being deceived with false teachings related to the secessionists; it more generally involves one committing other types of sin (3:4-9; cf. 1:9; 2:1, 15–17). If so, then the Johannine author might suppose that congregants who embrace the false beliefs of the secessionists and "antichrists" invalidate their faith, whereas congregants who commit sins unrelated to the secessionists may be authentic believers who are nonetheless in danger of apostasy by committing other acts of "lawlessness" (3:4). However, in 3:4-9 a dichotomy between sins of false beliefs and other sins is seriously weakened by the fact that this pericope about sin also seems related to deception (3:7), hence false beliefs. Even so, in 1 John a case could be made for a distinction between sins—some do not lead to death, another one does (5:16–17). These lines are not drawn, however, between false beliefs and lawless or unrighteous deeds, as we shall see below.

Option number three suggests the shame in 2:28 constitutes a loss of eschatological reward rather than loss of faith or eternal life. The loss of such reward is related to the imperative warning against deceivers in 2 John 8: "Watch yourselves so that you do not lose what we have worked for but [that] you may receive a full reward."[227] The formulaic exhortation βλέπετε is used in other New Testament passages not only to introduce warnings for the faithful to be on the alert for false teachers (e.g., Mark 8:15; 12:38; Col 2:8; Phil 3:2) but also for staying alert until the end of the age (Matt 24:4; Mark 13:5, 9; Luke 21:8; cf. 1 Cor 10:11–12). The passage is related to the *parousia* in which the full "reward" probably implies heavenly rewards (cf. Rev 3:11; 11:18; 22:12/Isa 40:10; Mark 9:41; Matt 5:12, 46; 10:41–42; Luke 6:23, 35; 1 Cor 3:10–15).[228] It should be noticed, however, that the language in 2 John is corporate

---

226. The introductory καὶ νῦν and addressing the reader as τεκνία may suggest a new pericope at 2:28. See Thompson, *1–3 John*, 84 for a list of commentators who suggest this break.

227. The "you . . . we . . . you" pattern, supported by B and Sahidic textual witnesses, is probably more authentic than the smoothed out "you . . . you . . . you" pattern (ℵ, A) or "we . . . we . . .we" (*TR*). Metzger, *Textual Commentary*, 719, is correct that the awkward pattern best explains the others and that internally the sentence reads, "that you do not destroy the things that we, apostles and teachers, wrought in you."

228. The thought in John 4:36 may also be interpreted in terms of the disciples receiving wages for

and addresses the "elect lady" (v. 1), which stands for the entire congregation who originally read this letter. The "we" probably refers to the elders who "worked" (v. 8) at evangelizing the region and mentoring converts in the congregation. This congregation is in danger of losing some of its members to the false teachings of the "antichrist" (vv. 7, 9). *It faces the danger of losing eschatological reward in the sense of losing some of its congregation members to false teachings.* The rewards and punishments pertaining to individuals are not specifically identified in 2 John 8. Verse 9 says that if an individual goes "too far" he/she does not abide in Christ's teaching and does not have God; namely, that person is not recognized as a believer. If anything the context of verses 8–9 supports the idea that the Johannine community itself may lose its full reward at the eschaton if some of its members are led astray. A *full* reward for the community probably means that all its members persevere with the community until the end. None of the members departs from the Johannine group. If so, then if the community receives anything less than a full reward, this would mean that some of its members had been deceived and left the community.

On the balance of things, our exploration leads us to suggest that option 2 or 3 seems to be the best way to interpret 1 John 2:28. Option 2 warns that some authentic believers in the community are in danger of committing apostasy, and they will be shamed by punishment at the second coming if they fall away. Option 3 warns that the community might lose some of its members to deception and thus be ashamed because it loses its full reward of possessing all its members at the second coming. Option 3 is more consistent with the inauthentic picture of defectors the author normally tends to portray.

ON SINNING AND NOT SINNING
(1 JOHN 3:4-10; CF. 1:8—2:2; JOHN 5:14)

Problematic with 1 John is the apparent contradiction between the believing community as unable not to sin in 1:8–2:2 and yet not able to sin in 3:4–10 and 5:18. The author is fully aware that Christian brothers and sisters do commit sin (1:8–10; 2:1; 5:16–17), and yet those "born of God" (i.e., Christian brothers and sisters!) do *not* sin. The discrepancies have been interpreted numerous ways, none of which is without weaknesses.[229] Some of the more prominent views are the following: 1) The

---

working in God's "harvest." On the apocalyptic emphasis of this verse, see Schnackenburg, *Epistles of John*, 285. Differently, Bultmann, *Johannesbriefe*, 108, suggests the possibility that this reward refers to eternal life (cf. 1 John 2:25).

229. For various views and supporters, see Kubo, "1 John 3:9," 47–56; Lieu, *Johannine Epistles*, 58–65; Brown, *Epistles of John*, 413–15. The position of Bogart, *Orthodox and Heretical Perfectionism*, is primarily argued in View 3 in the main text below.

contradiction is real or involves two different levels of redaction. 2) 1 John 1:8–10 and 3:4–10 are directed at the opponents who make the claim to be absolutely sinless, or differently, the two passages may be directed at two different schisms in the community. 3) The Johannine community is sectarian and created their own view of perfectionism (3:4–10), which statements turned out to be "overkill" against their response to the schismatics' claims implied in 1:8–10. 4) The Johannine claim for Christian sinlessness is more idealistic than actual. 5) Two different types of sin are involved, e.g., witting and unwitting. 6) The present tenses related to sinning in 3:4–10 and 5:18 refer to believers not being able to continue the practice of habitual sinning, whereas 1:8–10 responds to the opponents' false claims that they are not guilty of sin and have no principle of sin.

The correct answer may not rest squarely on any one position; there may be some validity to a few of these. View 5, however, seems less possible at 3:4–10 than 5:16–17. We do not see a dual meaning for "sin" in the former passage as in the latter.[230] The Johannine author seems to posit instead a universal aspect related to sin in 3:4: "sin is lawlessness."[231] The concept of "lawlessness" (ἀνομία) is often found in eschatological and apocalyptic texts (e.g., Matt 24:12; *Did.* 16.4; *Apoc. Pet.* 1.3) and is relevant for understanding the doctrine of antichrist/Satan (cf. 2 Thess 2:3–8). The association between the antichrist and lawlessness is also found in our text, and at least the former of these relates to the doctrine of the secessionists (2:18; cf. 3:4). A sharp contrast is set up between those who commit lawlessness in 3:4 and those who continually abide in Christ in 3:6.

A clue to interpreting this obtuse passage does not rest on its providing an exhortation for Christians to become sinless but on its intention to help the readers discern between children of God and children of the devil (3:7a, 10). This would be helpful in order to offset the coming of the many antichrists in 4:1–6; albeit, a clear connection between these opponents and their view of sin is difficult to establish. In any case, it may be safe to suggest that false teachers, past and present and future, may be proven for what they are by the fact that they commit unrighteous acts and do not love the Johannine community. Differently, authentic believers practice righteousness, love one another, and have God's "seed" in them; namely, they are born of

---

230. Here if the author wished to make a distinction, it would have been helpful to use another word for sin apart from ἁμαρτία/ἁμαρτάνω, such as ἀγνόημα (the sin of ignorance), πταίω (to err, stumble), or ὀφείλω (to incur moral debt). But the Johannine author is notorious for pouring multiple meanings into the same word.

231. The word for lawlessness is probably not associated with Mosaic Law but has more to do with not practicing righteousness (1 John 2:29; 3:7f; 5:18), violating God's commands (2:3–8; 3:22–24; 2 John 6; i.e., believe Jesus is the Christ and love one another), and perhaps not doing God's will (2:17; 5:14).

the Spirit.²³² As a rule they cannot be involved in the same practices as those who are of the spirit of antichrist without invalidating their own confession.²³³

Our perspective here discerns the practices of the Johannine community and presumably those of the followers of the antichrists through the concept of validity/invalidity. This should be expected if one of the primary problems in the letter relates to the danger of being deceived, and this problem is certainly not lost in 3:4–10 (e.g., 3:7). Some of tests that validate or falsify one's faith include walking in darkness or in light (1:6), keeping or not keeping divine commands (3:24), hating or loving fellow believers (3:14–15), and having God's spirit or the spirit of error (4:13).²³⁴ Whether previous apostates were still influencing members (2:27), or a new threat was influencing them (2 John 7–9), or both, it is quite possible that Johannine claims emphasizing the nature of Christ and avoiding sin are some sort of response to this influence. The author may be qualifying misperceptions his readers might have, and one of these might be that it is permissible to sin since they are inevitably sinners anyway (1 John 1:8, 10).²³⁵

If the opponents have a distorted view of sin, some argue that the Johannine author has picked up the language of that false view in 3:9 in saying that believers cannot sin. According to this view, the opponents may have considered themselves as sinless because God's "seed" dwelt in them. Our author responds that the true possessors of God's seed abides in Jesus and has the Spirit abiding in them (3:6–9), yet in picking up the opponents' language the author creates difficulties with his earlier sayings in 1:8–10.²³⁶ This interpretation is certainly possible but seems to stand or fall based on a mirror-read of what the opponents might have believed. Other scholars have argued that the tension between 1:8—2:2 and 3:4–10 may be alleviated through the Greek tenses these passages use. The present tense of sinning (e.g., ἁμαρτίαν οὐ ποιεῖ) in 3:4–10 suggests that believers do not make a continual practice or lifestyle of sin. For the Gentile members of the community, at least, this no doubt reflected their own habits prior to encountering Jesus and being born of God. Zerwick suggests the aorist tense means to "commit sin in the concrete, commit some sin or other" ²³⁷ (cf. 2:1–2), while the present tense (3:6, 9) means to "be

---

232. John 3:3–7/Ezek 36:26–27; cf. John 16:7–11; 1 John 2:20, 27; 3:24; 4:1–6, 13; Rom 8:14–17.

233. For other prominent interpretations of the "seed," see Lieu, "What Was," 467–72; Brown, *Epistles of John*, 408–11.

234. Cf. Lieu, *Johannine Epistles*, 51–52, who refers to Law, *Tests of Life*.

235. In 1 John 2:1 individual acts of sin rather than a habitual state of sin may be implied by the subjunctive aorist ἵνα μὴ ἁμάρτητε ("so that you may not sin"); so Brooke, *Johannine Epistles*, 23.

236. Cf. Painter, "Opponents," 57. Similarly, Bogart, *Orthodox and Heretical Perfectionism*, opines that the Johannine author is responding to the opponents by doing some "overkill."

237. Zerwick, *Biblical Greek*, 82 (§251). On this reading the aorist may be ingressive (begin com-

a sinner, as a characteristic <<state>>."[238] If the believer is born of God, then this person "cannot continue the sinful life that was his before his regeneration."[239] This view seems to have more merits than setbacks,[240] especially when we read Paul making a similar argument about sin in Rom 6:1–15 (esp. vv. 1, 2, 15). Such passages emphasize that a sinful lifestyle of the believer must not continue. A new kind of *halakhah* has been established through Jesus—the believers must "walk" as Jesus walked (1 John 2:6). They must imitate Christ and conduct themselves as he would. This includes living in the "light" or union with God (1:7),[241] living in righteous behavior (2:29), living in love (e.g., 2:10), and living in the truth of what they have been taught (2 John 4; 3 John 3–4).[242] *A two-way motif is presented here, where the "children of God" are walking in the light, while those walking not in the light but in darkness are "children of the devil" (1:6–7; 3:10).*

Perhaps the author expects the community to follow the same standard as the paralytic is expected to follow after Jesus heals him and says, "Sin no more" (John 5:14; cf. 1 John 2:6). It is doubtful that Jesus expects the man he healed to never commit another sin again, especially given that if such was the expectation and he were to sin again, a worse fate than paralysis would come upon him. A present-tense imperative is used (μηκέτι ἁμάρτανε), suggesting the man was to put an end to a lifestyle of continual sin rather than never commit any individual acts of sin. Incidentally, we notice that in 5:14 the fate worse than paralysis probably refers to eternal death as the consequence of sinful living.[243] Such a lifestyle leads to the "resurrection of condemnation" (cf. 5:28–29). This story points beyond itself to imply conversion for the readers. That it takes place at the pool of Bethesda may suggest for the Johannine audience a type of baptism, and Jesus saying "sin no more" implies

---

mitting this or that sin) and the present tense is stative (be a sinner); cf. Turner, *Grammatical Insights*, 151; 1 John 3:6 NET.

238. Zewick, *Biblical Greek*, 82. Less convincing is the gnomic present of Wallace, *Greek Grammar*, 524–25.

239. Zerwick, *Biblical Greek*, 82. Painter, *Epistles of John*, 227 (cf. 231) understands 3:6, 9 as a "characteristic way of being."

240. Some admitted setbacks are these: would John expect his audience to capture the nuances in the Greek tense? Also 1 John 1:8 and 5:16 seem awkward if the present tense on sin as continual is stressed in these verses, but then again they appear in passages distinct from 3:4–10. It is also possible that John or a later redactor may have used inconsistent grammar at times.

241. Cf. Strecker, *Johannine Letters*, 29–30.

242. See Merwe, "Matter of Fellowship," 544–55.

243. Likewise, in inferior manuscripts that have the story (e.g., D), when Jesus tells the woman caught in adultery to "sin no more" (μηκέτι ἁμάρτανε) she is expected to abandon her lifestyle of sexual immorality rather than become perfectly sinless (John 8:11).

that up to this point the man's previous sins have been cleansed.[244] In essence, Jesus warns the man not to fall away to sin now that his life has been changed. To this we might add the notion that in other New Testament epistles the emergent Christians are to avoid the practice of numerous vices that mark the lifestyle of unbelievers, even though it is apparent that Christians back then (and now) still commit individual acts of sin mentioned on those lists from time to time (e.g., Gal 5:19–21; 1 Cor 6:9–10; 1 Pet 4:3–4). The aspect of sin as a lifestyle being incompatible with believers in 1 John 3:4–10 is captured well by an illustration from F. F. Bruce:

> A sinful life does not mark a child of God, so that anyone who leads such a life is shown thereby not to be a child of God. When a boy goes to a new school, he may inadvertently do something out of keeping with the school's tradition . . . to be told immediately, "That isn't done here." A literalist might reply, "But obviously it *is* done; this boy has just done it"—but he would be deliberately missing the point . . . the rebuke is that such conduct is disapproved of in this school, so anyone who practises it can normally be assumed not to belong to the school. There may be odd exceptions, but that is the general rule.[245]

It is also significant that in the very passage where the Johannine author claims believers cannot sin, Jesus alone is the only example of a person who has no sin (1 John 3:5).

SIN THAT LEADS TO "DEATH" (1 JOHN 5:16–17; CF. 2:22–23; 3:14–15, 23–24; 4:2–3; 2 JOHN 7)

The author mentions two types of sin in 1 John 5:16–17: one leads to death and the other does not. If a believer sees a "brother" committing a sin not leading to death, the believer should pray so that God may give "life" to the one who is sinning.[246] The term "brother" or "brothers and sisters" (ἀδελφός/ ἀδελφοί) represent fellow believers among the Johannine community who have already passed from death to life (3:13–14; cf. 2:9–10; 3:10, 15–17; 3 John 3–5). As elsewhere in this epistle, "life" refers to eternal life (2:25; 3:14; 5:13, 16, 20; cf. John 5:24). The "sin leading to death"

---

244. On the latter point cf. Barrett, *John*, 255: "sin *no more* suggests that sins up to this point have already been dealt with. . . . The χεῖρόν τι can hardly be anything other than the Judgement (cf. v. 29)."

245. Bruce, *Epistles of John*, 90.

246. The person giving life may refer to either God or the human intercessionist via his prayers according to God's will. The idea comes close to James 5:20. In both cases there is a possibility for backslidden Christians to be restored in faith. Despite the claim of Bultmann, *Johannesbriefe*, 11, that 1 John 5:14–21 is written by a later redactor, most scholars consider this final pericope to be written by the same author as 1 John 5:1–13. See Strecker, *Johannine Letters*, 198–200.

In the Footsteps of Judas and Other Defectors

has been interpreted numerous ways.[247] These include: 1) a sin that leads to physical death,[248] 2) sinning in defiance or a "high hand,"[249] 3) a mortal sin as distinguished from what later became known as venial sins,[250] 4) blasphemy of the Holy Spirit,[251] or 5) a sin committed by unbelievers rather than believers.[252]

The best option, however, is to associate the "sin leading to death" with apostasy.[253] More specifically, 1 John seems to imply that certain beliefs and practices identify God's children and the children of the devil and antichrist. If a presumed child of God believes and acts in ways that align that individual with children of the devil, then it would stand to reason that such a person does not have eternal life. That person has committed a sin leading to death. The Johannine author does not bother to identify this sin, it seems, because he assumes his community can determine for themselves how it is committed. Their previous experience with the behavior of apostates who left their community would seem to be a vital gauge for determining this.

What is not entirely clear to us is which particular beliefs and practices the audience would have recognized as hallmarks that reflect the behavior of the defectors they experienced within their community. Perhaps the suggestions presented below may be combined to get an idea of these hallmarks. First, a denial of having sinned (1 John 1:8–2:2; cf. John 9:39–41) may have been associated with a repudiation of the sacrificial purpose of Jesus' death to take away the sins of the world (1 John 1:6; 2:2; cf. John 1:29). If so, this may be one of those markers. Second, the children of God and the children of the devil are identified in ethical terms as to whether or not they practice righteousness and love fellow believers (1 John 3:10; cf. 2:29).[254] Children of the devil do not practice righteousness (3:4–15). Third, in 3:23–24 God gives a commandment for the Johannine community to believe on the name of God's Son, Jesus the Christ (cf. 2:22–23; 4:14–15; 5:1, 4b–5), which stands on at least equal footing with the command to love one another (cf. 4:7–12; 4:16–5:3; 2 John 5–6). In a word,

---

247. For a survey of different perspectives, see Scholer, "Sins within," 233–38; Brown, *Epistles of John*, 613–18; Kim, *Apostasy Embedded*, 271–312.

248. E.g. Lev 10:1–2; Deut 22:25–26; *Jub.* 33.12–18; Acts 5:1–11; 1 Cor 5:5; 11:30.

249. E.g., Num 15:30–31; *Jub.* 21.22; 1QS 8.21–9.2; Heb 10:26–27; cf. *Jub.* 26.34; *Herm. Sim.* 6.2.1–4.

250. E.g., Tertullian, *Modesty* 2, 19; Hippolytus, *Haer.* 9.7.

251. Mark 3:29; Matt 12:32; Luke 12:10.

252. 1 John 3:6–9; 5:18. See further Scholer, "Sins within," 230–46. Marshall, *Epistles of John*, 178, 248, affirms instead that John seems to be referring to sin in general in 1 John 3, and it is not likely that he would expect his readers to anticipate at an earlier point (3:4–9) where he was heading with his definition of sin at a later point (5:18).

253. E.g., Beutler, *Johannesbreife*, 130; Griffith, *Keep Yourselves from Idols*, 144–46; Painter, *Epistles of John*, 319 (reject confession of faith); Brown, *Epistles of John*, 636 ("the sin of the secessionists").

254. In 2:29 it is possible that the author aligns himself with the Pauline tradition: cf. Yarbrough, *1–3 John*, 170–71.

the Johannine version of the great commandment from the Synoptic Gospels (e.g., Matt 22:37-40) seems to revise "love God with all your heart" to "believe in Jesus as the Christ," and "love your neighbor" has been transformed to "love one another" (cf. 1 John 3:23).[255] The Johannine author seems to view the Father and Son as one, so that to deny the Son is to deny the Father and to confess the Son is to confess the Father also (2:23). Hence, to believe Jesus as the Christ and Son of God is in fact to believe God. Moreover, in 1 John the barometer for determining one's love for God is whether one loves the children of God (5:1-2); a person cannot love God if he or she hates the "brothers and sisters" (3:15; 4:20-21).[256] Fourth, in terms of beliefs the apostates and opponents make false claims about Jesus (2:22-23; 4:2-3; 2 John 7). They deny him as "Christ," the Messiah. The meaning of "come in the flesh" (1 John 4:2; cf. 4:3) probably suggests the opponents did not believe that what Jesus did in the flesh during his earthly ministry was related to his being Messiah: "every spirit that confesses Jesus as the Christ who has come in the flesh . . ." (4:2; cf. 2:22; 2 John 7; John 11:27; 20:31; Acts 5:42; 8:5; *Barn.* 5:10-11).[257] The opponents are considered followers of the "antichrist" who are controlled by the "evil one" in the world (1 John 4:1-6; cf. 2:13-14; 5:19; John 12:31; 16:11; 2 John 7).

Thus, *the "sin leading to death" becomes the perfect nemesis of those things which are most vital to the Christian faith: belief in Jesus as Christ and Son of God, loving others, turning away from sin, and living in righteousness.* A person who denies such basic tenets exemplifies the character and deeds of the devil's children, the secessionists, and the many antichrists that threaten the community. For the author, such a person, no doubt, "abides in death" (cf. 1 John 3:14-15)

The Johannine author does not encourage praying for those who commit the sin leading to death, but he does not forbid it either (5:16). The author does not say one way or another if prayer could be effective in such instances. Presumably the decision is left to the one doing the praying, as long as praying for such a person

---

255. The author also affirms that the one who keeps God's commandments abides in God, and the verification of God abiding in the believers is that God has given the Spirit to them (1 John 3:24; cf. 2:20-27; 4:1-6, 13).

256. Johannine thought tends to combine the concepts of hate with murder and death, which also become ways for determining the children of the devil (3:10-15).

257. See Griffith, "Non-Polemical Reading," 267-72. A present rather than perfect tense in 2 John 7 is used: ". . . many deceivers have gone out into the world, people who do not confess Jesus as Christ coming in the flesh" (NET), but this nuance may not alter the meaning. Be that as it may, our perspective of Jesus as the Christ in these passages does not stand or fall on the particular translation we have chosen. Witherington, *Letters and Homilies*, 1.494, for instance, translates "Jesus Christ in the flesh has come" (4:2) and affirms, "The added word 'Christ' may just indicate that they did not think that Christ had come in the flesh as of yet, and so they denied that this Jesus who had lived and died was that Christ come in the flesh."

In the Footsteps of Judas and Other Defectors

does not come against God's will (cf. 5:14–15).[258] We do notice, for example, in the Johannine Jesus' prayer to the Father before his arrest that he mentions Judas' upcoming destruction but does not pray for his restoration (John 17:12).[259]

If the "sin leading to death" in 1 John 5:16–17 is apostasy and the denial of basic tenets of faith such as in 3:23–24, what then would be considered a sin "not leading to death"? Frustratingly the concept of loving the world involves principles rather than concrete examples (2:14–17). We are also told that the world is hostile to the believers (3:13), belongs to the Evil One (5:19), and that deceivers reside there (2 John 7). The author paints a negative portrait of the world, it seems, because he does not want his members to depart from the community to the world. Significant in this regard is that the Johannine community may function similar to modern new religious movements that socially insulate their members from contacts with the outside world in order to protect them from defecting.[260] Assimilation with the world betrays a temptation especially relevant to Gentile Christians (cf. 1 John 2:14–17).[261] It is possible that 5:21 speaks of the sin of assimilation in terms of idolatry: "little children, keep yourself from idols." Raymond Brown, however, opines that this verse means the secessionists have become, as it were, "idols" by attempting to seduce the covenant community from the one true God revealed in Christ Jesus.[262]

Even so, in the Johannine community's time and culture idolatry may be understood rather literally, unlike Western culture today. The elder's community lived in Ephesus, which had a large Gentile population with many followers of the goddess Artemis/Diana (e.g., Acts 19). Without further qualification, the abrupt ending at 1 John 5:21 may have led some in the community to read this verse literally. It is important to mention that idol meats became a problem resurfacing within Christian communities in the first century, including cities of Asia Minor in communication

---

258. This aspect nonetheless seems left up to the discernment of those who pray to discern God's voice on the matter. Certainly, God may lead those who pray to stop interceding for someone. Yarbrough, *1–3 John*, 312, references Jer 7:16; 11:14; 14:11, in which God tells Jeremiah to stop praying for compatriots. Another popular example we might add is 1 Sam 16:1 even though "prayer" is not mentioned.

259. See Von Wahlde, "Judas," 175.

260. See Wright, *Leaving Cults*; Wilson, *Leaving the Fold*, 122.

261. Anderson, "Antichristic Errors: Proselytization," 225–37, stresses the problem of assimilation in the Johannine community but thinks this may involve the rise of emperor worship in the late first century (237, 240; cf. idem, "Antichristic Errors: Flawed Interpretations," 206). Differently Trebilco, *Early Christians*, 385–93, claims the Johannine group exhibits a "low level" of assimilation and participation with the dominant culture because of its strong boundaries, and the "in-group" language in 1 John evinces very little acculturation with the world; 2 John and 3 John, however, show more signs of acculturation.

262. Brown, *Epistles of John*, 627–29, 641.

with Ephesus (Rev 2:14, 16, 20–22; cf. Acts 15; 1 Cor 8–10). The author's ambiguity at the end may include assimilation. It is not entirely clear whether 5:21 is meant to be understood metaphorically, literally, or both.[263] Perhaps this is deliberate so that the author could spread his net as wide as possible and affirm that Jesus is the true deity (5:20); therefore, *belief in any other deity is false*, whether Artemis, Caesar, idol foods, false beliefs that replace Jesus' lordship, or the Evil One who has in his power all those who belong to the world (5:19).

Typical temptations Christians may have faced included compromising with idolatrous practices, sexual sin ("lust of the flesh"), greed (Judas' sin), and so on.[264] As in many communities, divisions in the house churches and being at variance with fellow believers would perhaps take place and may be one of the reasons why the author repeatedly stresses love and loving one another (e.g., 1 John 3:17; 4:7–20). More specifically, the elder warns that the mandate to love includes loving fellow believers who are poor; in fact, love is authenticated when the community members do works to help needy brothers and sisters. To neglect such deeds violates the command to love one another (3:17–18). Such sins may be presumed among those that believers commit and need to confess (1:8–9).

Restoration is made possible as described in 5:16–17, which in some ways resembles the parting comments given by other early Christian writers to their respective communities (Gal 6:1; Jas 5:19–20; Jude 22–23). The elder, however, emphasizes prayer for the failed individual; Paul, James, and Jude desire their readers to play a more active role in the restoration. And differently than the Johannine community, Jude challenges his audience to restore the false teachers who were corrupting their communities! Both James and Jude consider the ones that need to be restored as apostates. For Paul the one that needs to be restored is committing vices that lead to exclusion from God's kingdom, but it is not clear whether the individual from Galatians 6:1 is already apostate. Elsewhere it is evident in Paul that apostates could be restored (e.g., 1 Cor 5:5b). What is the Johannine author's perception of the individual's status who could be restored to the community?

What almost seems to be a contradiction in 1 John 5:16 is that the person whose sin is "not leading to death" must be restored to eternal "life." In what sense could the

---

263. See Brown, *Epistles of John*, 625–26, for ten options. To these views may be added Griffith, "Non-Polemical Reading"; idem, *Keep Yourselves from Idols*, 204–8, who reads 5:21 rhetorically as a condemnation of Israel's apostasy.

264. We might add the adulterous woman's sin to be sexual (John 8:11; cf. 5:14). The earliest manuscripts, however, omit this story. The washing of feet in John 13:8–10 probably does not refer to post-conversion sins that individuals commit; it alludes to the atoning aspect of Jesus' death and also perhaps water baptism (1 John 1:7; cf. Rom 6:1–4). This would account for both the severity of Peter's exclusion from Jesus if he were not washed and why Judas is not "clean."

sinning believer ("brother/"sister") be given eternal life if he/she already has it? One possible solution is to interpret 5:16 in the sense of a reconfirmation or renewal of eternal life that is already possessed.[265] On the other hand this person needs prayer in order to be given "life." When we combine this aspect with the repetitive way the believer needs to be categorized as one that is not committing a sin leading to death (ἁμαρτάνοντα ἁμαρτίαν μὴ πρὸς θάνατον . . . τοῖς ἁμαρτάνουσιν μὴ πρὸς θάνατον), the assumption might be that this believer is *capable* of committing the sin leading to death. In other words, *a sin not leading to death might fester into one that does over time if there is no prayer offered to the sinning brother and no confession of sins.*[266] The Johannine author does not seem to speculate on whether such an individual ultimately possesses or does not possess eternal life at a given moment when committing the sin "not leading to death"—that this sinner is considered a believer suggests *yes, this person has eternal life*; that this believer needs to be given "life" again suggests *no, this person does not have eternal life*. The main point is that this person can be restored from his or her ambiguous status betwixt and between life and death.

In 5:16–17, then, we may be left with not only two distinct perspectives on sin, but also two perspectives on apostasy: 1) there are apostates who have committed the sin that leads to death; they live in spiritual death; and 2) there are brothers and sisters who commit sins that do not automatically lead to death; they might still eventually become spiritually dead, but the community can offer prayers for their restoration.[267] This perspective on 5:16–17 opens up the possibility that certain sins can indeed unravel a believer who has passed from death to life (3:14), and reverse the process so that the believer passes from life to death. If so, then 5:16–17 supports the possibility of a genuine believer falling away. Such an unsettling picture is quickly alleviated by the author stressing assurance to his community by affirming that God is involved in protecting them (1 John 5:18; cf. John 17:6, 11–12, 15; 10:28–29).[268]

---

265. Cf. Scholer, "Sins within," 240. For several interpretative options on why the "brother" needs "life," see Bass, *That You May Know*, 168–70.

266. Notice that forgiveness of sins is contingent upon confession in 1 John 1:9. Similar to my view is Smalley, *1, 2, 3 John*, 298; Marshall, *Epistles of John*, 248–59.

267. An interesting story is attributed to John the apostle in Ephesus, according to Clement, *Quis div.*, in Eusebius, *Hist. eccl.* 3.23. John entrusted a young man to a bishop who baptized and mentored the youth. This convert eventually fell into the company of robbers and became one himself, falling away from his faith. When John returned, the bishop claimed that the youth was "dead to God." John was able to restore the youth who repented, and he was baptized once again. Of course we do not know the validity of the story, but it at least portrays the restoration of an apostate by a person who is traditionally claimed as the author of 1 John.

268. Variant manuscripts and possible translations of 1 John 5:18 (. . . ὁ γεννηθεὶς ἐκ τοῦ θεοῦ τηρεῖ αὐτόν . . .) make this passage difficult to interpret, but essentially the two best views seem to be either that Jesus is the one who is "born of God" and protects/keeps the believer (e.g., "he who was born of God protects him," ESV), or God protects/keeps the believer who is born of God ("God protects the

In Johannine thought, since sin leading to death involves a denial of the Father as well as the Son (2:22–23), such apostates cut themselves off from the very being who would otherwise preserve them.

DIOTREPHES: AN INAUTHENTIC CHRISTIAN LEADER (3 JOHN 9-11)

The elder commends the believers named Gaius and Demetrius while at the same time he denounces a leader named Diotrephes. Gaius' hospitality toward itinerant preachers is set in contrast with Diotrephes' inhospitality. Nothing is really said about Diotrephes' beliefs; his conduct is what the elder condemns. If there were an acute problem with this leader's teachings, we assume the Johannine author would have mentioned it.[269] The conflict centers on a power struggle between Diotrephes and other Christian leaders. Diotrephes loves to put himself first (ὁ φιλοπρωτεύων) and not accept the authority of the elder and his colleagues (v. 9). He speaks against them, does not receive traveling believers into his house church, and prevents others who would do so, expelling them from the church (vv. 9–11).[270] This leader exercises enough authority over the congregation to be able to expel other members. The elder indirectly considers Diotrephes to be an evildoer (vv. 10–11). Diotrephes is an example of an ambitious Christian who does not love the Johannine believers (cf. 1 John 3:10, 16–18).

What is striking here is that Diotrephes has a position of leadership in the Johannine community. He probably holds the rank of an elder-bishop or is in the process of becoming one.[271] *The Johannine author considers this leader to be a false believer*: Diotrephes and others who commit evil deeds "have not seen God" (v. 11). To be sure, technically speaking, no one has seen God (cf. John 1:18). But the elder is probably suggesting that by doing good and loving Christian brothers and sisters, a person demonstrates love for God; and in Johannine thought if a person like Diotrephes does not love those whom he can see, he cannot love God, whom he

---

one he has fathered," NET). It is helpful to note that τηρέω is used in relation to both Jesus and God protecting the disciples in John 17, but because Jesus will be leaving them shortly on account of his upcoming death, he surrenders this task to the Father who will protect them from the "evil one" (John 17:15), very similar to 1 John 5:18.

269. Malherbe, "Inhospitality of Diotrephes," 222–32, rightly moves the debate away from the theological to one centering on hospitality. Hence discussions on Diotrephes' doctrinal position are of little value here. Contrast Käsemann, "Ketzer und Zuege," 292–311.

270. Apparently, Diotrephes, Gaius, and the Elder belong to different congregations (cf. 3 John 3, 6, 9–10, 15). The content of his malicious words is not known, and his talking nonsense (φλυαρέω) is not used elsewhere in scripture; yet φλύαρος can mean gossipy, trifling, or nonsensical (cf. 1 Tim 5:13; 4 Macc 5:11).

271. Cf. Wengst, *Johannes*, 233.

cannot see (1 John 4:20–22; cf. 1 John 3:6; 4:12). Diotrophes' actions reveal that he does not really know God.

CONCLUSION

Our study accepts that the fourth gospel and the Johannine Epistles should be read together, and a two-level reading of this gospel informs us about the Johannine community's situation. This community presumably originated in Palestine, was expelled from a synagogue (cf. John 9:22; 16:1–4), and moved to Ephesus. In the new location Gentiles joined the Jewish believers in Christ. A significant faction within the group developed primarily over the nature of Christ. This resulted in a number of members defecting from the group (1 John 2:19). According to the Johannine "elder," they denied Jesus as the Christ (1 John 2:22–23). These experiences seem to have colored the way the Johannine community and its leaders perceive apostates and the negative way the fourth gospel often portrays the Judeans who reject Jesus.

In John's gospel the Judeans are spiritually blinded (John 12:37–41; cf. Isa 6). Despite what seems to be the inevitable course of divine sovereignty, the author supports both divine initiative and human responsibility. We have argued through John's gospel and its Isaianic echoes that, whether by the devil or directly by God, God is in some sense involved in the obduracy of "the Jews." Their blindness is a result of divine judgment brought about by their earlier rejection of the revelation of God disclosed through Jesus and their own scriptures (cf. John 5–6). Nevertheless some "Jews" do believe, but a large number fall away on account of Jesus' messages that suggest his preexistence and ultimate authority (6:59–66; 8:30–58). Evidently, for the Johannine community, to accept Jesus as Christ is to accept his preexistence and deity (e.g., 1:1–18; 5:18; 20:28; 1 John 5:20). Among the dissenters is a group of Judeans who are precipitate defectors that become hostile towards Jesus and try to stone him on two different occasions because of what they perceive as blasphemous claims that he makes (John 8:30–58; 10:30–33). There also seems to be another group of "Jews" in the fourth gospel that are "Crypto"-believers. They choose to remain in the synagogue rather than face hardships by openly following Jesus (e.g., 12:42–43). Once Jesus is crucified and exalted, however, all "peoples" will be drawn and given to him by the Father in accordance with Isaianic prophecy, both Jews and Gentiles (12:32; cf. 6:44; Isa 54–56). Unlike the religious leaders who expel the followers of Jesus from the synagogue, the one who comes to Jesus and continues to believe in him will not be cast away from him (John 6:37). As the ideal shepherd, he will protect his flock from external harm (10:1–30; cf. 18:8–9).

The Gospel of John and the Epistles of John

Johannine literature stresses the assurance of the believer's salvation as a way of preventing another group defection from within the community (e.g., 20:31; 1 John 5:13). Some of the apostates from Ephesus are still disturbing the Johannine group (1 John 2:18, 26), and false prophets who come in the spirit of "antichrist" may be another threat on the horizon (1 John 4:1–6; 2 John 7–9). We are not told, however, what the defectors think about their own relationship with God and Jesus. It is possible that they still affirm Jesus as Christ but not in terms of the Johannine community's definition that affirms him as preexistent deity. Apostates are normally portrayed in the literature as false believers (John 6:64–65, 70–71). In the Johannine Epistles, defectors who went out from among the believing community in Ephesus never really belonged to the spiritual fellowship of the group (1 John 2:19), and Diotrophes, a leader in the Johannine community, is a false believer (3 John 9–11). The general emphasis of the epistles is to provide the believers with discernment and assurance. Those who keep on believing have eternal life and those who keep on sinning as a lifestyle abide in death (1 John 3:14). In the fourth gospel defectors among the Jewish disciples of Jesus have not truly understood and believed his words (John 6). Judas is viewed as the representative defector. He has always been a false disciple, a child of the devil, and his fate will be eternal destruction (John 6:70–71; 13:2; 17:12).

Nevertheless, if the norm presented in Johannine literature is that apostates are spurious believers, there are important exceptions to rule. The notion of abiding in Christ includes perseverance to the extent that those who are already abiding in Christ must continue to do so or be cut off from Christ and eschatologically destroyed (John 15:1–6). The command to abide in Jesus' love weighs heavy on this interpretation. Preludes to such judgment may be found in Jesus' warning to the man he heals at the pool of Bethesda and in the thief's intention in the message of the Good Shepherd (5:14; 10:10a). Other warnings include that if believers fail to abide in Christ they will experience shame at his second coming (1 John 2:28), and if they are finally led astray by deceivers, the Johannine leaders and community will lose its full "reward" (2 John 8).

Moreover, as in the Synoptic Gospels, Jesus claims to his followers that falling away in the face of persecution amounts to the loss of eternal life: the person who loves his life will lose it (John 12:25). Hence, it seems that in Johannine literature the previous apostates who embraced false teachings were never true believers, but true believers may become apostates due to persecution and failing to continue abiding in Christ. For the Johannine community, then, not all sins and apostasies should be treated alike. The sin of apostasy leads to eternal death, but if the community sees a fellow believer committing a sin not leading to "death," (i.e., not committing apostasy) they are to pray for the person's restoration (1 John 5:16–17). That these believers need to be restored back to "life" opens up the possibility that, in Johannine thinking, certain sins apart from apostasy may also unravel the faith of authentic Christians. We have suggested that these sins have to do with assimilation to the attitudes of the host society of the community that belongs to the "world" (e.g., 1 John 2:15–17; 3:17; cf. 3:1–10; 5:21; John 5:40). The Johannine author maintains strong boundary lines between insiders and outsiders.

What we have in Johannine literature, then, is not one perspective on apostasy but two. Those who have fallen away were never genuine Christians, but those who are in danger of falling away are. Among the options we have suggested, one that may be prominent is based on the labeling of an opponent using status degradation. In such labeling, those who were once identified with a respective community are later denounced as outsiders having nothing to do with the community, and their previous participation is viewed in some sense as a façade.

In a general way, John's view of apostates from the community resembles the Matthean view of false prophets that claim to follow Christ. The nature of apostasy in the Johannine and Matthean texts in this regard focus primarily on deception. Both gospels nonetheless affirm the possibility of genuine Christ-followers committing apostasy; Matthew more so than John. A distinctive aspect in the latter is that those who left the group are outsiders who might be attempting to influence some members. In Matthew the false prophets are not necessarily apostates, but imposters who may still play an active role within the Matthean community. It is not clear that they have ever left the group. And whereas in Matthew the false prophets practice lawlessness or unrighteous deeds contrary to the Law as interpreted by Jesus, in John the primary point of contention with the defectors is that they deny Jesus as Messiah. The false prophets in Matthew confess Jesus as the Christ, but they do not live in a way that honors that confession.

The Johannine writings agree with the Synoptic texts that apostates will be judged with eschatological destruction. With Mark, John does not portray Judas' physical death. He remains a recalcitrant figure to the end. A glaring difference is that Judas is viewed as never being truly a genuine follower of Jesus in John. No restoration is given to Judas in John's gospel, and perhaps significantly, although 1 John provides the hope of restoration through prayer of those who commit sins "not leading to death," no intercession is recommended for the apostate.

Conclusion

Throughout this study of the Synoptic Gospels, Acts, and Johannine writings, we have *identified the communities* that confess Jesus as the Christ and found them to be quite diverse. Mark and Luke-Acts address primarily Gentile audiences, the former set in Rome. The Johannine texts reflect a mixture of Jews and Gentiles who locate their ultimate setting in western Asia Minor. The Matthean communities are comprised mostly of Jewish Christ-followers from Palestine and Syria. Likewise, we have encountered a variety of the communities' opponents. They are sometimes outsiders, such as the Pharisees in Matthew and hostile Gentiles in Acts. Other times they are deceptive insiders who attempt to seduce Christ's followers, such as Matthew's false prophets, or outsiders who were once insiders, such as the defectors in the Johannine writings. Each of the communities faces unique situations. Mark's concern centers on a recent persecution of Christ-followers that was brought on by imperial Rome, and this gospel seeks the restoration lapsed believers who had denied Christ through this ordeal. Matthew confronts lawless behavior and false teachers, the Johannine community censures apostate disciples and those who deny Jesus as the Christ, and the disciples in Luke-Acts, among other things, must persevere through temptations related to greed. The Lukan Paul, moreover, faces opposition from other Christ-followers who believe his teachings signal the abandonment of the Mosaic Law. Discord among the Christ communities, some of which consider other Christ communities to be apostate, will remain evident as we examine the rest of the New Testament writings in subsequent volumes.

In this study we have observed the *nature of apostasy* in terms of unbelief, persecution, false teachings, and immoral behavior. The gospel writers present Israel's unbelief towards the message of Jesus as the Christ, and these authors generally interpret this as a type of apostasy that rejects God's prophetic plan for God's people. Israel's inability to find faith in Jesus as Messiah is due to their obduracy towards him as God's appointed messenger, a sign that the gospel writers associate with Israel's rebellion in Isaiah 6. In Mark, this obduracy takes place as a result of divine judgment, and not only is Israel hardened but also Jesus' relatives and his closest disciples. In Matthew the people harden their own hearts, but the disciples of Jesus are presented as having spiritual insight. In Acts, the mixed results of belief and unbelief among people of the Diaspora who hear the gospel bring about God's plan of salvation to the Gentiles. One emphasis distilled from the Johannine author is that a number of "Jews" believe in Jesus but then reject him later on, suggesting perhaps that the author's community encountered Christ-followers whom they perceive as apostates.

The authors consider persecution to be another cause of falling away, Mark and Matthew more so than Luke and John. In all four gospels Jesus anticipates that some of his disciples will abandon him rather than face imprisonment and physical harm, and he warns them against losing eternal life in order to preserve their mortal life. In the Synoptic texts he warns that they will be denied access to his kingdom in the age to come if they deny or are ashamed of him in the present age. The second "seed" in the parable of the Sower falls away due to persecution in Mark and Matthew. Mark's gospel seems motivated to highlight suffering and persecution as threatening the loss of faith because the community it addresses suffered mistreatment under Emperor Nero in Rome. Luke admits that persecutions can result in Christians falling away (e.g., Luke 9:24–26), but he mitigates such thoughts in order to portray an idealistic picture of Paul and other apostles as brave stalwarts of the faith who refuse to succumb to spiritual abandonment in the face of opposition. John likewise admits defection through persecution (John 12:25; 13:38), but the author's main concern turns on his community's belief in Jesus as the preexistent Christ. The group that departed from the community in 1 John probably maintained their confession as Christ-followers but did not believe that Jesus is preexistent or God.

A third venue for apostasy centers on false teachings and abusive leadership in the Christ-communities. In the Synoptic Gospels Jesus warns his disciples that if they cause "little ones" who trust in him to fall away they will be punished severely. Matthew warns his auditors against following false prophets who practice lawlessness, and in the Mount Olivet discourse Jesus warns that the increase of false leaders and messiahs will lead astray the Christ-followers before the close of the present age. In 3 John one of the leaders in the community, Diotrephes, rejects the Johannine author's authority.

Finally, Christ-followers are in danger of committing apostasy through immoral behavior, whether practicing vices, assimilating to the beliefs of outsiders, or engaging in loveless behavior towards others. In Luke-Acts greed contributes to the downfall of Christ-followers such as Judas and Ananias and Sapphira. In John's community, assimilation with the "world" leads to alienation from God. In Matthew

Jesus' followers must be morally prepared for his second coming; they must avoid drunkenness and abusing others or they will face divine judgment when their Lord returns. In the story of the Sheep and Goats, the goats' failure to perform works of love results in divine punishment on judgment day. To violate the command of loving one's neighbor as oneself is to commit lawlessness. For the Johannine community, abiding in Jesus' command to love one another is central to abiding in communion with him; the alternative is to abide in death and apostasy.

The *consequences of apostasy* often anticipate a final judgment against apostates when Christ returns (Mark, Matthew, Johannine writings). Those who repudiate Christ, whether verbally or through their conduct, will not be recognized by Christ in the age to come. Their punishment is described as being cast into "fire" (Mark, Matthew, John) or "outer darkness" (Matthew), and those who know God's will but fail to do it will receive a greater judgment than those who do not know God's will (Luke). Temporal chastisement imposed on rebellious congregation members includes their expulsion from the community with the hope that such individuals would seek forgiveness and be restored (Matthew). The Prodigal Son in Luke's famous parable is restored to his father's house once again, and the audience of Acts is encouraged to pray for the restoration of people like Simon Magus (Acts). The Johannine writer encourages the community to pray for the restoration of those whose sin is not leading to death, but there is no incentive to pray for the apostate. Peter's denial of Jesus is coupled with remorse in the gospels, and he is restored in all the narratives, but in Mark's gospel he shares a hardened state with the other disciples, and their restoration is less pronounced. Differently, Luke plays down Peter and the disciples' abandonment from Jesus in the passion narrative.

Through our study of this body of literature a *comparative approach* to the subject of apostasy reveals some noticeable differences among the emergent Christian communities, as we have mentioned above. Several more are worth pondering.

First, in Matthew the crowd Jesus speaks to in parables is spiritually blind as an effect of their own doing rather than as a judgment from God (as in Mark and John). Moreover, the disciples of Jesus in Matthew maintain spiritual insight, and Jesus gives them special authority in spiritual matters. In Mark, similar to the crowd and Jesus' opponents, the disciples are callous. Their spiritual status in Matthew perhaps functions as a way of legitimizing the authority of Matthew's community leaders, whereas Mark's community learns that even Jesus' most intimate followers and family members can be obdurate and deny him. Such a thought instructs the auditors to examine themselves and seek restoration if they had denied Christ through recent persecutions.

Second, unlike Mark and Matthew, Luke's narratives play down the notion of falling away through persecution in an effort to portray Jesus and his apostles as heroic examples of perseverance. In Luke's version of the parable of the Sower, temptation rather than persecution becomes the cause of the second seed falling away, and perseverance is the preventative. An exception to this norm of mitigating spiritual danger behind persecution is seen by Luke's unique perspective of blaspheming the Holy Spirit (Luke 12). Jesus' opponents, the scribes and Pharisees, commit the unpardonable sin in Mark and Matthew, but in Luke the sin is committed by Christ-followers who renounce Christ despite divine assistance when being threatened by outsiders. Luke nonetheless presents a competing example of restoration for Peter who denied Christ during his arrest.

Third, although both Johannine and Matthean writers denounce false teachers, a distinctive aspect in the former is that the apostates have left the community but still might be influencing its members. The false prophets in Matthew, on the other hand, are imposters rather than defectors, and they might be playing an active role within the Christ community. The Johannine writer claims that the apostates primarily deny Jesus as the Christ; the false prophets in Matthew confess Jesus as the Christ, but their lawless living repudiates that confession.

The different communities of the gospels, and sometimes their opponents, confessed Jesus as the Christ even though they did not believe and practice the same things. Since we do not possess firsthand records from the opponents, we are dependent on the viewpoints of the gospel writers. For all we know, some of the opponents in these gospels might have considered themselves to be righteous in the sight of God and Christ, and from their perspective the gospel writers and their communities had become apostate. What we have in the gospels, Acts, and Johannine writings, then, is *perceived* apostasy. The apostate is identified as such by another group or person who is doing the labeling.

One final difference worth mentioning is Judas' apostasy and judgment. In Mark he is portrayed as a disciple that falls away, remains obdurate, and will finally be condemned by God. He is not the remorseful disciple that Matthew portrays but a recalcitrant individual. In Luke-Acts, he is a disciple who apostatizes, meets a gruesome death in a field, and his office must be replaced by another disciple because he has been excluded from God's kingdom. Likewise, he is possessed by Satan. For the Johannine author, Judas is a representative defector whose condemnation is sealed as the son of destruction. Judas was always a wolf among sheep. The very first time he appears in this gospel he is called a devil. We therefore perceive conflicting portraits of Judas: he is a bona fide follower of Christ who betrays him and falls away in Mark and Luke, and yet in John he is never truly a believer in the first place. He also dies two different deaths: one by a suicidal hanging as an apparent sign of his remorse (Matthew) and the other by having his entrails spilled out as an indication of divine punishment (Luke-Acts).

These snippets describing first-century emergent Christian congregations and their views of apostasy suggest that these communities did not all act, think, or believe alike. The authors maintain their own respective agendas in these gospels, and the writings reflect different situations encountered by the communities. We have noticed also some cultural, ethnic, and socioeconomic differences among the early Christ-followers. They come from diverse geographic settings, encounter unique challenges, and interpret the Mosaic Law differently. Exactly who becomes identified as an apostate seems relative to the respective Christ-community that is making the claim, and, due to the stigma and shame attached to such phenomena, it seems that few would care to remember accurate details about apostates among their members. In volumes 2 and 3 of this work we will continue pursuing the concept of apostasy as it relates to diversity among the New Testament communities.

Bibliography

Allison, Dale C. *The Intertextual Jesus: Scripture in Q.* Harrisburg, PA: Trinity, 2000.
———. "Was There a 'Lukan Community?'" *IBS* 10 (1988) 62–70.
Allison, Dale C., and W. D. Davies. *A Critical and Exegetical Commentary on the Gospel According to Saint Matthew.* 3 vols. ICC. London: T. & T. Clark, 1988–94.
Anderson, Bernhard W. "Exodus Typology in Second Isaiah." In *Israel's Prophetic Heritage: Essays in Honor of James Muilenburg,* edited by Bernhard W. Anderson and Walter Harrelson, 177–95. London: SCM, 1962.
Anderson, Paul N. "Antichristic Errors: Flawed Interpretations regarding the Johannine Antichrist." In *Text and Community: Essays in Memory of Bruce M. Metzger,* edited by J. Harold Ellens, 1.197–216. NTM 19. Sheffield: Sheffield Phoenix, 2007.
———. "Antichristic Errors: Proselytization Back into Jewish Religious Certainty—The Threat of Schismatic Abandonment." In *Text and Community: Essays in Memory of Bruce M. Metzger,* edited by J. Harold Ellens, 1.217–40. NTM 19. Sheffield: Sheffield Phoenix, 2007.
Ashton, John. *Understanding the Fourth Gospel.* Oxford: Clarendon, 1991.
Baird, J. Arthur. "A Pragmatic Approach to Parable Exegesis." *JBL* 76 (1957) 201–7.
Balch, David L., editor. *Social History of the Matthean Community: Cross-Disciplinary Approaches.* Minneapolis: Fortress, 1991.
Banks, R. J. *Jesus and the Law in the Synoptic Tradition.* SNTSMS 28. Cambridge: Cambridge University Press, 1975.
Barbour, John D. *Versions of Deconversion: Autobiography and the Loss of Faith.* SRC. Charlottesville: University of Virginia Press, 1994.
Barclay, John M. G. "Deviance and Apostasy: Some Applications of Deviance Theory to First-Century Christianity." In *Modelling Early Christianity: Social-Scientific Studies of the New Testament in Its Context,* edited by Philip F. Esler, 114–27. New York: Routledge, 1995.
———. "Paul among Diaspora Jews: Anomaly or Apostate?" *JSNT* 60 (1995) 89–120.
———. "Who Was Considered an Apostate in the Jewish Diaspora?" In *Tolerance and Intolerance in Early Judaism and Christianity,* edited by Graham N. Stanton and Guy G. Stroumsa, 80–98. Cambridge: Cambridge University Press, 1998.
Barclay, John M. G., and Simon J. Gathercole, editors. *Divine and Human Agency in Paul and His Cultural Environment.* LNTS 335. London: T. & T. Clark, 2006.
Bardy, Gustave. *La Conversion au Christianisme durant les Premiers Siècles.* Théologie 15. Paris: Aubier, 1949.

Bibliography

Barrett, C. K. *A Critical and Exegetical Commentary on the Acts of the Apostles*. 2 vols. ICC. Edinburgh: T. & T. Clark, 1994–98.

———. *The Gospel according to St. John: An Introduction with Commentary and Notes on the Greek Text*. 2nd ed. Philadelphia: Westminster, 1978.

———. "I Am Not Ashamed of the Gospel." In *Foi Et Salut Selon S. Paul (Épître Aux Romains 1,16)*, Markus Barth and C. K. Barrett et al., 19–50. AnBib 42. Rome: Pontifical Biblical Institute, 1970.

Barstad, Hans M. *A Way in the Wilderness: The Second Exodus in the Message of Second Isaiah*. JSSM 12. Manchester: University of Manchester Press, 1989.

Barth, Gerhard. "Matthew's Understanding of the Law." In *Tradition and Interpretation in Matthew*, Günther Bornkamm, Gerhand Barth, and Heinz Joachim Held, 58–164. NTL. London: SCM, 1963.

Barton, Stephen. "Can We Identify the Gospel Audiences?" In *The Gospels for All Christians: Rethinking the Gospel Audiences*, edited by Richard Bauckham, 173–94. Grand Rapids: Eerdmans, 1998.

Bass, Christopher D. *That You May Know: Assurance of Salvation in 1 John*. NAC Studies in Bible and Theology. Nashville: B. & H. Academic, 2008.

Bassler, Jouette M. "The Galileans: A Neglected Factor in Johannine Community Research." *CBQ* 43 (1981) 243–57.

Bauckham, Richard. "The Audience of the Fourth Gospel." In *Jesus in Johannine Tradition*, edited by Robert T. Fortna and Tom Thatcher, 100–111. Louisville: Westminster John Knox, 2001.

———. "For Whom Were Gospels Written?" In *The Gospel for All Christians: Rethinking the Gospel Audiences*, edited by Richard Bauckham, 9–48. Grand Rapids: Eerdmans, 1998.

———. "James and the Jerusalem Community." In *Jewish Believers in Jesus: The Early Centuries*, edited by Oskar Skarsaune and Reidar Hvalvik, 55–95. Peabody, MA: Hendrickson, 2007.

———. "The Parable of the Royal Wedding Feast (Matthew 22:1–14) and the Parable of the Lame Man and the Blind Man (Apocryphon of Ezekiel)." *JBL* 115 (1996) 471–88.

———. "The Parable of the Vine: Rediscovering a Lost Parable of Jesus." *NTS* 33 (1987) 84–101.

Bauder, W. "Fall, Fall Away." In *NIDNTT* 1.606–8.

Bauer, Walter. *Orthodoxy and Heresy in Earliest Christianity*. Philadelphia: Fortress, 1977.

Beale, G. K. "Isaiah VI 9–13: A Retributive Taunt against Idolatry." *VT* 41 (1991) 257–78.

Beardslee, William A. "Saving One's Life by Losing It." *JAAR* 47 (1979) 57–72.

Beasley-Murray, George Raymond. *John*. WBC 36. Nashville: T. Nelson, 1999.

———. "The *Parousia* in Mark." *RevExp* 75 (1978) 565–81.

Beavis, Mary Ann. *Mark's Audience: The Literary and Social Setting of Mark 4.11–12*. JSNTSup 33. Sheffield: JSOT Press, 1989.

Becker, Adam, and Annette Reed, editors. *The Ways That Never Parted: Jews and Christians in Late Antiquity and the Early Middle Ages*. Minneapolis: Fortress, 2007.

Berkouwer, G. C. *Faith and Perseverance*. Studies in Dogmatics. Grand Rapids: Eerdmans, 1958.

Bertram, Georg. "μωρός κτλ." In *TDNT* 4.831–47.

———. "στρέφω." In *TDNT* 7.713–29.

Best, Ernest. *Following Jesus: Discipleship in the Gospel of Mark*. JSNTSup 4. Sheffield: University of Sheffield, 1981.

Betz, Hans Dieter. *The Sermon on the Mount: A Commentary on the Sermon on the Mount, including the Sermon on the Plain (Matthew 5:3—7:27 and 6:20-49)*. Hermenia. Minneapolis: Fortress, 1995.

Beuken, W. A. M. "Servant and Herald of Good Tidings: Isaiah 61 as an Interpretation of Isaiah 40–55." In *The Book of Isaiah = Le Livre d'Isaïe: Les Oracles et Leurs Relectures Unité et Complexité de L'Ouvrage*, edited by Jacques Vermeylen, 411–41. BETL 81. Leuven: Leuven University Press, 1989.

Beutler, Johannes. *Die Johannesbriefe*. RNT. Regensburg: Pustet, 2000.

Bieringer, Reimund, D. Pollefeyt, and F. Vandecasteele-Vanneuville, editors. *Anti-Judaism and the Fourth Gospel*. Louisville: Westminster John Knox, 2001.

Bird, Michael F. "The Unity of Luke-Acts in Recent Discussion." *JSNT* 83 (2007) 425–48.

Black, C. Clifton. *Mark: Images of an Apostolic Interpreter*. SPNT. Columbia: University of South Carolina Press, 1994.

Black, Matthew. *An Aramaic Approach to the Gospels and Acts*. 3rd ed. Oxford: Clarendon, 1967.

Blank. J. *Krisis: Untersuchungen zur johanneischen Christologie und Eschatologie*. Freiburg: Lambertus, 1964.

Blinzler, Josef. "The Jewish Punishment of Stoning in the New Testament Period." In *The Trial of Jesus: Cambridge Studies in Honour of C. F. D. Moule*, edited by Ernst Bammel, 147–61. SBT 2/13. London: SCM, 1970.

Bock, Darrell L. *Acts*. BECNT. Grand Rapids: Baker Academic, 2007.

———. *Blasphemy and Exaltation in Judaism and the Final Examination of Jesus*. Tübingen: Mohr/Siebeck, 1998.

———. *Luke*. 3 vols. BECNT. Grand Rapids: Baker, 1994.

Bogart, John. *Orthodox and Heretical Perfectionism in the Johannine Community as Evident in the First Epistle of John*. SBLDS 33. Missoula, MT: Scholar, 1977.

Borchert, Gerald L. *Assurance and Warning*. Nashville: Broadman Press, 1987.

———. *John*. 2 vols. NAC 25A, B. Nashville: Broadman & Holman, 1996–2002.

Borgen, Peder. *Bread from Heaven: An Exegetical Study of the Concept of Manna in the Gospel of John and the Writings of Philo*. NovTSup 10. Leiden: Brill, 1965.

Borig, Rainer. *Der Wahre Weinstock: Untersuchungen zu Jo 15, 1-10*. SANT 16. Munich: Kösel, 1967.

Bornkamm, Günther. "The Authority to 'Bind' and 'Loose' in the Church in Matthew's Gospel: The Problem of Sources in Matthew's Gospel." In *Jesus and Man's Hope*, 37–50. A Perspective Book: A Festival on the Gospels. Pittsburg: Pittsburg Theological Seminary, 1970–71.

Boucher, Madeleine. *The Mysterious Parable: A Literary Study*. CBQMS 6. Washington: Catholic Biblical Association of America, 1977.

Bovon, François. "Il a bien parlé à vos pères, le Saint-Esprit, par le prophète Ésaïe (Actes 28:25)." In *L'oeuvre de Luc: Études d'exégèse et de théologie*, 145–53. LD 130. Paris: Cerf, 1987.

———. *Das Evangelium nach Lukas*. Vols. 3, 4. EKK 3. Zurich: Benziger, 2001, 2009.

———. *L'Évangile selon saint Luc*. Vols. 1, 2. CNT 3A, B. Geneva: Labor et Fides, 1991, 1996.

———. *Luke the Theologian: Fifty-Five Years of Research (1950–2005)*. 2nd ed. Waco, TX: Baylor University, 2006.

Bowker, J. W. "Mystery and Parable: Mark 4:1–20." *JTS* 25 (1974) 300–317.

Boyarin, Daniel. "Justin Martyr Invents Judaism." *CH* 70 (2001) 427–61.

Bibliography

Braun, Herbert. "πλανάω, πλανάομαι, ἀποπλανάω, ἀποπλανάομαι, πλάνη, πλάνος, πλανήτης, πλάνης." In *TDNT* 6.228–53.

Brawley, Robert L. *Luke-Acts and the Jews: Conflict, Apology, and Conciliation.* SBLMS 33. Atlanta: Scholars, 1987.

———. *Text to Text Pours Forth Speech: Voices of Scripture in Luke-Acts.* ISBL. Bloomington: Indiana University Press, 1995.

Breytenbach, Cilliers. "Identity and Rules of Conduct in Mark: Following the Suffering, Expecting the Coming of Son of Man." In *Identity, Ethics, and Ethos in the New Testament*, edited by Jan G. van der Watt and assisted by François S. Malan, 49–75. BZNW 141. Berlin: de Gruyter, 2006.

Brinkerhoff, Merlin B., and M. L. Mackie, "Casting off the Bond of Organized Religion: A Religious-Careers Approach to the Study of Apostasy." *RRelRes* 34 (1992) 235–53.

Brodie, Thomas L. *The Gospel according to John: A Literary and Theological Commentary.* New York: Oxford University Press, 1993.

———. "Luke 9:57–62: A Systematic Adaptation of the Divine Challenge to Elijah (1 Kings 19)." In *SBLSP 1989*, edited David J. Lull, 237–45. Atlanta: Scholars, 1989.

———. "Luke the Literary Interpreter: Luke-Acts as a Systematic Rewriting and Updating of the Elijah-Elisha Narrative." PhD diss., Pontifical University of St. Thomas Aquinas, Rome, 1981.

———. "Towards Unraveling the Rhetorical Imitation of Sources in Acts: 2 Kgs 5 as One Component of Acts 8,9–40." *Biblica* 67 (1986) 41–67.

Bromley, David G. "The Social Construction of Contested Exit Roles: Defectors, Whistleblowers, and Apostates." In *Falling from the Faith: Causes and Consequences of Religious Apostasy*, edited by Bromley, 19–47. SFE 95. Newbury Park, CA: Sage, 1988.

———, editor. *Falling from the Faith: Causes and Consequences of Religious Apostasy.* SFE 95. Newbury Park, CA: Sage, 1988.

———, editor. *The Politics of Religious Apostasy: The Role of Apostates in the Transformation of Religious Movements.* RelAT. Westport, CT: Praeger, 1998.

Brooke, Alan England. *A Critical and Exegetical Commentary on the Johannine Epistles.* ICC 43. Edinburgh: T. & T. Clark, 1912.

Brown, Nobel B. "The Concept of Apostasy in Jewish and Christian Apocalyptic." PhD diss., Southern Baptist Theological Seminary, 1963.

Brown, Raymond E. *The Community of the Beloved Disciple.* New York: Paulist, 1979.

———. *The Death of the Messiah: From Gethsemane to the Grave: A Commentary on the Passion Narrative.* 2 vols. ABRL. New York: Doubleday, 1994.

———. *The Epistles of John.* AB 30. Garden City, NY: Doubleday, 1982.

———. *The Gospel according to John.* AB 29, 29A. Garden City, NY: Doubleday, 1966–70.

———. *An Introduction to the New Testament.* ABRL. New York: Doubleday, 1997.

Brown, Schuyler. *Apostasy and Perseverance in the Theology of Luke.* AnBib. Rome: Pontifical Biblical Institute, 1969.

Bruce, F. F. *The Book of the Acts.* Rev. ed. NICNT. Grand Rapids: Eerdmans, 1988.

Büchsel, Friedrich. "δέω." In *TDNT* 2.60–61.

Bultmann, Rudolf. *Die Drei Johannesbriefe.* KEK 14. Göttingen: Vandenhoeck & Ruprecht, 1969.

———. *The Gospel of John: A Commentary.* Translated by G. R. Beasley-Murray. Oxford: Blackwell, 1971.

———. *The Johannine Epistles: A Commentary on the Johannine Epistles*. Translated by R. Philip O'Hara with Lane C. McGaughy and Robert Funk, edited by Robert W. Funk. Hermenia. Philadelphia: Fortress, 1986.

———. *Theology of the New Testament*. Translated by Kendrick Grobel. 2 vols. New York: Schribner, 1951–55.

Burnet, Régis. *L'évangile de la trahison: Une biographie de Judas*. Paris: Seuil, 2008.

Burridge, Richard A. "About People, by People, for People: Gospel Genre and Audiences." In *The Gospel for All Christians: Rethinking the Gospel Audiences*, edited by Richard Bauckham, 113–45. Grand Rapids: Eerdmans, 1998.

———. *What Are the Gospels?: A Comparison with Graeco-Roman Biography*. SNTSMS 70. Cambridge: Cambridge University Press, 1992.

Carmignac, J. "Fais que nous n'entrions pas dans la tentation." *RB* 72 (1965) 218–26.

Carson, D. A. *Divine Sovereignty and Human Responsibility: Biblical Perspectives in Tension*. London: Marshall, Morgan & Scott, 1981.

———. *The Gospel according to John*. Grand Rapids: Eerdmans, 1991.

———. "Reflections on Christian Assurance." *WTJ* 54 (1992) 1–29.

Carter, Warren. *Matthew and the Margins: A Socio-Political and Religious Reading*. JSNTSup 204. Sheffield: Sheffield Academic, 2000.

———. *Matthew: Storyteller, Interpreter, Evangelist*. Peabody, MA: Hendrickson, 1996.

———. "Matthew's Gospel: Jewish Christianity, Christian Judaism, or Neither?" In *Jewish Christianity Reconsidered: Rethinking Ancient Groups and Texts*, edited by Matt Jackson-McCabe, 155–79. Minneapolis: Fortress, 2007.

Cassidy, Richard J. *Jesus, Politics, and Society: A Study of Luke's Gospel*. Maryknoll, NY: Orbis, 1978.

Celsor, Scott. "The Human Response in the Creation and Formation of Faith: A Narrative Analysis in John 12:20–50 and Its Application to the Doctrine of Justification." *HBT* 30 (2008) 115–35.

Cerfaux, Lucien. "Fructifiez en Supportant (l'éprouve) à propos de Luc 8,15." *RB* 64 (1957) 481–91.

Chalcraft, David J., editor. *Sectarianism in Early Judaism: Sociological Advances*. BibleWorld. London: Equinox, 2007.

Chennattu, Rekha M. "The Covenant Motif: A Key to the Interpretation of John 15–16." *Transcending Boundaries: Contemporary Readings of the New Testament: Essays in Honor of Francis J. Moloney*, edited by Rekha M. Chennattu and Mary L. Coloe, 141–59. BSR 187. Rome: LAS 2005.

Chenoweth, Ben. "Identifying the Talents Contextual Clues for the Interpretation of the Parable of the Talents (Matthew 25:14–30)." *TynBul* 56 (2005) 61–72.

Childs, Brevard S. *Isaiah*. OTL. Louisville: Westminster John Knox, 2001.

Chilton, Bruce. "Jews in the NT." In *ABD* 3.845–48.

Claybrook, Frederick W. *Once Saved, Always Saved?: A New Testament Study of Apostasy*. Lanham, MD: University Press of America, 2003.

Cohen, Shaye J. D. *The Beginning of Jewishness: Boundaries, Varieties, Uncertainties*. HCS 31. Berkeley: University of California Press, 1999.

———. "Crossing the Boundary and Becoming a Jew." *HTR* 82 (1989) 13–33.

———. "A Virgin Defiled: Some Rabbinic and Christian Views on the Origins of Heresy." *USQR* 36 (1980) 1–11.

Collins, Adela Yarbro. *Mark: A Commentary*. Hermeneia. Minneapolis: Fortress, 2007.

Bibliography

Collins, Raymond F. *Sexual Ethics and the New Testament: Behavior and Belief.* CompNT. New York: Crossroad, 2000.

Conzelmann, Hans. *Acts of the Apostles: A Commentary on the Acts of the Apostles.* Hermenia. Philadelphia: Fortress, 1987.

———. *The Theology of St. Luke.* Translated by Geoffrey Buswell. Philadelphia: Fortress, 1982.

Cosgrove, Charles H. "The Divine DEI in Luke-Acts: Investigations into the Lukan Understanding of God's Providence." *NovT* 26 (1984) 168–90.

Crossan, John Dominic. "Mark and the Relatives of Jesus." *NovT* 15 (1973) 81–113.

Cullmann, Oscar. *Prayer in the New Testament.* Translated by John Bowden. OBT. Minneapolis: Fortress, 1995.

Culpepper, R. Alan. *The Anatomy of the Fourth Gospel: A Study in Literary Design.* FF. Philadelphia: Fortress, 1983.

———. "Anti-Judaism in the Fourth Gospel as a Theological Problem for Christian Interpreters." In *Anti-Judaism and the Fourth Gospel*, 61–82. Louisville: Westminster John Knox, 2001.

———. *John, the Son of Zebedee: The Life of a Legend.* 2nd. ed. SPNT. Edinburgh: T. & T. Clark, 2000.

Culpepper, R. Alan, and Gail R. O'Day. *The Gospel of Luke, the Gospel of John.* NIB 9. Nashville: Abingdon, 1995.

Cunningham, S. *Through Many Tribulations: The Theology of Persecution in Luke-Acts.* JSNTSup 142. Sheffield: Sheffield Academic, 1997.

Daly-Denton, Margaret. "The Psalms in John's Gospel." In *The Psalms in the New Testament*, edited by Steve Moyise and Maarten J. J. Menken, 119–38. NTSI. London: T. & T. Clark, 2004.

Danker, Frederick W. *Luke.* PC. Philadelphia: Fortress, 1987.

Davies, W. D. *The Setting of the Sermon on the Mount.* Cambridge: Cambridge University Press, 1964.

Davis, John Jefferson. "The Perseverance of the Saints: A History of the Doctrine." *JETS* 34 (1991) 213–28.

Deines, Roland. *Die Gerechtigkeit der Tora im Reich des Messias: Mt 5,13–20 als Schlüsseltext der matthäischen Theologie.* WUNT 177. Tübingen: Mohr/Siebeck, 2005.

———. "Not the Law but the Messiah: Law and Righteousness in the Gospel of Matthew—An Ongoing Debate." In *Built upon the Rock: Studies in the Gospel of Matthew*, edited by Daniel M. Gurtner and John Nolland, 53–84. Grand Rapids: Eerdmans, 2008.

Delling, Gerhard. "τάσσω, etc." In *TDNT* 8.27–31.

Deming, Will. "Mark 9.42—10.12, Matthew 5.27–32, and *b. Nid.* 13b: A First Century Discussion of Male Sexuality." *NTS* 36 (1990) 130–44.

Derrett, J. Duncan M. "Ánanias, Sapphira, and the Right of Property." In *Studies in the New Testament*, 1.193–201. Leiden: Brill, 1977.

———. "Law in the New Testament: *Si scandalizaverit tem anus tua abscinde illam* (Mk. IX.42) and Comparative Legal History." In *Studies in the New Testament*, 1.4–31. Leiden: Brill, 1977.

———. "Simon Magus (Acts 8,9–24)." *ZNW* 73 (1982) 52–68.

deSilva, David A. "Exchanging Favor for Wrath: Apostasy in Hebrews and Patron-Client Relationships." *JBL* 115 (1996): 91–116.

———. "Hebrews 6:4–8: A Socio-Rhetorical Investigation." *TynBul* 50 (1999): 33–57, 225–35.

———. *An Introduction to the New Testament: Contexts, Methods & Ministry Formation.* Downers Grove, IL: InterVarsity, 2004.

Desjardins, Michel. "Bauer and Beyond: On Recent Scholarly Discussions of αἵρεσιν in the Early Christian Era." *SC* 8 (1991) 65–82.

Dinkler, Erich. "Jesu Wort vom Kreutztragen." In *Signum Crucis: Aufsätze zum Neuen Testament und zur christlichen Archäologie*, 77–98. Tübingen: Mohr/Siebeck, 1967.

Dobbeler, Stephanie von. "Auf der Grenze: Ethos und Identität der matthäishen Gemeinde nach Mt 15,1–20." *BZ*, n.s., 45 (2001) 55–79.

Dodd, C. H. *Parables of the Kingdom.* Rev. ed. London: Collins, 1961.

Domeris, William R. "The Confession of Peter According to John 6:69." *TynBul* 44.1 (1993) 155–67.

Donahue, John R., and Daniel J. Harrington. *The Gospel of Mark.* SP 2. Collegeville, MN: Liturgical, 2002.

Dov, Noy. "Apostasy." In *Encyclopaedia Judaica*, edited by Cecil Roth and Geoffrey Wigoder, 3.201–16. Jerusalem: Keter, 1972.

Draper, Jonathan A., editor. *The Didache in Modern Research.* AGJU 37. Leiden: Brill, 1996.

Duling, D. C. "Kingdom of God, Kingdom of Heaven." In *ABD* 4.49–69.

Dunn, James D. G. *The Acts of the Apostles.* EpC. Peterborough: Epworth, 1996.

———. "Prayer." In *DPL*, 621–22.

———. *The Parting of the Ways: Between Christianity and Judaism and Their Significance for the Character of Christianity.* London: SCM, 1991.

———. *Unity and Diversity in the New Testament: An Inquiry into the Character of Earliest Christianity.* 2nd ed. London: SCM, 1990.

Eakin, Frank E. "Spiritual Obduracy and Parable Purpose." In *The Use of The Old Testament in the New and Other Essays: Studies in Honor of William Franklin Stinespring*, edited by James M. Efird, 87–109. Durham, NC: Duke University Press, 1972.

Easton, Burton Scott. *The Gospel according to St. Luke: A Critical and Exegetical Commentary.* Edinburgh: T. & T. Clark, 1926.

Ehrman, Bart D. *The New Testament: A Historical Introduction to the Early Christian Writings.* 2nd ed. New York: Oxford University Press, 2000.

Ermoni, V. "Abjuration." In *Dictionnaire D'Archéologie Chrétienne et de Liturgie*, edited by Fernand Cabrol, 1.98–104. Paris: Letouzey et Ané, 1907.

Esler, Philip F. *Community and Gospel in Luke-Acts: The Social and Political Motivations of Lucan Theology.* SNTSMS 57. Cambridge: Cambridge University Press, 1987.

Eugen Drewermann. "Fürbitte für einen Verzweifelten." In *Judas, wer bist du?*, edited by R. Niemann, 29–43. Gütersloh: Gerd Mohn, 1991.

Evans, Craig A. "The Function of Isaiah 6:9–10 in Mark and John." *NovT* 24 (1982) 124–38.

———. "Is Luke's View of the Jewish Rejection of Jesus Anti-Semitic?" In *Reimaging the Death of the Lukan Jesus*, edited by Dennis D. Sylva, 29–56. AM, Theologie, 73. Frankfurt: Anton Hain, 1990.

———. "The Jewish Christian Gospel Tradition." In *Jewish Believers in Jesus: The Early Centuries*, edited by Oskar Skarsaune and Reidar Hvalvik, 240–77. Peabody, MA: Hendrickson, 2007.

———. *Mark 8:27—16:20.* WBC 34B. Dallas: Word, 2000.

Bibliography

———. *To See and Not Perceive: Isaiah 6.9–10 in Early Jewish and Christian Interpretation.* JSOTSup 64. Sheffield: Sheffield Academic, 1989.

Feldman, Louis H. *Jew and Gentile in the Ancient World: Attitudes and Interactions from Alexander to Justinian.* Princeton: Princeton University Press, 1993.

Feldmeier, Reinhard. *Der erste Brief des Petrus.* THKNT 15/1. Leipzig: Evangelische Verlagsanstalt, 2005.

Fitzmyer, Joseph A. *The Acts of the Apostles.* AB 31. New York: Doubleday, 1998.

———. "And Lead Us Not into Temptation." *Biblica* 84 (2003) 259–73.

———. *The Gospel according to Luke: A New Translation with Introduction and Commentary.* 2 vols. AB 28, 28A. Garden City, NY: Doubleday, 1981–85.

Foakes-Jackson, F. J. "Apostasy." In *Encyclopaedia of Religion and Ethics*, edited by J. Hastings, 1.623–25. Edinburgh: T. & T. Clark, 1908.

Forkman, Göran. *The Limits of the Religious Community: Expulsion from the Religious Community within the Qumran Sect, within Rabbinic Judaism, and within Primitive Christianity.* ConBNT 5. Lund: Gleerup, 1972.

France, R. T. *The Gospel of Mark: A Commentary on the Greek Text.* NIGTC. Grand Rapids: Eerdmans, 2002.

Francis, Leslie J., and Yaacov Julian Katz, editors. *Joining and Leaving Religion: Research Perspectives.* Leominster, UK: Gracewing, 2000.

Freed, Edwin D. "*Ego Eimi* in John 1:20 and 4:25." *CBQ* 41 (1979) 288–91.

———. *Old Testament Quotations in the Gospel of John.* NovTSup 11. Leiden: Brill, 1965.

Frenschkowski, Marco. „Galiläa oder Jerusalem? Die topographischen und politischen Hintergründe der Logienquelle." In *The Sayings Source Q and the Historical Jesus*, edited by A. Lindemann, 535–59. BETL 158. Leuven: Leuven University/Peeters, 2001.

Frend, W. H. C. *Martyrdom and Persecution in the Early Church: A Study of a Conflict from the Maccabees to Donatus.* Oxford: Blackwell, 1965.

Fuller, Reginald H. "The Son of Man: A Reconsideration." In *The Living Text: Essays in Honor of Ernest W. Saunders*, edited by Dennis E. Groh and Robert Jewett, 189–206. Lanham, MD: University Press of America, 1985.

Fusco, V. "Luke-Acts and the Future of Israel." *NovT* 38 (1996) 1–17.

Gale, Aaron M. *Redefining Ancient Borders: The Jewish Scribal Framework of Matthew's Gospel.* London: T. & T. Clark, 2005.

Gaventa, Beverly Roberts. *The Acts of the Apostles.* ANTC. Nashville: Abingdon, 2003.

Geldenhuys, Norval. *Commentary on the Gospel of Luke.* NICNT. Grand Rapids: Eerdmans, 1952.

George, Augustin. "La Conversion." In *Études sur l'Oeuvre de Luc*, 351–68. SB. Paris: Gabalda, 1978.

———. "Par le Doigt de Dieu (Lc 11,20)." In *Études sur l'Oeuvre de Luc*, 127–32. SB. Paris: Gabalda, 1978.

Gibbs, Jeffrey A. *Matthew 1:1—11:1.* Concordia Commentary. St. Louis: Concordia, 2006.

Giesen, H. "σκανδαλίζω *skandalizō* / σκάνδαλον, ου, τό *skandalon*." In *EDNT* 3.248–50.

Glasson, T. Francis. *Moses in the Fourth Gospel.* SBT 40. Naperville, IL: Allenson, 1963.

Gnilka, Joachim. *Johannesevangelium.* NechtB 1. Würzburg: Echter, 1983.

———. *Das Matthäusevangelium.* 2 vols. HKNT. Freiburg: Herder, 1986–88.

———. *Das Verstockung Israels: Isaias 6:9–10 in der Theologie der Synoptiker.* SANT 3. Munich: Kösel, 1961.

Goldingay, John. *Isaiah.* NIBCOT 13. Peabody, MA: Hendrickson, 2001.

Goodman, Martin. "The Function of the Minim in Early Rabbinic Judaism." In *Geschichte—Tradition—Reflexion: Festscrift für Martin Hengel zum 70. Geburtstag*, edited by Peter P. Schäfer, 1.501–10. Tübingen: Mohr/Siebeck, 1996.

———. *Mission and Conversion: Proselytizing in the Religious History of the Roman Empire*. Oxford: Clarendon, 1994.

Gosling, F. A. "Oh Judas! What Have You Done?" *EvQ* 71.2 (1999) 117–25.

Grant, Frederick C,. and Halford E. Luccock. *General Articles on the New Testament. Matthew. Mark*. IB 7. New York: Abingdon-Cokesbury, 1951.

Green, Joel B. *The Gospel of Luke*. NICNT. Grand Rapids: Eerdmans, 1997.

Gregg, Brian Han. *The Historical Jesus and the Final Judgment Sayings in Q*. WUNT 2/207. Tübingen: Mohr/Siebeck, 2006.

Grelot, Pierre. "Note sur Actes xiii, 47." *RechBib* (1981) 368–72.

Griffin, M. T. "Nero." In *ABD* 4.1076–81.

Griffith, Terry. "'The Jews Who Had Believed in Him'" (John 8:31) and the Motif of Apostasy in the Gospel of John." In *The Gospel of John and Christian Theology*, edited by Richard Bauckham and Carl Mosser, 183–92. Grand Rapids: Eerdmans, 2008.

———. *Keep Yourselves from Idols: A New Look at 1 John*. JSNTSup 233. Sheffield: Sheffield Academic, 2002.

———. "A Non-Polemical Reading of 1 John: Sin, Christology and the Limits of Johannine Christianity." *TynBul* 49 (1998) 253–76.

Guelich, Robert A. *Mark 1—8:26*. WBC 34A. Dallas: Word, 1989.

Guignebert, Charles. "'Les demi-chrétiens et leur place dans l'Eglise." *RHR* 88 (1923) 65–102.

Gundry, Robert H. *Mark: A Commentary on His Apology for the Cross*. Grand Rapids: Eerdmans, 1993.

———. *Matthew: A Commentary on His Handbook for a Mixed Church under Persecution*. 2nd ed. Grand Rapids: Eerdmans, 1995.

Haar, Stephen. *Simon Magus: The First Gnostic?* BNZW 119. Berlin: de Gruyter, 2003.

Hadaway, C. Kirk. "Five Types of Apostates." *UM* 9 (January 1992) 26–34.

Hadaway, C. Kirk, and Wade Clark Roof. "Apostasy in American Churches: Evidence from National Survey Data." In *Falling from the Faith: Causes and Consequences of Religious Apostasy*, edited by David G. Bromley, 29–46. SFE 95. Newbury Park, CA: Sage, 1988.

Haenchen, Ernst. *The Acts of the Apostles: A Commentary*. Translated by Bernard Noble and Gerald Shinn, updated by R. McL. Wilson. Philadelphia: Westminster, 1971.

———. *John: A Commentary on the Gospel of John*. Translated by Robert W. Funk, edited by Robert W. Funk with Ulrich Busse. Vol. 1. Hermeneia. Philadelphia: Fortress, 1984.

Hagner, Donald A. *Matthew*. 2 vols. WBC 33A, B. Dallas: Word, 1993–95.

———. "Matthew: Apostate, Reformer, Revolutionary?" *NTS* 49 (2003) 193–209.

———. "Matthew: Christian Judaism or Jewish Christianity?" In *The Face of the New Testament: A Survey of Recent Research*, edited by Scot McKnight and Grant R. Osborne, 263–82. Grand Rapids: Baker Academic, 2004.

Hanges, James C. Review of *Prädestination und Verstockung: Untersuchungen zur frühjüdischen, paulinischen und johanneischen Theologie* by Günter Röhser. *CRBR* 9 (1996) 262–64.

Hannah, D. D. "Isaiah within Judaism of the Second Temple Period." In *Isaiah in the New Testament*, edited by Steven Moyise and Maarten J. J. Menken, 22–27. The New Testament and the Scriptures of Israel. London: T. & T. Clark, 2005.

Bibliography

Hanson, Anthony Tyrrell. *The Prophetic Gospel: A Study of John and the Old Testament.* Edinburgh: T. & T. Clark, 1991.

Harner, Philip B. *What Are They Saying about the Catholic Epistles?* New York: Paulist, 2004.

Harrill, J. Albert. "Cannibalistic Language in the Fourth Gospel and Greco-Roman Polemics of Factionalism (John 6:52–66)." *JBL* 127 (2008) 133–58.

Hartman, Lars. *Prophecy Interpreted: The Formation of Some Jewish Apocalyptic Texts and of the Eschatological Discourse in Mark 13 Par.* ConBNT 1. Lund: Gleerup, 1966.

Harvey, A. E. "Forty Strokes Save One: Social Aspects of Judaizing and Apostasy." In *Alternative Approaches to New Testament Study*, edited by A. E. Harvey, 79–96. London: SPCK, 1985.

Hauck, Friedrich. "Παροιμία." In *TDNT* 5.854–56.

Hays, Richard B. *Echoes of Scripture in the Letters of Paul.* New Haven, CT: Yale University Press, 1989.

Heise, Jürgen. *Bleiben: Menein in den Johanneischen Schriften.* HUT 8. Tübingen: Mohr/Siebeck, 1967.

Hemer, Colin J. *The Book of Acts in the Setting of Hellenistic History.* Edited by Conrad H. Gempf. WUNT 49. Tübingen: Mohr/Siebeck, 1989.

Hengel, Martin. *The Johannine Question.* Philadelphia: Trinity, 1989.

Hill, Craig C. *Hellenists and Hebrews: Reappraising Division within the Earliest Church.* Minneapolis: Fortress, 1992.

———. "The Jerusalem Church." In *Jewish Christianity Reconsidered: Rethinking Ancient Groups and Texts*, edited by Matt Jackson-McCabe, 39–56. Minneapolis: Fortress, 2007.

Hill, David. "False Prophets and Charismatics: Structure and Interpretation in Matthew 7.15–23." *Biblica* 57 (1976) 327–48.

Hirschberg, Peter. "Jewish Believers in Asia Minor according to the Book of Revelation and the Gospel of John." In *Jewish Believers in Jesus: The Early Centuries*, edited by Oskar Skarsaune and Reidar Hvalvik, 217–40. Peabody, MA: Hendrickson, 2007.

Hofius, Otfried. "Erwählung und Bewahrung: Zur Auslegung von John 6,37." In *Johannesstudien: Untersuchungen zur Theologie des Vierten Evangeliums*, edited by Otfried Hofius and Hans-Christian Kammler, 81–86. WUNT 88. Tübingen: Mohr/Siebeck, 1996.

Hollenbach, B. "Lest They Should Turn and Be Forgiven: Irony." *BT* 34 (1983) 312–21.

Holz, T. *Untersuchengen über die alttestamentliche Zitate bei Lukas.* Berlin: Akademie-Verlag, 1968.

Hooker, Morna D. *The Gospel according to Saint Mark.* BNTC. Peabody, MA: Hendrickson, 1993.

Horbury, William. "The Benediction of the *minim* and Early Jewish-Christian Controversy." *JTS* 33 (1982) 19–61.

———. "Extirpation and Excommunication." *VT* 35 (1985) 13–38.

Horn, Friedrich Wilhelm. *Glaube und Handeln in der Theologie des Lukas.* Rev. ed. GTA 26. Göttingen: Vandenhoeck & Ruprecht, 1986.

Horn, Siegfried H. "The Divided Monarchy: The Kingdoms of Judah and Israel." Revised by P. Kyle McCarter. In *Ancient Israel: From Abraham to the Roman Destruction of the Temple*, edited by Hershel Shanks, 129–99. Rev. ed. Washington, DC: Biblical Archaeology Society, 1999.

Horrell, David G. "The Label Χριστιανός: 1 Pet. 4:16 and the Formation of Christian Identity." *JBL* 126.2 (2007) 361–81.

Hultgren, A. J. *The Parables of Jesus: A Commentary.* BIW. Grand Rapids: Eerdmans, 2000.

Humbert, Alphonse. "Essai d'une théologie du scandale dans les Synoptiques." *Biblica* 35 (1954) 1–28.

Hunsberger, Bruce. "Apostasy: A Social Learning Perspective." *RRelRes* 25 (1983) 21–38.

———. "A Reexamination of the Antecedents of Apostasy." *RRelRes* 21 (1980) 158–70.

Iersel, Bas M. F. van. "Failed Followers in Mark: Mark 13:12 as a Key for the Identification of the Intended Readers." *CBQ* 58 (1996) 244–63.

———. "Het begrip σκάνδαλον κτλ in het Nieuwe Testament." *VoxT* 35 (1965) 33–41.

Incigneri, Brian J. *The Gospel to the Romans: The Setting and Rhetoric of Mark's Gospel.* BIS 65. Leiden: Brill, 2003.

Jackson-McCabe, Matt. "What's in a Name? The Problem of 'Jewish Christianity.'" In *Jewish Christianity Reconsidered: Rethinking Ancient Groups and Texts*, edited by Matt Jackson-McCabe, 7–38. Minneapolis: Fortress, 2007.

Jacobs, Janet Liebman. *Divine Disenchantment: Deconverting from New Religions.* Bloomington: Indiana University Press, 1989.

Jaubert, Anne. "L'image de la Vigne (Jean 15)." In *Oikonomia: Heilsgeschichte als Thema der Theologie: Festschrift für Oscar Cullmann*, edited by Felix Christ, 93–99. Hamburg: H. Reich, 1967.

Jefford, C. N. "Mark, John." In *ABD* 4.557–58.

Jeremias, Joachim. *New Testament Theology.* Translated by John Bowden. New York: Scribner, 1988.

———. *The Parables of Jesus.* Translated by S. H. Hooke. 2nd rev. ed. London: SCM, 1972.

———. "πολλοί." In *TDNT* 6.536–45.

———. *The Prayers of Jesus.* SBT 2/6. London: SCM, 1967.

Jervell, Jacob. *Die Apostelgeschichte.* KEK 3. Göttingen: Vandenhoeck & Ruprecht, 1998.

———. *Luke and the People of God: A New Look at Luke-Acts.* Minneapolis: Augsburg, 1972.

———. "Paulus—Der Lehrer Israels: Zu den apologetischen Paulusreden in der Apostelgeschichte." *NovT* 9 (1967–68) 164–90.

Jindra, Ines Wenger. *Konversion und Stufentransformation: Ein kompliziertes Verhältnis.* Munich: Waxmann Münster 2005.

Johnson, Luke Timothy. *The Gospel of Luke.* SP 3. Collegeville, MN: Liturgical, 1991.

———. "On Finding the Lukan Community: A Cautious Cautionary Essay." In *SBLSP 1979*, 1.87–100. Missoula, MT: Scholars, 1979.

Jossa, Giorgio. *Jews or Christians? The Followers of Jesus in Search of Their Own Identity.* WUNT 202. Tübingen: Mohr/Siebeck, 2006.

Jung, Chang Wook. "Main Thrust of the Sentence(s) in 1 John 3:19–20: Encouragement or Warning?" *Neot* 41 (2007) 97–111.

Käsemann, Ernst. "Ketzer und Zuege." *ZTK* 48 (1951) 292–311.

Kaufman, Stephen A., editor-in-chief. *Targum Lexicon: A Lexicon to the Aramaic Versions of the Hebrew Scriptures from the Files of the Comprehensive Aramaic Lexicon Project* (CAL). Cincinnati: Hebrew Union College, Jewish Institute of Religion, 2004.

Keener, Craig S. *A Commentary on the Gospel of Matthew.* Grand Rapids: Eerdmans, 1999.

———. *The Gospel of John: A Commentary.* 2 vols. Peabody, MA: Hendrickson, 2003.

Kelber, Werner H. *The Kingdom in Mark: A New Place and a New Time.* Philadelphia: Fortress, 1974.

———. *Mark's Story of Jesus.* Philadelphia: Fortress, 1979.

Bibliography

———. *The Oral and the Written Gospel: The Hermeneutics of Speaking and Writing in the Synoptic Tradition, Mark, Paul, and Q.* Philadelphia: Fortress, 1983.

Kellenberger, Edgar. "Heil und Verstockung: Zu Jes 6,9f. bei Jesaja und im Neuen Testament." *TZ* 48.2 (1992) 268–75.

Killgallen, John J. "Persecution in the Acts of the Apostles." In *Luke and Acts*, edited by Gerald O'Collins and Gilberto Marconi, translated by Matthew J. O'Connell, 143–160, 245–50. New York: Paulist, 1991.

Kim, Dongsu. *An Exegesis of Apostasy Embedded in John's Narratives of Peter and Judas against the Synoptic Parallels.* SBEC 61. Lewiston: Mellen, 2004.

Kimelman, R. "*Birkat Ha-Minim* and the Lack of Evidence for an Anti-Christian Jewish Prayer in Late Antiquity." In *Jewish and Christian Self-Definition*, edited by E. P. Sanders, 2.226–44. Philadelphia: Fortress, 1981.

Kingsbury, Jack Dean. "Conclusion: Analysis of a Conversation." In *Social History of the Matthean Community: Cross-Disciplinary Approaches*, edited by David L. Balch, 259–69. Minneapolis: Fortress, 1991.

———. *Conflict in Mark: Jesus, Authorities, Disciples.* Minneapolis: Fortress, 1989.

———. *Matthew as Story.* Rev. ed. Philadelphia: Fortress, 1988.

———. *The Parables of Jesus in Matthew 13: A Study in Redaction-Criticism.* London: SPCK, 1969.

———. "The Rhetoric of Comprehension in the Gospel of Matthew." *NTS* 41 (1995) 358–77.

Kippenberg, H. G. "Apostasy." In *The Encyclopedia of Religion*, edited by Mircea Eliade, 1.353–56. New York: Simon & Schuster, 1995.

Klassen, William. "The Authenticity of Judas' Participation in the Arrest of Jesus." In *Authenticating the Activities of Jesus*, edited by Bruce Chilton and Craig A. Evans, 389–410. NTTS 28/2. Leiden: Brill, 2002.

———. *Judas: Betrayer or Friend of Jesus?* Minneapolis: Fortress, 1996.

Klauck, Hans-Josef. *Die Johannesbriefe.* EdF 276. Darmstadt: Wissenschaftliche Buchgesellschaft, 1995.

Klein, William W. *The New Chosen People: A Corporate View of Election.* Grand Rapids: Zondervan, 1990.

Klink, Edward W. "Expulsion from the Synagogue? Rethinking a Johannine Anachronism." *TynBul* 59 (2008) 99–118.

———. "The Gospel Community Debate: State of the Question." *CBR* 3 (2004) 60–85.

———. *The Sheep of the Fold: The Audience and Origin of the Gospel of John.* SNTSMS 144. Cambridge: Cambridge University Press 2007.

Kloppenborg, John S. *Excavating Q: The History and Setting of the Sayings Gospel.* Minneapolis: Fortress, 2000.

Koet, Bart J. "Isaiah in Luke-Acts." In *Isaiah in the New Testament*, edited by Steve Moyise and Maarten J. J. Menken, 79–100. NTSI. London: T. & T. Clark, 2005.

———. "Paul in Rome (Acts 28,16–31): A Farewell to Judaism?" *Bijdragen* 48 (1987) 397–415.

Köstenberger, Andreas J. "John." In *CNTOT*, 415–512.

———. *John.* BECNT. Grand Rapids: Baker, 2004.

Kowalski, Beate. *Die Hirtenrede (Joh 10,1–18) im Kontext des Johannesevangeliums.* SBB 31. Stuttgart: Katholisches Bibelwerk, 1996.

Kubo, Sakae. "1 John 3:9: Absolute or Habitual?" *AUSS* 7 (1969) 47–56.

Kühschelm, Roman. *Verstockung, Gericht une Heil: Exegetische und bibeltheologische Untersuchungen zum sogenannten <<Dualismus>> und <<Determinismus>> in Joh 12,35-50*. BBB 76. Frankfurt: M. Anton Hain, 1990.

Kysar, Robert. "Anti-Semitism and the Gospel of John." In *Anti-Semitism and Early Christianity: Issues of Polemic and Faith*, edited by Craig A. Evans and Donald A. Hagner, 113-27. Minneapolis: Fortress, 1993.

———. "The Dismantling of Decisional Faith: A Reading of John 6:25-71." In *Critical Readings of John 6*, edited by R. Alan Culpepper, 161-81. BIS 22. Leiden: Brill, 1997.

———. *John: The Maverick Gospel*. Atlanta: John Knox, 1976.

———. Review of *Der Wahre Weinstock*, by Rainer Borig. *JBL* 89 (1970) 259-60.

Lake, Kirsopp, translator. *Eusebius: The Ecclesiastical History*. LCL. Cambridge, MA: Harvard University Press, 1926-32.

Lambrecht, Jan. "A Note on Mark 8.38 and Q 12.8-9." *JSNT* 85 (2002) 117-25.

———. "Relatives of Jesus in Mark." *NovT* 16 (1974) 241-58.

Lampe, G. W. H. "'Grievous Wolves' (Acts 20:29)." In *Christ and Spirit in the New Testament*, edited by Barnabas Lindars, Stephen S. Smalley, and C. F. D. Moule, 253-68. Cambridge: Cambridge University Press, 1973.

———. "St. Peter's Denial and the Treatment of the Lapsi." In *The Heritage of the Early Church: Essays In Honor of Georges Vasilievich Florovsky on the Occasion of His Eightieth Birthday*, edited by David Neiman and Margaret A. Schatkin, 113-33. OrChrAn 195. Rome: Pontifical Institutum Studiorum Orientalium, 1973.

Lampe, P. "ἵνα." In *EDNT* 2.188-89.

Lane, William L. *The Gospel according to Mark*. NICNT. Grand Rapids: Eerdmans, 1974.

Lange, Armin. *Weisheit und Prädestination und den Textfunden von Qumran*. STDJ. Leiden: Brill, 1996.

Law, Robert. *The Tests of Life: A Study of the First Epistle of St. John*. Kerr Lectures 1909. Edinburgh: T. & T. Clark, 1909.

Lehnert, Volker A. *Die Provokation Israels: Die paradoxe Funktion von Jes 6,9-10 bei Markus und Lukas: Ein textpragmatischer Versuch im Kontext gegenwärtiger Rezeptionsästhetik und Lesetheorie*. NTDH 25. Neukirchen-Vluyn: Neukirchener, 1999.

Leroy, Herbert. *Rätsel und Missverständnis; ein Beitrag zur Formgeschichte des Johannesevangeliums*. BBB 30. Bonn: P. Hanstein, 1968.

Lieu, Judith M. "Blindness in the Johannine Tradition." *NTS* 34 (1988) 83-95.

———. *The Theology of the Johannine Epistles*. NTTh. Cambridge: Cambridge University Press, 1991.

———. "What Was from the Beginning: Scripture and Tradition in the Johannine Epistles." *NTS* 39 (1993) 458-77.

Litwak, Kenneth Duncan. *Echoes of Scripture in Luke-Acts: Telling the History of God's People Intertextually*. JSNTSup 282. London: T. & T. Clark, 2005.

Lohfink, Gerhard. "Der präexistente Heilsplan." In *Neues Testament und Ethik: Für Rudolf Schnackenburg zum 75*, edited by Helmut Merklein, 110-33. Freiburg: Herder, 1989.

Lohmeyer, Ernst. *Das Evangelium des Markus*. KEK. Göttingen: Vandenhoeck & Ruprecht, 1967.

Löverstam, Evald. *Spiritual Wakefulness in the New Testament*. Translated by W. F. Salisbury. LUÅ, n.f., avd. 1, bd. 55, nr. 3. Lund: Gleerup, 1963.

Luz, Ulrich. "Die Jünger im Matthäusevangelium, *ZNW* 62 (1971) 141-71.

Bibliography

———. *Matthew: A Commentary*. Translated by James E. Crouch, edited by Helmut Koester. 3 vols. Hermeneia. Minneapolis: Fortress, 2001-7.

Maccoby, Hyam. *Judas Iscariot and the Myth of Jewish Evil*. New York: Macmillan, 1992.

Maddox, Robert L. *The Purpose of Luke-Acts*. SNTW. Edinburgh: T. & T. Clark, 1985.

Malatesta, Edward. *Interiority and Covenant: A Study of εἶναι ἐν and μένειν ἐν in the First Letter of Saint John*. AnBib 69. Rome: Pontifical Biblical Institute, 1978.

Malherbe, Abraham J. "The Inhospitality of Diotrophes." In *God's Christ and His People: Studies in Honour of Nils Alstrup Dahl*, edited by Jacob Jervell and Wayne A. Meeks, 222-32. Oslo: Universitetsforlaget, 1977.

Malina, Bruce J., and Jerome H. Neyrey. "Conflict in Luke-Acts: Labeling and Deviance Theory." In *The Social World of Luke-Acts: Models for Interpretation*, edited by Jerome H. Neyrey, 97-122. Peabody, MA: Hendrickson, 1991.

Malina, Bruce J., and Richard L. Rohrbaugh. *Social-Science Commentary on the Synoptic Gospels*. 2nd ed. Minneapolis: Fortress, 2003.

Manson, T. W. *The Sayings of Jesus: As Recorded in the Gospels according to St. Matthew and St. Luke*. London: SCM, 1950.

———. *The Teachings of Jesus: Studies of Its Form and Content*. Cambridge: Cambridge University Press, 1935.

Marcus, Joel. *Mark: A New Translation with Introduction and Commentary*. 2 vols. AB 27, 27A. New York: Doubleday, 2000-2009.

Marguerat, Daniel. "The Enigma of the Silent Closing of Acts (28:16-31)." In *Jesus and the Heritage of Israel: Luke's Narrative Claim upon Israel's Legacy*, edited by David P. Moessner, 284-304. LIntI 1. Harrisburg, PA: Trinity, 1999.

———. "La Mort d'Ananias et Saphira (Ac 5.1-11) dans la Stratégie Narrative de Luc." *NTS* 39 (1993) 209-26.

Marshall, I. Howard. "Acts." In *CNTOT*, 513-606.

———. *The Acts of the Apostles: An Introduction and Commentary*. TNTC. Grand Rapids: Eerdmans, 1980.

———. *The Gospel of Luke: A Commentary on the Greek Text*. NIGTC. Exeter, UK: Paternoster, 1978.

———. *Kept by the Power of God: A Study of Perseverance and Falling Away*. 3rd ed. LES. Carlisle: Paternoster, 1995.

———. *Luke: Historian and Theologian*. CEPBT. Grand Rapids: Zondervan, 1970.

Martin-Achard, Robert. "Sagesse de Dieu et sagesse humaine chez Ésaie." In *Maqqél Shâqédh: La branche d'amandier. Hommage à W. Vischer*, edited by W. Vischer, S. Amsler, et al., 137-44. Montpellier: Causse Graille Castelnau, 1960.

Martyn, J. Louis. *History and Theology in the Fourth Gospel*. 2nd ed. Nashville: Abingdon, 1979.

Marxsen, Willi. *Mark the Evangelist: Studies on the Redaction History of the Gospel*. Translated by J. Boyce et al. Nashville: Abingdon, 1969.

Mateos, Juan. "Análisis semántico de los lexemas ΣΚΑΝΔΑΛΙΖΩ ΣΚΑΝΔΑΛΟΝ." *FN* 2 (1989) 57-92.

Matera, Frank. *What Are They Saying about Mark?* New York: Paulist, 1987.

McGrath, James F. *John's Apologetic Christology: Legitimation and Development in Johannine Christology*. SNTSMS 111. Cambridge: Cambridge University Press, 2008.

McKnight, Scot. *A Light among the Gentiles: Jewish Missionary Activity in the Second Temple Period*. Minneapolis: Fortress, 1991.

———. "Matthean Community." In *DLNT*, 724–25.
McKnight, Scot, and Hauna Ondrey. *Finding Faith, Losing Faith: Stories of Conversion and Apostasy*. Waco, TX: Baylor University Press, 2008.
McLaughlin, John L. "Their Hearts Were Hardened: The Use of Isaiah 6,9–10 in the Book of Isaiah." *Biblica* 75.1 (1994) 1–25.
Meadors, Edward P. *Idolatry and the Hardening of the Heart: A Study in Biblical Theology*. London: T. & T. Clark, 2006.
Meeks, Wayne A. "The Man from Heaven in Johannine Sectarianism." *JBL* 91 (1972) 44–72.
———. "Simon Magus in Recent Research," *RelSRev* 3.3 (1977) 137–42.
Meier, John P. *A Marginal Jew: Rethinking the Historical Jesus*. 3 vols. ABRL. New York: Doubleday, 1991–2001.
———. "Matthew, Gospel of." In *ABD* 3.623–40.
Menken, Martinus J. J. "The Old Testament Quotation in John 6,45: Source and Redaction." *ETL* 64 (1988) 164–72.
———. *Old Testament Quotations in the Fourth Gospel: Studies in Textual Form*. CBET 15. Kampen: Kok Pharos, 1996.
Menzies, Robert P. *Empowered for Witness: The Spirit in Luke-Acts*. JPSSS 6. Sheffield: Sheffield Academic, 1994.
Merrill, Eugene. *Qumran and Predestination: A Theological Study of the Thanksgiving Hymns*. STDJ 8. Leiden: Brill, 1975.
Merwe, Dirk G. van der. "'A Matter of Having Fellowship': Ethics in the Johannine Epistles." In *Identity, Ethics, and Ethos in the New Testament*, edited by Jan G. Van der Watt and assisted by François S. Malan, 535–63. BZNW 141. Berlin: de Gruyter, 2006.
Metzger, Bruce M. *A Textual Commentary on the Greek New Testament*. 2nd ed. Stuttgart: Deutsche Bibelgesellschaft/United Bible Societies, 1994.
Meyer, Ben F. "Many (=All) Are Called, but Few (=Not All) Are Chosen." *NTS* 36 (1990) 89–97.
Michaelis, W. "ὁδός." In *TDNT* 5.70–75.
Michaelis, Wilhelm. "πίπτω, πτῶμα, πτῶσις, ἐκπίπτω, καταπίπτω, παραπίπτω, παράπτωμα, περιπίπτω." In *TDNT* 1.161–73.
Milikowsky, C. 1988. "Which Gehenna? Retribution and Eschatology in the Synoptic Gospels and in Early Jewish Texts." *NTS* 34 (1988) 238–49.
Mitchell, Margaret M. "Patristic Counter-Evidence to the Claim that 'The Gospels Were Written for All Christians.'" *NTS* 51 (2005) 36–79.
Moloney, Francis J. *The Gospel of John*. Edited by Daniel J. Harrington. SP 4. Collegeville, MN: Liturgical, 1998.
Moore, George Foot. *Judaism in the First Centuries of the Christian Era: The Age of the Tannaim*. 2 vols. Cambridge, MA: Harvard University Press, 1966.
Motyer, Stephen. *Your Father the Devil?: A New Approach to John and "the Jews."* PBTM. Carlisle: Paternoster, 1997.
Moyise Steve, and Maarten J. J. Menken, editors. *Isaiah in the New Testament*. NTSI. London: T. & T. Clark, 2005.
Myllykoski, Matti. "James the Just in History and Tradition: Perspectives of Past and Present Scholarship (Part 1)." *CBR* 5 (2006) 73–122.
Nanos, Mark D. "Paul's *Reversal* of Jews Calling Gentiles 'Dogs' (Philippians 3:2): 1600 Years of an Ideological Tale Wagging an Exegetical Dog?" January 17, 2008. Online: http://www.marknanos.com/Phil3Dogs-Reverse-1-17-08.pdf.

Bibliography

Neusner, Jacob, translator. *The Mishnah: A New Translation*. New Haven, CT: Yale University Press, 1988.

Newman, Barclay Moon, and Eugene Albert Nida. *A Handbook on the Acts of the Apostles*. UBS Handbook Series. New York: United Bible Societies, 1993.

Neyrey, Jerome H. *Honor and Shame in the Gospel of Matthew*. Louisville: Westminster John Knox, 1998.

———. *An Ideology of Revolt: John's Christology in Social-Science Perspective*. Philadelphia: Fortress, 1988.

———. "The Symbolic Universe of Luke-Acts: 'They Turn the World Upside Down.'" In *The Social World of Luke-Acts: Models for Interpretation*, edited by Jerome H. Neyrey, 271–304. Peabody, MA: Hendrickson, 1991.

Nolland, John. *The Gospel of Matthew: A Commentary on the Greek Text*. NIGTC. Grand Rapids: Eerdmans, 2005.

———. *Luke*. 3 vols. WBC 35A, B, C. Dallas: Word, 1989–93.

O'Toole, Robert F. "'You Did Not Lie to Us (Human Beings) but to God' (Acts 5,4c)." *Biblica* 76 (1995) 182–209.

Obermann, Andreas. *Die christologische Erfüllung der Scrift im Johannesevangelium: Eine Untersuchung zur johanneischen Hermeneutik anhand der Schriftzitate*. WUNT 2/83. Tübingen: Mohr/Siebeck, 1996.

Oepke, Albrecht. "ἀπόλλυμι, ἀπώλεια, Ἀπολλύων." In *TDNT* 1.394–97.

———. ἐξίστημι." In *TDNT* 2.459–60.

Oropeza, B. J. "Apostasy in the Wilderness: Paul's Message to the Corinthians in a State of Eschatological Liminality." *JSNT* 75 (1999) 69–86.

———. "Echoes of Isaiah in the Rhetoric of Paul: New Exodus, Wisdom, and the Humility of the Cross in Utopian-Apocalyptic Expectations." In *The Intertexture of Apocalyptic Discourse in the New Testament*, edited by Duane F. Watson, 87–112. SBLSS 14. Atlanta: Scholars, 2002.

———. "Judas' Death and Final Destiny in the Gospels and Earliest Christian Writings." *Neot* (forthcoming).

———. *Paul and Apostasy: Eschatology, Perseverance, and Falling Away in the Corinthian Congregation*. WUNT 2/115. Tübingen: Mohr/Siebeck, 2000. 2nd ed.: Eugene, OR: Wipf & Stock, 2007.

———. "What Is Sex? Christians and Erotic Boundaries." In *Religion and Sexuality: Passionate Debates*, edited by C. K. Robertson, 27–63. New York: P. Lang, 2006.

Overman, J. Andrew. *Matthew's Gospel and Formative Judaism: The Social World of the Matthean Community*. Minneapolis: Fortress, 1990.

Paffenroth, Kim. "The Stories of the Fate of Judas and Differing Attitudes toward Sources." *Proceedings* 12 (1992) 67–81.

Paget, James Carleton. "Definition of the Terms Jewish Christian and Jewish Christianity in the History of Research." In *Jewish Believers in Jesus: The Early Centuries*, edited by Oskar Skarsaune and Reidar Hvalvik, 22–52. Peabody, MA: Hendrickson, 2007.

Painter, John. *1, 2, and 3 John*. Collegeville, MN: Liturgical, 2002.

———. "Monotheism and Dualism Reconsidering Predestination in John 12:40." In *Transcending Boundaries: Contemporary Readings of the New Testament: Essays in Honor of Francis J. Moloney*, edited by Rekha M. Chennattu and Mary L. Coloe, 119–39. BSR 187. Rome: LAS, 2005.

———. "The 'Opponents' in 1 John." *NTS* 32 (1986) 48–71.

———. *The Quest for the Messiah: The History, Literature and Theology of the Johannine Community*. Nashville: Abingdon, 1993.

Pancaro, Severino. *The Law in the Fourth Gospel: The Torah and the Gospel, Moses and Jesus, Judaism and Christianity according to John*. NovTSup 42. Leiden: Brill, 1975.

Pao, David W. *Acts and the Isaianic New Exodus*. WUNT 2/130. Tübingen: Mohr/Siebeck, 2000.

Partridge, Christopher, and Helen Reid, editors. *Finding and Losing Faith: Studies in Conversion*. Milton Keynes: Paternoster, 2006.

Pearson, Birger A. "A Q Community in Galilee?" *NTS* 50 (2004) 476–94.

Parsons, Mikeal C., and Richard I. Pervo. *Rethinking the Unity of Luke-Acts*. Minneapolis: Fortress, 1993.

Pesch, Rudolf. *Das Markusevangelium*. HTKNT 2/1–2. Freiburg: Herder, 1977.

———. *Die Apostelgeschichte*. EKK 8/2. Zürich: Benziger, 1986.

Pesch, Wilhelm. *Matthäus als Seelsorger*. SBS 2. Stuttgart: Katholisches Bibelwerk, 1966.

Peterson, Dwight N. *The Origins of Mark: The Marcan Community in Current Debate*. BIS 48. Leiden: Brill, 2000.

Peterson, Robert A. "Perseverance and Apostasy: A Bibliographic Essay." *Presbyterion* 16 (1990) 119–25.

Phillips, Gary A. "History and Text: The Reader in Context in Matthew's Parables Discourse." *Semeia* 31 (1985) 111–38.

Pietersen, Lloyd. "Despicable Deviants: Labeling Theory and the Polemic of the Pastorals." *SocR* 58 (1997) 343–52.

Pilgrim, Walter E. *Good News to the Poor: Wealth and Poverty in Luke-Acts*. Minneapolis: Augsburg, 1981.

Polhill, John B. *Acts*. NAC 26. Nashville: Broadman, 1992.

Porter, Stanley E. "Mt 6:13 and Lk 11:4: 'Lead Us Not into Temptation.'" *ExpTim* 101 (1989–90) 359–62.

———. *Paul in Acts*. Peabody, MA: Hendrickson, 1999.

Powell, Mark Allan. *What Are They Saying about Acts?* New York: Paulist, 1989.

———. *What Are They Saying about Luke?* New York: Paulist, 1989.

Preston, J. J. "Expulsion" In *The Encyclopedia of Religion*, edited by Mircea Eliade, 5.233. New York: Simon & Schuster, 1995.

Rad, Gerhard von. *Old Testament Theology*. Translated by D. M. G. Stalker. 2 vols. New York: Harper, 1962–65.

Räisänen, Heiki. *The Idea of Divine Hardening: A Comparative Study of the Notion of Divine Hardening, Leading Astray, and Inciting to Evil the Bible and the Qur'an*. PFES 25. Helsinki: Finnish Exegetical Society, 1976.

Rapske, Brian. "Opposition to the Plan of God and Persecution." In *Witness to the Gospel: The Theology of Acts*, edited by I. Howard Marshall and David Peterson, 235–56. Grand Rapids: Eerdmans, 1998.

Rebell, Walter. "'Sein Leben Verlieren' (Mark 8.35 Parr.) Als Strukturmoment Vor- und Nachösterlichen Glaubens." *NTS* 35 (1989) 202–18.

Reim, G. *Studien zum altestamentlichen Hintergrund des Johannesevangelims*. SNTSMS 22. Cambridge: Cambridge University Press, 1974.

Reinhartz, Adelle. "The Johannine Community and Its Jewish Neighbors: A Reappraisal." In *What Is John?*, edited by Fernando F. Segovia, 2.111–38. SBLSymS 7. Atlanta: Scholars, 1998.

Bibliography

Rensberger, David. "Anti-Judaism and the Gospel of John." In *Anti-Judaism and the Gospels*, edited by William R. Farmer, 120–57. Harrisburg, PA: Trinity, 1999.

Rhoads, David M. *Reading Mark: Engaging the Gospel.* Minneapolis: Fortress, 2004.

Rhoads, David M., Joanna Dewey, and Donald Michie. *Mark as Story: An Introduction to the Narrative of a Gospel.* 2nd ed. Minneapolis: Fortress, 1999.

Ridderbos, Herman N. *The Gospel of John: A Theological Commentary.* Translated by John Vriend. Grand Rapids: Eerdmans, 1997.

Robbins, Vernon K. *Exploring the Texture of Texts: A Guide to Socio-Rhetorical Interpretation.* Harrisburg, PA: Trinity, 1996.

———. *Jesus the Teacher: A Socio-Rhetorical Interpretation of Mark.* Minneapolis: Fortress, 1984.

———. *New Boundaries in Old Territory: Form and Social Rhetoric in Mark.* ESEC 3. New York: P. Lang, 1994.

———. "The Social Location of the Implied Author of Luke-Acts." In *The Social World of Luke-Acts: Models for Interpretation*, edited by Jerome H. Neyrey, 305–32. Peabody, MA: Hendrickson, 1991.

Robertson, A. T. *Word Pictures in the New Testament.* 6 vols. Nashville: Broadman, 1930.

Robinson, John A. T. "The Destination and Purpose of St. John's Gospel." *NTS* 6 (1960) 117–31.

Rohrbaugh, Richard L. "The Pre-Industrial City in Luke-Acts: Urban Social Relations." In *The Social World of Luke-Acts: Models for Interpretation*, edited by Jerome H. Neyrey, 125–49. Peabody, MA: Hendrickson, 1991.

Röhser, Günter. *Prädestination und Verstockung: Untersuchungen zur frühjüdischen, paulinischen und johanneischen Theologie.* TANZ 14. Tübingen: Francke, 1994.

Roskam, Hendrika N. *The Purpose of the Gospel of Mark in Its Historical and Social Context.* NovTSup 114. Leiden: Brill, 2004.

Rosscup, James E. *Abiding in Christ: Studies in John 15.* Grand Rapids: Zondervan, 1973. Reprint: Eugene, OR: Wipf and Stock, 2003.

Rothfuchs, Wilhelm. *Die Erfüllungszitate des Matthäus-Evangeliums: Eine biblisch-theologische Untersuchung.* BWANT 8. Stuttgart: W. Kohlhammer, 1969.

Russell, D. S. *The Method & Message of Jewish Apocalyptic, 200 BC–AD 100.* OTL. Philadelphia: Westminster, 1964.

Saldarini, Anthony J. *Matthew's Christian-Jewish Community.* CSJH. Chicago: University of Chicago, 1994.

———. *Pharisees, Scribes and Sadducees in Palestinian Society: A Sociological Approach.* BRS. Wilmington, DL: M. Glazier, 1988. Rev. ed.: Grand Rapids: Eerdmans, 2001.

Salevao, Iutisone. *Legitimation in the Letter to the Hebrews: The Construction and Maintenance of a Symbolic Universe.* JSNTSup 219. Sheffield: Sheffield Academic, 2002.

Sand, Alexander. *Das Gesetz und die Propheten: Untersuchungen zur Theologie des Evangeliums nacht Matthäus.* BU 11. Regensburg: Pustet, 1974.

Sanders, Jack T. *The Jews in Luke-Acts.* Philadelphia: Fortress, 1987.

Sandmel, Samuel. *Anti-Semitism in the New Testament?* Philadelphia: Fortress, 1978.

Sandt, Huub van de, editor. *Matthew and the Didache: Two Documents from the Sam Jewish-Christian Milieu?* Minneapolis: Fortress, 2005.

Sato, Yoshiaki. "Martyrdom and Apostasy." In *Eusebius, Christianity, and Judaism*, edited by Harold W. Attridge and Gohei Hata, 619–34. Detroit: Wayne State University Press, 1992.

Sawyer, John F. A. *The Fifth Gospel: Isaiah in the History of Christianity.* Cambridge: Cambridge University Press, 1996.

Schenke, Ludger. "Das Johanneische Schisma und die 'Zwölf' (Johannes 6,60–71)." *NTS* 38 (1992) 105–21.

Schereschewsky, B.-Z. "Apostate." In *The Principles of Jewish Law*, edited by Menachem Elon, 377–79. Jerusalem: Keter, 1975.

Schiffman, Lawrence H. *Who Was a Jew?: Rabbinic and Halakhic Perspectives on the Jewish-Christian Schism.* Hoboken, NJ: Ktav, 1985.

Schlier, Heinrich. "ἀρνέομαι." In *TDNT* 1.469–73.

———. "ἀφίστημι, ἀποστασία, διχοστασία." In *TDNT* 1.512–14.

Schmidt, Ulrich. "Zum Paradox vom 'Verlieren' und 'Finden' des Lebens" *Biblica* 89 (2008) 329–51.

Schnackenburg, Rudolf. *The Gospel according to St. John.* Translated by Kevin Smyth. 3 vols. HTKNT. London: Burns & Oates, 1968, 1980, 1982.

———. *The Gospel of Matthew.* Translated by Robert R. Barr. Grand Rapids: Eerdmans, 2002.

———. *The Johannine Epistles: Introduction and Commentary.* Translated by Reginald and Ilse Fuller. New York: Crossroad, 1992.

Schneck, Richard. *Isaiah in the Gospel of Mark I–VIII.* BIBALDS 1. Vallejo, CA: BIBAL, 1994.

Schneemelcher, Wilhelm, editor. *New Testament Apocrypha.* Translated by R. McL. Wilson. 2 vols. Louisville, KY: Westminster John Knox, 1991–92.

Schneider, Gerhard. *Die Apostelgeschichte.* 2 vols. HTKNT 5. Freiburg: Herder, 1980–2002.

Schnelle, Udo. *Einleitung in das Neue Testament.* Uni-Taschenbücher. Göttingen: Vandenhoeck & Ruprecht, 1994. ET: *The History and Theology of the New Testament Writings.* Minneapolis: Fortress, 1998.

———. *Das Evangelium nach Johannes.* THKNT 4. Leipzig: Evangelische Verlagsanstalt, 1998.

Scholer, David M. "Sins within and Sins without: An Interpretation of 1 John 5:16–17." In *Current Issues in Biblical and Patristic Interpretation: Studies in honor of Merrill C. Tenney Presented by His Former Students*, edited by G. F. Hawthorne, 230–46. Grand Rapids: Eerdmans, 1975.

Schreiner, Thomas R., and Ardel B. Caneday. *The Race Set before Us: A Biblical Theology of Perseverance and Assurance.* Downers Grover, IL: InterVarsity, 2001.

Schrenk, Gottlob. "ἐκλεκτός." In *TDNT* 4.181–92.

Schuchard, Bruce G. *Scripture within Scripture: The Interrelationship of Form and Function in the Explicit Old Testament Citations of the Gospel of John.* SBLDS 133. Atlanta: Scholars, 1992.

Schürmann, Heinz. *Das Lukasevangelium.* HTKNT 3. Freiburg: Herder, 1969.

———. "Die Warnung des Lukas vor der Falschlehre in der 'Predigt am Berge' Lk 6,20–49." *BZ*, n.s.,10 (1966) 57–81.

Schweizer, Eduard. *The Good News according to Luke.* Translated by David E. Green. Atlanta: John Knox, 1984.

———. *The Good News according to Mark.* Translated by Donald H. Madvig. Richmond: John Knox, 1970.

Scott, J. Martin C. "Jews or Christians?: The Opponents of Jesus in the Fourth Gospel." In *Jesus and Paul: Global Perspectives in Honor of James D. G. Dunn, a Festschrift for His 70TH Birthday*, edited by B. J. Oropeza, C. K. Robertson, and Douglas C. Mohrmann, 83–101. LNTS 414. London: T. & T. Clark, 2009.

Bibliography

Seccombe, David. "Luke and Isaiah." *NTS* 27 (1981) 252–59.

———. "The New People of God." In *Witness to the Gospel: The Theology of Acts*, edited by I. Howard Marshall and D. Peterson, 349–72. Grand Rapids: Eerdmans, 1998.

Segal, Alan F. "Matthew's Jewish Voice." In *Social History of the Matthean Community: Cross-Disciplinary Approaches*, edited by David L. Balch, 3–37. Minneapolis: Fortress, 1991.

———. *Two Powers in Heaven: Early Rabbinic Reports about Christianity and Gnosticism*. Studies in Judaism and Late Antiquity 25. Leiden: Brill, 1977.

Segovia, Fernando F. *The Farewell of the Word: The Johannine Call to Abide*. Minneapolis: Fortress, 1991.

Shellard, Barbara. *New Light on Luke: Its Purpose, Sources and Literary Context*. JSNTSup 215. London: T. & T. Clark, 2002.

Sherkat, Darren E., and John Wilson. "Preferences, Constraints, and Choices in Religious Markets: An Examination of Religious Switching and Apostasy." *SF* 73 (1995) 993–1026.

Sim, David C. *The Gospel of Matthew and Christian Judaism: The History and Social Setting of the Matthean community*. SNTW. Edinburgh: T. & T. Clark, 1998.

———. "Matthew 7.21–23: Further Evidence of Its Anti-Pauline Perspective." *NTS* 53 (2007) 325–43.

———. "Matthew's Anti-Paulinism: A Neglected Feature of Matthean Studies." *HvTSt* 58 (2002) 766–83.

Simon, Marcel. "From Greek Hairesis to Christian Heresy." In *Early Christian Literature and the Classical Intellectual Tradition: In Honorem Robert M. Grant*, edited by William R. Schoedel and Robert L. Wilken, 101–16. ThH 54. Paris: Éditions Beauchesne, 1979.

Skarsaune, Oskar. "Jewish Believers in Jesus in Antiquity—Problems of Definition, Method, and Sources." In *Jewish Believers in Jesus: The Early Centuries*, edited by Oskar Skarsaune and Reidar Hvalvik, 3–21. Peabody, MA: Hendrickson, 2007.

Sloyan, Gerard S. *What Are They Saying about John?* New York: Paulist, 1991.

Smalley, Stephen S. *1, 2, 3 John*. WBC 51. Dallas: Word, 1984.

Smith, C. W. F. "The Mixed State of the Church in Matthew's Gospel." *JBL* 82 (1963) 149–68.

Smith, D. Moody. *John*. ANTC. Nashville: Abingdon, 1999.

———. *The Theology of the Gospel of John*. CNTS. Cambridge: Cambridge University Press, 1995.

Smith, Ralph L. *Micah–Malachi*. WBC 32. Waco, TX: Word, 1984.

Squires, John T. *The Plan of God in Luke-Acts*. SNTSMS 76. Cambridge: Cambridge University Press, 1993.

Stählin, Gustav. *Skandalon*. BFCT 2/24. Gütersloh: Bertelsmann, 1930.

———. "σκάνδαλον, σκανδαλίζω." In *TDNT* 7.338–58.

Stanton, Graham N. *A Gospel for a New People: Studies in Matthew*. Edinburgh: T. & T. Clark, 1992.

———. "The Origin and Purpose of Matthew's Gospel: Matthean Scholarship from 1945–1980." In *ANRW* II.25.3, edited by Wolfgang Haase, 1889–1951. Berlin: de Gruyter, 1985.

Starbuck, E. D. "Backsliding." In *Encyclopaedia of Religion and Ethics*, edited by J. Hastings, 2.319–21. Edinburgh: T. & T. Clark, 1908.

Stark, Rodney, and William S. Bainbridge. *The Future of Religion: Secularization, Revival, and Cult Reformation*. Berkeley: University of California Press, 1985.

Stark, Rodney, and William S. Bainbridge. "Of Churches, Sects, and Cults: Preliminary Concepts for a Theory of Religious Movements." *JSSR* 18 (1979) 117–33.

Stegner, William Richard. "Romans 9:6–29—A Midrash." *JSNT* 22 (1984) 37–52.

Stein, Robert H. *Luke*. NAC 24. Nashville: Broadman, 2003.

———. "A Short Note on Mark xiv.28 and xvi. 7." *NTS* 20 (1973–74) 445–52.

Stern, Sacha. *Jewish Identity in Early Rabbinic Writings*. AGJU 23. Leiden: Brill, 1994.

Steyn, Gert Jacobus. *Septuagint Quotations in the Context of the Petrine and Pauline Speeches of the Act Apostolorum*. CBET 12. Kampen: Kok Pharos, 1995.

Stibbe, Mark W. G. *John's Gospel*. NTR. London: Routledge, 1994.

Strauss, Mark L. *The Davidic Messiah in Luke-Acts: The Promise and Its Fulfillment in Lukan Theology*. JSNTSup 110. London: Sheffield Academic, 1995.

Strecker, Georg. "Zur Messiasgeheimnistheorie im Markusevangelium." *TU* 88; *SE* 3 (1964) 87–104.

Strecker, Georg. *The Johannine Letters: A Commentary on 1, 2, and 3 John*. Translated by Linda M. Maloney, edited by Harold Attridge. Hermeneia. Minneapolis: Fortress, 1996.

Strobel, A. *Untersuchungen zum eschatologischen Verzögerungsproblem auf Grund der spätjüdisch-urchristlichen Geschichte von Habakuk 2,2ff.* NovTSup 2. Leiden: Brill, 1961.

Swartley, Willard M. *Israel's Scripture Traditions and the Synoptic Gospels: Story Shaping Story*. Peabody, MA: Hendrickson, 1994.

Swetnam, James. "The Meaning of πεπιστευκότας in John 8.31." *Biblica* 51 (1980) 106–9.

Tabor J. D., and Arthur J. Droge, *A Noble Death: Suicide and Martyrdom among Christians and Jews in Antiquity*. San Francisco: HarperSanFrancisco, 1992.

Talbert, Charles H. *Reading Acts: A Literary and Theological Commentary on the Acts of the Apostles*. RNTS. New York: Crossroad, 1997.

———. *Reading the Sermon on the Mount: Character Formation and Ethical Decision Making in Matthew 5–7*. Grand Rapids: Baker Academic, 2004.

———. "Shifting Sands: The Recent Study of the Gospel of Luke." *Interpretation* 30.4 (1976) 381–95.

Tannehill, Robert C. "The Disciples in Mark: The Function of a Narrative Role." In *The Interpretation of Mark*, edited by William Telford, 134–57. IRT 7. Philadelphia: Fortress, 1985.

———. "Do the Ethics of Acts Include the Ethical Teaching in Luke?" In *Acts and Ethics*, edited by Thomas E. Phillips, 109–22. NTM 9. Sheffield: Sheffield Phoenix, 2005.

———. *Luke*. ANTC. Nashville: Abingdon, 1996.

———. "The Mission of Jesus according to Luke IV 16–30." In *Jesus in Nazareth*, edited by W. Eltester. BZNW 40. New York: de Gruyter, 1972.

———. *The Narrative Unity of Luke-Acts: A Literary Interpretation*. 2 vols. FF. Philadelphia: Fortress, 1986–90.

Taylor, Justin. "'The Love of Many Will Grow Cold': Matt 24:9–13 and the Neronian Persecution." *RB* 96 (1989) 352–57.

Theobald, Michael. "Gezogen von Gottes Liebe (John 6,44f) Beobachtungen zur überrlieferung eines johanneischen 'Herrenworts.'" In *Schrift und Tradition: Festschrift für Josef Ernst zum 70. Geburtstag*, edited by Knut Backhaus and Franz Georg Untergassmair, 315–41. Paderborn: F. Schöningh, 1996.

Thompson, Marianne Meye. *1–3 John*. IVPNTC. Downers Grove, IL: InterVarsity, 1992.

Thompson, Mary R. *The Role of Disbelief in Mark: A New Approach to the Second Gospel*. New York: Paulist, 1989.

Tiede, David L. *Prophecy and History in Luke-Acts*. Philadelphia: Fortress, 1980.

Tilborg, Sjef van. *Reading John in Ephesus*. NovtTSup 83. Leiden: Brill, 1996.

Bibliography

Tolbert, Mary Ann. *Sowing the Gospel: Mark's World in Literary-Historical Perspective*. Minneapolis: Fortress, 1989.

Trebilco, Paul R. *The Early Christians in Ephesus from Paul to Ignatius*. WUNT 166. Tübingen: Mohr/Siebeck, 2004.

Trumbower, Jeffrey A. *Born from Above: The Anthropology of the Gospel of John*. HUT 29. Tübingen: Mohr/Siebeck, 1992.

Tuckett, C. M. "Mark's Concerns in the Parables Chapter (Mark 4,1-34)." *Biblica* 69 (1988) 1-26.

Turner, Nigel. *Grammatical Insights into the New Testament*. Edinburgh: T. & T. Clark, 1966.

Tyson, Joseph B. editor. *Luke-Acts and the Jewish People: Eight Critical Perspectives*. Minneapolis: Augsburg, 1988.

Van Elderen, Bastiaan. "The Purpose of the Parables according to Matthew 13:10-17." In *New Dimensions in New Testament Study*. Edited by Merrill J. Tenney and Richard E. Longenecker, 180-90. Grand Rapids: Zondervan, 1974.

Van Hove, Alphonse. "Apostasy." *The Catholic Encyclopedia: An International Work of Reference on the Constitution, Doctrine, Discipline, and History of the Catholic Church*, edited by C. Herbermann et al., 1.624-26. New York: Encyclopedia Press, 1913.

Vielhauer, Philipp. "On the Paulinism of Acts." In *Studies in Luke-Acts: Essays Presented in Honor of Paul Schubert*, edited by Leander E. Keck & J. Louis Martyn, 33-50. Nashville: Abingdon, 1966.

Vogler, Werner. *Judas Iskarioth: Untersuchungen zu Tradition und Redaktion von Texten des Neuen Testaments und ausserkanonischer Schriften*. TANZ 42. Berlin: Evangelische Verlagsanstalt, 1983.

Volf, Miroslav. *Exclusion and Embrace: A Theological Exploration of Identity, Otherness and Reconciliation*. Nashville: Abingdon, 1996.

Von Staden, Heinrich. " Hairesis and Heresy: The Case of the Haireseis Iatrikai." In *Self-Definition in the Greco-Roman World*, edited by Ben. F. Meyer and E. P. Sanders, 76-100. Vol. 3 of *Jewish and Christian Self-Designation*. Philadelphia: Fortress, 1982.

Von Wahlde, Urban C. "Community in Conflict: The History and Social Context of the Johannine Community." *Interpretation* 49 (1995) 379-89.

———. "The Johannine 'Jews': A Critical Survey." *NTS* 28 (1982) 33-60.

———. "Judas, the Son of Perdition, and the Fulfillment of Scripture in John 17:12." In *The New Testament and Early Christian Literature in Greco-Roman Context: Studies in Honor of David E. Aune*, edited by John Fotopoulos, 167-81. NovTSup 122. Leiden: Brill, 2006.

Vriezen, Th. C. "Essentials of the Theology of Isaiah." In *Israel's Prophetic Heritage: Essays in Honor of James Muilenburg*, edited by Bernard W. Anderson and Walter Harrelson, 128-35. New York: Harper, 1962.

Wallace, Daniel B. *Greek Grammar beyond the Basics: An Exegetical Syntax of the New Testament*. Grand Rapids: Zondervan, 1996.

Walton, Steve. "Acts: Many Questions, Many Answers." In *The Face of New Testament Studies: A Survey of Recent Research*, edited by Scot McKnight and Grant R. Osborne, 229-250. Grand Rapids: Baker Academic, 2004.

———. *Leadership and Lifestyle: The Portrait of Paul in the Miletus Speech and 1 Thessalonians*. SNTSMS 108. Cambridge: Cambridge University Press, 2000.

Wansbrough, Henry. "Mark 3, 21—Was Jesus Out of His Mind?" *NTS* 18 (1971-72) 233-36.

Watts, John D. W. *Isaiah. 1-33*. WBC 24. Waco, TX: Word, 1985.

———. *Isaiah. 34-66*. WBC 25. Waco, TX: Word, 1987.

Watts, Rikki E. *Isaiah's New Exodus and Mark.* WUNT 2/88. Tübingen: Mohr/Siebeck, 1997.

———. "Mark." In *CNTOT*, 111–249.

Weatherly, Jon A. *Jewish Responsibility for the Death of Jesus in Luke-Acts.* JSNTSup 106. Sheffield: Sheffield Academic, 1994.

Wehnert, Jürgen. *Die Reinheit des 'christlichen Gottesvolkes' aus Juden und Heiden: Studien zum historischen und theologischen Hintergrund des sogenannten Aposteldekrets.* FRLANT 173. Göttingen: Vandenhoeck & Ruprecht, 1997.

———. *Die Wir-Passagen der Apostelgeschichte: Ein lukanisches Stilmittel aus jüdischer Tradition.* GTA 40. Göttingen: Vandenhoeck & Ruprecht, 1989.

Wengst, Klaus. *Das Johannesevangelium.* 2 vols. THKNT 4. Stuttgart: W. Kohlhammer, 2000–2001.

———. *Der erste, zweite und dritte Brief des Johannes.* ÖTKNT 16. Gütersloh: Gütersloher, 1978.

Wenkel, David H. "Imprecatory Speech-Acts in the Book of Acts." *AsJ* 63 (2008) 81–93.

Whedbee, J. William. *Isaiah and Wisdom.* Nashville: Abingdon, 1971.

Whiston, William, translator. *The Works of Josephus: Complete and Unabridged.* Peabody, MA: Hendrickson, 1987.

Wiarda, Timothy. *Peter in the Gospels: Pattern, Personality and Relationship.* WUNT 2/127. Tübingen: Mohr/Siebeck, 2000.

Wiefel, Wolfgang. *Das Evangelium nach Matthäus.* THKNT 1. Leipzig: Evangelische Verlagsanstalt, 1998.

Wikenhauser, Alfred. *Das Evangelium nach Johannes.* RNT 4. Regensburg: F. Pustet, 1957.

Wilckens, Ulrich. *Das Evangelium nach Johannes.* ATD 4. Göttingen: Vandenhoeck & Ruprecht, 1998.

———. "ὑποκρίνομαι, συνυποκρίνομαι, ὑπόκρισις, ὑποκριτής." In *TDNT* 8.563–71.

———. "ὕστερος, ὕστερον, ὑστερέω, ἀφυστερέω, ὑστέρημα, ὑστέρησις." In *TDNT* 8.592–601.

Wildberger, Hans. *Jesaja*, vol. 3: *Teilband, Jesaja 28–39. Das Buch, der Prophet und seine Botschaft.* BKAT 10. Neukirchen-Vluyn: Neukirchener, 1982.

Williams, Catrin H. "The Testimony of Isaiah in Johannine Christology." In *"As Those Who Are Taught": The Interpretation of Isaiah from the LXX to the SBL*, edited by Claire M. McGinnis and Patricia K. Tull, 107–24. SBLSymS 27. Atlanta: Society of Biblical Literature, 2006.

Williams, James G. "Note on the 'Unforgivable Sin' Logion." *NTS* 12 (1965) 75–77.

Wilson, Brian R. *Magic and the Millennium: A Sociological Study of Religious Movements of Protest among Tribal and Third-World Peoples.* London: Heinemann, 1973.

———. *Religious Sects: A Sociological Study.* London: Widenfield, 1973.

Wilson, Stephen G. "Gentile Judaizers." *NTS* 38 (1992) 605–16.

———. *The Gentiles and the Gentile Mission in Luke-Acts.* SNTSMS 23. Cambridge: Cambridge University Press, 1973.

———. *Leaving the Fold: Apostates and Defectors in Antiquity.* Minneapolis: Fortress, 2004.

———. *Related Strangers: Jews and Christians, 70–170 C.E.* Minneapolis: Fortress, 1995.

Wilson, Walter T. "A Third Form of Righteousness: The Theme and Contribution of Matthew 6.19—7.12 in the Sermon on the Mount." *NTS* 53 (2007) 303–24.

Winbery, C. L. "Abiding in Christ: The Concept of Discipleship in John." *TTE* 38 (1988) 104–20.

Bibliography

Witherington, Ben. *The Acts of the Apostles: A Socio-Rhetorical Commentary.* Grand Rapids: Eerdmans, 1998.

———. *John's Wisdom: A Commentary on the Fourth Gospel.* Louisville: Westminster John Knox, 1995.

———. *Letters and Homilies for Hellenized Christians: A Socio-Rhetorical Commentary on Titus, 1–2 Timothy and 1–3 John.* Downers Grove, IL: IVP Academic, 2006.

Witmer, Stephen. "Overlooked Evidence for Citation and Redaction in John 6.45a." *ZNW* 97 (2006) 134–38.

Wolter, M. "παράπτωμα, ατος, τό *paraptōma*." In *EDNT* 3.33–34.

Wright, Stuart A. *Leaving Cults: The Dynamics of Defection.* SSSRMS 7. Washington, DC: Society for the Scientific Study of Religion, 1987.

Xavier, A. "Judas Iscariot in the Fourth Gospel: A Paradigm of Lost Discipleship." *Indian Theological Studies* 32 (1995) 250–58.

Yarbrough, Robert W. *1–3 John.* BECNT. Grand Rapids: Baker Academic, 2008.

York, John O. *The Last Shall Be First: The Rhetoric of Reversal in Luke.* JSNTSup 46. Sheffield: JSOT Press, 1991.

Zerwick, Maximilian. *Biblical Greek: Illustrated by Examples.* Translated by Joseph Smith. Rome: Scripta Pontificii Instituti Biblico, 1963.

Zerwick, Maximilian, and Mary Grosvenor. *A Grammatical Analysis of the Greek New Testament.* Unabridged 3rd rev. ed. Rome: Editrice Pontificio Istituto Biblico, 1988.

Zumstein, Jean. *La Condition du Croyant dans L'Évangile selon Matthieu.* OBO 16. Göttingen: Vandenhoeck & Ruprecht, 1977.

Zwiep, Arie W. *Judas and the Choice of Matthias: A Study on Context and Concern of Acts 1:15–26.* WUNT 2/187. Tübingen: Mohr/Siebeck, 2004.

———. "Judas and the Jews: Anti-Semitic Interpretation of Judas Iscariot, Past and Present." In *Jesus and Paul: Global Perspectives in Honor of James D. G. Dunn, a Festschrift for His 70th Birthday*, edited by B. J. Oropeza, C. K. Robertson, and Douglas C. Mohrmann, 72–82. LNTS 414. London: T. & T. Clark, 2009.

Ancient Sources Index

HEBREW SCRIPTURES/ SEPTUAGINT

Genesis
1–3	196, 198
15:4f	81
17:1–8	81
19:17	139, 178
19:26	178
22:11	83
29:31–33	207
49:27	142
50:20	117

Exodus
1:15–16	21
3:4	83
7:13	36
9:7	36
11:4–5	21
16	60
16:2–12	167
16:17–18	80
17:2	153
19:5	201
19:11–20	170
32:32	116
33–34	175

Leviticus
2:13	55
10	152
10:1–2	220
10:6	153
12:6	99
17:4	147
17:7	65
17:9	147
17–18	123
19:17	74
19:18	34
19:33–34	94
20:3–5	147
23:29	152
24:10–16	54

Numbers
11:22	167
13–14	167
14:19	124
14:22	153
14:35–37	153
15:30–31	139, 220
15:39	120
16:41–49	153
21:6	153
25:9	153
26:54	80
32:15	120
35:8	80

Deuteronomy
2:7	53
5:16–20	34
6:4–8	24, 34
6:16	153
8:3	170f
10:20	201
11:22	201
11:26	117

Ancient Sources Index

Deuteronomy (*continued*)

12:12	155
13	82, 120
13:1–18	165
13:10	127
13:13	127
14:27, 29	155
17:5	147
17:6	74
17:12	139
18:15	122, 167
18:15–20	152, 175
18:18	122
18:22	82
19:15	74
19:16–21	155
21:15	207
22:25–26	220
24:1	34, 124
24:3	124
25:5–6	34
26:17–19	117
27:26	200f
28	102
28–30	20, 152, 198, 201
29:3–4	36, 191
29:10–28	201
30:11–20	56, 117, 170
30:18, 20	201
31:18	120
32	87, 198, 201

Joshua

7	152
7:11	201
7:19	153
7:22–26	145
22:16–18	120, 124, 127
22:19	124
22:22	124
23:13	41, 71
24	201

Judges

2:3	41
2:19	120
8:27	41

1 Samuel

3:10	83
15:33	89
16:1	222
24:1–10	191

2 Samuel

7:12–16	170
12:5	182
15:12	183
15:20	133
15:31, 34	183
16:15	183
16:20–23	183
18:28	183
17:23–24	145
20:9–10	145

1 Kings

5:1–24	155
9:6	120
17:1–16	103
18:45–46	103, 155
19:4	103
19:8	103
19:19–21	126
22:19–23	19, 62, 191

2 Kings

1:4–12	152
2	103
2:23–24	152
4	103
5	152
6:32	152
7:2	152
7:19	152
8:10–15	152
15:4	22
15:27–30	22
15:32–16:9	22
15:35	22

1 Chronicles

16:13	79

2 Chronicles

7:19	120
11:15	65
27:2	22
29:19	124

Nehemiah

2:19	124
6:6	124

Esther

7:9–10	21

Job

1–2	62
3:1–12	147
9:8	169
17:7	193
18:5–6	90
29:14	78

Psalms (MT/ LXX[MT])

1:6	56
2:7	103, 112
7:15–16	68
13[14]:4	84
15[16]:10	68, 112
16:9–10	170
17:30	63
22	146, 188
34:19	146
40[41]:9–10	37, 146, 182f
43[44]:18–19	178
48[49]:7–8	39
48[49]:13	39
48[49]:15	39
52[53]:5	84
54[55]:13–15	183
58[59]:3–6	84
63[64]:3	84
68[69]:22–29	143, 146, 148f
77[78]:17–20	167
77[78]:23–31	60, 167
77[78]:41	153
77[78]:56	153
78:24	167
78:37	155
88[89]:3–4	113
88[89]:33–37	113
89:2–37	170
93[94]:4	84
105:36	41
105[106]:25	167, 169
105[106]:30LXX	169
108[109]:6–8	148
108[109]:8	143, 148f
108[109]:13	148
108[109]:13	148
108:21	83
110	120
115:4–8	21
124[125]:5	84
129:3	83
131[132]:11–12	113
135[134]:15–18	21
139:5–6	41
139:8	83
140[141]:9	41, 84

Proverbs

1:5	26
3:23	182
9:9	26
10:9	120
11:19	117
13:9	90
14:27	117
16:1, 4, 9	117
16:18–19	66
16:33	117
18:21	117
19:21	117
20:20	90
20:24	117
21:30–31	117
24:20	90
24:22	182
26:27	68
28:15	142
31:21	33

Isaiah

1	111
1:2–4	20
1:3–7	201

Ancient Sources Index

Isaiah (*continued*)

1:5–9	20
1:14–18	20
1:16–20	20, 22
1:23	20
1:24	13
1:29–31	20, 201
2:2	112
2:3	169
2:6–9	20
2:11–17	20
2:18	20
3:1–9	20
3:8–9	20
3:12	20
3:16	20
3:25–26	20
4:4	201
5	197, 199
5:1–7	20, 33, 68, 200f
5:8–22	146, 200
5:9	146
5:11–24	20f
5:13–30	20
5:19	104
5:20	197, 199
5:24	201
5:25	146
5:30	197
6:1–13	19f, 175, 190–99, 226, 229–30
6:8	20
6:10–11	16–23, 45f, 66f, 106, 108–110, 113, 146, 175, 190–99
6:13	20f, 201
7:9–13	20
7:14	53
8:14–15	118
8:16–22	22, 197
9:1–2	13
9:2–6	197
9:8–13	22
10:20–22	21, 81
11	16
11:11	21
11:11–16	81
13:21	65
14:26	104
19:1	20f
19:3–17	104
19:11–12	20f
21:11–12	90
24:17–23	129, 141
24:18	68
25:1	104
25:6	78, 168
26:32	13
28:5–13	21
28:7	13
28:10	13
28:12	21
28:13	178
28:16	22, 118
28:16–20	13
29:6	58
29:9–14	21, 197
29:13	33, 68
29:18–19	21, 197f
30:1	146
30:1–7	21
30:9–11	21
30:15	22
30:18	200
30:20–22	21
31:1	146
31:1–3	21
31:6	22
32:1–5	21
33:17–22	21
34:5	182
34:9–10	65
34:14	65
34:16–17	104
35:1	65
35:1–10	21
35:5	197
37:31–32	81
38:18	68
40:2	104
40:5	104, 106, 112
40:10	214
40:21	104
40:24	28
41:4	169
41:9	80
42:1	103f
42:1–9	80, 197

Ancient Sources Index

42:6–7	13, 21, 55, 104, 112, 115, 197	55:3	112f
		55:3–56:8	170
42:16–20	21, 112	55:4	172
42:17	178	55:5	168f
42:18–19	197f	55:6	168f
43:2	45	55:7–8	104, 113
43:5	53	55:9–13	168
43:7	115	55:10–11	27, 113, 115f, 168f
43:8	21, 197f	55:10–56:1	168f
43:10	80, 169	55:12–13	169
44:1–2	80	55:13–56:8	172
44:9–20	21	56:4	115
44:25	178	56:5	172
44:26	104	56:7–8	112, 169f, 172
44:28	172	56:8–11	168
44:28–45:6	116	56:10	197f
45:3–7	197	57:4	182
45:4	80	58:6–7	94, 103
45:14–26	116	59:10	197
45:21	104	60:1–3	13, 55, 197
46:3	21	60:21	68
46:5–7	21	61	16
46:10–11	104	61:1–2	103f, 119
46:13	112	61:1–11	21
48:4–8	21	61:10	78
48:12–15	80, 169	61:13	68
48:16	104	63	16
49:1	80	63:2–6	56
49:6	13, 55, 111–13	63:9–14	153
49:6–9	103f, 115, 197	63:17	21, 191
51:4–5	55f, 116	63:18	172
51:12	169	64:11	172
52:10	112	65:8–16	32
52:13–53:12	104, 116, 146	66:5	32
52:13	16	66:10	115
52:15	16, 67	66:24	45
53	26f		
53:1	191	**Jeremiah**	
53:5–6	16	2:21	201
53:11–12	16	2:19	124
54–56	168f, 200, 226	3:13	201
54:6	80	3:14	127
54:7	172	4	201
54:10	172	7:16	222
54:11–14		9	201
168–70		11:14	222
54:13	168f, 171f	13:16	182
55:1–56:11	112f, 168–72	14:11	222
55:1–5	115, 168–72	15:16	170f

Ancient Sources Index

Jeremiah (*continued*)

18:2	144
19:1	144
21:8	117
23:1–4	186
23:3–6	81
31:27–38	24
31–33	201
31:3	175
31:33	169
38:3	175
39:7–9	144
45:4	68

Ezekiel

1	19
3.1–3	170f
3:7	24
3:11	24
3:20	206
3:27	24
12:2	24
15	199, 201, 206
16	111
17:2	17
22:27	142
18	206
18:21–31	206
23	111
24:21–23	152f
25:26–27	191
33:9–19	206
34:1–11	81, 186, 206
34:10	186f, 206
34:30	53, 186
36:25–27	169, 194, 206, 217
38:22	58

Daniel

2:5	155
6:12	116
7:13	122
7:21–25	26f
9:9	127
9:24–27	26f, 146
11:41	69
12:1	81
12:2	113
12:12–14	81

Hosea

1	22, 111
2	111
2–6	201
4:17	41, 71
7:13	146
9:12	146
11:4	175

Joel

2:32	81

Amos

1:1	22
2:4–4:11	22
3:2	84
6:1	146
7:2–4	83

Micah

2:1–3	146
4:6–7	81

Habakkuk

2:3–4	89
2:6	17

Zephaniah

3:3	142
3:11–13	81

Zechariah

11.4–7	186
11:12–13	144
11:17	187
12:10–13:1	36
13:7	26, 36, 42, 45, 71, 131, 146, 187
13:8–9	45

Malachi

3:1	16

APOCRYPHA

Tobit
3:6	149
8:15	79
4:10–11	145

Judith
5:1	71

Wisdom
2:10–20	146
3:1–9	146
3:9	79
4:3–4	28
5:6	56
10:7	139
14:11	41, 71
16:20	170
19:10–12	167
2:23	196

Sirach
6:20	200
10:12	127
23:14	147
23:25	28
27:8	78
27:23	41
28:6	200
33:1	63
36:10	81
39:26	55
40:15	28
46:1	79
47:22	79
48:10	133

Baruch
5:2	78

Susanna
33	33

55–59	89

Song of the Three
1:9	124

Additions of Esther
13:9	83
14:17	83

1 Maccabees
2:15	124
6:10	127

2 Maccabees
1:24	83
5:8	124
6:21	115
7	44

4 Maccabees
5:11	225
13:14–15	70
15:3	113
17:11–24	76
18:21	193

2 Esdras (cf. 4 Ezra)
1:19	60
4:28–32	24
8:3	80
8:41–44	27
9:31–37	24, 27

NEW TESTAMENT

Matthew
1:23–25	49, 53
3:2	23
3:7	49
3:8–19	23, 92
3:10	55, 69, 202
3:12	202

Ancient Sources Index

Matthew (*continued*)

3:13–17	17
3:15	78
4:1	62
4:1–11	70, 75
4:2	49
4:15	13
4:17	67
4:18	75
4:23	52, 67, 95
4:24	49
5–7	55–63, 96
5:1–2	55, 68
5:3	49
5:5–9	56
5:6	78
5:10	78
5:12	214
5:13	55, 126
5:14–16	55, 90
5:17–20	49–54, 61, 84, 96, 122
5:19	97
5:20	78, 97
5:21–48	53, 56, 61
5:22	49, 53, 56, 97
5:25–26	49
5:28–30	42f, 53, 56, 71f, 96f
5:29	126
5:32	53
5:34	53
5:43–48	61, 74
5:46	214
5:47	49, 74
6:1	54
6:1–4	94
6:6–10	92
6:7	49, 74
6:9–13	59–63
6:14–15	56, 61
6:16	49
6:19	49
6:19–34	69
6:24	49, 207
6:25	60
6:32	49
6:33	78
7:1	56, 61
7:2	26, 56
7:5	58
7:6	58f
7:7–8	66
7:12	50, 53f, 61, 94, 96
7:12–26	68
7:13–14	56–58, 82, 155
7:15	88, 142
7:15–23	51, 57f, 80–88, 96
7:17–20	69
7:19	55, 57
7:21–23	57, 60, 64, 70, 79, 80–88, 92, 96f, 205
7:21–27	54f, 57
7:24–27	58, 92, 94, 96
7:28–29	49, 55, 68, 96
8:3	53
8:4	53
8:10–12	49, 55, 68, 78, 80, 88f, 90f, 93
8:18–20	69
8:22	53
8:24–26	58, 75
9:3	53f
9:8	68
9:9–11	53, 74
9:16–17	53
9:20	53
9:25	49
9:33	68
9:34	32, 49
9:35	52, 67, 95
9:36	71
10:1–8	67, 75
10:4	143
10:5–6	49
10:6	71, 120
10:8–10	69
10:9	49
10:14–15	92
10:16–18	49, 52, 55, 70, 87f, 95
10:16–39	69
10:20–24	66, 70, 81
10:25–39	49, 76, 81
10:26	70
10:28	56, 69–73, 97, 186, 205
10:31	70
10:32–33	40, 53, 69–73, 83f, 96, 135, 205
10:32–39	96, 126
10:37	207

10:38	69–73, 96, 205	13:39–42	51, 68, 71, 84, 89, 92, 202
10:38–42	211	13:41	203
10:39	39, 96, 135, 205f	13:43	23, 78
10:41–42	92, 214	13:45–46	49
11:1	67	13:47–50	79, 89, 91–95
11:6	178	13:51	67
11:7	68	13:52	53
11:11–15	53, 94	13:54	52, 95
11:15	23	13:57	69, 178
11:16–17	94	13:58	75
11:21	147	14:5	68
11:25–27	53, 66, 95, 108, 175	14:14	68
11:28–30	53, 95	14:21	49
12:1–14	50, 53	14:28–31	58, 75
12:9	52, 95	14:30	75
12:11	141	14:31	75
12:14	49	14:36	53
12:16	53	15:1	49
12:18–21	49, 80	15:1–9	52
12:22–32	49, 95, 135	15:2–20	53
12:24	66	15:5	49
12:28	53	15:7–13	49, 68, 83, 91
12:30	49, 65	15:12–14	49, 68f, 141
12:31–32	32, 65, 220	15:16–20	50
12:33	51, 68f	15:21–28	49, 59
12:36–42	49, 63–66	15:24	71, 120
12:43–45	63, 94f, 150	15:30	49
12:46–50	66, 68, 94	15:31–32	68
12:50	54, 60, 68	16:1–12	49
13:1–23	27, 65	16:6	52, 88
13:4–6	69, 201	16:8	75
13:7	69	16:11–12	52
13:8	65, 92	16:16–18	73, 75, 182
13:9	23, 66	16:19	53, 73, 75
13:10–17	66–68, 76, 95	16:21	49
13:11–15	26, 65, 67, 73, 95, 133	16:22–23	75, 182
13:12	196	16:24–27	69–73, 96, 135, 205, 284
13:16	67	16:25	39, 71, 135, 206
13:17	53	16:27	53, 92
13:19	68	16:28	83
13:20	65, 69–73, 96, 181, 205	17:12	146
13:21	30, 58, 69–73, 96, 181, 205	17:14	68
13:22	69	17:17	75
13:23	65, 92	17:20	75
13:24–30	79, 82, 91–95	17:24–25	53
13:30	202	17:27	41, 69
13:35–36	67f	18:1–14	41f, 69–74, 95, 97
13:36	68, 75	18:6–9	45, 56, 82, 94, 96f, 126, 140, 147f
13:36–43	79, 91–95		

Ancient Sources Index

Matthew (*continued*)

18:10	94
18:12–14	60, 74, 94, 97
18:15	71
18:15–20	13, 72–77, 84, 95
18:17	49
18:18	53
18:20	53
18:21–35	56, 61, 74, 94
18:26	74
18:28–30	88
18:29	74
19:2	68
19:16–30	69, 92
19:19	94
19:28	83
19:29	35
20:1–16	49, 94
20:18	146
20:19	49
20:25	49
20:28	80, 146
20:29	68
21:5–7	49
21:8–11	68
21:19	69, 92
21:24	92
21:28–32	54, 60, 78f, 91
21:29	79
21:31	60, 78
21:32	78
21:33–46	78, 91
21:40–44	79
21:41–43	53, 69, 78, 92
21:43–45	49, 51, 53, 68, 92
22:1–14	77–80, 91, 94f
22:12	97
22:13	55, 89, 97
22:14	77–80
22:15	49
22:29	49
22:34–41	51, 54, 61, 82, 88
22:37–42	94, 96, 221
22:39	94
22:66–71	120
23:1	68, 95
23:1–36	49
23:2–3	49, 52f, 95, 120
23:5	56, 120
23:7–10	52, 76
23:11–12	66
23:13–15	89, 120, 147
23:16–22	49, 52, 147
23:19	49
23:23	49f, 53, 89, 147
23:24	49
23:25	89, 147
23:26	49
23:27–29	51, 68, 84, 89, 147
23:33–36	56, 84
23:34	70
23:37	108
24:1–3	86, 90
24:4	57, 88–91, 214
24:4–28	80–88, 90
24:9	49, 76, 93
24:10–12	51, 57, 69, 76, 80–88, 90, 96, 141, 203, 205, 216
24:13	70, 80–88, 96
24:14	49, 93
24:20	53
24:22–31	57, 76, 80–88, 96, 141
24:24	51, 76, 82, 96
24:26	82
24:31	202
24:36	184
24:37–44	78f, 88f
24:38	58
24:42–51	76, 78f, 88–93, 96, 138
24:42–26:30	94
25:1–13	56, 78f, 88–91
25:1–46	91–95
25:11	83
25:12	84f, 88
25:14–30	49, 79, 92
25:29	26, 196
25:30	55, 88, 97
25:31–32	49, 53, 83, 93, 202
25:31–46	83, 92–95
25:34–35	94, 132
25:41	84, 202
25:45	94
25:46	78, 202
26:13	49
26:14–16	76
26:21–25	76, 143
26:22	76

26:24	64, 76f, 97, 145–50	2:29–34	31
26:25	76	3:1	19
26:26–28	57, 80, 146	3:2	19
26:29	78, 83, 90	3:5–6	33
26:31	69, 71, 73–77, 131, 188, 203	3:7–10	19, 31, 49
26:33–35	69, 73–77	3:11	34
26:36–46	133	3:13–19	75
26:38	88	3:14	19, 36
26:39	62, 86	3:17	11
26:41	62, 88	3:19	143
26:42	54, 60	3:19–30	135
26:46–50	76	3:21	15, 31–38, 45f
26:49	76	3:22–30	24f, 31–34, 45f
26:56	69, 73–77, 187	3:29	29, 199, 220
26:57	49	3:30	32
26:63–65	53f, 134	3:31–35	15, 31, 33–38, 45f, 66
26:69	75, 132	4	197
26:70–75	69, 73–77, 84, 132	4:1–9	24–31, 46f
26:75	55	4:2	33
27:1–5	73–77, 97, 143	4:3	23
27:6	49	4:5–6	201, 25–31
27:9–10	144	4:7	47
27:19	78	4:9	23–27
27:23–24	77	4:10–12	14, 16–24, 31–33, 36, 45–47, 66–68, 191
27:33	49		
27:41	49	4:11	23f, 33, 106
27:46	49, 188	4:12	11, 133
27:57	49	4:13–20	25–31, 45–47
28:7–10	55, 75	4:16–17	15, 25–31, 181
28:16–20	49, 53, 55, 75	4:18–19	25–31, 47
28:17	75	4:21–36	31–33, 45f
28:19	93	4:23–25	23–27, 45f, 67, 88, 196
		4:26–32	24
		4:33	23, 191
		4:34	17, 23f
		4:35–41	31f, 35
		5:8–13	31
		5:9	11
		5:17–25	31
		5:21–34	31, 35
		5:31	32
		5:41	11, 49
		6:1–6	15, 31, 33
		6:3	33, 69, 178
		6:7–13	14, 36, 75
		6:12	23
		6:14–15	32
		6:29	35
		6:30–44	31, 35

Mark

1:1–4	11, 16, 22f
1:12–15	22f, 31, 49, 62
1:17–20	14, 22
1:23–27	31
1:32–34	31
1:38	19
2:1–12	31
2:5	35
2:7	33
2:10	19
2:13	31
2:14	14
2:16	32
2:23–28	33
2:24	32

Ancient Sources Index

Mark (*continued*)

6:35	31
6:37	11
6:45–51	31, 35
6:52	17, 25, 31, 33–38, 45f, 67
6:53–55	31, 152
7:1–23	11, 33, 122
7:6–7	11
7:10–13	11, 35
7:11	49
7:14–15	23f, 31
7:19	53
7:24–30	35
7:31–37	36
7:33	31
7:34	11, 49
7:42	11
8:1–13	31, 35
8:14–21	17, 24, 35
8:15	29, 88, 214
8:17–18	11, 17, 25, 29, 33–38, 45f, 193
8:22–26	36
8:23	31
8:27	16
8:29	14, 182
8:31–9:1	38
8:32–33	28, 182
8:34–38	15, 29f, 35, 37–41, 45f, 70, 135, 184, 206, 211f
9:1	38
9:12	19
9:23	86
9:30–50	38
9:31	146
9:32	17, 33
9:33–37	42–44
9:34	32
9:35	38
9:38–39	83
9:40	49
9:41	214
9:42–50	28f, 41–47, 55f, 71, 140, 147f, 203
9:44	146
9:49–50	55
10:1	31
10:6	33
10:15	29, 72
10:17–22	28, 30, 40, 45
10:19	33, 35
10:28–30	14f, 30, 33f, 40
10:32–45	38
10:43	38
10:45	26, 146
10:46–52	31, 35
10:52	16
11:1	16
11:8	31
11:13–14	30f
11:25–27	40, 44, 56, 61, 66
11:32	31
12:1–12	24, 32
12:2	30
12:9	29
12:12	17, 31
12:19	33
12:24	33
12:28–34	23, 33, 40
12:37	17
12:38	88, 214
12:40	29
12:42	11
13	80
13:5–6	29f, 36, 82, 85f, 88, 214
13:7–13	81
13:9	30, 36, 86, 88, 214
13:10	13
13:12	15, 29, 34, 46, 81
13:13	29, 35, 81, 146
13:14	87
13:17	147
13:20	29, 80, 86
13:21–23	29f, 36, 82, 86, 88, 141
13:32	184
13:33	25, 30, 86, 88
13:33–37	88
13:34	14
13:35	88
13:37	25, 29f, 36, 86, 138
14:1–11	30
14:7–8	35
14:10–11	30, 36, 40, 47, 143
14:12	19
14:17	41
14:18–21	30, 36f, 143, 183

Ancient Sources Index

14:21	15, 26, 29, 31, 33–38, 40, 44–46, 64, 85, 145–50	3:3	23
		3:6	103, 113, 126, 131
		3:7–14	23, 109
14:24	16, 26, 146	3:11	101
14:27	28f, 31, 33–38, 40–42, 45f, 85, 131, 188, 203	3:17	202
		4:1–13	70, 103
14:28	12, 13, 38, 40, 46	4:2	107, 127
14:29–30	28, 36f, 41	4:5–8	23, 135
14:31–42	36, 46	4:13	62f, 107, 113, 127f
14:32	133	4:14–31	103f, 119, 157
14:35–36	62, 86	4:19	103
14:37–38	29f, 36, 46, 63	4:21	104
14:43–46	15, 30f, 36f, 46	4:29	118, 120, 144
14:50	14, 29, 33–38, 40, 45f, 85, 187	4:32	120
		4:38–41	152
14:60	134	4:43	105
14:61–64	54, 134	5:1	107
14:62	29	5:11	101, 150
14:66–72	14f, 33–38, 40, 45f, 132	5:15	118, 131
15:8–15	31	5:17–26	103, 152
15:15–16	11	5:20	131
15:21	35	5:22	150
15:22	11	5:28	101, 150
15:34	188	5:32	23
15:39	11, 35	5:38	104
15:42–46	35	6:7	107
16:1–8	38	6:16	143–45, 148
16:6–7	12, 13, 37f, 40, 46	6:17–19	103
		6:18	131
		6:20	119
Luke		6:22	118
1:1–4	98–100, 102, 104–06, 116	6:23	119, 214
1:5–66	117	6:24–26	101, 128, 140f, 147
1:16	118, 133	6:27	138
1:17	109	6:35–37	56, 138, 140, 214
1:33	111	6:38	26
1:54–55	111	6:39–42	141
1:68–79	111	6:43–49	58, 82f
1:77	113	7:1–10	129
1:78–79	103	7:16	120
2:22	99	7:20–23	69, 118f, 128
2:25	111	7:27	178
2:27–32	103, 111	7:29–30	118f
2:30	113	7:30	104, 116
2:32	111f	7:30–35	108
2:34	118, 136	7:36–50	119
2:37	127	7:39	118f
2:41	107	8:3	118
2:49	105	8:4–15	27, 126–31
3:2	107		

Ancient Sources Index

Luke (*continued*)

8:6–7	126–31, 158, 201
8:9–10	17
8:10	106–114, 131
8:13	28, 63, 126–31, 157, 181
8:14	107, 126–31, 158
8:16–18	26
8:18	66, 88, 93, 196
8:19–21	66, 93
8:21	107, 131
8:26–39	119
8:40–56	152
8:45–47	184
9:1	148, 152
9:10–17	103
9:11	103
9:13	131
9:21–22	105, 133, 135
9:23–26	39f, 70, 113, 126, 128, 132f, 135–39, 158, 184, 206, 211f, 230
9:31	104
9:32–33	131
9:35	80
9:40–41	131
9:44–45	131, 143, 146
9:47	150
9:48	127
9:49–50	63, 83
9:50	49
9:51	133
9:57–62	125, 178, 184
10:13–15	118, 140, 147
10:14	139
10:17–20	107, 149
10:20	107, 116
10:21–23	108, 175f
10:23–24	131
10:25	113, 119
10:25–37	119, 138
11:1	107
11:2–4	59–63, 128, 130, 157
11:14–19	119, 135
11:15	33
11:18–22	107, 135
11:19	63
11:23	63
11:24–26	63–65, 150
11:28	107, 131
11:31–32	118
11:37–54	118f
11:42–47	138, 140, 147
11:52	140
12	232
12:1	88, 118, 141f
12:4–12	70, 128f, 135–38, 148, 158
12:8–9	40, 70, 84, 132, 135–38, 158
12:10	135–38, 151, 158, 220
12:11	153
12:13–21	101, 119
12:22–34	101, 119
12:33	138, 150, 184
12:34–40	88f, 138–43
12:35–48	90, 138–43, 158
12:42	131
12:–48	88, 148
12:51–53	118
12:54–56	131
13:1	101
13:5	107
13:10–17	118
13:22	83
13:23–30	56, 83
13:26–27	83, 127
13:28–29	89, 118
13:33	105
13:34–35	99, 108, 110, 116, 131
13:36	104
13:46	107
14:1–2	107, 119
14:12–14	119
14:14	70, 130
14:15	90, 107
14:15–24	77, 101, 107, 119
14:25–35	101, 126, 184
14:26	118, 207
14:27	135, 184
14:33	101, 150
14:34	55
14:35	23, 55, 131
15:1–2	108, 119
15:1–32	118–21, 159
15:3–7	71
15:6	189
15:17–32	108, 118–21
15:32	113
16:1–13	151
16:9	132

16:10–12	139	21:9	105, 132
16:17	122	21:10–36	80, 135–38
16:19–31	70, 101, 108, 118f, 128, 137, 140, 149, 158	21:12–19	81, 118, 128f, 135–38, 153
		21:20–24	87, 99, 113
16:25	118	21:24	110, 131
16:27–31	108	21:26	81, 128
16:28	149	21:34–36	88, 128f, 138–43, 158
17:1–4	41f, 61, 71, 74, 105f, 109, 128, 138–43, 147f, 157f, 203	22:2–6	143, 148f, 158
		22:3	107, 150f, 154
		22:4, 6	143–45, 148
17:5	140	22:7	105
17:11–19	119	22:15–16	133
17:21–23	141	22:17–23	148
17:25	105	22:19	13
17:26–30	139	22:21–22	104f, 116, 133, 140, 143–45, 157
17:27–33	58, 158, 178		
17:32–33	39, 70, 113, 129, 133, 135, 138–43, 148, 158, 206	22:28	63, 90, 128, 130, 132
		22:30	149
18:1–8	126–130	22:31–34	107, 109, 131–35, 138, 159
18:7–8	80, 126–31, 157	22:37	104f, 146
18:9–25	118f	22:39–43	119, 133
18:17	72, 127	22:40	63, 128, 130, 157
18:18–29	101, 113, 128	22:42	62
18:22	150	22:44–45	131, 133
18:28	150	22:46	63, 128, 130f, 133, 157
18:29 30	35	22:47	143
18:31–34	104, 131, 143, 146	22:48	143
19:1–10	101, 119, 129, 150	22:53f	113, 137
19:3–4	131	22:54–62	131–35, 159
19:9	113	23:2	120, 157
19:10	116, 120	23:4	120
19:11	131	23:5	157
19:11–27	49, 92	23:12	101
19:22–26	128	23:14	120, 157
19:26	93, 139, 196	23:20	120
19:41–44	99, 108	23:24	108
19:44–48	118, 131	23:29–31	99
20:9–15	108	23:34	111, 136
20:17	118	23:35	80
20:19	108	23:43	70, 137, 158
20:20	143	23:45	132
20:27	104	24	105
20:35–36	70	24:3	118–21
20:46	88, 142	24:7	105
20:47	139	24:9	149
21:5	128	24:12–35	132
21:5–37	129	24:14	118–21
21:6	99	24:16	131
21:8	88, 131f, 138–43, 214	24:19	120

Ancient Sources Index

Luke (*continued*)

24:25–27	104f
24:26	105
24:27	105f, 108
24:31	131
24:33	149
24:36–43	129
24:38	150
24:44–47	105f, 116, 131, 183
24:49	132

John

1:1	161, 165, 194, 210
1:1–18	196f, 226
1:4–5	195, 197
1:6	195
1:7	170, 195
1:9	164
1:10–11	195, 198, 207
1:12	195
1:13	194f
1:14	161, 165, 171, 173, 194f, 210
1:15	164, 194
1:16	167
1:17	167
1:18	161, 165, 175, 210, 224
1:19–27	164f, 167
1:29–34	197, 207, 220
1:30	164
1:31	167
1:35–41	195
1:39	172
1:41	183
1:45	167, 175
1:46	166
1:47–49	166, 183, 187
2:13–22	172f, 196
2:15	173
2:23	165, 199
2:24–25	183, 187
3:1–14	176, 194, 196
3:2	163
3:3–5	172, 194, 217
3:6–7	217
3:13–15	176, 167, 194
3:15–16	171, 176, 186, 195
3:16–17	185, 190, 195, 207
3:18–20	195, 197, 207
3:19–21	172, 182, 192, 194f, 197f
3:22–26	163
3:27	179
3:29–30	164
3:31	194
3:33–34	171, 175
3:36	171, 185, 195, 199, 208, 211
4:10–15	196
4:22	165
4:24	172f
4:31–34	196
5:1	174
5:14	215–19, 223, 227
5:16	191
5:17–18	161, 165, 174, 188, 191f, 226
5:19	192
5:21	175
5:23	170
5:24	171, 194f, 219
5:28	211, 218
5:29	185, 211, 218f
5:30	173
5:31–47	167, 174
5:38	171, 177, 180, 199
5:39	167
5:39–47	171, 199
5:40	172, 177, 195, 228
5:41	64
5:42	187
5:43	177
5:44	207
5:45	167
5:46	175, 198
6	167–71, 175, 200, 204, 210, 216
6:1–4	201
6:1–16	167
6:7	191
6:12	173
6:14	167, 175
6:15	179f
6:16–21	169
6:22–59	173
6:26–27	179f
6:29	195
6:30–35	167, 180, 196
6:35–47	170f, 171–77, 179f, 195
6:36	171, 199
6:37–44	189f, 195, 171–77, 204, 226
6:40	171
6:41–45	166–77, 178f, 195, 226

6:47–51	170f, 207	8:32	166, 188, 195
6:48–59	170f, 175	8:35	208
6:51	169	8:37–44	166, 196
6:52	166f, 173, 177	8:44–47	166, 191, 194, 196, 198f
6:54–58	170, 180, 183, 208	8:48	165f
6:59	171, 173, 177, 226	8:51–55	190, 196
6:60–66	164, 171, 178–81, 196, 226	8:52	166
6:61	167, 173, 203	8:56–58	175, 196
6:62–64	176, 195	8:58–59	161, 187f
6:63	172, 176, 208	9	181
6:64–71	178–81, 182–85, 194, 201f, 209, 212, 227	9:2	191
		9:5–34	197
6:65	176	9:16	199
6:67–69	167f, 175, 177–81	9:17	175
6:70–71	143, 166, 177–81, 187, 212, 227	9:22	161, 183, 198f, 226
		9:24–25	199
7:1	166	9:29	199
7.12	165	9:31	174
7:17	174, 195	9:34–35	172f, 198
7:19–23	165, 167	9:35–38	175, 199
7:26–27	183	9:39–41	17, 198–99, 207, 220
7:30	188	10:1–31	185–90, 226
7:31	165, 199	10:4	173
7:32	163, 165, 188	10:6	196
7:33–34	168, 196	10:10–11	185–90, 194, 203, 227
7:35	164, 196	10:14	84
7:36	196	10:15–18	194
7:37–38	172	10:16	168, 170
7:40	167	10:17	191
7:41–42	183	10:20	165
7:44	188	10:22	176
7:45	163, 165	10:22–39	188
7:47	165	10:25	199
7:48	199	10:26	194, 198f
7:50	163	10:27	183, 204
7:52	166	10:28–33	161, 165, 172, 185–90, 192, 204, 224, 226
8	188		
8:3	163	10:31–36	165
8:11	218, 223	10:34–35	171
8:12	197, 207	10:37–38	189, 195
8:14	183	10:39	188
8:20	188	10:41	164
8:21–27	187f, 196, 207	10:42	165, 199
8:28	176, 187, 199	11:9–10	182, 197
8:29	173, 188	11:11–16	196
8:30–31	165f, 178–82, 188f, 195, 199, 208	11:23–25	171, 196
		11:32	164, 194
8:31–59	164, 166, 178–82, 189, 196, 226	11:45–48	165, 199
		11:51–52	170

John (continued)

Reference	Pages
11:57	165, 188
12:4–6	143, 182–85
12:11	165, 199
12:16	175f
12:18	191
12:20–22	164
12:23	206f
12:25	39, 174, 186f, 199–208, 227, 230
12:26	207
12:27–36	191
12:28	168, 183, 191
12:31	173, 192, 207, 221
12:32–34	170, 175f, 196, 226
12:35	182, 192, 197
12:36	195, 197
12:37–41	17, 72, 175f, 190–99, 226
12:42–43	161, 163, 165, 199, 208, 226
12:45	175
12:47	207
13	202
13:2	143, 166, 182–85, 227
13:10–11	182–85
13:12–17	13
13:18	182f, 191
13:19–30	143, 182–85, 197, 209
13:33–34	187f, 194
13:35–38	13, 55, 132, 180, 187f, 190, 194, 207, 230
14:3	190
14:6	192
14:7–11	161, 175, 192, 196
14:10	200, 202, 208
14:17–23	200, 202, 208
14:21–24	190, 208
14:25	203
14:26	176, 208
14:30	207
15:1–6	174, 199–208, 227
15:6	181, 185, 199–208, 211f
15:7	180, 202
15:7–17	199f, 203
15:8	180
15:9	194
15:10	186, 190, 200, 202
15:13–15	135, 187
15:16–19	183, 201
15:18–27	203, 207
15:18–16:24	203
15:20	190
15:21–24	174, 199, 203
15:25	183, 191, 203
15:26–27	176, 203, 208
16:1–4	161, 163, 173, 177, 188, 199–208, 226
16:4–24	203
16:7–15	176, 202, 217
16:11	207, 221
16:13	208
16:16–19	196
16:20–22	168, 188
16:25	196
16:28	194
16:29	196
16:31–32	187f, 203
16:33	207
17	189, 225
17:2	189
17:5	194
17:6	189f, 194f, 224
17:9	189f
17:11–23	190, 192, 224
17:12	172, 182–85, 186f, 189–91, 203, 222, 224, 227
17:13–16	207
17:14	190, 194
17:15	62, 190, 224
17:17	190
17:20	164, 189
17:24	189
18:2–5	143, 185
18:3	163, 166
18:8–10	172, 187f, 190, 226
18:12–13	166
18:15–18	132, 166, 187, 207
18:25–27	132, 187, 207
18:28	123
18:36	172
19:11	182–85
19:24	183, 191
19:28	183
19:35	160
19:36–37	183, 191
19:38	163
20:9	175f
20:10	132

Ancient Sources Index

20:21	195
20:22	202, 208
20:23	73
20:28	161, 165, 169, 226
20:31	162, 171, 177, 227
21	164, 187
21:3	188
21:10	188
21:12–17	183, 187
21:15–19	207
21:20	182
21:24	160
21:30	182

Acts

1:1–3	99
1:5	118
1:6–7	105, 113, 131
1:8	100, 103, 109, 111f, 118, 132
1:15–26	104, 143–51, 158
2:14	103
2:17–23	105, 111, 113
2:21	117
2:22	146, 157
2:23	104–6, 111, 116, 146, 157
2:24	146, 157
2:33	104, 131
2:36	105
2:37–40	117
2:38	109, 111, 150, 155
2:39	103f, 111, 115f, 150
2:40	113
2:41	118, 157
2:42–47	13, 101, 104, 113, 116, 127, 150f, 155
3:14–21	103–5, 108–11, 122, 131, 133, 136
3:22–23	120, 122, 152f
3:24	115
3:25	110
3:26	104, 116
4:1–4	118f, 127, 150
4:3–23	136
4:5–21	105, 108
4:6	115
4:8	137
4:12	113
4:20	131
4:23–31	104, 116, 133
4:27	101, 104–6
4:28–31	104–6, 116, 137, 150, 157
4:32–37	101, 150f
4:33	153
4:34	115
4:36	11
5	101
5:1–10	145, 150–55, 158f, 220
5:3	154, 193
5:11	145, 152, 155, 220
5:13–14	151f
5:14–15	103, 118, 152
5:16–17	119, 152
5:17–40	136
5:20	113
5:27	70
5:28	142
5:36–37	106, 115, 127
5:38–39	104
5:42	221
6–7	108, 121–26, 136, 157
6:3	131
6:7	118, 121, 130
6:9–12	122
6:10	137
6:11	54
6:13–14	122
6:15	136f
7:2	111
7:37	122, 152
7:39–43	108, 120–22, 139
7:42	108
7:51	116, 136
7:51–59	54, 108, 111, 122, 134, 137
7:52	104f, 122
7:57	116
7:58	136
7:60	108, 111, 134
8	10, 114, 155
8:1–4	122, 133f
8:4–24	158
8:5	103, 221
8:9–24	86, 127, 142, 151, 154–56, 158
8:26–40	103, 155
8:30–35	104, 146
8:37–38	127
8:39–40	155
9:1–2	122, 134

Ancient Sources Index

Acts (*continued*)

9:1–20	4, 104, 114	13:43–45	106–14, 116, 118f, 130, 136
9:4	83	13:46–48	106–14, 103f, 114–17, 131, 157
9:6	105		
9:7	131	13:48	106–114, 114–117, 127
9:11	122	13:50–51	30, 133
9:15	103f	14:1–2	118f
9:16	105	14:3	116, 130
9:17	136	14:5–6	133
9:29–30	11, 103	14:8–11	103
9:32–35	103, 152	14:15	109, 116
9:35	109, 118	14:19–21	133
9:36–42	151f	14:22	105, 126–32
9:42	118, 152	14:27	115
10	114	14:35	131
10:1–6	104	15:1–30	51, 103, 113, 121–26, 131, 157, 223
10:22	100		
10:23	131	15:4	104, 115, 121–26
10:28–29	123	15:5	118, 121–26, 181
10:36–43	104f	15:7	103f
10:41	104	15:11	116
10:42	146	15:13–19	105
10:43	104f	15:17	93, 116
10:45	115, 123	15:19	109, 116
11:1	127	15:20, 29	121–26, 123
11:1–3	123	15:22	104
11:4–18	123	15:25	104
11:8	131	15:26	128
11:15–18	103f, 113, 155	15:32	132
11:19	8, 113, 118, 133	15:35–36	51, 99
11:21	105, 109	15:36–41	51
11:23	116, 126–31	15:37	11
11:27–30	151	15:39	11
11:28	98	15:41	132
12:1–2	149	16:3	124
12:10	127	16:5	132
12:12	11	16:7	153
12:21–25	11, 145	16:6–8	99, 103
13:1	102	16:10–17	98f
13:5	11	16:14	104
13:6–11	120, 130, 142, 145	16:16–24	111, 142, 151
13:12	127	16:17	113
13:13	11	16:19–36	136
13:14–50	106–14	16:20	99
13:17	104, 106–14	16:30f	113, 127
13:25–33	104, 106–14, 130, 136	16:37f	122
13:32–38	170	17:1–4	118
13:40f	88, 106–14	17:3	105
13:42	106–14, 126–31	17:4–5	100, 102, 119

Ancient Sources Index

17:6	131
17:11–12	102, 118f, 127, 131
17:17	100
17:26	113, 131, 146
17:30–31	104f, 116, 146
18:6	114, 136, 142
18:8	118, 126–31
18:12–17	3, 101, 136
18:18	124
18:21	104
18:22	51, 99
18:23	132
18:25f	100
18:27	181
19	222
19:1–7	164
19:8–10	107, 116, 127, 141
19:11–12	103
19:18	181
19:18–41	141
19:21	105, 133
19:23–20:1	111, 151
19:37–41	101, 111
20	209
20:1	111, 151
20:5	99, 124
20:5–15	98
20:16	86
20:17–35	124, 138–43
20:19	127f
20:22–23	104, 127, 133, 153
20:24	116, 126–31, 133, 138–43, 153
20:25	99, 133
20:28–31	88, 141f, 120, 138–43, 158
20:32	130
20:33–35	101, 151f
20:38	133
21:1	142
21:7	131
21:13	133
21:14	104, 133
21:17–26	51
21:18–19	126–31
21:20–21	4, 100, 118, 121–26, 157, 181
21:21–35	124
21:22–24	125
21:24	100
21:25	124, 181
21:26–36	124
21:28	4, 124
21:35	101
21:36	126–31
21:39	122
22:1	111
22:3–4	122
22:5	111
22:10	105
22:14	60, 104
22:15	103, 131
22:19	70
22:21	114
22:22–23	124, 158
22:25–29	122, 127
22:28	101
22:31–34	131–35
22:54–62	131–35
23:1	111
23:1–11	136
23:6–10	118, 130
23:11	133
23:16–31	101
23:26	100
23:1	70
23:11–22	105
23:27	122
24:3	100
24:5	9
24:15	130
24:26	101, 151
25:10	105
25:16	101
26:11	36, 131–36, 158
26:17–20	103f, 109, 112, 114, 116, 131, 133, 154
26:22–23	105, 130f
26:25	100
26:28	8
26:31	188
27:1–28:16	98
27:23–26	105
27:31	130
27:39	86
27:46	188
28	98, 101, 109f, 159, 199
28:17–23	106–114
28:23	118, 125

279

Ancient Sources Index

Acts (*continued*)

28:24–28	17, 106, 108–110, 112–14, 116, 118f, 125, 131, 133, 157
28:29	118, 125
28:30–31	110, 125

Romans

1:16	109
1:24–32	108, 197
2:18	86
4:12	123
4:21	182
5:12	196
6:1–15	218, 223
8:9	155
8:14–17	217
8:35	30
9:6–8	118, 179
9:22	155
9:24	118
9:31–33	41, 118, 182
10:4–10	125, 170
11	199
11:7–8	17, 110, 193
11:13–14	110
11:20	89
11:25–26	110
11:32	45
12:1–2	45
13:8–10	51
13:11–14	90
14	124
14:13–21	72
14:15	186
15:11	93
16:17	71
16:26	93

1 Corinthians

1:8	81
3:10–15	93, 153, 214
5:1–13	72, 74
5:5	74, 220, 223
6:9–10	88, 219
7:18	124
7:19	125
8–10	124f, 223
8:3	84
8:10–13	72
8:11	186
8:13	203
9:19–22	125
9:24–27	130
10:3–12	171
10:9–10	153
10:11–12	88, 214
10:13–14	63, 127
10:15–20	171
10:18	88
11:22	71
11:26	171
11:30	220
14:19	100
15:9	9, 134
16:13	88

2 Corinthians

3	125
3:14–4:4	17
3:16	133
4:3–4	27, 192
6:14	51
8:15	80
11:24	70
11:29	85, 203

Galatians

1:4	90
1:13	134
1:14	124
1:13–16	4
2	157
2:1–16	123, 125
2:3–6	125
2:4	123
2:11–15	123
2:12	123
3:10	115
3:10–25	125
3:26	115
4:9	133
4:14	128
5–6	124
5:1–6	51
5:4	85
5:6	125

Ancient Sources Index

5:15	88
5:19–21	219
6:1	223
6:6	100
6:10	94
6:12	51
6:15	125

Ephesians

1:3–14	60
2:1, 5	194
5:8	194
6:14	78

Philippians

2:14–16	55, 211
3:2–3	88, 124, 206, 214
3:4–8	4, 124
3:6	134
3:14	130
4:3	116

Colossians

1:13	194
2:8	214
2:13	194
3:11	125
3:13	61
4:6	55
4:10	11
4:11	98
4:14	98
4:16	100

1 Thessalonians

2:19	211
4:3–7	124
5:1–4	89
5:3–10	129
5:4–8	78, 88f

2 Thessalonians

1:4	30
2:3–4	51, 81, 84, 124, 182, 184
2:3–8	216
2:7–12	51, 84, 86, 182

1 Timothy

1:3	142
1:9	51
1:13	134
1:19–20	85, 142
2:4	45
4:1–3	86, 127, 142
4:11	11
4:12	71
5:13	225
6:2	71
6:9	127, 155

2 Timothy

2:12	40, 84
2:19	84
3:1–5	86, 142
3:11	30
4:3–4	120, 142
4:7	130
4:11	98

Titus

2:5	71
3:8	181

Philemon

24	11, 98

Hebrews

3:12	88f, 127
3:19	89
10:26–27	220
10:29	59, 85
10:38	139
10:39	155, 186
11:37	89
12:25	88, 120

James

1:2–4	128
1:12–14	62, 127
1:22–25	25
2:15–17	94
3:1	139
4:1–3	128
4:6	66

Ancient Sources Index

James (*continued*)

4:17	139
5:19–20	56, 85, 133, 220, 223

1 Peter

1:6	128
2:6–8	41, 118
2:9	194
2:12	55
3:1	55
3:16	55
4:3–4	219
4:7	88
4:12	45
4:16	8
5:13	11, 45

2 Peter

2:1	85f, 142, 186
2:1–22	86
2:2–3	139, 142, 186
2:9	63
2:12	59
2:13	128
2:16	59
2:21	139
2:22	59, 64
3:10–14	90
3:15–17	51, 86, 90, 186

1 John

1:3	200, 212
1:5–7	197, 220, 218
1:7	171, 218, 223
1:8–2:2	194f, 212, 214, 215–19, 220, 223f
2:3–5	190, 200, 216
2:6–8	208, 216, 218
2:8–14	197
2:9–10	188, 203, 208, 218f
2:11	192, 208
2:12	212
2:12–28	208
2:13–15	163, 192, 214, 221
2:14	180, 222
2:15–17	163, 174, 190, 196, 207, 213f, 216, 222, 228
2:18–19	86, 142, 179, 184, 206, 208–10, 212f, 216, 227
2:18–27	208, 211, 214
2:19	85, 161, 163, 178–81, 186, 201, 204f, 208–10, 212, 226f
2:20	217
2:20–27	221
2:22–23	178, 209, 219–25, 226
2:24	180, 200, 202, 208, 213
2:24–28	212
2:25	215, 219
2:26	186, 206, 209, 213, 227
2:27–28	208f, 213, 217
2:28	40, 208, 210–15, 227
2:29	216, 218, 220
2:29–3:10	211, 214
3:1	191, 212, 214, 228
3:2–9	212, 228
3:3	212, 228
3:4–10	214, 215–19, 228
3:4–15	220
3:6	212, 218, 226
3:7	212–14, 216
3:8	166, 196, 216
3:9	180
3:10	218f, 225
3:10–17	166, 192, 207f, 220
3:13–15	181, 185, 194, 219–25, 227
3:15–17	166, 176, 219, 221, 223, 225, 228
3:16–24	94, 190, 195, 200, 208
3:18	212, 223, 225
3:19–21	210
3:22–24	208, 212, 216f, 219–25
4:1	213
4:1–6	185, 190, 208–10, 212, 217, 219–25, 227
4:2–3	219–25
4:7–20	220, 223
4:10	176
4:12–17	208, 226
4:13	212, 217, 221
4:14–15	220
4:15–16	212
4:16–5:3	220
4:17	210
4:20–22	200, 221, 226
5:1	195, 220
5:1–2	220f

5:1–13	219
5:4–5	220
5:10	195
5:12–13	163, 171, 177, 195, 208, 212–14, 219, 227
5:14–15	216, 222
5:14–21	219
5:15–16	166, 185, 203, 219
5:16–18	172, 190, 205, 214–16, 218, 219–25, 228
5:19	207f, 221f
5:20	208, 210, 219, 226
5:21	212f, 222, 228

2 John

1–2	163, 180, 208, 215
4	213, 218
5–6	216, 220
7	215, 219–25
7–11	186, 208–10, 217, 227
8	210–15, 227
8–10	86, 88, 163, 180, 208, 215
9	213, 215
13	163

3 John

1–4	163, 218
3–5	219, 225
6	225
9–11	225–26, 227
15	225

Jude

4	86
4–19	206
5	186
10	59
11	166
12	69
22–23	85, 223

Revelation

2–3	93
2:2	142
2:4–5	81, 187
2:6	142
2:7	24f
2:9	166
2:10	81
2:11	24f
2:14	41, 86, 223
2:16	223
2:17	24f, 60, 170
2:20–22	86, 223
2:29	24f
3:3–5	78, 149, 190
3:4	78, 90
3:6	24f
3:8	190
3:9	166
3:10	128, 190
3:11	214
3:13	24f
3:19	115
3:20	173
3:22	24f
6:11	78
7	87
7:9–10	78, 93
9:12	146
10:9–11	171
11:14	146
11:18	214
12	87
12:9	196
13:8	116
13:9	24f
13:11–14	86
14:10–11	202
14:14–20	202
16:5	78
16:13	86
18:10–19	146
19:8	78
19:9	78
19:20	86
20:1–15	93
20:2	196
20:10–15	202
21:2	173
21:8	89, 202
21:22	173
22:12	78, 214
22:18–19	149

Ancient Sources Index

PSEUDEPIGRAPHA

Adam and Eve (Life of) *Vita*
12–16	196
Ahiqar	145

Apocalypse of Abraham
9.1	83
31.4–8	86

Apocalypse of Daniel
9.10–16	86

Apocalypse of Elijah
1.13–14	82, 86
3.1–5	82
4.15–25	82, 86
5.1	82

2 Baruch
7–12	58
10:6–7	146f
20.1–2	81
22.2	83
29.3–6	78
29.8	60, 170
48.34	86
51.15	39
70.2–7	82
85.13	56

3 Baruch
9.7	196

1 Enoch
5.7–8	79
12.3	149
38.2	146, 147
38.3	64, 147
38.5	111
40.9	113
46.6	40
48.8–10	40
60.7–24	78
62.8–13	129
62.14	78
80.7	82
81.4	149
89.12–76	186
89.13–27	142
91.7	82
91.18–19	56
93.9	82
95.3	111
95.4–7	146
99.11–16	146
100.1–2	82

2 Enoch
29.4–5	196
30.15	56
31.3	196
41.2	147

4 Ezra
2:13	81
2:20–23	94
4.12	147
5.1–2	82
5.18	142, 186
6.49–52	78
6:25	81
7:27	81
8.3	80
8.41–44	27
9.31	27
11.42	82
14.50	149

Joseph and Aseneth
14.7	83

Jubilees
1.23	194
1.29	79
10.21	124
15.33–34	32
21.22	220
22.16	123
23.16–24	82
26.34	220

30.20–23	149
33.12–18	220
36.9–10	149
48.15–18	62

Martyrdom & Ascension of Isaiah
1.5	78
2.4	124

Psalms of Solomon
3.16	113
14.2–4	68
14.10	113
15.4–5	45
16.7	41f
17.32	169
18.6	194

Sibylline Oracles
2.252–54	45
3.46–49	170
3.273–79	82
3.310	146f
3.689–92	58
7.149	60

Testament of Abraham
8	56
[B]10	149
[A]13	149

Testament of Job
18	113
49.2	149

Testament of the Twelve
(alphabetic tribal names below)

Testament of Dan
2.2–4	191

Testament of Gad
1.2–4	186

Testament of Issachar
6.1–4	142

Testament of Joseph
1.3	56
7.5	191

Testament of Judah
18.1–6	142
21.9	86
24.3	194

Testament of Levi
4.1	142
10.2–5	86, 142
14–15	82
16.3	86

Testament of Naphtali
4.1–5	142

Testament of Reuben
2.9	68

Testament of Zebulun
9	82

JOSEPHUS AND PHILO

Josephus

Ag. Ap.
1	100

Ant.
1.193	33
1.11.4[203]	139
2.16.5[333]	102
4.8.15 [219]	73
7.9.8[228–32]	145
10.8.2–3[142]	105
10.11.7[278–81]	102
10.53	133
10.142	117
11.8.6–7[340, 346]	124, 154
13.172f	117
16.397f	117
18.1.4[16–17]	111
18.17	165
19.8.2[343–50]	145
20.9.1[199]	111

Ancient Sources Index

Josephus (continued)

J.W.
1.5.2 [111])	73
1.18.3[357]	39
2.8.10[152]	134
2.119–66	117
3.8.5 [361–82]	76
4.5.3	153
5.472	81
7.11.1–4[441–53]	145

Life[Vit.]
49	73

Philo

Agriculture
102–04	56

Alleg.
3.75[213]	139
3.169–76	170

Conf.
34 [173]	83

Dreams
1.247f[42]	139

Flight
22[121]	139

Mut.
159–160	170

Spec.
1.316	34
2.27	153
3	170

Virtues
181[34]	139

QUMRAN/DEAD SEA SCROLLS LITERATURE

1QH
1.19–31	193
2.13	79
4.21f	129
7.29–31	129
9.1–10.4	193
10.22–29	165
11.12–14	194
14.17–18	45
15.12–22	193
18.10	129

1QS
1.9f	111
3.6–9	194
5.24–6.1	73
6.1–11	79
8.21–9.2	220
11.16f	129

4Q175
15–17	84

4Q180
1	193

4Q198
2	145

4Q339
	86

4Q340
	86

4Q375
	82

4Q378
	82

4Q385
	81

4Q418
fr.69.13	113

CD
1.7	68
2.2–13	193
3.20	113
4:3–4	79
5.20	86
7.21	86

Ancient Sources Index

8.8	139
9.2–8	73

CD-B

19.5–21	36, 179
19.16–17	179
20.4	169

EARLY JEWISH/RABBINIC LITERATURE

Mishnah

m. Abot

3.11A–B	124

m. Hagigah

2.1	147

m. Keritot

1.1	122

m. Makkot

3.10–15	134
3.12	70

m. Niddah

2.1	43

m. Pirke Abot

1.12	175

m. Sanhedrin

6.2	153
6.4	144
7.5	54, 122
10.1–2	76, 111, 170

m. Shabbat

7.1	139

m. Sotah

9.15	82

m. Yadayim

4.7	111, 165

Babylonian Talmud

b. Bekhorot

8b	55
60b	62

b. Berakot

64A	169

b. Megillah

17b	18

b. Niddah

13a–b	43

b. Tamid

32a	39

b. Yebamote

48b	194

Miscellaneous

Eighteen Benedictions

12	48f

Gen. Rabbah

27.27

Exod. Rabbah

28.1–3	170
	76

Mekilta Exod.

14:31	90

Shemahot | 153

Sifre Num.

6:24	90
11.22	167

Targ. Eccl.

6.6	149

y. Berakot

2.4.5	18

Ancient Sources Index

GRECO-ROMAN LITERATURE

Apuleius

Metam
11.7	102
11. 13	102

Herodotus

Histories
9.114–22	109

Homer

Illiad
22.405–515	109

Odyssey
23.248–96	109

Lucian

Alex. 102

(Ps.-)Longinus

Sub.
9.2	109

Pliny

Nat.
31.102	55

Pliny the Younger

Epistulae
10.96–97	15, 37, 134

Polybius

Histories
1.35–36	105
1.4.1–2	105

Quintilian

Inst.
2.13.12–13	109

Tacitus

Annals
15.44	15, 35, 87

NEW TESTAMENT APOCRYPHA & GNOSTIC LITERATURE

Acts of Thomas

46	64

Apocalypse of Peter

1.2	182
1.3	216
3	64

Gospel of Judas

35.27–36.4	144
44.21	144
44.23–45.2	143
45.11–12	143
46.19–20	144

Gospel of the Nazoreans

frag. 18	92

Gospel of Thomas

8	23
9	17, 27
21	23, 88
63	23
63–65	77
65	23
93	58
96	23

Gospel of Truth

21.11–14	193

22:2–20	193
33.15f	59

EARLY CHURCH FATHERS

Ambrose

Auxentius
8	39

Virg.
2.4[25]	39

Augustine

Doctr. chr.
3.16	39

Fel.
1.4	144

Nat. orig.
2.17	39

Mart. Habib. 39

(Ps.-)Barnabas

Ep.
4.14	80
5.10–11	221

Basil

Hom.
19	149

Clement of Rome

1 Clement
5.2–5	14, 29, 87
11.1–2	139
23.9	139
40:1f	115
46.8f	64, 120, 147f
58.2	116

2 Clement
3.2	70
4.5	84
5.2–4	70, 142
13.1–5	55
17.1	100

Clement of Alexandria

Miscellanies
7.12	84

Pseudo-Clementines

Recognitions
1.54	164
1.60	164
2.3	58
3.1.2	58
10.63	156

Homilies
20.21	156

Cyprian

Epistulae
55[48].7	39

Laps. 134
9.1–5	35

On the Glory of Martyrdom
17	39

Treatises
9	39, 84

Unit. eccl.
15	84

Didache

1.1	56
1.5	56
7:1	49
8.1–3	59, 62
8.10	49
8.10	49
11.7	136

Ancient Sources Index

Didache (*continued*)

15.3	73
16.3–5	81, 86–88, 142, 203, 216

Eusebius

Hist. eccl.

2.15.1–8	11, 14, 45
2.23.16	144
3.1.2	14
3.5.3	86
3.23	160, 224
3.24.6	48
3.39.14–16	11, 48
4.15	134
4.26.9	14
5.1	134
5.8	160
5.8.2f	48, 98
6.14.5–7	11
6.41	134
8.2.2–3	3, 134

Hermas (The Shepherd of)

Mand.

8.10	203
11.1[43]	86

Sim.

4.4	69
6.2.1–4	220
6.2.3	142
8.6.4	40
8.9.1	127
9.1.6	28
9.4.7	149
9.17.5–18.2	64
9.21.3	28, 40
9.21.1–3	201
9.26.3	39

Vis.

2.2	39, 115, 205
2.3.2	127
2.4.3	100
3.6.4	181
3.6–7	205
3.7.1	181
4.1.2	147
4.1.3	203
4.2	64
4.2.6	147

Hilary of Poiters

On the Trinity

10	39

Ignatius

Eph.

7	59, 142
9	142
10	88
16	142

Mag.

5.1	149

Phld.

2.1–2	142
3.2	115

Smyrn.

4.1	59
10.2	211

Irenaeus

Haer.

1.16.3	64
1.23	156
1.26	209
2.20.5	147
2.22.5	160
3.1.1	11, 45, 48, 98, 160
3.3.4	209
3.11.1	209
3.14.1	98
4.15. 2	80
4.28.1–2	147
4.36.6	78
5.35.1	78
36.3	88
36.6	79
42.7	64

Hippolytus

Haer.
6.2–15	156
9.7	220

John Chrysostom

Hom. 1 Cor
32[11]	39

Jerome

Epistulae
108.19	39

Justin

Apol.
1.16	84, 142
1.26	156
1.56	156

Dial.
120.6	156

Lactantius

Inst.
21	14

Origen

Cels.
2.11, 12	183

Comm. Jo.
2.14.100–1010	193
3.15.91–97	193

Comm. Matt.
12:14	71

Princ.
1.3	136

Papias

Frag. 18   143

Polycarp

Mart. Pol.
1.1	30
9–10	37

Phil.
7.2	62

Tertullian

Apology
5	14
21	14

Modesty
2	220
9.14	80
19	220
21	73

Nat.
1.7	14

Praescr.
22	160

Marc.
4	98
4.2	160
4.21	39
4.35	139

Scorp.
9	39

Author Index

Allison, Dale C., 27–28, 50, 56, 59, 62, 67, 73–74, 76, 84, 91, 94, 99, 147
Anderson, Bernhard W., 16
Anderson, Paul N., 161, 210, 222
Ashton, John, 161

Baird, J. Arthur, 23
Balch, David L., 49
Banks, R. J., 123
Barbour, John D., 3
Barclay, John M. G., 4f, 7, 26, 53, 121
Bardy, Gustave, 3
Barrett, C. K., 40, 70, 98, 107, 125, 134, 155, 172, 194, 196, 199, 203, 207, 219
Barstad, Hans M., 16
Barth, Gerhard, 50–52, 67, 75, 82
Barton, Stephen, 13
Bass, Christopher D., 213, 224
Bassler, Jouette M., 166
Bauckham, Richard, 14, 50, 79, 99, 162, 204
Bauder, W., 2, 127
Bauer, Walter, 2
Beale, G. K., 21
Beardslee, William A., 39
Beasley-Murray, G. R., 40, 181, 194
Bauer, F. C., 121
Beavis, Mary Ann, 11f
Becker, Adam, and Annette Reed, 4
Berkouwer, G. C., 6
Bertram, Georg, 55, 120
Best, Ernest, 16, 32, 36, 38
Betz, Hans Dieter, 55f, 58, 83
Beuken, W. A. M., 104
Beutler, Johannes, 220
Bieringer, Reimund, 164
Bird, Michael F., 98
Black, C. Clifton, 12

Black, Matthew, 19, 27, 138, 145
Blank. J., 192
Blinzler, Josef, 144
Bock, Darrell L., 54, 102, 107, 109, 113f, 123, 129, 141
Bogart, John, 215, 217
Borchert, Gerald L., 177, 188f, 202
Borgen, Peder, 167, 169
Borig, Rainer, 200, 205
Bornkamm, Gunther, 74
Boucher, Madeleine, 24–26
Bovon, Francois, 99, 103, 110, 120, 127, 135, 138
Bowker, J. W., 27
Boyarin, Daniel, 4
Braun, Herbert, 2
Brawley, Robert L., 102, 111
Breytenbach, Cilliers, 23, 34, 40, 44
Brinkerhoff, Merlin B., and M. L. Mackie, 3, 72
Brodie, Thomas L., 103, 126, 155
Bromley, David G., 2
Brooke, Alan England, 217
Brown, Nobel B., 2
Brown, Raymond E., 54, 75, 101, 160f, 164, 166, 172f, 179, 181, 186, 290, 294, 209, 211f, 215, 217, 220, 222f
Brown, Schuyler, 102, 128, 132, 136, 140, 148, 150f, 154
Bruce, F. F., 116, 134, 219
Büchsel, Friedrich, 73
Bultmann, Rudolf, 7, 177, 179, 215, 219
Burnet, Regis, 143
Burridge, Richard A., 13, 100

Caneday, Ardel B. 7, 86, 127
Carson, D. A., 26, 84f, 117, 173f, 179–81, 198, 201, 204

Carter, Warren, 49, 53, 63
Cassidy, Richard J., 101
Celsor, Scott, 195, 197
Cerfaux, Lucien, 127
Chalcraft, David J., 3
Chennattu, Rekha M., 200f, 203
Chenoweth, Ben, 92
Childs, Brevard S., 172
Chilton, Bruce, 166
Claybrook, Frederick W., 7
Cohen, Shaye J. D., 2, 4
Collins, Adela Yarbro, 12f, 30, 43
Collins, Raymond F., 30
Conzelmann, Hans, 103, 111, 123
Cosgrove, Charles H., 103, 105, 116f
Crossan, John Dominic, 34
Cullmann, Oscar, 63
Culpepper, R. Alan, 139, 160, 162, 175, 184, 196
Cunningham, S., 127

Daly-Denton, Margaret, 182f
Danker, Frederick W., 93
Davis, John Jefferson., 1
Davies, W. D., 27f, 50, 56, 59, 67, 73, 76, 84, 91, 94, 147
Deines, Roland, 52f
Delling, Gerhard, 115
Deming, Will, 43
Derrett, J. Duncan M., 44f, 152f
deSilva, David A., 7, 48
Dinkler, Erich, 39
Desjardins, Michel, 2
Dobbeler, Stephanie von, 52
Dodd, C. H., 67
Domeris, William R., 168
Donahue, John R., and Daniel J. Harrington, 28
Dov, Noy, 1
Draper, Jonathan A., 56
Duling, D. C., 59
Dunn, James D. G., 4, 7, 60, 151, 154

Eakin, Frank E., 22
Easton, Burton Scott, 126
Ehrman, Bart D., 49, 160
Ermoni, V., 1
Esler, Philip F., 100, 102
Evans, Craig A., 18–20, 37, 42–44, 49, 66f, 106f, 109, 111, 134

Feldman, Louis H., 3
Feldmeier, Reinhard, 36

Fitzmyer, Joseph A., 62, 98f, 101, 112, 133, 145
Foakes-Jackson, F. J., 1
Forkman, Göran, 74
France, R. T., 30, 33
Francis, Leslie J., and Yaacov Julian Katz, 2
Freed, Edwin D., 169, 188
Frenschkowski, Marco, 99
Frend, W. H. C., 82
Fuller, Reginald H., 176
Fusco, V., 110

Gale, Aaron M., 48–50
Gaventa, Beverly Roberts, 121
George, Augustin, 116
Gibbs, Jeffrey A., 57
Giesen, H., 2
Glasson, T. Francis, 200
Gnilka, Joachim, 68, 106, 173
Goldingay, John, 21
Goodman, Martin, 2
Gosling, F. A., 143
Grant, Frederick C,. and Halford E. Luccock, 42
Green, Joel B., 128
Gregg, Brian Han, 58, 70, 91, 118, 136, 140
Grelot, Pierre, 112
Griffin, M. T., 15
Griffith, Terry, 163, 180f, 220f, 223
Guelich Robert A., 11, 17, 23
Guignebert, Charles, 3
Gundry, Robert H., 11, 26f, 37, 39, 42f, 48, 50, 59

Haar, Stephen, 156
Hadaway, C. Kirk, 3
Haenchen, Ernst, 98, 160, 181
Hagner, Donald A., 49, 52f, 55, 75
Hanges, James C., 26
Hannah, D. D., 19
Hanson, A. T., 168
Harner, Philip B., 160
Harrill, J. Albert, 180
Hartman, Lars, 69, 82, 89
Harvey, A. E., 134
Hauck, Friedrich, 185
Hays, Richard B., 8
Heise, Jurgen, 204
Hemer, Colin J., 51
Hengel, Martin, 160
Hill, Craig C., 121f

Author Index

Hirschberg, Peter, 161
Hofius, Otfried, 204
Hollenbach, B., 18
Holz, T., 103
Hooker, Morna D., 43f, 86f
Horbury, William, 2, 161
Horn, Friedrich Wilhelm, 101
Horrell, David G., 9
Hultgren, A. J., 17f, 27, 61, 88f, 94
Humbert, Alphonse, 2, 41
Hunsberger, Bruce, 3

Iersel, Bas M. F. van, 16, 41, 44
Incigneri, Brian J., 41

Jackson-McCabe, Matt, 3
Jacobs, Janet Liebman, 72
Jaubert, Anne, 200
Jeremias, Joachim, 17–19, 39f, 59f, 62, 64, 78, 80, 91, 126, 133
Jervell, Jacob, 106, 109, 112, 118
Jefford, C. N., 11
Jindra, Ines Wenger, 2
Johnson, Luke Timothy, 99, 125, 130, 150–53
Jossa, Giorgio, 4
Jung, Chang Wook, 210

Kasemann, Ernst, 225
Kaufman, Stephen A., 18
Keener, Craig S., 63, 73, 167, 175, 184, 186, 190f, 196, 205
Kelber, Werner H., 12
Kellenberger, Edgar, 17
Killgallen, John J., 133
Kim, Dongsu, 178, 184, 187, 203, 220
Kimelman, R., 161
Kingsbury, Jack D., 36, 49, 54, 65, 67–69, 75, 108, 131
Kippenberg, H. G., 1
Klassen, William, 143, 147
Klauck, Hans-Josef, 160, 209
Klink, Edward W., 14, 165
Kloppenborg, John S., 99
Koet, Bart J., 103, 109
Köstenberger, Andreas J., 167, 170, 178, 180, 186, 194, 202, 207
Kowalski, Beate, 185
Kubo, Sakae, 215
Kühschelm, Roman, 191, 198
Kysar, Robert, 162, 166, 195, 197

Lake, Kirsopp, 3
Lambrecht, Jan, 33, 40
Lampe, G. W. H., 36, 142
Lampe, P., 18
Lane, William L., 25, 32
Lange, Armin, 193
Law, Robert, 217
Lehnert, Volker A., 22, 110
Leroy, Herbert, 196
Lieu, Judith M., 163, 192, 198, 212, 215, 217
Litwak, Kenneth D., 102, 106
Lohfink, Gerhard, 60
Lohmeyer, Ernst, 34
Löverstam, Evald, 129
Luz, Ulrich, 28, 54–57, 63, 66f, 70, 75–77, 82, 84, 90

Maccoby, Hyam, 143
Maddox, Robert L., 109
Malatesta, Edward, 200, 208f
Malherbe, Abraham J., 225
Malina, Bruce J., 28, 40, 42, 122
Manson, T. W., 18, 59, 61, 73, 84, 90, 116, 126, 131
Marcus, Joel, 16, 19, 23, 39, 43, 45
Marguerat, Daniel, 109, 152, 154
Marshall, I. Howard, 6f, 81, 89, 114, 117, 130, 135, 140, 153, 208, 213, 220, 224
Martin-Achard, Robert, 20
Martyn, J. Louis, 161
Marxsen, Willi, 12
Mateos, Juan, 2, 41
Matera, Frank, 12
McGrath. James F., 165, 198
Metzger, Bruce, 12, 40, 61, 71, 155, 192f, 214,
Michaelis, W., 2
McKnight, Scot, 2, 4, 54
McLaughlin, John L., 21
Meadors, Edward P., 22
Meeks, Wayne A., 156, 62, 194, 209
Meier, John P., 39f, 49, 59, 61f, 75, 79
Menken, Martinus J. J., 8, 168f, 182f, 192, 199
Menzies, Robert P., 135, 137
Merrill, Eugene, 193
Merwe, Dirk G. van der, 218
Meyer, Ben F., 79f
Michaelis, Wilhelm, 2, 57
Milikowsky, C., 41, 70
Mitchell, Margaret M., 50

Author Index

Moore, George Foot, 32
Motyer, Stephen, 181
Moyise, Steve, 8
Myllykoski, Matti, 34

Nanos, Mark D., 59
Neyrey, Jerome H., 7, 83, 118, 122
Neusner, Jacob, 124
Nolland, John, 80, 100, 120, 132, 140f

O'Toole, Robert F., 152f
Obermann, Andreas, 171, 191
Oepke, Albrecht, 34, 186
Ondrey, Hauna, 2
Oropeza, B. J., 1f, 7, 16, 20, 43, 134, 143
Overman, J. Andrew, 49f, 52, 71, 74

Paffenroth, Kim, 145
Paget, James Carleton, 3
Painter, John, 160f, 176, 183, 192, 217f, 220
Pancaro, Severino, 165
Pao, David W., 103, 110, 112, 153
Partridge, Christopher, and Helen Reid, 2
Pearson, Birger A., 99
Parsons, Mikeal C., 98
Pervo, Richard I., 98
Pesch, Rudolf, 25, 30, 34, 61, 110, 113
Pesch, Wilhelm, 71, 73
Peterson, Dwight N., 12
Peterson, Richard A., 1
Phillips, Gary A., 68
Pietersen, Lloyd, 206
Pilgrim, Walter E., 101
Polhill, John B., 112, 122
Pollefeyt, D. 164
Porter, Stanley E., 62, 112
Powell, Mark Allan, 102, 109
Preston, J. J., 1

Rad, Gerhard von, 22
Räisänen, Heiki, 79, 107, 191
Rapske, Brian, 124
Rebell, Walter, 39
Reim, G., 168
Reinhartz, Adelle, 161
Rensberger, David, 164
Rhoads, David M., 13, 29, 31, 38, 42
Ridderbos, Herman N., 174, 198
Robbins, Vernon K., 8, 24, 40, 100
Robinson, John A. T., 164
Rohrbaugh, Richard L., 28, 40, 42, 101

Röhser, Günter, 26
Roskam, Hendrika N., 12
Rosscup, James E., 200
Rothfuchs, Wilhelm, 67
Russell, D. S., 82

Saldarini, Anthony J., 52
Salevao, Iutisone, 7
Sand, Alexander, 51
Sanders, Jack T., 111
Sandmel, Samuel, 111
Sandt, Huub van de, 56
Sato, Yoshiaki, 3
Sawyer, John F. A., 8, 103f
Schenke, Ludger, 210
Schereschewsky, B.-Z., 1
Schiffman, Lawrence H., 4
Schlier, Heinrich, 2
Schmidt, Ulrich, 39, 135, 140
Schnackenburg, Rudolf, 72, 169, 175, 177, 181, 193, 195, 199, 202f, 215
Schneck, Richard, 16, 18
Schneider, Gerhard, 98, 107, 142
Schnelle, Udo, 48, 101, 161, 177, 203
Scholer, David M., 220, 224
Schreiner, Thomas R., 7, 86, 127
Schrenk, Gottlob, 130
Schuchard, Bruce G., 191
Schürmann, Heinz, 100, 141
Schweizer, Eduard, 42, 45
Scott, J. Martin C., 165
Seccombe, David, 103, 111
Segal, Alan, 2, 49
Segovia, Fernando F., 200, 204
Shellard, Barbara, 99, 101f
Sherkat, Darren E., and John Wilson, 3
Sim, David C., 51f
Simon, Marcel, 2
Skarsaune, Oskar, 3
Sloyan, Gerard S., 165
Smalley, Stephen S., 162, 211, 224
Smith, C. W. F., 91
Smith, Dwight Moody, 185, 195
Smith, Ralph L., 42
Squires, John T., 104f, 117
Stählin, Gustav, 2, 34, 41
Starbuck, E. D., 1
Stanton, Graham N., 48, 50
Starbuck, E. D., 1
Stark, Rodney, and William S. Bainbridge, 3
Stegner, William Richard, 8
Stein, Robert H., 13

Author Index

Stern, Sacha, 2, 4f
Steyn, Gert Jacobus, 102, 106, 146
Stibbe, Mark W. G., 166
Strauss, Mark L., 103
Strecker, Georg, 32, 179 196, 208, 212f, 218f
Strobel, A., 89
Swartley, Willard M., 16
Swetnam, James, 180

Tabor J. D., and Arthur J. Droge, 76
Talbert, Charles H., 51, 61, 100, 102f, 105, 156
Tannehill, R. C., 13, 35, 38, 102f, 128, 131, 137, 151
Taylor, Justin, 87
Theobald, Michael, 175
Thompson, Mary R., 32f
Thompson, Marianne Meye, 214
Tiede, David L., 101
Tilborg, Sjef van, 160
Tolbert, Mary Ann, 27f, 34
Trebilco, Paul R., 141f, 164, 186, 222
Trumbower, Jeffrey A., 177, 189, 193f, 204, 209
Tuckett, C. M., 19, 32
Turner, Nigel, 218
Tyson, Joseph B., 111

Van Elderen, Bastiaan, 67
Van Hove, A., 1
Vandecasteele-Vanneuville, F., 164
Vielhauer, Philipp, 98
Vogler, Werner, 37
Volf, Miroslov, 1
Von Staden, Heinrich, 2
Von Wahlde, Urban C., 166, 222
Vriezen, Th. C., 20

Wallace, Daniel B., 134, 218
Walton, Steve, 111, 142
Wansbrough, Henry, 33
Watts, John D. W., 169
Watts, Rikki E., 16, 18, 21, 32, 36, 42
Weatherly, Jon A., 111
Wehnert, Jürgen, 98, 123
Wengst, Klaus, 200, 225
Wenkel, David H., 155
Whedbee, J. William, 20
Whiston, William, 117
Wiarda, Timothy, 36
Wiefel, Wolfgang, 66
Wikenhauser, Alfred, 174
Wilckens, Ulrich 2
Wildberger, Hans, 21, 65
Williams, Catrin H., 191
Williams, James G., 32
Wilson, Brian R., 3
Wilson, Stephen G., 2f, 5, 29f, 35, 72, 103, 134, 181, 222
Wilson, Walter T., 58
Winbery, C. L., 184
Witherington, Ben, 111f, 154, 156, 162, 172, 221
Witmer, Stephen, 168
Wolter, M., 2
Wright, Stuart A., 29, 35, 222,

Xavier, A., 182

Yarbrough, Robert W., 220, 222
York, John O., 119

Zerwick, Maximilian, 172, 217f
Zumstein, Jean, 75
Zwiep, Arie W., 143–45

Subject Index

Abiding (in Jesus), 170–74, 180, 183f,
    199–217, 221, 227, 231
Accommodation, 4
Acculturation, 4, 222
Affliction (see Suffer)
Amputation, 44, 47
Ananias and Sapphira, 150–54, 159
Antichrist(s), 179, 184, 206, 208–10,
    214–17, 220–222, 227
Antinomian(ism) (see also Law), 50f, 82,
    86, 95
Anti-Semitic, 111, 143, 164–67, 184
Antioch (Syrian), 9, 49–51, 95, 99, 123
Antioch (Pisidia), 112–14
Antiochus Epiphanes, 44
Antithetical, 39
Apostasy (see also Unbelief, Persecution,
        Suffering, Vices),
    antagonistic, 29f, 59, 181, 210
    (in) communities (see Communities)
    consequences of, 7
    critical studies in NT, 6–7
    definition, ch. 1
    diversity of, 6–7
    gradual, 29f, 107
    nature of, 6
    perceived, 4–6, 51, 77, 86, 111, 148,
        165, 189, 197f, 205f, 210, 226,
        230, 232
    precipitate, 29f, 181, 226
Aramaic, 11, 14, 18, 27, 39f, 48f, 59f, 62f,
    73, 80, 89, 121f, 138, 145
Arminianism, ix, 7n19
Ashamed, 15, 37, 40f, 46, 70, 135, 138,
    210–15, 230
Asia Minor, 93, 99, 112, 118, 160, 222,
    229
Assimilation, 4–5, 121, 163, 207, 222f,
    228, 230

Assurance, 7, 57, 80, 124, 168, 170. 174,
    189, 203, 208, 210, 212, 224, 227
Authority of Disciples, 73–77

Baptism, John the Baptist, 23, 25, 57,
    100, 117f, 150, 154f, 163f, 174,
    194, 209, 218, 223
Behavior (see Moral Behavior)
Believe, Belief (see Faith; Unbelief)
Betrayal (see also Judas), 15, 27, 29f, 30,
    33–37, 44–47, 69, 72, 75, 81, 87,
    90, 105, 135
birkat ha-minim, 48, 161
Blasphemy, Blasphemy of the Holy Spirit,
    25, 31–34, 37, 46, 53f, 63, 95,
    122, 134–38, 151, 153, 158, 165,
    180, 189, 220, 226, 232
Blessings (see Curse)
Blindness, spiritual (see also Obduracy),
    ch. 2, 49, 65–68, 104, 107, 141,
    145f, 159, 172, 176, 178, 185,
    190–99, 207, 226, 231
Boundaries (see also Outsider), 3–5, 40,
    50, 53, 121, 165, 222, 228

Caesar (see also Nero), 120, 223
Calvinism, ix, 7n.19
Charismatic opponents, 51, 82
Children, 41–45, 71
Chosen (see Elect)
Christ (see Messiah)
Christian(s), Christianity (see
        Communities), 8–9
Christology, 53f, 102f, 161, 164, 171
Church, see Communities, Corporate
    Mixed church, 91f, 95
Circumcision, 5, 32, 51, 98, 100, 108,
    123–25, 157

297

Subject Index

Communities, 5–7
  Markan, ch. 1
  Matthean, ch. 2
  Lukan, 99–102 (ch. 3)
  Johannine, ch. 4
  Pauline (see Paul)
Condemn(ation), 37, 43, 51, 56, 58, 63, 69f, 76–78, 85, 89, 92, 94, 96, 101, 111. 140, 143–48, 150, 153, 195, 198, 218, 223, 225, 232
Confess, Confession (see Deny)
Convert, Conversion, 4, 29, 64, 69, 72, 100, 102, 114, 116, 118, 122f, 127, 129, 133, 136, 150, 154–56, 160, 164, 194, 205, 211, 215, 218, 223f
Corporate/Collective body, people, groups, nations, 64, 73, 79, 81, 87, 93, 115, 145, 172f, 175f, 179, 189, 212, 214
Covenant, 20f, 42, 55–57, 113, 115, 120, 124, 168, 170–73, 179, 199–201, 222
Covetousness (see Greed)
Coward(ice), 43, 132
Cross, Crucifixion, 15, 31, 35–41, 46, 63, 70, 86, 108, 111, 135, 139, 171, 176f, 184, 199, 207, 209, 226
Crowds, 17, 22–26, 31–33, 46, 55–58, 66f, 71, 75, 95, 131, 138f, 144, 168, 170, 176f, 191, 193, 195–99, 204, 231
Crypto-Christian, 173, 178, 208, 226
Curse(s), 20, 30, 36f, 48, 54, 56, 68, 134, 145–55, 187, 198

Dark(ness), 21, 24, 77, 90, 92f, 163, 182, 185, 191f, 194f, 197–99, 209, 217f, 231
Deaf (see Blindness)
Death, 15f, 20, 22, 30, 38–41, 44, 46, 56f, 70, 76f, 81, 86, 99, 104f, 111, 122, 124, 130, 133–37, 140, 143–54, 158, 166, 171, 176, 186, 194, 206–08, 214, 218–28, 231–33
Deception (see False Teachings, Led Astray)
Deeds (see Works)
Deity of Christ, 53, 62, 169, 210, 223, 226f
Deliverance (see Salvation)

Demon(s), Demon-possession (see also Satan), 14, 32–34, 46, 63–65, 83, 95, 135, 148, 150f, 165f
Deny, Denial of Christ (see also Peter), 6, 15, ch. 1, 40, 43, 70, 84, 96, 128f, 132–37, 151, 187, 201f, 209–11, 221, 228–32
Destruction, Eternal destruction, 22, 41f, 48, 55f, 58, 71–73, 76, 78, 81, 89f, 96, 122, 129, 132f, 135, 139, 141, 145, 147, 152–55, 158, 171, 178, 182, 185f, 189, 201, 203f, 207, 214, 222, 227f, 232
Determinism, Arbitrary Choice of God (see also Predestination, Freedom), 8, 21f, 114–17, 175, 193–95, 198
Devil (see Satan)
Diaspora, 4–5, 53, 91, 101, 111, 121f, 124, 164, 230
Diotrephes, 225f
Disciples (see Peter, Judas, John, Authority of, Communities)
Disobedience (see Obedience)
Dogs, 15, 58f
"Drawn" by God (Johannine), 171–77
Drunk(ards), 20f, 88f, 92, 96, 138, 231

Ephesus, Ephesian, 99, 107, 111, 115, 120, 141f, 152, 158, 160, 163f, 178, 187, 209, 222–24, 226f, 230,
Ecclesiology (see also Community), 7n20, 102
Eighteen Benedictions (see *birkat ha-minim*)
Elect, Election, 7, 21, 79–81, 85–88, 91, 96, 115f, 130, 147f, 172, 182–84, 190, 201, 213, 215
End Times (see Eschaton)
Endurance (see also Perseverance), 29, 58, 81, 85, 87, 129–31, 180, 200
Eschaton, Eschatology (see also second coming), 7n20, 36, 41, 43f, 53, 55–63, 69, 70f, 77f, 80f, 83, 87f, 90–93, 96, 102, 107, 113, 122, 127f, 132, 136–41, 146f, 149, 155, 170–73, 194, 200–04, 207, 212–16, 227f
Essenes, 82, 117
Eternal Life (see also Salvation), 37, 39, 44–46, 56f, 70, 94, 96, 113–15, 129, 135, 139f, 149, 158, 162f,

Subject Index

167f, 170–74, 177, 185f, 189, 200, 207f, 211–15, 219f, 224, 227, 230
Ethics (see also Immorality), 2, 23, 40, 58, 60, 84, 94, 100, 128, 151, 200, 205, 212, 220
Eucharist (see Lord's Supper)
Exodus, New Exodus, 8, 16–18, 21f, 32, 35, 38, 46, 104, 130, 153, 169
Expulsion (see also Excommunication), 6, 73–75, 85, 150–54, 159, 161, 163, 178, 188, 203, 208, 231
Excommunication (see also Expulsion), 73–75, 84, 179

Faith, Faithfulness, 4, 9, 13–16, 25f, 29f, 35, 38, 42, 45, 52, 61, 63, 72, 75, 80–85, 88–96, 100, 102, 109, 118, 120f, 125, 128–35, 138–43, 152, 154f, 162, 164, 175–81, 190, 199, 203–214, 217, 219–24, 228–30
False teachings, false teachers/prophets 2, 29, 51f, 54, 57–59, 64, 71, 73–76, 79–88, 90, 94–97, 100, 107–09, 120–24, 141–43, 154, 156, 263, 204, 209–17, 221–30
Family, 15, 23, 31, 33–38, 42, 46, 66, 101, 135, 231
Food, food laws (see also Idol, Idol Meats), 5, 14, 53, 60, 123f, 148, 167–71, 179, 223
Foreknowledge, 37, 116, 182–84, 195
Foreigner (see Outsider/Insider)
Forgive(n), Forgiveness, 18f, 32f, 40, 44, 53, 56f, 59–63, 74–76, 96, 105. 111, 113f, 136f, 140, 151, 154, 199, 212, 224, 231
Fornication, Sexual vice, 42f, 123f, 195, 218, 223
Forsake, 20, 34, 36f, 62, 75, 97, 124, 140, 173, 188
Freedom (human), (see also Responsibility), 26, 86, 108, 114–17, 195
Fruit, bearing good fruit, 23, 27f, 30, 25, 51, 55, 68f, 78, 84, 92, 96, 127–31, 133, 151, 183, 196, 199–201, 205, 212

Galilee/Galilean, 12f, 22, 31, 41, 49f, 52, 95, 99, 166, 172, 174, 178
Gehenna (see also Hell), 15, 41–47, 56f, 70, 96f, 136f, 147, 158, 203

Gentile(s), 4–5, 11–13, 49, 52, 55, 59, 68, 71, 74, 78, 83, 89, 91, 93, ch. 3, 163–65, 196–99, 209, 217, 222, 226, 229f
Genuine (belief/believer), ungenuine, inauthentic, 23, 28, 76f, 84f, 127, 151, 154, 156, 171, 179, 181f, 184, 186, 201, 204–06, 208f, 213–15, 224–26, 228
"Given" by God (Johannine), 171–77
Gnostic(ism), 27, 51, 84, 156, 193f, 209
God-fearer(s), 100–102, 112, 114f
Grace, Gift, Favor, 26 66, 78, 76, 86, 92, 114, 116, 121, 130, 155, 170, 174, 176, 195, 212
Greed, Covetousness, 47, 76, 129, 143, 149–54, 157, 159, 182, 223, 229,

Hardened heart (see Obduracy, Blindness)
Heaven(ly) (see also Kingdom of God), 20, 50, 53, 59, 90, 105, 116, 138, 149,, 158, 167–70, 175, 180, 191, 202, 214
Hell, Hades, Outer Darkness (see also Gehenna, Judgment), 6, 42, 45, 56, 61, 70, 72, 77, 84, 89, 92f, 97, 140f, 147, 149, 158
Hellenism, Hellenize 4–5, 50, 99, 107, 121f, 134, 157f, 163
Heretics, heresy (see also False teachings/ beliefs), 2, 156, 161
Hireling, 185–89
Holy Spirit (see also Blasphemy of), 106, 136f, 150f, 164, 193, 200, 202f,
Honor, Dishonor (see also Ashamed), 34f, 40, 79, 83, 96, 99, 145, 228
Household, 42, 83, 89, 92, 94, 118, 138
Hypocrite, Hypocrisy, 20, 58, 76, 88f, 123, 138, 141, 205

"I am," 187–89, 194
Idol(atry), Idol meats , 53, 71f, 82, 108, 123f, 131, 141, 149, 222f
Immorality, moral failure (see also Moral; Ethics), 6, 20, 23, 42, 76, 86, 92, 94, 119f, 127, 129, 133, 138–43, 158, 197, 218, 229f
Individualism (see also Corporate), 116, 172–77, 183, 212
Intertextual (-ity), 7–8, 115, 177
Israel (see Jew)

299

Subject Index

James (brother of Jesus), 27, 34, 51, 62, 123–25, 223
Jerusalem, 9, 11f, 15f, 22, 25, 27, 31, 38–40, 46, 48, 51, 55, 70, 78, 83, 87, 99, 101, 104, 108, 110f, 118, 120–25, 130, 132, 135, 151, 154, 157, 163–65, 169, 172, 174, 181, 188, 191, 193, 196, 198
Jew, Jewish, Judaism (see also Diaspora), 3–4, 8, 11f, 17, 18, 24, 29, 32, 39–43, 48–65, 68, 73–80, 83, 87, 89–91, 95f, chs. 3, 4
Jewish Christian(s), 3, 11, 48, 52, 68, 74, 87, 89f, 101, 123–25, 157, 161, 163–66, 180f, 210
Jewish custom(s), 11, 99, 123–26
John the Baptist (see Baptism)
Judas (Iscariot), 15, 27, 30, 36–47, 52, 75–77, 85, 97, 106, 133, 143–51, 153f, 157f, 166, 177, 179f, 182–85, 188, 195, 202, 205, 209, 222f, 227f, 230, 232
Judgment (Divine Judgment, Final Judgment, Judgment Day), 6f, 18–23, 37, 40, 44f, 56, 58, 65f, 68–73, 76–80, 83, 88–97, 105, 110, 118, 136–41, 146–49, 151, 155, 158, 177, 192, 197f, 201f, 204, 207, 211, 213, 226f, 230–32
Justification (see also Righteousness), 7n.20, 20, 151, 167

Kingdom, Kingdom of God/Heaven, 12, 17, 22–25, 28, 32, 39, 43, 50, 57–60, 63–75, 77–80, 83f, 87, 89, 91–97, 101, 105–9, 123, 126, 128f, 135, 149, 158, 170, 172, 190, 194, 223, 230, 232
Knowledge (spiritual), Wisdom, Insight, 20, 26, 55, 66f, 68, 72, 92, 95, 117, 131, 195f, 199, 213

Law, Torah, Lawless(ness), 4, 20, 24, 34, ch. 2, 100, 121–26, 134, 157, 170f, 174, 214, 216f, 222, 228–32
Lex talionis (see also Reciprocation), 21, 45, 155, 197
Led astray, 46, 58, 80, 82, 88, 90, 120, 211, 215, 227
Life (see Eternal Life)
"Little Ones," 36, 41–43, 71f, 74, 95, 140
Light (Johannine), 163, 182, 191f, 195, 197–99, 217f

Logos, 162, 175
Lord's Supper, 148, 164, 170f, 176
Loss of Reward, 70, 93, 153, 212–15, 227
Lot's Wife, 139f
Loyalty (see Faith, Faithfulness; Betrayal)
Lust (see also Covetousness), 43, 56, 96, 128, 207, 223

Magic, Magician (Elymas, Simon), 21, 83, 120, 141f, 154–56, 158
Marginalize(d), 119–21, 140, 157f
Marriage, Intermarriage, 29, 77–80, 89, 124
Martyr, Martyrdom, 15, 39, 44, 69f, 81f, 96, 121, 129, 140, 149, 207
Messiah, messianic, 12, 31, 34, 37, 52–54, 60, 62, 65, 67, 75, 78, 80–82, 87, 90f, 96, 103, 107, 111, 116, 119–22, 132, 141, 161, 164, 178–83, 186, 188, 197, 209f, 221, 228–30
Monotheism, 100, 161
Moral Behavior (see Immorality, Ethics; Virtue(s), Vice(s), Obedience, Righteous), 84, 89, 195, 198, 205, 216, 231
Moses, 16, 52, 56, 105, 108, 122, 124f, 152, 157, 167f, 171, 175, 180, 195
Multitude (see Crowds)
Murmuring, 167–71, 173, 178,
Mystery, 17, 66, 144, 176, 194

Narrow way, door (see also Two Ways), 56–58, 83, 96
Nazarenes, 9, 48
Nero, 14–16, 35, 45, 87, 101, 151, 230
New exodus (see Exodus)

Obduracy, 8, ch. 1, 65–68, 74, 95, 104, 106–114, 122, 167, 189f, 196f, 199, 226, 229, 231f
Obedience, Disobedience, 14, 22, 31, 53f, 56, 60, 67, 93, 126, 153, 212f
Olivet Discourse, 80–88
Outsider/Insider, 16–19, 23–36, 46, 49, 55, 59, 71, 74, 89, 96, 100, 106, 129, 136, 140, 162f, 180, 185, 187, 192, 196, 206, 228, 229f, 232
Opponents, 5, 12, 17, 24, 29–34, 49–54, 63, 65, 68, 82, 100, 102, 109, 111, 120–25, 131, 136, 142, 157f, 163, 165f, 183, 186–89, 203, 206–10, 216f, 221, 228f, 231f

Subject Index

Oral Tradition, 13, 39, 92, 135, 211
Orthodoxy, 2

Pagan(s), 3, 5
Papias, 11, 13, 143
Parables (see also Scripture Reference Index)
    End Time, Miscellaneous, ch. 2
    Forgiveness, 61
    Interpretation and Obduracy, 17–27, 66–68
    Lost Sheep, 71, 97, 119
    Minas, 92f
    Prodigal Son, 107f, 119f, 159, 231
    Seven unclean spirits, 63–65
    Sheep and Goats, 93
    Sower, 23–31, 46, 63, 69, 96, 107, 126–31, 139, 157, 181, 201, 230, 232
    Talents, 92f
    Ten Virgins, 90f
    Thief in the Night, 88–90
        Wedding Banquet, 77–80
        Wheat and Tares, 91f
Parousia (see also Second Coming, Eschaton), 6–7, 13, 40, 70, 73, 79, 90f, 138f, 211f, 214
Patron-client, 100
Paul, Pauline Community/Teaching, 4, 11, 29, 37, 51f, 61, 72–74, 82, 86, 89, 94, ch. 3, 169 171, 179, 192, 199, 206, 209, 211, 218, 220, 223, 229f
Penance (see Repent)
Persecution, 14–16, 28–31, 33–47, 58, 69f, 80, 82, 84, 87, 96, 101, 106, 111, 122, 127–39, 149, 151, 157f, 166f, 174, 187f, 201, 203f, 207f, 211, 227, 229–32
Perseverance (see also Endurance), 7, 27, 35, 59, 70, 81f, 87f, 90, 98, 102, 114, 126–34, 148, 157–59, 173f, 177, 188–90, 204, 208f, 212f, 215, 227, 232
Peter, Peter's denials, 11–16, 27f, 36–40, 45f, 51, 73, 75, 84, 90, 97, 103, 105f, 116, 123, 125, 128, 131–39, 149–59, 164, 168, 177, 182, 187f, 201, 207, 223, 231f
Pharisees, 23, 27, 29, 49–52, 59, 64–68, 77f, 82, 95, 108, 117f, 120, 122f, 128, 134, 141f, 163, 165, 173, 181, 185f, 199, 229, 232

Preexistence, 161, 180, 187, 194, 209f, 226f, 230
Pigs, 58f
Plan of God, divine purpose/necessity, ch. 3, esp. 104–6
Poor, the, 42, 71f, 94, 101, 119, 140, 158, 181, 223
Prayer, 36, 38, 46, 59–63, 86, 96, 130, 132f, 148, 154, 156, 159, 189f, 219, 221–24, 228, 231
Predestination (see also Determinism), 19, 66, 94, 174, 177, 182f, 189, 192–95, 198
Pride, 20, 23, 66, 108, 119, 199, 207
Priests, chief, 31, 49, 76, 78, 120, 163, 165
Prodigal Son (see Parables)
Punishment, Divine (see Judgment)

Qumran, Qumran community (see also Essenes), 8, 36, 140, 165, 179, 193f, 206

Racism (Prejudice), 1, 167
Reciprocation (see also *lex talionis*), 44, 56, 61, 66, 70, 96, 190, 197
Reconciliation, 13, 32, 44
Religious authorities/leaders, 27f, 31f, 45f, 49, 53, 66, 77f, 89, 91, 95, 108, 119–21, 135, 165, 173, 185, 187, 220
Religious wars, 1
Renunciation (see also Deny), 15, 36f, 134, 232
Repent, Repentance, 16, 18–23, 25f, 36f, 44, 46, 64, 66, 71, 74, 76f, 95, 102, 108–110, 113, 116, 133, 137, 140, 144, 154–56, 159, 184, 194, 198, 205, 224
Restore, Restoration, 6, 12f, 16, 20f, 28, 36–38, 40, 46, 55, 65, 73–75, 80, 85, 97, 105, 108, 110, 112, 119f, 128, 130–33, 137, 156, 159, 164, 266, 169–72, 180, 187f, 200f, 205, 207, 219, 222–24, 228–32
Resurrection, 12, 38, 41, 44, 70, 75, 102, 104f, 112–14, 118, 129–32, 151, 170f, 176, 207, 218
Remnant, 21, 27, 42, 45, 81, 86f, 112, 130, 168, 197
Responsibility (human), 18–27, 37, 55, 64, 66–68, 77, 87, 94f, 106f, 111, 114–17, 139, 146, 173–177, 185f,

301

Subject Index

Responsibility (human) (*continued*), 189f, 193, 195f, 198, 208, 213, 226
Reversal, 36, 83, 119–21, 125, 134, 155, 199
Rhetoric, 51, 55, 83, 109, 159, 223
    Of comprehension, 65
    Of suspense/suspension/silence, 38, 109f, 155
Rich, Riches (see also Greed), 30, 69, 128f, 158f
Righteous/Righteousness, unrighteous, 7f, 21, 36, 45, 50–58, 64, 67f, 70, 78, 83f, 89–92, 96, 113, 119, 122, 130, 149, 151, 154, 168, 171, 197, 206, 211, 214, 216, 218, 220f, 228, 232
Rise Again (see Resurrection)
Rome, Roman, ch. 1, 71, 99–101, 105–07, 109–112, 118–122, 125, 133, 156, 187, 229f

Sabbath, 5, 53, 165
Sadducees, 23, 117, 163, 165
Salt(iness), 55, 96
Salvation, 3, 7, 22, 55, 57, 74, 81f, 87, 96, 101, 103, 106f, 110, 112–21, 125, 127f, 130, 133, 138f, 146, 149f, 155–57, 168, 170–77, 195, 198, 207, 227, 230
Samaritan(s), Samaria, 111, 114, 150, 154–56, 172, 176
Sanhedrin, 108, 122, 134, 163
Satan (the Devil, Evil one), 27f, 31, 62, 70, 73, 75, 107, 312, 143, 148–51, 154, 158, 182, 190, 192f, 196, 198, 216, 221f, 232
Schism(s), 161, 163f, 178, 204, 210, 216
Scribes, 23, 26–28, 32, 44, 49f, 52, 57, 64–68, 76, 95, 108, 120, 126, 142, 163, 179, 232
Scriptures (Israel's), 8, 11, 22, 43, 54, 62, 65, 100–02, 105f, 111, 114, 117, 145–47, 152, 157, 162, 165, 169, 196, 200
Secessionists, 163, 178, 205, 208–210, 212, 214, 216, 220–22
Second Coming, 6f, 12, 40, 85, 90f, 128, 130, 137, 138, 210–15, 227, 231
Sect, Sectarian, 3n.12, 15, 42, 49, 111, 163f, 201, 216
Sermon on the Mount, 55–63
Sexual Immorality (see Fornication)
Shame (see Ashamed)
Shepherd, 36, 42, 71, 142, 185–89, 226f
Simon Magus, 154–56, 159
Sin (see Sinner; Sinning; Vices, Idolatry, Fornication, Greed)
Sinner(s), 23, 59, 71, 73f, 108, 119–21, 158, 166, 180, 217f, 224
Sinning (Johannine view), 215–25
Son of God, 34f, 37, 53f, 162, 166, 208, 221
Soteriology (see also Salvation), 7n20
Stephen, 108, 121f, 133–37
Status degradation, 206, 228
Stumbling block, 35, 41–43, 71f, 75, 97, 118, 140, 147, 149, 178, 182, 216
Suffer(ing), 14, 16, 30f, 36–46, 63, 69, 71f, 81, 86, 89f, 97, 104, 129, 133–38, 145–47, 158, 171, 208, 211, 230
Suicide, 76f, 144f, 158, 233
Synagogue, 11, 52–54, 68, 70–72, 75, 88, 95, 100, 103, 107, 109, 112, 161–66, 171–74, 178, 181, 198f, 203, 208, 210, 226

Tax Collectors, 23, 48, 71, 74, 108, 119f
Tempt(ation), 30, 36f, 43f, 59–63, 70–73, 96, 126–32, 139, 143, 157, 190, 207, 222f, 229, 232
Testing, Trials, 250, 30, 58, 62, 126–28, 138, 153
Torture, 14f, 44f, 47, 89, 134, 149
Two-Level reading (Johannine), 161–63, 180, 185, 187, 209, 226
Two Ways, 8, 56f, 218

Unbelief, 19, 34, 43, 68, 75, 106–10, 114, 118, 157, 165, 189, 191, 197f, 229f
Unclean spirits (see Demons)
Unfaithful (see Faith, Faithfulness)
Unpardonable sin (see Blasphemy)

Vice(s), 20, 43, 89, 96, 151, 171, 182, 219, 223, 230
Vine (Jesus as the), 199–208
Virtues, 4, 109

Watch Motif, 88–90
Wealth (see Rich, Riches)
Will of God/Lord, 26, 34, 51, 54–60, 65f, 75, 78, 84, 96, 117, 148, 173f, 216, 219, 222, 231
Wisdom (see Knowledge, spiritual)

Subject Index

Woe saying(s), 62, 76, 101, 140f, 145–47
Women, 12, 35, 38, 119f, 147, 281, 223
Works, Deeds, 32, 52, 55, 57, 68, 70, 78, 83, 85f, 89f, 92, 94, 96, 138, 180, 182, 195, 197f, 214, 221, 223, 225, 228, 231
World (Johannine view), 163, 174–76, 190, 194–97, 203, 207, 210, 220–23, 228, 230

Zealots, 82
Zion, 130, 168f, 172

www.ingramcontent.com/pod-product-compliance
Lightning Source LLC
Chambersburg PA
CBHW081824230426
43668CB00017B/2370